ASHLEY HUTCHINGS:
THE AUTHORISED BIOGRAPHY

THE GUV'NOR AND THE RISE
OF FOLK-ROCK
1945-1973

by Brian Hinton and Geoff Wall

Helter
Skelter
Publishing

First edition published in 2002 by Helter Skelter Publishing
4 Denmark Street, London WC2H 8LL

Copyright © 2002 Brian Hinton and Geoff Wall

Cover design by Paul McEvoy at Bold
Typesetting by Caroline Walker
Printed in Great Britain by The Bath Press, Bath

A CIP record for this book is available from the British Library

ISBN 1-900924-32-3

Ashley on stage at the Whittlesey Barn Barbecue, near Peterborough. 2nd June 1968

For Kay Hutchings, Maidie Hinton and Jean Wall

ACKNOWLEDGMENTS

From Geoff Wall – It remains a giant step from writing opinionated magazine articles to biographer, so my grateful thanks to Ashley for his faith, friendship and trust.

From Brian Hinton – I second that emotion and the same applies to Eileen for whom Ashley will always be Tyger.

Special thanks from both authors to the following, without whom....

Julian Bell for reading the completed manuscript and showing us a way through, as well as his many detailed corrections. Ian Maun for his encouragement, meticulous proof-reading and unstinting help. Steve Sheldon [it was all his fault!] and Teri Anderson, John O'Regan for making introductions, Ian Burgess and Mark Fuller for their enthusiasm and helpfulness, and Ian and Stephanie Rennie. All of these are true keepers of the flame of Fairport and beyond.

We owe a particular debt to the near-legendary tape archives of Brian New – saved in the nick of time from the Lewes floods – which have enabled us to completely re-evaluate the musical achievements of the various line-ups of the Albion Country Band. Profound thanks too to fellow archivists Clinton Heylin and Ian Maun – again – for priceless insights into live performances by early Fairport.

Thanks to the following for delving back into their memories of Ashley at various stages of his career...

Kay and Greg Hutchings.
Kingsley Abbott, Judy Dyble, Anders Folke, Iain Matthews, Simon Nicol and Richard Thompson.
Martin Carthy, Keith Dewhurst, Andy Irvine, Maddy Prior, Sandy Roberton, Gay and Terry Woods.
Steve Ashley, Shirley Collins, Sue Draheim and John Kirkpatrick.
Clive Gregson, Andy Roberts and John Tams.

Dave Griffin and Derek Bigwood for PC and AppleMac Air-Sea rescue and support.

Mandy Brereton, Tim Chambre, Chris Clark, Alan Clayson, Nigel Cross, David Harris, Chris Heasman, Clinton Heylin, Brian Hopper, Patrick Humphries, Adrian Jurd, Vic King, Mimi Lee, Jeff Lewis, Dr Neil Philip, Jane Pieri, Nigel Robinson, Ian Robson, Gordon Rowe, Neil Wayne and Hazel Wilkerson. And last but certainly not least, Mike Fuller, who over the last two years has been forced to look at us through his TV documentary viewfinder whilst we interrogated Ashley and chums.

All photographs used within this book come from Ashley's collection. Whilst the publishers have made every reasonable effort to trace the copyright owners for any or all the photographs in the book, there may be some omissions of credits for which we apologise. We shall be very happy to attribute any such credits in a second edition.

Recommended websites include Ashley's www.ashleyhutchings.com and Steve Sheldon's www.folkicons.co.uk

"The Ledge" is a quarterly magazine produced by the Friends of Fairport available from Ian Burgess, 83 Windway Road, Llandaff, Cardiff, South Glamorgan CF5 1AH. e-mail: ian@unhalfbricking.freeserve.co.uk

CONTENTS

CONTENTS

PREFACE

Thanks for opening this book, particularly if you've already paid for it. It's about a man described as "a *very* significant figure" in the development of folk rock, and because the chap doing the describing was one Richard Thompson, you can be assured that these pages will be indispensable reading. Richard's comment is breathtakingly modest of course, for he himself was at Hutchings' side with his own prodigious talent. But then every prodigious talent on the British folk scene plays alongside Hutchings at some stage – his ability to pick a team is a key part of this story.

Ashley and I got to know each other through a long running TV project. In these middle years of life our respective vintages make no distinction, but around 1970, the half decade that separates our birthdays was a canyon. He, "Tyger" Hutchings, and his fellow musicians had already risen to cult status, whereas my friends and I were still mere students. It was upon us, in our tatty flats where dope and patchouli perfumes mingled with a faint whiff from the gas meters, that the gorgeous chords of Fairport fell. Our final exams were bungled to cheap red wine and Steeleye Span. We started our careers to the Albion Band. This young audience was the bed-rock of folk rock – it was the generation which bought the new sounds invented by Hutchings and his wonderful colleagues and to that extent we helped make their work possible. Admittedly, it was an easier job to buy an LP than to invent a whole musical genre and rise to cult status, but I like to think we did our bit. My own friends were certainly fired up by the new movement that made folk what we'd now call "cool", and stirred passionate debate between modernisers and traditionalists. It galvanised the folk clubs, those vital social hubs where newcomers mixed with the greats, mild mixed with bitter and, best of all, girls mixed with boys. Among my chums were a highly talented bunch, on the gig circuit themselves and poised on the edge of turning professional. They revered the hallowed circle around Hutchings and drew enormous inspiration from it. It was *the* sound of our young lives. As life would have it, in the end these students gave up music to concentrate on Proper Jobs. But conversely, one friend who had a Proper Job had already packed it up to become a professional musician. His name was (and still is) John Tams. Hutchings recruited him for the ground breaking *Son Of Morris On*, then again for the National Theatre productions. It's no coincidence that John was to become a towering talent in his own right – Hutchings, with the natural instinct of a second generation bandleader, had typically spotted the potential.

That little snapshot is of one consumer's eye view of the early years of Ashley Hutchings' career. The tracks I originally played on the Dansette still prickle the hairs on my neck every time I play them on CD and such enduring quality is way beyond mere nostalgia. The tracks – scores of tracks – that Ashley's laid down subsequently comprise many more favourites. So how have they come about, what stories weave around them?

Well, this book will be a revelation. The authors, Geoff Wall and Brian Hinton, have already found it revealing and as fine music journalists and critics, their opinion is sound. Simon Nicol described their subject as an "*eminence grise*" at the age of twenty and yet this is the first time that the subject has been documented in any detail. In Ashley's story there's a musical past which you may be lucky enough to recall, a present which you will understand the better. And a tale of how it all joined up in the energising invention of folk rock from where so much music has flowed.

Mike Fuller
TV Director of "Ridgeriders"

PART ONE

FAIRPORT CONVENTION

"Ashley is a centrally important figure in the last thirty-odd years of British culture. I think that it's very important to have someone like Ashley exploring the possibilities of the tradition. And bringing it in various way in to the public focus."
— Richard Thompson

Fairport Convention. l-r: Martin Lamble, Simon Nicol, Judy Dyble, Richard Thompson, Iain Matthews, Ashley Hutchings. 1967

1:1
THE PROSPECT BEFORE US

When BBC Radio 2 listeners voted for *their* fifty most influential folk albums of all time, five albums within the 'Top Ten' were the work of, or the inspiration of one man, Ashley Hutchings. These included Steeleye Span's *Please To See The King* [9], Shirley Collins' *No Roses* [8], the Albion Band's *Rise Up Like The Sun* [5], Ashley's *Morris On* [3], and Fairport Convention's *Liege & Lief* [1].

Ashley Hutchings first came to fame as bass guitarist with Fairport Convention, in their explosive prime in the late sixties. On his instrument, he was as musically inventive as Phil Lesh of the Grateful Dead, and as melodic yet unshowy as Chris Hillman of the Byrds. Just as Hillman can be seen as an architect of Americana, or alt country, so Hutchings can be seen as the man principally responsible for the contemporary roots scene. Among his close musical associates stand John Tams, Graeme Taylor, Show of Hands, Chris While and Julie Matthews...right up to the current Albion Band.

This book is the first to trace exactly how crucial Ashley was to Fairport's redefinition on *Liege & Lief* of English rock music by infusing it with the spirit of traditional song. Here were the old, dark, dangerous roots music of the English peasantry – music that looks despair in the eyes and then spits in its face.

It was a vision that has sustained Hutchings ever since, through his formation of Steeleye Span and the various incarnations of the Albion Band. This book traces that progress, and his growing obsession with a specifically English tradition. The narrative takes us to the break-up of the Albion Country Band in 1973, the turning point in Ashley's career.

His influence can be felt in the drum 'n' bass stylings of Eliza Carthy's *Red*, in the powerhouse folk-rock of the Oyster Band, and in the inventiveness of Albion Band offshoots like The Home Service. Fellow visionaries Shirley Collins, Martin Carthy, Richard Thompson, Simon Nicol, Steve Ashley and John Kirkpatrick, are all extensively interviewed here, along with Ashley's own family.

Mercurial and passionate, he has turned his back several times on fame and fortune in order to pursue his dream of restoring English folk music to its natural audience. Percy Grainger wrote of "the cruel treatment meted out to folksingers as human beings (most of them died in poor-houses or in other downhearting surroundings) and at the thought of how their high gifts oftenest were allowed to perish unheard, unrecorded and unhonoured". If Ashley Hutchings' life has had one single unifying purpose it has been to honour those forgotten folksingers, and preserve their tradition by making it new.

Ashley Stephen Hutchings was born during wartime, on January 26th 1945, and grew up amongst the leafy, middle-class slopes of Muswell Hill. He currently lives within a similar Sheffield city environment. His up-market apartment has a neat and business-like appearance, almost like a Show Home. There are few homely touches other than the framed photographs of his father's dance band and a meticulously arranged record collection. In person, he is a mass of contradictions: restless but firmly rooted in his own eccentric Englishness, meticulous in dress and speech but a man whose every fibre resists the *status quo*. He is always on the road to another gig, or recording session, or broadcast, yet has never learnt to drive. He played at the wildest venues the sixties had to offer, but never took part in the drugs culture, and will find bits of fluff to pick up from the best swept floor. When we arrived to disrupt his ordered life, he produced thirty years of ephemera that were locked within a battered suitcase. Brian's academic zeal lighted upon this musty heap of mildew and we spent two full days sorting this detritus into neat piles, thus saving a priceless archive. Ashley threw windows open in an effort to dispel the pungent reek, but failed. What we glimpsed during this process were tantalising clues to a forgotten heritage. By the time we left, everything was back in its place and Ashley back in charge of his burrow. His good grace was an example to us all. Here is a man both engagingly modest, yet suffused with his own ego and imagination.

Most of all, he is a magician. You are just admiring his craftmanship or careful research, and then he suddenly hits you with a concept so ridiculous and jaw-dropping in its inventiveness, it's like a thump in the stomach. He can make the hair at the back of your neck quiver, not only with his instrumental prowess (underrated as that still is) but with the force of his mind.

There's something shamanic about all this, the kind of wild hot-wiring in the brain which was unleashed in the sixties, and often conceals itself in nostalgia and melancholy. The writer Michael Moorcock can pull off the same trick, as can movie director John Boorman, myth-makers both. Indeed, one of the best ways to look at Hutchings, both as a builder and breaker of rock bands, and in terms of his restless creativity, is as a film-maker of the megalomaniac stamp of Orson Welles. Ashley, too, is larger than life, a man who wants to do everything, taking on all the big themes, battling with the big corporations. Stubbornness and self-belief. Always moving on.

Ashley is a man of nervous animation, in motion geographically, spiritually and in terms of his romantic entanglements. The strange journey we are about to relate involved a series of visits conducted jointly by Ashley and us, to the places that have mattered most to him. Also in attendance was the affable Mike Fuller, director of TV's "Ridgeriders", filming the event for a TV documentary which follows the writing of this biography. Interviews held *in situ* often brought out memories buried for decades, but suddenly prompted by the very surroundings where they first arose. We have visited, in turn, the mock Tudor house where Ashley grew up, 'Fairport', the house just a mile or so up the road, central London, rural Sussex, and the two crucibles where he helped construct British folk rock, Farley Chamberlayne (near Winchester) where Fairport rehearsed *Liege & Lief* and Winterbourne Stoke (near Salisbury) where Steeleye Span first came together. Private places all, but with a public resonance.

Within early Fairport Convention, Ashley was very much in control. He stood at the back with the rudimentary sound control, getting the levels right. And even though he stood in the shadows, he seemed to be very much the captain of the ship. Fairport's lead guitarist Richard Thompson: "He was the first to become a full-time musician. It was Ashley's band, he was always the moving force behind the direction and the policy all the way into folk-rock and into the traditional revival. Simon Nicol, the one original Fairport member still with the band: "You need a pecking order and someone with whom the buck stops." Richard Thompson: "And where the list starts. Ashley is a compulsive list writer." Simon: "The amount of biros that man must have used over the last 35 years! It must be a swimming pool full of biro ink."

Ashley's stepmother Kay talked to us in their family home. The walls are jam-packed with landscape paintings by Ashley's father. A typical fifties mum, she royally entertained us with tea and cakes, and after some initial nervousness settled down happily to chat. She also showed an incisive ability to dissect both Ashley's and our characters. It took us back to a wintry lunchtime at Winchester's Tower Arts Centre where we met her son for the first time as he decanted himself from the tour bus. After initial pleasanteries we drove to a pub literally in the shadow of a monumental sculpture of King Alfred, and Ashley, the stern entrepreneur, put us through our audition. It was like being examined by a fierce searchlight…and we passed! Perhaps Brian, the mad poet, and Geoff, the unflappable Civil Servant reflect the two poles of Ashley's personality. Now, in a mock tudor house at Muswell Hill, Kay filled in some of the gaps.

"Quite a brilliant family, the Hutchings. We have Diane Harmer, an astro-physicist in the family. Greg (Ashley's brother) is very interested in astronomy. Ashley was very, very earnest, and very keen on getting groups together. At the beginning it had to be anybody who could afford an instrument. He's got over enormous difficulties. I'm sure that he starved although he's never said anything to us. For such a fussy person he seems to sleep down anywhere. He's driven. You couldn't live with him – he's always on the phone. But with his dad, although he had his music and painting, he took time for us and decorating. He was very good in the garden – a family man. Whereas with Ashley everything comes second to music. Although he's very fond of Blair his son. I just often try to imagine what Ashley would be like now without Blair, because it has altered him a lot. He's a lovely and intelligent little boy."

"I think it's destiny. Ashley would go out and Joe Boyd would be standing there. He seemed to move on – one person taught him something and the next person did. He's the original wandering minstrel. Way back to Shakespeare's day. He's got the power of concentration. He can't stop. His mother and Grandma were the same. It's funny – some of the Hutchings can be very rude indeed. It is the Huguenot trait." Ashley can trace his family back to the Huguenots who fled religious persecution in France.

Ashley wrote of *himself*, introducing his one-man show playing the folk-song collector Cecil Sharp, that he would be best remembered "for his pioneering work in popularising folk-songs and folk-dances in England in recent times, and the chief figure in the electric folk music". We think it goes even deeper than that, and that Hutchings has helped redefine the notion of what it is to be 'English', at a time when such questions are of burning relevance.

1:2
TWANGIN' N' A-TRADDIN'

Mock Tudor, Muswell Hill

Ashley's childhood roots in the solid ground of North London were to define much of his later musical career. He was brought up on Durnsford Road, between Muswell Hill and Bounds Green, in a mock Tudor four bedroomed house – little changed to this day – facing a recreation park and swimming pool.

Richard Thompson's *Mock Tudor* album contained a lot of subtext about the early Fairport days. Kingsley Abbott was a friend of early Fairport and went on to become a teacher and a highly regarded expert on sixties music. Similarly he puts social circumstances in focus. "The Durnsford Road parade very much sums up the aspiring nature of the period. They are big houses, and situated opposite a park. There was a real mix of people who lived there: the Wyvills in 139. Rosie and Clarry in 141, a brother and sister who were really whacky old people. She was like Miss Haversham, forever waiting for the love of her life to return. She kept all the wedding clothes. There were just so many stories in that road."

"The Wyvills always had an open house for Sunday tea. It was a very, very whacky little parade of houses, and in that respect it was quintessentially English. The whole thing of Englishness is the containment of eccentricity, and it was all there, and more. Somebody like Alan Ayckbourn could make wonderful plays around there. There was this mock horror of going south of the river. Going down through Kentish Town to places like the West End, was a very, very frequent Saturday drive. There is this terminology of place names – Golders Green, Palmers Green, Muswell Hill. That feel of North London being a nice, safe place. Around the corner from me, literally half a minute's walk away were Ronnie Carroll and Millicent Martin."

Close neighbours included entertainer and some-time Goon, "Professor" Bruce Lacey and Brian Wyvill, who befriended the young Richard Thompson at William Ellis school, and also knew Simon Nicol, from the Muswell Hill Methodist Youth Club.

Ashley by Len Hutchings. 1957

But even within this sheltered Mock Tudor home environment some things were kept secret. Ashley: "I can't tell you much about my natural Mum. All I know for sure is that her name was Vera and that she committed suicide by coal gas poisoning, when I was five. I don't remember anything about that. Maybe I wiped it from my mind. I went for many, many years, right up to adulthood without knowing as it was kept from me. A few threads were eventually pulled together in my mind, and I'd see the odd photograph on the mantlepiece of an Aunt or Grandmother. Eventually, because I didn't want to confront my Father or Kay, I went to Somerset House in a lunchtime, when I was working as a journalist in my late teens, and I got a copy of her Death Certificate. I tracked it down and there it was – the name Vera, and her suicide. I wasn't sure whether Kay was my natural Mother. It was a shock to read "Suicide". To go back to work and do an afternoon's work after that was quite numbing."

"But I didn't confront my parents. It was partly to do with my Englishness, and reticence, and it's partly to do with the early sixties, because no one would dream of not bringing it up now. But it was a different era. I didn't brood on it. I filed it away in my brain and carried on. Thinking there will be a time when it will be suitable to talk about this. But the loner comes into it now, because I didn't share that information. I didn't share it with a friend. I didn't share it with my Mother or my Father. I didn't share it with anyone."

My earliest memories are at Sheen Court Boarding School near Worthing in Sussex, and quite clearly I was sent there to be away from all the problems that were involved. Because not only did my Mother die, but my Father very quickly found Kay, and within a very short time they married. What I remember is about a year at Boarding School which I hated, and where my pathological hatred for onions was developed. 'You can't leave the table until you've eaten all those boiled onions!' If you talk to any of the musicians I've worked with, they'll say: 'Oh yes, Ashley. He hates onions!' It is the thing which has attached to me and has stayed all my life. In fact the interesting thing is that the earliest memories I have are very much a blueprint for my life."

Kay Hutchings' recalled: "I remember upsetting him once talking about Deanna Durbin, and I said that her legs were quite fat – "What do you mean? Why are they fat?" He couldn't understand. He had an eye for the women even then."

Ashley and father at Sheen Court Boarding School, Worthing. 1951

Ashley: "My other vivid memories are in playgrounds, kissing the girls. Linda Hagger sitting on my lap, when all the other boys were running around, kicking balls or whatever. I also had a remarkably intimate and precocious sexual relationship with the two girls next door, Jill and Sue, at the very, very young age of six or seven. So that female interest was obviously there from very early days."

"I didn't pass my Eleven Plus and for one good reason, because I didn't do my study for the relevant subjects. This attitude carried on through my Senior years in the very Empiric sounding Cecil Rhodes Comprehensive School, which was literally a quarter of a mile from my house, just across the Recreation Ground."

"It's not worth listing the paltry certificates that I got at school. I enjoyed schooldays because of the freedom I had, the girls, the sports and because of the fact that people liked me. Really the studies were a side item. It didn't worry me at all, because I wasn't into being academic. I was more interested in how I looked and whether my quiff was in place. In no way was I academic, that all came later. It might go some way to explain that when I got the folk-bug I poured myself into Libraries and books, which I hadn't done at school. Trying to skive off lessons. You could say that like one of my heroes, Bert Lloyd, I was self-educated."

"And then my brother Greg arrived when I was 13 years old. Although he's virtually a generation apart and we're not really close, I do think of him as being a brother and not a step-brother."

"At 15 I started to hate my quiff and wanted to get rid of it. I was still very clean cut but had taken to wearing suede shoes to school, and a cut-away collar shirt. The school uniform was Royal Blue but we somehow got special dispensation to wear what we liked. So we were wearing Navy Blue jackets. Like rebels. No blazers. And quite hip looking in a scandalous way."

Members of Cecil Rhodes football team. 1959-1960. Ashley is second from the right – front row.

By now, he had acquired a nickname, 'Tyger' Hutchings – from his tigerish aggression on the football field. The spelling, though, could only have come from the poem by William Blake of that same title, in *Songs of Innocence and Experience*. Here is a source of unquenchable energy, "burning bright/in the forests of the night", equally apt for Hutchings' air of mystery and sheer bloody-mindedness. Bryan King, another of Ashley's boyhood friends, was nicknamed Lyan, to match. "We weren't real tearaways. It was establishing a "we are different and that we don't just want to be plebs" persona. We weren't Rockers or Teddy Boys. I started to develop good friends at this time. Special friends, most of whom I subsequently lost touch with."

His stepmother gave us further insights into the youthful Hutchings. "At school he could tell people what to do and they would follow him. He was a natural leader. We had to put his own door bell on, with 'Tyger' – his nickname – written on it because we got fed up with answering the door. The bell went into his room in the front where 'everything' happened in there. He wrote "Kip Out" on the door for us not to go in. K-I-P OUT."

The young Hutchings grew up with Radio Luxembourg. His first musical passion was early rock'n'roll, "greasy kid's stuff" as Bob Dylan was to describe it. Even then he would buy original US pressings rather than British reissues. Like so many others, he listened covertly, under the bedclothes, to Radio Luxembourg's nocturnal emissions. He heard Presley's '*Heartbreak Hotel*', and fell madly in love with this blend of passion and energy.

It was the skiffle craze which enabled the young Hutchings to first play in public, just like the Beatles. "I bought a bass guitar when I was 16, and have stuck with it ever since". He has since progressed from tea-chest to Fender, but the principle is much the same, to give a band 'bottom', rocking the foundations and leading from the back. At its best, its a sneaky instrument, rhythm and melody together, and it suits his secretive nature. Ashley was as absorbent as blotting paper, soaking up all kinds of musical experiences, with a mental stamina and openness to new sounds which has served him well down the years.

His quest for the musical philosopher's stone was "exhaustive". "My week might very often be taken up with six nights out, and each night a different musical form. Jazz clubs, folk clubs, classical concerts, R&B clubs like Cooks' Ferry Inn, the Flamingo, the Marquee". Firing his young imagination, and giving it wings with which to fly.

So when did he first start playing music? "I suppose he was about twelve. His father made him a tea-chest bass for skiffle. He played Lonnie Donegan's '*Freight Train*' – that went on for hours. We became very unpopular along this road with all the noise. I'll tell you one thing about Ashley, he's very intolerant about music! He only likes what he likes. He'd come away when he was little from a child's party if they weren't playing the right music. I can remember him storming in from next door: "Well, I'm not going there again!" "Why? What's the matter?" "They keep playing that song, *Wonderful, Wonderful Copenhagen!*"

"Ashley loved the theatre too. He had a toy theatre and he'd love you to be ill, so that he could set up his theatre and do a show. He does super voices. He used to read Tin Tin to his brother Greg and do all the different voices. They used to call us "The Actor's Family" and the first thing he did was "*The Mummers Play*." He must have been nine or ten. I can remember him practicing his lines all day – "Is there a Doctor in the house? Yes, there is a Doctor!" He played The Doctor of Physick."

Kay stresses his sense of independence, even as a young boy. "Ashley is

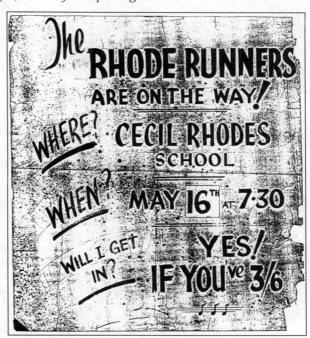

Ashley's School band poster drawn by Len Hutchings

very self-taught – very motivated. He was never without a piece of paper and a pencil. Always writing." Oddly he didn't actually have any music lessons. "Ashley and his father didn't seem to be able to learn music. They've got such a natural ear – they can tell you any note, and just join in. They originally had brass bands in the family I think."

Ashley's father was a self taught pianist who led his own dance combo, Leonard Hutchings and the Embassy Five. Ashley: "My Dad was a very talented Sign Writer, employed by the Post Office. His chief job was painting tiny, intricate lettering and numbers on switchboards. He'd often bring them back. I can picture them now, little white plastic discs which would go in the switchboards. He would travel around. And out of hours, he would paint and sell his paintings. I imagine his earnings were supplemented by playing piano in the bands. The earliest memory I have of music is my Father playing piano in the house, when I was seven years old. So I was born and brought up with the sound of piano, his favourites Errol Garner and Art Tatum."

Kay added "Leonard used to paint Nipper, the logo for His Masters' Voice, at Hampstead. When we first got married Ashley had been sent to a little Boarding School in Worthing, but he came home for the holidays and was crying in his porridge not to go back. I said: "Right – just go to Christmas!" Kay laughingly added "He was a good little boy as long as we did what he wanted!"

Even when young, "He loved cowboys and the Saturday morning pictures. There would be a knock at the door, and I'd open it to "They've got me ma!" He loved Randolph Scott. He always had his gun. And yet in early band photos, he was always dressed differently to the rest of the band. He loved to be different and dressed in collar-less shirts. He was quite a nervous young boy who was frightened of dying."

"He was very influenced by Country Music when he was young. I can't remember what the first single he bought was, but it was probably The Everly Brothers. I think that Bob Dylan cast a large shadow over him, and still does. I see a lot of Leonard in Ashley especially when he frowns when playing the bass. Leonard was very serious looking when he played piano. And then of course he went to Cecil Rhodes, the Senior College over there, and that's when he used to play every Saturday night. He used to take his little group over there. I and his Aunty used to creep over when it was dark, to look in the window. He was 16 and it was a terrible noise! But all the girls were looking on. It wasn't folk, it was rock and roll, long before the Beatles."

Ashley and his brother Greg in the garden at Durnsford Road. 1965

Ashley had other kinds of heroes: "I've always loved Westerns, ever since I was a kid. I played with toy cowboys and indians, soldiers and cavalry, by myself for hours and hours in the garden, hiding them in the rockery. Apaches attacking the cavalry. I never played with anyone else and would happily play by myself for hours. I suppose it started with an interest in the Old West at a very young age, and then when I started to pay attention to Pop Music, it was Elvis Presley and 'Heartbreak Hotel' on Radio Luxembourg. I remember it clearly as absolutely knocking me back and me thinking: "Wow! That sounds so exciting, and it sounds so American!" It doesn't sound like Ronnie Hilton! Because the Fifties were very English, very staid. I think beige is a better word than grey, for what England was in the early fifties."

Like many others, Ashley turned his gaze towards the neon-coloured utopia of America. He absorbed every aspect of Americana. "Initially I was influenced by the clean-cut look of Tab Hunter and Frankie Avalon. Then it changed and I got a bit more rough and ready after that. By the time Fairport started, I was wearing the fringe buckskin jacket. I was never interested in being a Mod, because that was following a trend. I didn't want to follow trends. I wanted to establish a trend."

"There's no question that I was fascinated by Americana in my teens. That manifested itself most strongly when I got involved in the blues. Because I really, really got deeply into the blues, not just R&B, but all the different strands of blues, Mississippi Delta Blues, Chicago blues. I went to see everyone that I could see. You see how that focused, intense interest in a form, has stayed with me. When I do my research, I do it more thoroughly than anyone I know."

"Quite early on, I developed my interest in clothes, fashion and being a bit sharp. I had to be one step ahead. In my teens, I would go out of my way to try and look different, to get clothes that no one else had got. This extended to trips up to the West End, to seek out one of only two shops that I knew of, who imported American clothes. I would save up all my pocket money and buy a button-down collar shirt. I got them from Krantz in Shaftesbury Avenue. Eventually, when I went to work in town, I would again save up my money, and be the first to buy a lightweight American jacket. A quite hip Dion jacket. For a short while when the Beatles came on the scene, I started wearing a collar-less jacket. I'd have probably been the only one in my area, my street certainly, with one of those jackets."

Ashley crossed paths with his infamous Muswell neighbours, the Ravens – with the Davies Brothers – who later to become the Kinks. "I came across them. I played football against them once for my school team when Ray and Dave Davies were at the William Grimshaw School. Dave played against my Cecil Rhodes School. We got whacked. Dave was pretty tough and Ray was pretty tall so we didn't stand much of a chance. Quite early on of course, they had great success with 'You Really Got Me' in 1964. We were nothing, we were still messing around. The Kinks' management pushed them into the debutante circuit. They played Blaises and clubs like that in hunting pink. I saw them play at North Bank Youth Club in Muswell Hill but I never saw any of their onstage fighting."

"When I first heard the Beatles on DJ Brian Matthew's BBC Light Programme, they sounded magnificently raw. I saw them on early evening, teatime TV, for the first time during their 'Love Me Do' period, and just thought they were fantastic. They made me think that I wanted to be in a band for the first time." The Byrds, one of Ashley's great influences, were affected in exactly the same way.

Unlike them, Ashley was not so enamored by Dick Lester's *A Hard Day's Night*, and he went off the Beatles very quickly. "I saw the band and was very taken by them early on. We played Beatles songs in the first group that I formed with my 16 year old school friends. I can't remember what we called ourselves. We didn't do gigs, we just formed a little group. I said: "I'll play bass", and someone said: "I'll play drums" and so on." Ashley laughingly added, "We ended up with four rhythm guitarists. Many fell by the wayside, and only two of us carried on playing instruments. But that's always the way. I was interested in the Mersey Sound for about a year and then R&B Blues overtook the Beatles' music in my affections."

1:3
WINGS

Ashley's early attempts at band-leading were with youth club combos. As Simon Nicol later told journalist Pamela Longfellow, "every time I'd go to the Local Youth Club to stir things up, there'd be Tyger in some blues band or other. It was an endless succession".

REMEMBER....
REMEMBER....
THE FIFTH OF DECEMBER
THE STILL WATERS
RHYTHM & BLUES
DANCE

ST. GEORGE'S HALL 7.45
BOTTOM OF
MUSWELL HILL 4/-

Martin & Son (The Harewood Press), 2a Cross Key Square, Little Britain, London. E.C.1

Still Waters poster drawn by Len Hutchings

Ashley comments "I loved the Stones. I queued up and saw them at the Club Noreik in Seven Sisters Road at the very beginning, when they had just recorded '*Come On*' and were Brian Jones's band. The British blues revival's founding fathers, Cyril Davies and Alexis Korner weren't my favourites, but once I was hooked on R&B, I took in everything and got as deeply into it as I could. When you think how scruffy those bands were they did affect our dress sense. I look back at the old photos and we had a kind of R&B look to us. It's that Stones' pose where we're copying Jagger, from 1965 onwards, through my first proper group, The Still Waters, who became The Blue Reeds, who then became Dr K's Blues Band. In each case it was just an extension of the predecessor. Different individuals would come in, but it was basically the same group of people, and we became a band that developed and improved. We had Rick Kay on keyboard, who was the Dr K. Mick Haase who was singing and playing harmonica. John Daniels who was my school friend. We were the only two from my school. I can't remember whether we auditioned for these bands. You would bump into people and things developed. There's one photo of me playing bass guitar with Dr K's Blues Band, with the band's name painted on it by my father. I was the only one in the band who

Back garden, Durnsford Road. 1966

had his guitar painted with the name. No-one else would think of it.

"We liked John Mayall and people like that, but we were actually delving much deeper into the blues. We saw a lot of the black guys who would come over solo and take on a backing band. Howling Wolf, Jimmy Reed, Little Walter with The Moody Blues or Brian Auger's Trinity, the Groundhogs or the Downliners Sect backing them. They'd wheel over a great old blues man, probably rehearse for half an afternoon and then they were off on tour. For the next couple of years I was totally, totally taken over by the blues and R&B. By 1964, Dr K's Blues Band were quite a good blues band playing pubs and small clubs, outside of Muswell Hill, but not out of London though.

"Then I met Simon and Dr K came to an end. I have to say what angels my parents were, because they allowed our blues band to rehearse in my front room for some considerable time. Probably two years. I'm eternally grateful to them because we didn't have any money and we couldn't have afforded a rehearsal Hall. My front room in Durnsford Road was certainly where it all came together. Then that was superseded by The Ethnic Shuffle Orchestra, an acoustic group with Simon. Again we practised at my house.

"At this time I was heavily influenced by The Byrds and their look. I had to wear glasses and got a pair of those square ones that Jim McGuinn made popular. The Byrds certainly influenced my dress sense. I wore a fringe jacket with a scarf, grew a beard and had very shaggy hair. The usual kind of thing!"

Wings
Hutchings/Ken Nicol

When The Byrds flew in then the dance began,
We all were lifted up on Californian wings,
And over London streets in the drizzling rain
We danced to the sound of Rickenbacker strings.
It was the kick-start that our young and precious lives needed then,
So we started on our long and winding trail,
And we played...

And soon we found that we could fly ourselves,
We all were lifted up on sturdy, home-made wings,

And in '69, in the Summertime
We danced to the sound of flying fiddle strings.
And all the rules and safety-first were left unheeded then,
With the confidence of youth we couldn't fail,
No more...

But now the years have flown and our lives have grown
And we're held aloft by torn and tattered wings,
And over city streets in the pouring rain
We still dance to the sound of thumb-and-fingered strings.
Now the screens are where our children make their music now,
But soon enough they'll find their fledgeling wings,
And they'll play......

Money was in short supply. "After watching Spurs I used to walk back after the game. A distance of about five miles. In those days you did. I often think that one of Richard's most evocative songs is *'Walking The Long Miles Home'* because that's exactly what we did. You saw your girlfriend home, missed the last bus and walked all the way home. And in those days you'd walk through London at 1 o'clock in the morning and there was no problem."

Some things have not changed though. For Ashley, Simon is "still the cheeky kid with an acoustic 12-string technique to leave his contemporaries dumb-struck. The baby of the group, with the oldest head, the broadest shoulders, the widest vocabulary."

Ashley moved into an upstairs flat at Fairport house, a mile down the road from his home. Simon would spend much of his time practising jug-band music in Ashley's spare bedsitter. The Nicols moved fifty yards up the road, and rented out the house, still to be found with its nameplate on the corner of Fortismere Avenue and Fortis Green Road.

More than thirty years on, as we sat in the relaxed setting of a Muswell Hill bistro, Richard Thompson wandered in, affable and slightly lost-looking despite his imposing height. Then Simon Nicol joined us a few minutes later, exuding bonhomie. Once the two were together they seemed to lock into a private code of shared experience, two schoolboys out of *Just William*, with us at times struggling to get serious answers out of them. We found it difficult to tie them down until Ashley, the stern Headmaster, arrived and took charge. Richard still seems surprisingly shy for such a big man, but once his mind locks on to a subject, his intellect flashes like a sabre. Simon seems almost uncertain under the bonhomie, and at times, unjustly does himself down. His rapier wit can be cutting, almost like as a defence mechanism. He is far more complex than his genial stage presence suggests. As the evening progressed, there was one magical moment with the trio, sitting in a row, eating pasta. What flowed between the three was a masculine tenderness and a shared respect that was touching. The years seemed to roll back and you saw the chemistry between them effervescing.

Later, in the steady drizzle which somehow seemed archetypal English, 'Fairport' loomed above us, solid and slightly menacing. The three became animated as the memories flooded back. Mike Fuller circled, his camera tracking us like prey, as we clustered around Fairport's ceramic nameplate. The house name is next to a ship in sail on stormy seas, made to look like the natural grain of wood.

Simon: "My Father was a doctor, and his GP practice was downstairs and we had the upper floors. I lived there until I was 13. It was a sadness when we moved out, and my Mother was reduced to renting it our to ne'er-do-wells such as Ashley, who polluted the place with his music and his red painted ceiling."

Richard: "During rehearsals the fire-station short-wave radio would come over the PA system, which added a certain unexpected element to our music. I think Simon had an AC30. I had a Selmer Selectatone, which is a princely amp, all of 20 watts. I think we had a PA and I expect that we sounded utter crap!"

Ashley: "It's a massive house and we had two floors with about six people living there. We didn't rent the ground floor, but we had the upper floors. I had a room on the first floor and I painted it bright red all over. Well it was 1967! There was the room where we used to rehearse, and that's where Fairport convened. We were trying to get Fairport off the ground and were very committed to playing, getting gigs and trying to make a go of it.

"As soon as I left school I was very lucky and fell on my feet. A County Councillor recommended me to a teacher at school for the job as a Trainee Journalist. I joined *Furnishing World* as a Reporter. I remember being 17 years old at a Press Reception, thrown in with all these hard-bitten journalists. During this time I took my first flight, going to Guernsey to report on the Tomato Board. But I can't remember exactly what this had to do with furnishing!

"I worked for Mercury House Publications who were based in Waterloo. So I learnt my trade that included how to report and how to make up pages. I went to typing and shorthand evening classes. That's where it all came together and I quickly moved on from *Furnishing World* to *Advertiser's Weekly*. I then took a break and worked for a very forgettable year in an export company. I returned to publishing, this time not writing, but as Personal Assistant to Alfred Morgan of Alfred Morgan Publications. Which was in the same building as Haymarket Press. Alfred Morgan, was the sidekick, the buddy, the leading light, along with the young, thrusting Michael Heseltine, future deputy Prime Minister, of that publishing group. One of my workmates was the young Tariq Ali, fresh from Oxford but not yet famous as a political agitator. Personal Assistant means that I wasn't writing, I was taking phone calls, liaising with Departments, talking to Editors. Quite a responsible job in which my Management skills developed. There came a point when I'd been in it for about a year, and Fairport had just started, and we thought that we'd got something. We'd done some all-nighters and managed to get a gig at Middle Earth. I thought: "If we're going to take this any further, I will have to do it full time. I will have to give up my job and get those gigs." We didn't have a proper manager. So I'd go out there and try to get some work. Kingsley used to bring food parcels containing bread, apples and the like to keep me going through the hard months while Fairport was trying to get established. I well remember ducking down and hiding from the Rent Collector. Eventually we did start to make a living, but it was very tough in the beginning."

Journalism must have had a positive effect on how Ashley came to take material, shape it, edit it and present it to the audience. "I think so. What you're obviously getting now is my developing an interest in literature, writing and words. The words are coming through now, very strongly. But thanks to journalism, I was also being able to package and present material in a user-friendly way.

"If I hear early recordings of Fairport on stage, I'm embarrassed by my delivery, because I did most of the spoken introductions between numbers. I'm conveying information but am embarrassed by how quiet, laid-back and incoherent I was sometimes.

A 4-CD compilation, '*The Guv'nor*' opens with a period piece, the Ethnic Shuffle

Orchestra recorded, at 'Fairport', strumming and strutting their way through *'Washington at Valley Forge'*, a Stateside sounding piece. After a bit of general chat, Hutchings sings in an American accent and plays acoustic upright bass, Simon Nicol and Steve Airey play acoustic guitars, one 'Willy' toots kazoo and Bryan King scrubs his washboard: all join in the chorus, in a blokeish manner. The whole thing is amateurish, good-natured, slightly out of tune, and fun, like a piece by the early Bonzo Dog Band.

"The Ethnics were playing American jug band, wash-board music. I'd moved on from the blues. We'd listen to the original recordings obtained from Dobells, the London book and record shop, and I gained quite an extensive knowledge of the idiom

Ethnic Shuffle Orchestra. 1966. Front l-r: Simon Nicol, Bryan King, Ashley. Back l-r: Willy, Steve Airey

from Gus Cannon and so on. Jug Bands were prevalent in the Sixties. There was Jim Kweskin's Jug Band of course, but we always went back to the originals, back to the recordings from earlier in the century to get material. We never really did any gigs, it was just fun. Very quickly, we formed what became Fairport." It's interesting to see the trans-Atlantic parallels – in America, The Grateful Dead, Country Joe & The Fish, Lovin' Spoonful all evolved from jug bands into psychedelia.

It was at Muswell Hill Methodist Youth Club that the Ethnic Shuffle Orchestra first played a public gig in "jug band style", and word began to spread about the precocious musical talents of Tyger and Simon. Kingsley Abbott recalls that "Ashley was a little older than the rest of us by three or four years. I suppose that he was seen as something of a father figure to the group, in the early days. He was also charming and my wife-to-be remembers him seeing her safely up the road in snowy weather to make sure she was all right".

Simon said in an interview with Mick Donovan. "He had a very clear idea of where he was going. He was the visionary. He knew the elements that he needed to make a band. I was one of the elements, and we all started playing off one another".

Ashley diary. 1966

Thompson agrees, talking to *Flypaper*. "Ashley was usually the motivation force …
who'd administrate things, and figure out the best stuff to do. We'd always discuss
it, but he'd be the best to organise it".

Ashley's private diaries for 1965 and 1966 reveal his life at the time, a carefully
annotated mix of watching TV, going to parties, small-time gigs, clothes buying
trips to the West End, rehearsing nights with the lads, and dates with girls. Perhaps
the most significant entry…

Wednesday 6th July 1966:
Evening: Called on Si. We went to "J.B" (public bar!) I suggested forming a "Folk-
Rock" group with him and Rich Thompson. We agreed to give it a go. Went back to
his place after and we thought up numbers to do.

Richard Thompson, shy and tongue-tied, had replaced Jeff Kribbet for a one-off
Dr K's Blues Band gig: "Ashley must have liked me and said 'Why don't you play
with us?', so I started playing with him and Simon and various drummers". In turn,
Hutchings would sometimes sit in with Thompson's school band, "mostly vocal,
rock and roll, playing like The Who, doing the blues and Chuck Berry". Future
Strangler Hugh Cornwell was their usual bassist. Ashley was "so chuffed playing
with Richie "that I decided to knock the other bands on the head and just play with
him and Simon. Jug bands didn't get that much call for, and those blues groups, well
I'd had enough of that".

Thompson found Nicol a willing musical foil to his lead guitar flourishes, and Hutchings rock solid on bass. The three began playing barmitzvahs and weddings – as Simon recalled, "once a week if we were lucky … a lot of people used to get married". For Thompson, it was "the usual sort of juggy band thing with one amplifier between three guitars and half a drum kit". Introduced by a mutual friend as "just as good a guitarist as Hank Marvin" – Thompson would come out "with this free-form, liberated music", as Simon described it. Richard points out that the electric guitar was not always king in those early years. "There was an occasional acoustic band which was myself and Simon, Ashley and their friend Judy Dyble – I think it was a four piece – and we'd do the odd folk club like that around 1966".

Among a floating personnel of percussionists, Shaun Frater became the drummer of choice. It was a mutual friend, Richard Lewis, whose vast record collection was often raided by Hutchings for new material, who suggested the name 'Fairport Convention', with some of the ornate mystery of the West Coast groups – The Mystery Trend, the Association – whose reputation was starting to spread via pirate radio, and whom Ashley witnessed in Rome. For this friendliest of groups, it was all too appropriate that their name should sound so inclusive, so companionable. You can all join in.

Fairport Convention first played as such at a private party in Leaside Avenue, Muswell Hill, on 15th April, 1967, however when the band won what could laughably be called a residency at Golders Green Bowling Alley, they appeared here

Tim Turner's Narration playing the bowling alley. 1967

for one gig as 'Tim Turner's Narration' – a name taken from British cinema's '*Look at Life*'. Simon doubled on banjo and violin, and Richard would occasionally pick up a mandolin. Photographs survive of the bowling alley gig: in one, Hutchings sings while Thompson watches, in another the positions are reversed, and Ashley lurks at the back, feet splayed, already master of his instrument. WEM speakers litter the stage.

But ambition burned in Ashley's brain, and one must put down to him the wording of a mysterious message in May 6th's *Melody Maker*, announcing with something nearing desperation (or hope) that "Fairport Convention stays home tonight, patiently awaiting bookings", together with a phone number, TUD 0718. Plenty else was happening.

John Mayall's Blues Breakers, featuring 'guitar boss' Peter Green, were playing the back room of the Manor House. Meanwhile, the 'happening band of 1967', Family, were headlining an all-nighter at Bath Rectory, hippie pranksters the Spontaneous Music Ensemble were at the Little Theatre Club in St Martin's Lane, and Humphrey Lyttleton was in Highgate Village. As to Fairport, a further entry announced that 'Fairport Convention gives up hope. Goes to Highgate Odeon'.

The band's first public gig under their new name was held on 27th May 1967. The gig was billed in *Melody Maker* as "Become converted, Fairport Convention happen at St Michael's Hall, Golders Green, opp Woolworths. Advance tickets 5s". A special poster announced "A Mass Conversion to the Fairport Convention", as if they were a Billy Graham prayer meeting, and featured a madonna and a candle around whose flame was the legend 'Post Renaissance Rock'. On the advance tickets, designed by Thompson, the lead guitarist had drawn around his own hand: the information is printed on the elongated fingers and thumb.

The gig was booked from 7.30 to 10.30, tickets 6 shillings on the door. About twenty brave souls turned up to watch Fairport play Love's *'Seven and Seven Is'*, a Chuck Berry song, the Byrds' *'My Back Pages'*, and an obscure B side from the same band which Hutchings was keen on playing, *'Hey Joe'*, as popularised by Hendrix.

In a photo of an unknown early gig Ashley stands off to the right, in a dark velvet shirt and black silk scarf, looking steely and watchful. Thompson stands stage centre, shadowed – as is Hutchings – on the thick curtains behind. Nicol is just

Fairport Convention's debut gig. Drawn by Richard Thompson. 1967

off to the left, sitting down. Frater is dressed in black and sits bolt upright. The stage equipment is again rudimentary, with only one mike. They all seem boyish, but serious, lost in their music. It could be a trick of the camera, but Thompson seems to be wearing a fur hat, or maybe it's just his collar-length hair: the overall look is more suburban than hippie.

The whole band were relaxed on stage that night, all except Frater, a fact that did not escape

Fairport Convention early gig. 1967. l-r: Simon Nicol, Martin Lamble, Ashley Hutchings, Richard Thompson

Martin Lamble, "this kid with a delicate face and sad eyes", who had come along with Abbott. He announced at the end of the gig that he "wanted to play drums for that band." The evening made a profit of £5, which the band spent on a Chinese meal.

Abbott recalls "At that point it was definitely Ashley who was the one who was most interested in chatting. The rest hung back, in the undergrowth so to speak. The following week. I remember Simon and Ashley coming around. Martin was talking drumming and I was talking material. That's where the link came."

"Simon and Tyger were presented in our lives as a duo. Although I would say that Tyger had the West Coast/Pop knowledge. Simon was certainly a precocious character at that time, whereas Ashley was more genteel. Ashley was like a big, overseeing benign person."

Simon Nicol described best the transition between all that had gone before and the new band. "By the time we started doing the Byrds stuff, the washboards had been put away I think you can say about Fairport that certainly for a long time, there weren't two shows that were the same". Hutchings still jokes on stage about two schoolboys in short trousers and dirty knees – Simon and Richard – knocking on his front door, and the three listening open-mouthed to a new song on the radio, '*Mr Tambourine Man*', with chiming guitars and angelic harmonies. The Byrds were certainly to be crucial, as Hutchings' later song '*Wings*' so poignantly recalled. Thompson himself acknowledges that "we began to be very influenced by them, although old Tyger seemed to be more attached to Phil Ochs". In every sense, electricity was in the air.

There is an argument that the genesis of Fairport occurred in Ashley's front room as opposed to 'Fairport' itself. Abbott: "It certainly would have occurred in Durnsford Road, but it depends in fact where you think the beginning of Fairport Convention lies. Whether it was the Simon-Tyger axis or when Richard came aboard. Martin Lamble and I were at University College School. We were all talking in the same nice Middle Class voice." Listening to Ashley on early radio broadcasts, this is readily apparent. "There were so many overlaps. In fact there was a group of Brian Wyvill's who actually called themselves "The Clique", and that would have been a lot of people who formed the majority at the front of the audience at that first gig. That was the key cross-over point. Highgate. Muswell Hill.

"All the images that one has of growing up listening to Children's Favourites on a Saturday morning with Uncle Mac, schoolboys in caps, short grey trousers. Probably a little bit closer to *Jennings* than *Just William*. There was no cussing. Nobody was a smoker, nobody was a drinker. Scarves were worn with pride. It wasn't purposefully thought out, that's just how it was. Basically all of those areas of North London were reasonably comfortably off areas. There was nobody that was coming from a poor surrounding. It was a nice, safe area.

"Remember that also on the Durnsford Parade was Bruce Lacey. If you went into Bruce's hall you encountered a full-sized stuffed camel. There was all manner of visiting friends, a very left-field set of people, from Spike Milligan on down. Milligan was North Finchley. He wasn't that far away. There were strands of infiltration of that style of humour that eventually came to the Bonzos, to Bob Kerr's Whoopee Band and The Alberts. There was a particular book that Judy would always crease up about and we all loved called *Eleanor Gording Smith's Great Messy Book*. Just a series of line drawings of things like how to repair your own watch." It sounds almost Ronald Searle-ish.

"Fairport was always characterised by good humour and Judy's memories are of always laughing. There was never anything remotely like arguments. If people felt miffed about something, they just stayed quiet. They'd sit quietly in the van or something. The essence was "if we're going to do this, let's enjoy it!". Everybody contributed to the whole."

"Initially, the shape of the band was from Ashley. He related very much to what the Byrds were doing with electrified folk music and electrified country music. Tyger's bass lines were very inventive and melodic, and they were gentle. He would fill little spaces with lovely little runs, that just sat right." He would let that bass drive the song along in a way that few others did. Simon was as solid as a rock, his rhythm anchored everything. Simon was struck by Creedence Clearwater Revival's marvellous rhythmic poke. And then to stick Richard on the top of that, with what he was doing. Right from day one it was something special. Other bands that we would go and see then were R&B bands or Soul bands. Finesse and musicality weren't usually high up on the list. I didn't know anybody else who was playing that singer-songwriter material. There was a finesse, there was a humour and very obvious musicality."

Martin Lamble replaced Shaun Frater on drums in June 1967: his first gig with the band, held at a strip club 'Happening 44' in Gerrard Street, Soho was seen by the rest of the band as a "public audition". Indeed, it was in these rather seedy surroundings that their future manager Joe Boyd first saw Fairport. The club was owned by Jack Braceland, who had run a nudist colony in Watford – the mind boggles – and also did the light-show at UFO: he is the man who swaps mohair for tie-dies in Richard Thompson's song 'Cooksferry Queen'.

'Happening 44' was a strip club in the daytime, just a little hole in the wall. Mick Farren had a Saturday night residency with the Social Deviants. Here is a side of the 60s just as mythically potent as love-ins and LSD orgies. Here is the world of *Performance* and the sinister fictions of Iain Sinclair. Farren: "The back room was filled with cans of ancient porn loops and bits of bondage hardware that were now and again dragged out to be part of the show. Serious gangsters of the Richardson family in camel-hair coats would shoulder their way down the stairs thinking the gaff was still a late-night drinker. Strippers from other clubs would sometimes shake it with the band in stockings and G-strings like their equivalent of sitting in."

When Fairport returned to this psychedelic dungeon in July, Lamble was the undisputed master of the drum stool. Keith Moon made just such a public takeover bid at an early Who gig, and in his radically different way, Lamble was as integral to the soft rock of Fairport as Moon's scatter gun approach for Townshend and company. Pete Frame, of *Rock Family Trees* fame, described brilliantly Lamble's approach, which "sometimes has the bass drum motif blanching and other times is so gentle that only an almost imperceptible cymbal is heard". This subtle style meshed perfectly with Hutchings' fluid bass runs,

Photo: Anders Folke

Happening 44, Soho. 22nd June 1967

already aiming more for melody than simply anchoring the sound.

The band quickly established a firm foothold in the capital's most fashionable night-spots. They spent the Summer of Love playing support acts at venues like the Electric Garden, in Covent Garden, later to be renamed 'Middle Earth' (and now, in the way of such things, the offices of a city law firm). Their audience at such late nights might rarely have broken into triple figures, but they were generally people who mattered. The band began to be noticed in the media rather more quickly than if they had been based in, say, Scunthorpe. Fairport also began to criss-cross this subterranean circuit with other bands on their way up in the world: Blossom Toes, The Action (later Mighty Baby), the Alan Bown Set and Eclection (with Trevor Lucas). The latter were exploring much the same folk-rock as Fairport.

For transport, the band had an old green Commer Van, with the band sitting in the back on top of their upright Marshall amps. At this point, neither Richard nor Tyger showed any interest in driving, and Simon was still under the legal age to do so. Their manager, Keith Roberts began to drive the van, and used it for romantic assignations with female fans. Fairport themselves were "sweet and innocent" of such things at the time, except for – in Abbott's words – "Tyger, 'the oldest person in the world' (Simon being the youngest)" who was known to enjoy the occasional love affair. "He would tell us younger mortals, with a suggestion of a twinkle in his eye, that he liked older girls as they brought "experience" to the situation".

Ashley: "At one point I put the little finger on my left hand out, and I went to the Doctor. He put it in a splint and said: "Don't take that off! Don't move it. It's got to heal properly." But we had some important 'Underground' club gigs in Central London coming up. I couldn't play with a splint on my finger, and I wasn't prepared to cancel the gigs. So I just took it off and we played. As a consequence, my finger never healed properly. So all my life I've played with my "Trigger Finger" clicking. I've got something on it at the moment which loosens it, but its natural state is to click. I've also got a broken finger at the top. But that is on my right hand, so it's not as important. I do sometimes play with the first two index fingers on the right hand, but the top of one is broken and never healed properly. I never got on with a plectrum."

Seeing people like Clapton, of course, made the young Fairport assess their own aptitude. "Although we believed in the band, early on," Ashley explains, "we couldn't quite believe in the abilities of each other perhaps, until it was pointed out to us. Until Joe Boyd raved over Richard and the band in general. And not until the press notices came out and said what a very interesting band this is, would we actually believe it. When you're that close to people you take it for granted. Even Richard, we didn't think of him as a god. He was Richard, our mate, who played very good guitar. We needed outside people to point out the strengths of the band."

That self-deprecation is a very English characteristic. "We felt that our main strength was the songs and the fact that we had an ear for good literate songs. In fact if you had asked us we would have probably said we are doing the best songs. We didn't just lift a song, we arranged it. For example, our arrangement of 'Chelsea Morning' is incredibly complicated. There's an ascending run that the bass and the two guitars play, an effect which is almost orchestral. Our arrangements were very carefully worked on. I think we put our own character into them. 'Suzanne' is another case in point. It doesn't sound anything like Leonard Cohen or indeed Judy Collins doing it. It has this very strong rhythmic staccato thing which is all based around the drum kit."

Someone might say: "I've found this great song called 'Jack O'Diamonds' and people won't know this song. Dylan wrote this song with Ben Carruthers, and it's really interesting." You pick up your instruments and you work out the arrangement by playing together. Basically Fairport were a working band, a band which relied upon playing together and being close to each other, physically. And those arrangements were all just hammered out. "It's a method that I have continued with through all my subsequent bands. If I think back to early Fairport, that was probably the high point of that way of working. For example, the hammering out of folk-rock arrangements, for traditional folk songs rocked up, no one had done before. There was no blueprint, so we had to work it all out together. Today, it's relatively easy for the current Albion Band to use a traditional folk song. You just sit around and play it. Because the blueprint has been set out and the band will know what to play and what not to play, because of what has gone on before.

"I would say there was a special atmosphere in Fairport that has never been recreated. If you ask Simon or Richard I bet they would say the same. It's all to do with youth, but also with the things that come out of youth. It's the fact that you have this enthusiasm and bravery which you are never able to hang on to as you get older. This devil-may-care bravery. That doesn't tend to happen when you get older. I certainly wouldn't do it now. There was a very special atmosphere in early Fairport that I have never recreated. I don't think you can. When I was young we had this devil-may-care recklessness. Money is the last thing on the agenda. And that's why sadly in later life, people fell out with Joe Boyd. He simply didn't keep clear records of monies that were in and monies that were out. But at the time money just didn't come in to it."

Comparing the sixties to now, Ashley recalled that "Fairport's 30th anniversary Cropredy reunion set possessed a very special warmth, the first line-up in particular, when doing '*Time Will Show The Wiser*' and '*Jack O'Diamonds*'. It was a very special show. Lots of things come into your head in that situation: it makes you feel young again, but it's not that pure and simple. You're aware of sharing it this time. First time around you were not sharing it with the audience. You were doing what you wanted to do, on stage, and you hoped they would like it. And eventually they might buy an album. But all those years later, you're doing the songs, not just for yourself any more. You're performing them and you know that there are 20,000 people out there saying: "Oh, they're doing THAT ONE! Great. I like that one too!" And it's a very different feeling. With early Fairport, an audience were almost eavesdropping on what we were doing. There were absolutely no concessions to what an audience might like. You got boredom and a bit of abuse. In 1976 they were still objecting to it. Some guy stood up in the Albert Hall and bellowed out: "This is not Folk Music!"

We asked Kay Hutchings whether there was much of a camaraderie between the parents of the band members. "Oh yes. We used to ring up and talk to each other. Simon's mother used to come here. We used to grumble about them all of course: "What are they doing?" "Fancy that!" and "Look at their hair!"

Judy Dyble recalled "I remember going home from these gigs and the birds would be singing and you'd shout "SHUT UP!" My Mother would have put a hot-water bottle in my bed, at 10 o'clock at night when she would have gone to bed, and made me a flask of coffee. I'd arrive home to this cold hot-water bottle and cold flask of coffee." You get the feeling that all the parents of Fairport all knew one another. "My parents said that Richard's parents came round to see them. They were a bit worried. Ashley's mother was as well. They must have talked to each other, in the very formal way that parents did in those days, and decided they had to let us do it, I suppose. Later I discovered that my parents had been terrified."

Kingsley remembers walking around Muswell Hill with Ashley during the day – the band would rehearse in the evenings, with visitors banned from the premises – and how "even at these early stages, he was well aware that Fairport could not exist for long as a covers band, no matter how good or interesting this was. The future lay in developing their own original material".

The two worked jointly on ideas for songs, sitting near Les Aldrich's Music Shop. "Some of these were heavily influenced by the Keith Reid school of songwriting, as '*Whiter Shade of Pale*' swept all before it in the summer of 1967. I remember that we had a lot of fun trying to work up a line about everyone spilling out of the Tolly (Tollington – local Muswell Hill Secondary School) at the end of the school day. We came up with ideas, and rough structures for three or four songs, one of which '*Reasons for Leaving*' was less awful than the others". Another original song was given the title '*No 1 Loser*', loosely based on the Phil Ochs song '*Flower Lady*'.

It was during that summer Ashley first met Ann Shaftel, a remarkable American girl, who was visiting London with George Galt, a fine harmonica player. The two became great friends of the Fairport coterie, and when Galt returned to America alone, Ashley began an intense romantic and spiritual relationship with Ann.

She introduced him to paintings and fine arts (her study area) and the two did the rounds of London and Paris museums, galleries and movie houses. They became lovers – in fact Hutchings would say she was his first "grown-up" love. Ann would be influential in the early years of Fairport, providing them with imported US albums of Tim Hardin, the Youngbloods, Ritchie Havens, John Fahey and the like. Crucially, she was to later introduce them to the music of The Band when she came back a year later from the States with a copy of *Music From Big Pink* – the group's seminal first album, and The Byrds' *Sweetheart Of The Rodeo,* both massive influences on Fairport's music. Shaftel's relationship with Hutchings was to surface and re-surface a number of times in his later life.

Ashley: "One hot summer day, we decided that it would be nice for me to have my ear pierced. So Ann got an ice cube, a needle and started the operation. Remember this was 1967 and no-one had ear-piercing in those days, and no-one really knew how to do it. So about midway through the 'operation', when the needle was halfway through the ear, the ice cube had melted down her hand, and the remainder of it was done without anesthetic. Worthwhile, because as far as I was aware, I was the only person in Muswell Hill with an earring. That was one example of just how far I would go in an effort to be a trend-setter."

To underline the financial hardship that Ashley was experiencing Ann recalled when she was to meet Ashley at the National Gallery. He was very late because he couldn't afford the tube fare and had to walk most of the way from Joe Boyd's flat in West London. This hardship was soon to be a thing of the past.

1:4
FROM LEASIDE AVENUE TO HAPPENING 44

Before the Summer of Love had grown autumnal, the band had added a female singer. This pattern has recurred throughout Ashley's subsequent musical life – almost all the bands he has led since have focused on a distinctive and assertive female singer. It is no slight on 18 year old library assistant Judy Dyble to say that she was the least assertive of them all: her wispy vocals were so much of their time, and perhaps reflective of a softer, more compliant form of femaleness, pre-Germaine Greer. Ashley has always been an 'equal opportunities' employer, though time has not dealt kindly with the reason he gave back in 1973 for having chosen his first female colleague, "because we were sure bands had to have a chick, and Judy lived round the corner from me".

Kay Hutchings remembers Judy being "very shy. She lived around the corner and used to sew all the lace on Ashley's shirt cuffs." Judy: "The first gig I did with them, was the day my sister got married in 1967, and I had to be bridesmaid. I went to the reception, then rushed home, got changed and went off to play on this houseboat on the Thames, which promptly sank. There was this sudden cry of "Abandon ship!!!" And things developed from there."

For a rock band to have a female singer in those days was something of a break-through, so unusual that Judy was featured in a *Melody Maker* article titled 'Handbags and the Bandwagon'. In Fairport, the reliance on vocal harmonies, centred on the male/female dynamic *did* draw on the softer aspects of the early Jefferson Airplane, circa *Surrealistic Pillow*. The way that Thompson's jaunty guitar wound around a solid yet fluid rhythm section was also reminiscent of Kaukonen, Casady and Dryden at their best. Ashley's bass patterns embroidered rather than thumped, drawing pretty patterns down in the deep. Ann Shaftel remembers walking into Biba's boutique in Kensington with Ashley. A record was playing and Ashley said that it was obviously American because of the bass line!

Simon Nicol could lay down power chords just like Kantner, but without talking to interviewers like a stoned Bertrand Russell. Fairport were never to follow the political stridency of such albums as Jefferson Airplane's *Volunteers*, or the heavy acid sound and song-suites of *After Bathing at Baxters*, let alone espouse the acid-rock lifestyle. If the Airplane acted as a role model it was for their general air of being disaffected, sparky avatars of youth culture, as Ashley's fine poem about seeing Grace Slick on TV, "electric in electric blue", twenty years later, so neatly encapsulates.

**Sonnet – On seeing Grace Slick unexpectedly in a
1987 television rock spectacular.**
And suddenly you burst upon the screen,
Electric, in electric-blue and bear-
Ing little sign of mellowing, a mean,

Wide streak of blue rebellion in your hair;
That rebel-yell as potent now as when
It heralded experimental thought
And deed. That entertaining starship then,
By all that's good, how could it come to nought?
The rot, perhaps it's true, could not be stopped,
Like thinning hair, a thickness at the waist
Or rigid lines drawn down the years that cropped
Up in the most unblemished face of Grace.
Today, by chance, I came upon my youth,
Rebellious, proud and just a bit uncouth.

It was Radio 1 DJ Tommy Vance who first coined the phrase 'The English Jefferson Airplane' in describing Fairport Convention. Was it an apt description? Simon: "Well, we were about the same number of people in the band and I can imagine Jorma Kaukonen and Ashley exchanging notes. There was a chick singer up front, and there was approximately the same number of syllables in the names." Richard humorously adds: "I think about six syllables was a minimum at that point for a band name. At that stage of our respective careers, they were probably good and dynamic, and we were a bit weedy with our 15 watt Silver Selectatone amps."

Misspelt as Judy Dyboe, their new singer was quoted that December in *Disc* to the effect that "anyone who dares compare us with the Jefferson Airplane will be pelted with bad herrings". Why then did the band play its own version of the Airplane's '*Plastic Fantastic Lover*', alongside other psychedelic delights like Paul Butterfield's '*East West*' and the Left Banke's '*Walk Away Renee*'?

Dyble lived in Bounds Green. "There was this great Pentagon type looking place in the middle of Muswell Hill that the buses used to go round. That was where we all hung around." She would walk past his house every day, on her way to the bus-stop. Judy: "Fairport was really nice. The neighbours used to complain about Simon organising motor-bike races round the garden. They came along and said I could live in a van with them, which I did". It sounds like a cleaned-up version of Snow White and the Seven Dwarfs! She recalls pre-Fairport playing "hackneyed folk songs" like '*The Water Is Wide*' when she joined, soon supplanted by fresh material. "We were always influenced by the music we had heard most recently. For a while it was Clarence Ashley and Tex Isley, then we saw Eric Clapton, so of course we became a blues band for a time".

Dyble played "a battered old black autoharp, with an added pickup." – When this eventually broke, DJ John Peel paid for its replacement, an electric version. It was part of the prevailing style. So too were Jim and Jean. Kingsley Abbott had their rare LP on Verve, and from it Phil Ochs' '*Flower Lady*', Dylan's '*Lay Down Your Weary Tune*' – then unavailable as sung by its composer – and Emitt Rhodes' '*Time Will Show The Wiser*' all entered the Fairport repertoire. Mimi Farina was Joan Baez's sister and she added her sweet voice to her partner Richard Farina on '*Reno, Nevada*' which was covered by Fairport. By adding Dyble to their line-up, Fairport could tackle exactly the kind of boy and girl vocal harmony soft rock which was proving so popular in hip circles in the States.

Dyble's first official gig with the band was at the UFO club, supporting Syd Barrett's Pink Floyd, and playing two sets to a comatose audience. At the time there was an extraordinary opening up of English culture. Fairport were very much a product of all that.

Ashley: "I hadn't thought that it must have been unusual to have on the bill, a poet, a folk-rock band, a fire-eater, a light show, and some freaky far-out music. It's just part of what we did. It was the norm. What would have been strange is turning up at one of these clubs and just having a couple of folk-rock bands. Totally unheard of – which of course is what you get now. Nowadays everyone is just pigeonholed into their musical slot."

"When you were working in places like the UFO – the whole point of 'The Underground' was a coming together of avant garde music, rock music, poetry, drama, people like The Living Theatre. I didn't have much to do with it, but you couldn't avoid it then. You'd play a bill and there would be a poet and a there would be a bit of performance art, and you playing your folk-rock, and then some freaky sound band, sub-Pink Floyd kind of band. It was all mixed up together and you got used to it."

"But the spots that we'd be playing weren't the prime spots. We might get an all-nighter at The Speakeasy Club and there would be let's say for example, Tim Hardin, supported by Tyrannosaurus Rex and Fairport Convention. We'd have the first spot and the last spot. So we'd go on at 11.30pm and 5am in the morning. And what do you do in between. Tyrannosaurus Rex get the 1am and 4 am, and the prime spot at 2am in the morning was Tim Hardin. We tended to play to the people who were coming in, and to the people who had nowhere to go, before the milkman arrived. It was our equivalent of paying the dues that the old rock & rollers played going around the Palais, or the bluesmen, the dues that they paid playing the bars in Chicago. You learnt because the audience was very often not listening, chemically enhanced and under the influence, you learned to perform. You learned that it wasn't good enough to just put your head down and ignore them. They were a tough audience. Not tough in terms of throwing things, they had seen it all, they were bored. You had to pay decent money to get in to these places, so it wasn't yobs off the street. Very often record company people were in the audience and other musicians. So it was tough in that respect, but you became a band. Stamina was important. You built that up."

"The Clubs weren't all identical. At the lower end of the scale you'd have Happening 44 which was a scruffy strip club, whilst at the top end you'd have the Cromwellian and Blaises, which were Society-type venues. But it was all fascinating. Most had tiny stages and light shows. Undoubtedly the venues in the provinces were the best gigs. Because there you played to people who really cared, people who tuned into BBC DJ's John Peel or David Symonds. They listened to programmes like Top Gear and therefore knew the music. So when you went to clubs like Mothers or Van Dikes, they were full of youngsters who really loved the music, sat down, and listened. And what was also great about those days, (and you don't get it nowadays), was you could go back to one of those clubs three times a year. They wouldn't have had enough of you. Nowadays you've got to wait two years before you can go back anywhere. The venues simply won't book you. In those days, your regular appearances fuelled the interest and it gathered momentum. It was like seeing your local football team. And they'd notice that there were one or two new songs in the set."

"Today it's a completely different attitude. There's too many performers all vying for the same venues. There's fewer venues. You're also now competing with the World musicians who are coming over. So you're not only competing with other British performers, you are now vying with the world. Another thing which has changed radically is that you had other bands who were real friends. We were never in opposition to the likes of Family and Soft Machine. They were mates. "Are you on there? We're playing there and we'll come and see you". They did their spot, you watched them, you did your spot and they watched you. Family were one of our favourites. Obviously we played with the likes of Edgar Broughton, the Crazy World Of Arthur Brown, Blossom Toes – all those great names that we remember, we played with, regularly."

There can be little doubt that the healthy university and college cheque books later effectively killed the once thriving nationwide club circuit. "Because they could afford it, they were greatly abused. Their Social Secretaries were very often held to ransom by the band's management, and paid enormous amounts of money to get the music they wanted. Eventually that greed killed the golden goose. The powers that be stopped the budgets and suddenly from having all that wonderful music at the universities and colleges, it was cut down to a trickle. The music world never quite recovered."

"I think we did better in more intimate clubs, because we were quiet, subtle and our lyrics were important. We also liked to talk to the audiences. 95% of the acts just announced the song's title and then played. Fairport were known as being a friendly, chatty group, but it was a style that didn't translate too well to Festivals. The acts that did well within that arena, needed a strong focal point. I was there when Jethro Tull broke through. People just couldn't believe this guy Ian Anderson, standing on one leg, playing the flute. Prior to that, we played gigs with them and there was an equality. But they did that festival and became something else. There can also be little doubt that when bands went to America they came back with a different attitude that was somehow harder. There was an intangible something that had definitely gone by the early seventies."

Judy commented "UFO, Middle Earth and The Roundhouse were wonderful places when gigs were playing, but if you saw them in daylight, they were awful. I wasn't even aware of The Roundhouse being a huge circular place until the daylight. It just seemed like a whole warren. Because of all the lights and the dope that was going on, you didn't really notice it."

Ashley might well have noticed how, as Syd Barrett grew ever more unpredictable, it was their bass player who laid out the steady basis for their wild improvisations, and who acted as the band's mastermind. Fairport, though, were never to embrace technicolour light shows: their own stance on stage was more mysterious, oddly confident, moodily self-sufficient.

Judy told *Hokey Pokey* of one magical evening, when they emerged from the Electric Garden, "before it was Middle Earth, and Richard and I wandered outside and we saw what must have been the last lamp-lighter lighting those gas lamps in Covent Garden". Thompson himself, remembered Middle Earth as "a basement right off the square, when it was a fruit and veg market. We'd go to the sausage sandwich stall and there was this incredible collision of cultures – freaks in their long hair and kaftans, market workers with their flat caps and the leather, and people coming out of the opera in evening clothes and tafetta – it was like acid without the acid".

Judy: "Someone would hear something and say: "Oh that's interesting!". And we'd all listen and suddenly become converts. In Portobello Road Market there was this set of instruments, and it was a double bass and a violin and a drum kit, and they lit up. They had like white perspex and they all lit up. We made Ashley buy this great bass which he was always into collecting. He had one which was very strange, and took it home on the Tube. It resembled a huge lit-up banjo and subsequently appeared on the front of *The Hornsey Journal*. I remember that Martin said he could play violin and they fixed the violin up with all those little guitar amplifiers. So there was Martin playing an amplified violin."

"My autoharp was the first amplified or electric autoharp in London. I had a stereo one custom-built. I think that John Peel had the other. It was a wonderful instrument and although I don't play it much nowadays, I still give it a polish now and then. It was easy to play but very hard to tune. That was a real problem because I had to tune it before we went on stage. The end of the guitar strings would stab you necessitating tape being stuck on your fingers. No wonder The Carter Family looked so miserable! The autoharp was originally played flat, and I couldn't do that, and somebody else – The Lovin' Spoonful, I saw them play it upright. I loved the sound of dulcimers. There turned out to be a little man who lived in Bounds Green who made dulcimers. I used it in the band but never could play it very well. They used to fall off my lap. I used to stick them on with Bluetack. I played recorders badly. Especially on our freeform bits of recorder playing which I tried to redo, on stage at our Cropredy 30th Reunion."

Roger Simpson took some priceless photographs inside Fairport house. One of these featured Ashley's banjo bass, later given a starring role on 'Top of the Pops'. Martin looks pensive, and Judy sits on his drum kit, lettered with the band's name in hippie script, with the 'i' of Fairport surrounded with petals. *Very* '67.

The Hornsey Journal proudly declared that "The group of four boys and a girl take their name from Fairport House, where they rehearse over a doctor's surgery after surgery hours". Among those pictured is "Tyger Hutchins, aged 22". Georgie Fame caught them at the Speakeasy, and "the pop star expressed keen approval. They play American West Coast songs, folk-rock, and blues, and write some of their numbers." The group's managers are given as John Penhallow of Greenham Road, Muswell Hill and Keith Roberts. Not for long …

Ashley: "Originally I was trying to run the band, then we had a friend who helped and tried to get gigs. We stumbled along for about six months, and then one day whilst we were playing the bottom of the bill at the UFO Club in Tottenham Court Road, that's when Joe Boyd appeared.

Joe Boyd had been stage manager at the 1965 Newport Folk Festival, where Dylan first went electric, and moved to London as the local representative of Elektra records. He produced records by the likes of Leon Rosselson, Alasdair Clayre and

The Hornsey Journal. 11th August 1967

the early Incredible String Band. Boyd was also 'musical director' at UFO, in the Tottenham Court Road. He described the club to *Melody Maker*'s Chris Welch as "a place for experimental pop music and also for the mixing of the medias, light shows, and theatrical happenings".

Kingsley Abbott remembers UFO. as being extremely full that crucial night, "Fairport were supporting Pink Floyd, and they played their usual good first set, well received by an audience who were all sitting or lying on the floor of the old ballroom. I doubt that many of them could have stood up for too long, but they gave the band a laid-back ovation". During the interval, Joe Boyd came backstage to offer the band a management deal. "Tyger was excited and impressed with Joe's credentials, which fitted well with where Fairport's interests lay at that time. I doubt that they would have gone with just anyone at this stage: they would have seen through the usual rock biz hustlers".

"In classic Tin Pan Alley style", says Ashley, "this American breezed into the dressing room and said "Hey you guys are great and would you like to make a record?" Ashley was impressed. "I think it was his voice to start with – he spoke with such authority. I don't think that we knew a lot about him or his pedigree until later. We just read the *International Times* and knew that he and Hoppy Hopkins ran the UFO Club. It was a certainly a great bonus to us once it was unfolded exactly what this very young man had achieved in his time. Which was fantastic because he'd recorded Rambling Jack Elliott and Derrol Adams over here in England. He'd come over with the blues package and the old guys. In such a short time he'd done an awful lot and it was great to hear the stories."

As to Joni Mitchell, Joe Boyd had met her at the Newport festival in 1967, and she came over to England that same year. "She was looking for a publishing deal over here. I introduced her to David Platt at Essex Music, who made her some kind of advance".

Ashley: "If you listen to '*Cactus Tree*' on Joni Mitchell's *Song To A Seagull* – Joe's the one who "sends her letters in his facts and figures scrawl." There's three verses. One's about David Crosby, who takes her sailing. Another's about Michael from the mountains, and the third's about Joe, who sends her letters. One magical day I went to call on Joe in Notting Hill and he said "My friend Joni Mitchell is over from the States, and I walked into a room and she was there. It was just her and me, and we had a little chat. I commented that "We do one of your songs". "Oh that's nice – I've got lots more!" Sadly I never met her after that. She had a classic beauty, her bone structure and face is beautiful.

"Through knowing Joe we were able to have access to demos from Essex Music of Bob Dylan, Robbie Robertson, the Band and Joni material on white label demos that pretty well no-one else knew about in Britain. The Dylan material came primarily from me. I was a great, great Dylan fan and sought out the most obscure Dylan stuff."

Ashley continues, "We played with Tim Buckley at the Middle Earth. But you didn't meet Buckley – you stood next to him and he was in another world. I saw Leonard Cohen at the BBC whilst he recorded a session and had a nice chat with him. He was a lovely man and I much admire him to this day.

"There was no feeling that Fairport surrendered the direction of the band to Joe. Joe's style of production and management is very laid back. He'll choose the right people and then he'll let them get on with it. Pick the right team and that's half the problems solved. He allowed us great freedom and occasionally he'd try and push in one direction or another, but it wasn't bombastic. What attracted him to the band was "their eclecticism, doing American songs in an English way". This was thanks to Ashley's guiding influence, though Boyd attempted to distance the band from this second-hand material as quickly as possible, perhaps wrongly as he latterly admits on the sleevenotes to the reissued *Heyday*.

Boyd was fixated with the band's young lead guitarist: "I would try gently to push the group in the direction of doing what Richard wanted to do." So where did this leave Ashley, the elder statesman of the group? One can see the grounds for future conflict. Meanwhile, Boyd put the band on £10 a week each, and signed them to Track records – who paid for much-needed new equipment. Boyd also signed the band to his own Witchseason company. In an advert in *Oz* magazine, it was claimed that Witchseason "takes care of your head". In the band's first official publicity shot, Ashley has hands on belt and a gypsy scarf round his neck, seemingly standing in front of the rest. Simon is almost lost in the foliage, a magic place that was actually in the garden at Fairport. It oddly prefigures the front cover of their third album.

There's a fine line between artistic values in what you wish to achieve, and the commercial aspirations of a record company. Ashley: "I can remember Joe Boyd saying to me, at the front of the Marquee Club in Wardour Street in London, in what must have been late 67, he wanted us to do some interviews and me, standing up to him, toe-to-toe and arguing that we didn't want to do interviews. And him saying: "Come on. You've got to live in the real world! You've got to embrace and play the game." And me, being wet behind the ears, but supported by Richard and the others, digging in our heels naively saying "We're artists! We don't want to talk to hacks about our music!"

Early set lists were always written and handed out by Tyger, though much of the on-stage patter came from the self-confident Nicol. Seemingly not a man troubled by self-doubt. For audiences at the time, Hutchings was the band's mastermind, plotting at the back when not adjusting the sound levels, a mysterious figure often dressed in black. A man whom Simon Nicol described as being "the original alchemist and ringmaster." It was also Hutchings who seemed the most creatively restless, always looking to move on. The sort of person who can see around corners.

One of his set lists survives from late summer 1967, and shows Ashley already adept at pacing a set. First up is the hippie anthem, Dino Valente's '*Let's Get Together*', followed by the tale of lost love that is '*One Sure Thing*'. Next is the Phil Ochs song '*Flower Lady*'; '*Chili Beans, Warm*

FAIRPORT CONVENTION

Date sheet for next 7 days

Friday 22nd March	Meet at 83, 6.00 p.m. Session at Sound Techniques 7-12 p.m.
Saturday 23rd March	Meet at Simon's 3.00 p.m. Carlton Ballroom Erdington. Stop overnight.
Sunday 24th March	Play Frank Freeman Sunday Club. Kidderminster.
Monday 25th March	Practise at Poland Street. 6.00 p.m. onwards.
Tuesday 26th March	Meet at Simon's 1.00 p.m. Play College of Commerce, Manchester.
Wednesday 27th March	Meet at Simon's 4.30 p.m. Session at Sound Technique 6.00 -12.00 p.m.
Thursday 28th March	Meet at Simon's 4.30 p.m. Play Guildford School of Art.
Friday 29th March	Meet at Siverstein's Studio 3.30. Session from 4.00 p.m.-7 p.m.

Witchseason's weekly date sheet. 22nd-29th March 1968

The Fairport Convention	Management: John Penhallow, Witchseason Productions Ltd., 83 Charlotte Street, London, W.1. 01 636 9436	Agency: The Bryan Morrison Agency Ltd., 142 Charing Cross Road, London, W.C.2. TEM 0171/0606	Recording: Joe Boyd, 01 636 9436

'The' Fairport Convention. First publicity shot. l-r: Richard Thompson, Ashley Hutchings, Simon Nicol, Judy Dyble, Martin Lamble

Nights', is an early composition by the band, a guitar-led instrumental. To follow, Dylan's slow blues *'Takes A Lot To Laugh'*, Joni Mitchell's *'Both Sides Now'* – not the over-familiar standard it is now – and *'Season Of The Witch'*, the sinister and malevolent Donovan song which gave Witchseason its name. This is a band already prepared to take risks. *'Lay Down Your Weary Tune'*, another Dylan song, and then Eric Andersen's delicate *'Violets Of Dawn'*. The set ends with Richard Farina's *'Reno, Nevada'*, and the Paul Butterfield instrumental *'East-West'*. These are two guitar showcases on which Thompson would stretch out – on a good night – almost to infinity, over a rhythmic pattern set up by the power trio of Hutchings, Nicol and Lamble.

Those who saw Fairport way back then remember crafted gems – never to be etched on vinyl – like Bob Dylan's *'Chimes of Freedom'* and *'My Back Pages'*, or Tim Hardin's *'Hang Onto A Dream'* and *'The Lady Came From Baltimore'*. Less expected is a brooding *'Hey Joe'*, the Byrds' *'So You Wanna Be A Rock N' Roll Star'*, Phil Ochs' savage song *'Crucifixion'* and Love's frenetic *'Seven and Seven Is'*. Bacharach-David's *'My Little Red Book'* – another early Fairport favourite – was also covered by Love, an early Elektra signing which predated and out-toughed the Doors.

Songs like these give Fairport a more threatening image than that of paisley pop: Ashley was to locate a similar mixture of pastoral charm and murderous intent in the folk tradition. The dichotomy has run throughout his work, and helps give it resonance. Love purveyed a similarly unsettling mix of idealism and menace. A rumour circulated that they had murdered their roadie, and two of the band were subsequently convicted for the 'donut stand' robberies, while lead singer Arthur Lee is currently in prison on gun charges. Fairport were not peaceniks either, maintaining a North London cool. And at the heart of their sound and image was the unsmiling Hutchings (actually the warmest hearted of the lot).

As to Jefferson Airplane, the band certainly performed '*Plastic Fantastic Lover*': Whether they also covered '*White Rabbit*' is more in doubt. Reflecting Ashley's roots with Dr K, they unleashed blues standards like Buddy Guy's '*Messin With The Man*' and the Eric Clapton showcase '*Stepping Out*', with Thompson playing God. Even more intriguing are a scattering of original compositions, like '*Decameron*', '*Ghetto*', '*Sun Shade*' and '*The Lobster*', a setting of a George D. Painter poem. Some of this self-written material surfaced on their debut album, or on radio sessions: some didn't. None of this did.

The band continued to play all the best psychedelic dungeons, venues best portrayed in Norman Wisdom's unintentionally hilarious film *Sauce for the Goose*, with a spectacularly hairy and unwashed Pretty Things, playing in a provincial basement. Fairport first visited the newly named Middle Earth, at 43 King Street, Covent Garden, on the 26th August, with three return gigs in September. The booking on the 30th was billed as 'Turn on to the Fairport Convention and the Dreamland Express, plus Herbal Mixture and John Peel'. Fairport were perceived as part of a whole agenda: soft rock, soft drugs, free love and joss sticks, with a light show if you were lucky.

Fairport opened the bill at London's Saville Theatre on 1st October, alongside hard hunk Tim Rose and psychedelic warlords Keith West's Tomorrow. Joe Boyd acted as compere. After the interval, the Incredible String Band previewed 'world music', twenty years early, followed by headliners the Pink Floyd, with Syd Barrett still in one mind.

Days later, Fairport appeared at 'Intake 7' at Sussex University, a Fresher's Ball for new students at the trendiest academic institution of the time. None of Fairport actually went to college: they played at the venues instead, to students much their own age and mentality For some, they provided more of an education than their official tutors! The review in the varsity magazine was titled 'Fairport Steal The Show': a "comparatively little known group from London thrilled" those who caught their act. "I found the

Middle Earth, Covent Garden. 26th August 1968

balance of their sound was a little top heavy at times, and the autoharp and girl's voice were often hard to hear, although this was probably due as much to the poor acoustics as to anything else. The lead guitarist's playing certainly put him in the Eric Clapton class, whilst the second guitarist played fine harmonies and accompanying melodies as the bass guitarist wandered into beautiful tunes all by himself".

For Kingsley Abbott, too, "Tyger appeared to be the guiding hand at this stage; as the oldest the others looked to him to produce the set list decisions and direct things on stage. Away from the stage it seemed to be very democratic". They were billed as 'England's Top West Coast Group' when they played a discotheque at the Railway Hotel, Wealdstone, a pub well known as an early gig venue for bands like the Who.

Back at Middle Earth by the end of October, Fairport were listed above the likes of 'Mimi and Mouse' and 'The Blues Communion', as part of an evening which stretched from 10.30pm to dawn. Just right for young fans from outside London, who could combine the gig with somewhere cheap to stay for the night. Also on the bill were 'feature films/short films/poetry/guest musicians' and the whole experience cost 10/- for members, and £1 for guests. The previous night had seen John Peel as resident DJ, and the Nice. According to Abbot, Fairport's early gigs were "sparsely attended, but the people who were seeing them were people of influence in the business".

Disc for 23rd December note that "newish group the Faiport Convention knocked

Photo: Kingsley Abbott

Fairport Convention outside a cinema, on a walk between sets at the Speakeasy Club. 14th December 1967. l-r: John Penhallow, Ashley Hutchings, Martin Lamble, Richard Thompson

out the entire London Speakeasy Club on Thursday with some super-bright new sounds, the like of which we ain't heard in a long time". Cilla Black is "glimpsed freaking out to the Convention". Photographs survive of the band cramped in a corner. In another shot, a bespectacled Dyble cradles an autoharp. Best of all is a the band offstage, outside a cinema, with a startled John Penhallow, and Ashley in leather jacket, a black silk tie inside his open necked shirt, scholarly glasses, and a neat beard and moustache.

Abbott was less keen on out-of-town gigs. "These trips were not too much fun in an old Commer van. We would allow extra time for breakdown possibilities. There wasn't that much gear to hump in, but everybody carried things in. Simon and Ashley would do most of the electrics, again there was so little. A small Marshall stack. Very basic PA hardware. Those very early gigs at The Middle Earth, the Uni's, the Clubs, that we visited in the early days, set the bedrock for the band. Had it involved harsher characters, it might not have developed in the way it did."

Middle Earth, Covent Garden. 23rd December 1967

1:5
TAKING FLIGHT

There was still one piece of the jigsaw to add. Ashley had been phoning round music agencies, looking for a male singer. A timely call to Deram label A&R man, Tony Hall, came through when Hall was in his office talking to Steve Hiett, the lead singer of the English 'surfer' band, Pyramid. Hiett suggested that one of his own band members, a vocalist, might be just the man that Fairport were looking for: Ian Matthews MacDonald – better known as Iain Matthews, after he dropped his surname to avoid confusion with saxophonist Ian MacDonalds of King Crimson. Pyramid had been managed by Jonathan Weston, also manager of Procol Harum, but when he went bankrupt, Pyramid folded. To supplement his income, Iain was working in a shoe shop in London's famously fashionable Carnaby Street. It was the break he needed. Joe Boyd, Richard, Judy and Ashley had already heard Pyramid play at what Boyd shrugs off as a 'stupid boutique' in Fulham Road in West London. Iain himself had seen Fairport's show at the Saville Theatre, when working as a roadie for Denny Laine.

In late September the *Finchley Press* reported that a Muswell Hill pop group had just visited a recording studio, name-checking "Simon Nichol [sic] and Tyger Hutchings." It was during one of Fairport's early visits to Sound Techniques that Iain showed up. "Ian quietly watched and took everything in that day, and was soon in the band, adding a new vocal direction".

Matthews turned up at the studio with a suitcase

Falmer House, Brighton poster. 28th February 1968

containing all his worldly possessions, including some treasured Ritchie Havens, Tim Hardin and Byrds LPs: "I just observed the first day because they were cutting a track. Ashley was very obviously a guiding light. Even on that first day it was apparent that Ashley and Joe Boyd, and Richard to a lesser extent, were the ones that were pushing the band's direction. But I really think Joe was the one with vision. Although he gives the impression that he was rather distant from it all, I think any major decision that was made in Fairport during the first five years was either instigated or cemented by Joe. Who suggested that I come into the band? Joe Boyd! Who suggested Sandy come in? Joe Boyd! Who suggested I leave? Joe Boyd! Who suggested Swarbrick come in? Joe Boyd!" It had also been Joe Boyd who confided to Ashley at the time of Judy's imminent sacking that the band was firing the wrong singer, saying "Judy was an honest vocalist whereas Iain had never sung an honest note in his life."

"Very silently, Joe was the guiding light in those early years," Iain continues. "Joe gave Ashley access to all the Joni Mitchell demos. She hadn't made a record. Joe had the ear of Warner Brothers and he knew Joni. Same with the Dylan stuff – it all came on acetate from Joe. But to give Ashley credit, although Joe was the provider, Ashley saw the right stuff. He realised what was going to work and what wasn't. I think the reason that I took the path I did was to celebrate the song, and I'm sure that Ashley would say the same thing. I was never into bands like Yes and I never really got the blues thing apart from Fleetwood Mac. On the first album I just worked with Richard adding lyrics. But that gave me an incentive to try a complete song. And strangely enough, I never wrote with Ashley. I'd just started getting into some folk things. For the first dozen dates, I just sang about four numbers".

A suited smoothie to Fairport's bohemian sloppiness, Iain was a year younger than Hutchings, and he had at one time been an apprentice with Bradford Football Club. He was born in Scunthorpe, well outside Fairport's North London axis, and had gigged with local bands at home before coming down to London in 1966 to work with Pyramid. He joined Fairport as a singer, though he played a pair of huge floor-mounted congas. Writer Kingsley Abbott opines, "They were looking to strengthen vocally as a way of broadening the band, broadening the material, and broadening the sound. Iain was from a different strata with different reference points and he didn't mix socially with the others. At their communal Brent flat, he'd barely come into the other rooms. Simon's room was the biggest and the one that was the shared sitting room. Richard had a much smaller room that was a no-go area."

Judy Dyble started to feel uneasy about the presence of this newcomer: "I don't think our voices matched particularly well. I remember feeling quite sad when I found out that Iain and the others had recorded a couple of tracks for the album when I hadn't even been asked to learn the song". She was not the last singer to make much the same complaint in bands controlled by Ashley.

Iain's sweet vocal style on both sides of the band's debut 45 which combines 'If I Had a Ribbon Bow', first recorded by Maxine Sullivan in 1936, with 'If (Stomp)', co-written by MacDonald and Richard Thompson. 'If I Had a Ribbon Bow' uses Tristan Fry, a session player later of Sky, on vibes, and is a jaunty, slightly winsome affair. Simon Nicol recalled to Fairport Convention biographer Patrick Humphries, that the band had a "terrible time" laying it down in the studio. "John Wood (who was resident engineer and co-owner of the studio) had to snip it all together on an Ampex 4-track vertical machine. He was less than enthusiastic".

Ashley: "'Ribbon Bow' was from Joe Boyd's collection, and Judy was largely instrumental in agreeing to do that song as a single. Joe and Judy simply said 'That's quite a good one. Let's do that'. It was totally unlike our style, but these were the days when anything could get into the charts: '*Granny Takes A Trip*' etc, and it got a lot of radio play. It was r e c o r d e d c o m p l e t e l y separately as a single and was only released as a single track."

Judy: "It was really funny doing the r e c o r d i n g because I was playing the harmonium and my feet wouldn't reach the pedals. So Ian or Simon, was actually laying on the floor working the pedals. I knew nothing about

Photo: Kingsley Abbott

Witchseason's Ribbon Bow poster. 1968

recording. It's amazing how time just disappears when you're in a studio. You go in at three o'clock in the afternoon, and the next time you look out of the window – there's only ever one window – it's four o'clock in the morning, and somebody would go and get cream cakes. I never thought about how much it would cost to record. Most of Fairport's singles were unlike their contemporaries. '*Meet On The Ledge*' was different to anything else, so was '*Si Tu Dois Partir*'. '*Ribbon Bow*' is a really good song. I sing it sometimes when I'm just standing alone or walking around a field. I can still remember all the words."

Away from the studio, the on-stage vocals often seemed to lack cohesion. Kingsley Abbott: "On stage, leads were taken by Judy, Judy and Iain combined, or by Richard. Simon would take the occasional stage lead, one being on '*Plastic Fantastic Lover*', a Jefferson Airplane cover. Richard was still unconfident about

Witchseason's poster. 1968

singing, yet produced the most effective rendition of '*Jack O'Diamonds*'". Ashley generally remained mute."

Joe Boyd had firm views on the direction he wanted the band to follow. He introduced them quickly to new material and encouraged them to vocal strengths. The recording sessions proceeded without delay. Abbott believes the band's new manager "tried to shake Fairport up, make them quit looking and acting like schoolkids. Christ, they weren't even into dope".

Fairport's self-titled debut album was released in the UK during June 1968. Boyd's company, Witchseason, prepared an advertisement in which the band are playing on the roof of a Gothic-style house, centred on a giant's head. Judy Dyble is stage left. A ghoulish Thompson, Nicol and a serious Hutchings cluster around Lamble's drum kit. The group's name is outlined as if in smoke from the twin chimneys. Dyble commenting on the imagery reminiscent of Mervyn Peake's fictional creation of Gormenghast castle, recalled, "I wish I had one of those. A friend has got one and they put it in the attic because the kids were scared of it." Another advert carried the following blurb, heavy with hippie understatement, pronounced, 'Fairport Convention does not turn you on. That's something you'll have to organise for yourself. Won't blow your mind. Try Vietnam for best brain-blowing results. *Fairport Convention* is a Polydor LP put together by unusual personalities for that insignificant minority of seekers to whom real music, oddly enough, seems to matter'.

It's long been assumed that the '*Ribbon Bow*' single on Track was the band's first studio excursion, but Ashley explains "We did some demos, two of these were [Joni Mitchell's] '*Both Sides Now*' and '*One Sure Thing*'. We did a couple of things at Sound Techniques and that was our first exploration of a studio, but if you ask any of us, you won't get many good words said about our first album. Richard, Simon and I don't think much of it. I doubt if Iain does either. The followers of the music, the punters seem to enjoy this album more than we do. There's a lot of sentimentality to it in a way. How many people, when they're young, make great first albums? Not many. You could say The Band's first album was great, but they weren't young. They'd gone through many changes. So with Fairport Convention, this was really only the second time we'd been into the studio. We made a couple of demos, and then we were in there making our first ever album. So we were a bit in awe. It took blooming ages – we'd have fifteen takes getting one backing track down. It doesn't flow like the others."

"Of all the albums, I think that this is the one that suffers the most from Joe being Joe – which is easy-going. I think that it needed a firm hand, and that it needed a producer to say 'No, that's not really good enough. Come back with four more songs that are better.' We said 'Let's do some new songs!', because at this time, our live set included mostly other people's material, mostly Leonard Cohen's, Joni Mitchell's, Eric Andersen's, and the material of Bob Dylan. So going into the studio we weren't going to do cover versions; we had to come up with our own material. It forced Richard and me to write. It feels a very sterile album to me. We were finding our feet really."

The sleeve of *Fairport Convention* wraps around like a gatefold, with the band emerging from the shadows cast by an antique Tiffany lamp – old-fashioned, restrained and slightly sinister, just like the music inside. A bearded Hutchings is furthest in the shadows, but also at the centre of the front cover. His hands join Nicol's and Thompson's, almost as if they are at a seance. Ashley: "It's very dated. The imagery and the artwork was very much of its time. We had very little to do with the cover – we were put in this Joni Mitchell-style environment with a Tiffany lamp, and it was suggested to us that certain things were put on the table. No symbolism there. The only thing that was personal to me was the blue marble, which I was given by Ann Shaftel. There's nothing symbolic about the Marx Brothers. We liked the Marx Brothers, but we were too young to know why. We were being moulded at that stage by the designers and producer."

Judy recalls that part of this process of image-creation included a radical style change for her: "Donald Silverstein, the photographer decided that I should be more made up, so they took me off to Mary Quant's, Zandra Rhodes' and Vidal Sassoon's. I had my hair cut and they showed me how to put on make-up. Zandra Rhodes was this wonderful and extraordinary woman, who lent me clothes for the album cover shoot. The very weird jacket had lipstick all over it but was probably very 'cool'. They even made me take off my glasses and wear contact lenses. I couldn't see a thing. The tears were running down my face, so I went back to my glasses. I remember that the shoot was very dramatically lit with us all supposedly looking cool and serious, which was a hoot because the band's persona was very laid back and life was a riot. Everyone had such a devastating sense of humour."

Melody Maker declared *Fairport Convention* to be "a nice, thoughtful, folk-tinged album, full of well thought-up sounds. Banjos, 12 strings, jugs and violins, as well as the conventional guitars provide a pretty clutter of sound. A deeply rewarding set, one that should be purchased by their fellow British groups who are often sadly ignorant of what is happening on their own doorstep".

The album bears this out; it is tasteful English folk-rock, which rocks surprisingly hard. Thompson brought his love for the conceptual work of composers like John Cage to the feast, a flirtation with the avant-garde which Fairport were to drop forthwith. Songwriting collaborations were to become a hallmark of those early Fairport albums. Richard: "Because we were feeling our way as writers, we really needed other people to bounce ideas off. I think if we'd written songs on our own, they'd have been worse than they already are. There's a few duffers on there anyway. Serious duffers. Well, you expect that on the first record. We were finding our feet in a recording studio. By our second album we were getting the noises down in the studio, the guitar sounds, the drum sounds, whatever they were, a lot better. It's been commented that Fairport were more of an American band at this stage, but I felt we were unformed. There was a real Britishness to it as well, a kind of Kinksian Britishness."

The careful programming of the album sets a precedent for the whole of Hutchings' subsequent career, and his role as sonic architect is everywhere. Typical of the subtlety is the choice of '*Jack O'Diamonds*' as the token Dylan cover: Thompson brought Ashley the rare 1965 single by Ben Carruthers and the Deep, which put a tune to a Dylan poem from the back sleeve of *Another Side*.

Descending piano notes lead into '*Portfolio*', an instrumental which closes side one of the original vinyl. Nicol's violin saws away, over Judy Dyble's piano. Tyger Hutchings is credited with bass guitar and jug, and receives co-writing credits with Judy Dyble. It was a song Dyble declared she had invented, though "Tyger added some bass to it."

Ashley and Richard share the credits for adapting George D Painter's poem '*The Lobster*', to a musical setting; it is extraordinary and in many ways, was the precursor to displays of Ashley's theatrical side. It remains one of most sinister things ever put on record. Richard recalls "It just seemed an interesting thing to try to adapt. I think Iain was interested in singing something like that." He laughingly added, "We didn't want to do *The Sound Of Music!*"

George D Painter is a distinguished Proust scholar who wrote one unutterably strange poetry collection called *The Road to Sinodun*. It deals with sexual jealousy, mental breakdown, and a strange epiphany on a hill near the Thames. The poet and anthology editor George MacBeth took some of its tightly rhymed short poems for his anthology *The Penguin Book of Sick Verse*, where Hutchings and Thompson discovered it. Iain Matthews gets the terror of the poem just right, half singing, half talking it. The musical time-line continued beyond Painter's book: the woman who provoked such ambivalent feelings – a fellow undergraduate at Cambridge – married Painter's rival, and produced a son Jack Monck, who played bass in Steve Miller's Delivery, who played the same rock clubs as Fairport, and later was bassist in Syd Barrett's short lived band Stars.

There exists a tantalising glimpse of an alternative debut album. Hand-written by Ashley, one can clearly see his original idea of placing cover versions on one side and Fairport originals upon the other.

Hutchings and Thompson co-wrote '*It's Alright Ma, It's Only*

Witchcraft' which twists a Dylan title to spin a tale of a hurricane coming, no less than a new age trembling in the wings (like Yeats' rough beast slouching towards Bethlehem), which is presaged by some new sounds brought over from "Frisco way". Its sequel can be heard thirty years later in Hutchings' affecting song, '*Wings*'.

For those who have since claimed that Hutchings' bass playing is better on

Fairport Convention. l-r: Martin Lamble, Richard Thompson, Ashley Hutchings, Judy Dyble, Simon Nicol, Iain Matthews

ideas than in execution, this album alone refutes any such nonsense utterly. The opening track is a kind of musical mission statement, with Thompson's curt breaks cut out of the precise swing of the rhythm section, in careful sympathy with Matthews' vocals. Hutchings plays masterful bass, strumming for emphasis, with

Ashley at the Speakeasy. 1968

sudden swoops up and down the register, as melodic in its own right as everything else (very tuneful drums, for a start). There is a sense of 'everybody playing' that one gets elsewhere in the Grateful Dead, or their English equivalent Mighty Baby, both led by a sophisticated bassist, releasing twin electric guitars to embroider rather than have to carry the rush of the music. For further confirmation, just listen to '*I Don't Know Where I Stand*', where Hutchings underpins the whole thing.

The album's closing track, '*M1 Breakdown*', begins with the sound of a transit van, and opens out into a hoe-down, with Jew's harp, much like the instrumentals purveyed by the Ethnic Shuffle Orchestra. A collaboration between Hutchings and Nicol, it contains a reference to the song

'*I've Been Everywhere, Man*'. Time has rendered '*M1 Breakdown*' – little more than a piece of comic fluff when it was written – tragically prophetic.

When folklorist Bob Pegg claimed the album was ruined by Dyble's recorder playing, Simon reacted angrily: "I like it. There were a lot of worse instrumentalists in the group at the time than Judy and there's a lot worse playing on that album". He points out that Fairport have always believed in swapping instruments, onstage and whilst recording. And songs. "'*One Sure Thing*' came from Harvey Brooks and Jim Glover's 1966 US album *Changes*, which also provided '*Lay Down Your Weary Tune*' and '*Flower Lady*' for their live shows. Judy remains fond of the debut album: "It was of the time. Everything I did seemed to be rather airy-fairy. I think it probably wasn't successful because there was no form to it."

A taster for the forthcoming album came with the band's first session for Radio 1's *Top Gear*. A cover of Dino Valenti's '*Let's Get Together*' has a girlish Dyble answering Iain's self assured lead lines, then Thompson breaking in with a perfect West Coast, liquid lead break, Hutchings bubbling underneath in counterpoint, with his bass well forward in the mix. The song ends with a low rumble. "Featuring the voice of Judy Dival" declares the show's co-host Tommy Vance, though he corrects this later.

He introduces '*One Sure Thing*' with the words "Put them all together, and they sound like this." Hutchings again swoops under Judy's fragile vocal, with Thompson supplying grace notes, with Ashley matching him, as Richard soars. Majestic, ragged, and far better than the album version. Autoharp and recorder come in over the booming bass, and then back to the vocal.

Vance offers, "Possibly England's version of the Jefferson Airplane" which his co-host John Peel ignores, going into a strange rap about all the wallpaper in Peel Acres having been stolen. Peel recovers sufficiently to cogently introduce a Dylan cover, '*Lay Down Your Weary Tune*'. Bass and drums lock into an energetic rhythm track, steady and reliable.

"They're singing about a Chelsea morning, no song about Fulham yet, I wonder how long it'll be" muses Peel, mixing football imagery, a Joni Mitchell song title and Fairport's oeuvre, as the band crash in. Ashley carries the rhythm with repeated notes for the chorus, then plunges down deep for the next verse. He has perfected the low rumble, while Thompson

Middle Earth, Covent Garden. 23rd February 1968

bides his time, then comes in unison with Hutchings for the finale. "The beautiful voice of Judy Dyble", Vance enthuses. All four broadcast tracks, later surfaced on the CD bootleg 'A Chronicle of Sorts'. The cover shot is one of the first of the six piece group, with Lamble in a brightly patterned shirt and central parted hair, and Hutchings clean shaven with curly hair, crouching in front of the band, and dead centre.

Journalist Michael White has commented on this strange photograph that "it is hard to dispel the scent of world-weariness permeating the otherwise confident tone their collective gaze conveys. Ashley Hutchings' cool frown. Martin Lamble's pensive expression, impatient, hands on hips; Iain Matthews over-the-shoulder glance, distracted, vulnerable. Judy Dyble and Simon Nicol: distant, dislocated: eyes searching beyond the moment. From the back a callow male in a striped T-shirt peers fixedly over the bridge of his nose. The stark black and white image echoes the comparative certainties of youth. Their expressions give the lie to the received popular wisdom of the era: all pervasive peace and love". A Byrdsian Californian cool is more like what they are exuding here.

As well as trendy venues like the Speakeasy, the band were starting to play provincial gigs like the Elbow Room, Aston. But it was at the heart of swinging London, at The Speakeasy Club, that Fairport met their most celebrated fan, Jimi Hendrix. Ashley clearly remembers one occasion when Hendrix borrowed his Fender bass. Here was a man who while looking to an unimaginable future was also "as good as any musician of the day playing music in conventional styles. He was as good a bass player as anyone. Picture the occasion: he was playing a bass strung the wrong way round, playing with a band he'd never played with before – and it was just terrific. He was a lovely guy, and just full of music. I met him a number of times. If there was music going on, Jimi wanted to play. He came up on stage, played my bass guitar, and then he played Richard's electric guitar. Because he was left-handed, he would be playing our guitars round the other way, upside-down, and making this fantastic music. We did 'Like A Rolling Stone' both times. And of course we shared the bill a few times, at Festivals. He epitomised that period, not just the garish clothes, but the fact that he just didn't care. He was a big man with a big personality in a big frame. He had massive presence and of course he had massive hair. A big crown of hair."

Kingsley Abbott recalls the Speakeasy appearance and a half-hour version of Dylan's 'Like A Rolling Stone'. "When Jimi played with them it was about 3.30 or 4.00 in the morning, when there were only between twelve to twenty people left in the club. Richard and Jimi took turns at exploratory solos, with both obviously enjoying each other's talent". Thompson felt as if he was meeting royalty. It was intimidating for a bunch of "young herberts trying to look cool and this extremely urbane and very bizarre looking, very handsome black man comes up on stage and says "Do you mind if I sit in?" He just played whatever we were playing, whether it was 'Absolutely Sweet Marie' or 'East West'". Simon told Mojo, "Jimi was very happy to get up onstage and bat it out with us. We did 'Hey Joe' a couple of times – it was in our repertoire, like Love's version – and the Butterfield track 'East West' we did most nights. He played Richard's guitar, Richard would grab mine, and I would grab a spare to play rhythm. He played with tremendous freedom".

Now that their debut album was safely completed – though not to be released for another six months – the band's gig sheet for January 1968 was healthily full, playing the 'New Roundhouse', the Bottleneck Blues Club the following day, then off to France for the Midem Festival. The band were still commanding around £75 a night.

Fairport played Middle Earth on their return, and *Melody Maker* singled out their sense of dynamics. "The FC have mastered the art of volume control, which makes listening to them a far more agreeable occupation that it is with some other groups who think volume equals music". Fairport were quick on the uptake, sourcing '*Suzanne*' from Cohen's debut album. As Hutchings told Patrick Humphries, "I remember very clearly the turnover of material around 1968 was incredible. We would learn new songs and perform them onstage almost weekly. There were country things: '*I Still Miss Someone*' by Johnny Cash, a version of '*My Dog Blue*' which the Byrds recorded, Glen D Hardin's '*Things You Gave Me*', and '*Morning Glory*' by Tim Buckley'".

Radio sessions of Fairport playing '*Marcie*' and '*Night in the City*' appear on *The Guv'nor* Vol 3 – as does a studio outtake of '*Both Sides Now*'. '*Chelsea Morning*' and '*I Don't Know Where I Stand*' had made it onto Fairport's debut album, and '*Eastern Rain*' – never recorded by its composer – would feature on the follow-up. Joni's songs seemed to fit both Judy Dyble's voice and – fortuitously – Sandy Denny's.

This was just the kind of material that the band liked best, slightly obscure, tuneful, a little odd, and lyrically subtle. The band's sound did correspond to a certain strain of American music. Scenemaker, Miles in *International Times* rather slightingly compared them to the Comfortable Chair, while Judy Sims in *Disc* wrote "they have a nice folky sound which reminded me of the Modern Folk Quartet, a Los Angeles band of two years back". What set them apart from such slightly smug West Coast harmony bands was the sheer muscle given by their rhythm section, the width of their repertoire, and Thompson's own explosive lead breaks. Yet still their guitarist was not satisfied. Richard: "I remember saying to Ashley after a gig that I was kind of embarrassed about doing the material we were doing, because we should have outgrown doing covers ... it somehow wasn't good enough. I just thought for a band to have credibility at that point you really had to write your own material. After the Beatles, anyone could do it. Otherwise the words that come out of your mouth could not be taken as seriously. I don't know if it was immediately after that, but stuff started to trickle through."

And so it did, with Hutchings, Thompson and MacDonald all supplying material, often in collaboration. But on-stage, Thompson continued to prefer to lurk at the back of the stage: "I'd be the JJ Cale hiding behind the Marshall stack. Coming forward to do a vocal was like walking through flames".

Although Fairport had a changing image, they always had a sense of the purity of sound. Ashley: "We were always a very strong song band. That was partly our upbringing. Partly the fact that there were people who'd played a lot of acoustic music, and knew the value of dynamics and clarity, and getting words over. And that is totally at odds with the style of many of the bands in the psychedelic scene who were into sounds and power. There were a lot of different types of skill in the band."

Fairport seemed to have a few songs – '*Reno, Nevada*' in particular, and '*East West*' where they did play long improvisations. "Ten minutes easily. Very often something longer. It was a different way of playing – we just don't do now. It would be so alien to me now. It was just a natural way of doing things in those days."

It's interesting that when they went to Cropredy and were playing the '25 years on' set, how different the sound was. In 1997, it was very odd for people in the audience, because you were going back some thirty years. Ashley: "It was very odd for all of us!" Simon Nicol: "Fairport are not like a re-creation band, and never has been. We were paying tribute to each of those periods, and I found that whole concert spread over the two days, to be one of the most exciting things I've ever done in my life. Because Ashley took charge of it and wrote such a brilliant skeleton on which to hang the music. He gave it a framework, starting it off with something left-field like '*Wings*', which was written with that retrospective ethos to it." Richard Thompson: "I think Fairport is a band to be proud of. So there's a good feeling about playing that repertoire. And also it's nice to play stuff that you kind of know but you don't know. To play a whole evening of that is quite a challenge but also quite stimulating. It's a revisiting, but inevitably you really don't go back there, you really have to reinterpret it."

Judy: "It was lovely playing with them all again at Cropredy. It was as though we were all eighteen and nineteen again."

Ashley: "The reinterpretation of '*Time Will Show The Wiser*' and '*Jack O'Diamonds*' with Richard was fantastic. Doing the narration at the side I got to hear the performance. I got people like Richard standing there sweating, and you don't get the chance to see and feel that as much when you're playing, because you're concentrating upon what you are doing."

Simon: "I don't remember there being a day when it stopped being a loose free-for-all, and then suddenly there was a gig and we had to get a repertoire together. It just gradually became more serious and the line-up became more stable. Fairport were a happy band. That real joy of life came across."

There was this idea of Fairport being almost like a test-bed or laboratory, trying different songs, trying different nuances. Richard: "For a while up until we took the very British direction, Fairport was a very experimental band. It was basically a folk-rock band in terms of styles and we tried a lot of different things. I think bands could be at that point. If you look at The Beatles in 1962 and 63, they were playing Country music, '*Besame Mucho*', and bit of R&B, standards, plus a little Tin Pan Alley, it was a lot more open."

Witnessing the band in the sixties, one felt that Fairport could have taken off in any direction. It seemed that the songs were very fluid, and their arrangements changed from night to night, especially the solos. Richard: "It was a musical situation in which anything was possible. One in which the audience wouldn't mind that experimentation happening. You had bands like Pink Floyd, Arthur Brown and Soft Machine, that were being very loosely structured, but played quite anarchistically. So the audience was prepared, you know. The audience were suitably psychedelicised."

On '*Reno, Nevada*' Fairport mutate into a cross between The Paul Butterfield Blues Band and the Grateful Dead, with wonderful, long improvisations. Simon: "Not the Dead themselves, but the Butterfields were a very important influence on me as a musician. Having gone to see them live, they were really exciting. It was the first time we heard that blend of straight-down-the-line, hard Chicago blues and then this free-form. I think I saw them at The Marquee. There was lots of Jazz improv. That's one thing about the Sixties – everything was there at once." Richard: "We took in everything from jazz to traditional folk and blues. I saw the Indo Jazz Fusions, High Level Ranters, Jesse Fuller at the Starting Gate in Bounds Green. The Watersons at the Black Bull, Whetstone. All kinds of stuff. The Marquee Club with The Who on Tuesdays and The Yardbirds on Fridays. Gary Farr and The T-Bones, Spencer Davis Group, Davy Jones and the Lower Third."

Fairport came through all those strange London clubs, the UFO, Middle Earth and Happening 44. Simon described them as being "Pretty chaotic, very disorganised, shambolic, and very, very tiring because it was the anti-going-to-bed club. We were no different from the audience. Everybody dressed the same. In many ways it's like going to a Fairport gig now." The band began to concentrate upon the

College circuit. It is no coincidence that the front cover of their second album *What We Did On Our Holidays* featured Fairport arriving at a gig at one of the newer, plateglass universities.

The college gigs were augmented by the larger clubs, with their own reliable audience – Van Dikes in Plymouth, Mothers in Birmingham, London's misnamed Country Club – who in turn had settled tastes in what bands they expected to see. As Matthews says "There were maybe ten or a dozen bands that you would see all the time", those also featured by John Peel on *Top Gear*, and reviewed favourably by 'underground' magazines like *International Times*. Thirty years on, much the same bands are still playing much the same circuit to much the same audience, albeit greyer and balder. It is to Ashley's credit that he has constantly sought out new audiences, and young musicians to play with.

At the start of 1968, the highlight of their second *Top Gear* session was the Eric Andersen song '*Violets of Dawn*', with Dyble at her most ethereal and strange, backed at first only by Nicol's rhythm guitar. Then a drum tap and the bass, leading into a slow march, with Hutchings as its stern musical major. Matthews joins in subtly, and Thompson embroiders over the top, then back to just Judy and guitar, before the band comes back again. Perfect dynamics, with its own subdued tension.

'*If I Had A Ribbon Bow*' is wheezy with a yearning vocal and bouncy guitar, a rocking harmonium, and Hutchings playing no more notes than he needs. The middle section sounds ghostly, with overdubbed recorders – a strange mix of the mediaeval, the swing era, and early hippie, with Judy's satisfied sigh at the end. They sounded closest to "quality pop" bands of the time like Honeybus, though the sparkling guitar playing was the main attraction, egoless and cheery in an era of over-serious blues masters.

Judy recalls that subsequent to '*Ribbon Bow*' being released, Fairport played a little club in Kidderminster. "I think that it was a Ballroom Dancing Club during the week, but on Saturdays it became a Youth Club. They decided to have a ribbon bow competition, and all these girls turned up in ribbon bows and I had to judge it. It was so hard to judge. And they were all not much younger than me."

The BBC Radio One sessions for Top Gear were far more flowing than other efforts had been. Ashley: "We were more at ease because we were playing live. We would simply go into a studio, sit around, all play live and then overdub. You would overdub vocals and a guitar solo perhaps. But, certainly you started by all playing live. Unlike the first album which was pieced together."

The single, '*If I Had A Ribbon Bow*' was released as a single on 23rd February, and got plenty of plays on Radio One and the pirate Radio Caroline. The local newspaper bore the headline 'Fairport Set Fair For The Future'. "Recording manager" Joe Boyd was pursuing "lucrative offers" for the band from the USA. A thousand psychedelic posters had been produced for sale in the West End: they featured an Aubrey Beardsley-influenced drawing of a 20s flapper, with curly hair, a matching bow, and four girls in witches hats emerging from her shoulders.

New Musical Express, then still a pure pop paper, described with approval "a delicate number with a fine gossamer-like texture, featuring the fragile willowy voice of the girl singer, and soft humming support from the rest of the group. There's a gently jogging rhythm, an unobtrusive backing of guitars and a very noticeable folksy quality."

For the musician's weekly bible, *Melody Maker*, their raver-about-town Chris Welch discerned "a quaint, sweet sound by quaint, sweet Judy Dyble and the lads of the Convention, one of London's more popular club groups". He remembers one night at the Speakeasy, when Lamble, "wearing an alarm clock around his neck, informed me that I was fat. Apart from that being a palpable falsehood, it should be known they are deserving of great success, and as they swing along like Benny Goodman (1935 band) meets Music and Movement. Could easily communicate with mothers and fathers as well as we hippies of the cool four million".

Another review talked of "the marvellous American style production, with drifting and clicking and vibes". It is often forgotten that even if Fairport weren't American, then Boyd definitely was, and he brings his transatlantic expertise to what is after all an American song. The gigs continued, regardless. February at Middle Earth, saw a "Fantastic Friday" with "an Incredible Double Equal Bill", shared with Blossom Toes. "Middle Earth has ten thousand square feet of space" the advert helpfully pointed out. Plenty of space to crash out in.

They also played a 'Field Day Dance' held by the Brighton Federation of Students at Falmer House. Also on the bill were Jethro Tull – who years down the track would use Fairport as a kind of grooming academy for new members. March brought the Elbow Room, Aston. "We can guarantee this soft folk rock group – but you must listen. Part of the 'avant-garde Pop Scene', held on Thurdays."

March 31st saw a special event at Middle Earth, entitled 'Albion Awakening'. In May, two days after Fairport had headlined there, the same venue hosted a 'Celebration for Albion' featuring Haps Hash and the Coloured Coat (nothing to do with Andrew Lloyd-Webber!). The poet Michael Horovitz would later edit an influential anthology of stoned poetry titled *Children of Albion*. The concept of Albion was part of the intellectual seedbed of the times, where William Blake met John Michell. Michell started the current vogue for earth mysteries. In a key article in *International Times*, Michell rediscovered in Europe a pre-Christian civilisation of neolithic hippies. The world he outlines is aligned to the matriarchy set out by Robert Graves in his strange 'grammar of poetic myth' *The White Goddess*, peaceful and productive, and has left its marks of tumuli, ley lines and megaliths. Earth mysteries.

For all the imagery, the band were neither overtly mystical or political. Kingsley Abbott: "Ashley was looking towards the future from very early on, wanting to map out a route. Richard was convinced that 1975 was going to be the apocalypse year and that something terrible was going to happen. There was a place that Martin and I used to go called The Process in Mayfair. I think it was Scientology-linked. It was a really cool little bar café in the basement. I went purely because it was a really nice, happy little club. I can remember when Love's *Forever Changes* album came out, I took it down and they put it on the record player, and everyone sat listening to it. There were all these thin bearded guys all dressed in black, but they never made any attempt to recruit us into anything. We weren't aware in the way we are nowadays, there was more interest in mysticism, in the Indian hippy trail bit. It was a bit of a dicey time in some ways in that all the way through the Fifties and the Sixties, the nuclear threat did hang pretty heavy on us. Certainly I grew up, I wouldn't say, in a permanent state of worry, but the apprehension was always there. Politics as we know it didn't really come in until the early Seventies with the various demonstrations in London about Vietnam. There were certainly a few CND demos that we went on. Martin was with his girlfriend Barbara when we first met Fairport, he met her on an Oxfam March."

Although Ashley never went to the place he commented "We were never interested in the occult, at all. It certainly didn't come into my realm of interest. For me, the supernatural only came in later, with my reading of the Child Ballads and getting interested in the folk tradition. A little bit is there in *Liege & Lief* but it comes to its height in *Full House*. That whole album, and sleeve notes are full of magic. But I'd left by then."

Meanwhile, back on *this* earth, Fairport then flew to the Casino in Montreux, far off their usual beaten track, for a forty-minute spot at the international television festival. The evening degenerated into a blues jam with 'god of hell fire' Arthur Brown, Blossom Toes and Brian Auger and his Trinity.

Chris Welch remembers "Fairport had to play to a largely unconcerned crowd of socialites in the Casino. They chattered noisily while the group tried to make piping recorders and pretty songs heard above the din." On to Paris, where Fairport made their first foray into a TV studio, to film three songs for French television's Bouton Rouge show.

The performance has survived on black and white video. '*Morning Glory*' starts with strummed chords, then Hutchings' bass plunge signals Iain to come in, singing with longing and sadness, over a simple three note recorder motif. Thompson suddenly bursts in with extreme self-confidence, with his trademark ferocity, working his way up the frets to a climax, then ebbing into musical embroidery, and back to the singing. The whole band play as a tight ensemble. '*Time Will Show the Wiser*' counterpoints bass growls and high squalls of notes on guitar, with Lamble driving things away from the back. There is something untamed in the music here, belying the band's stationary stance onstage. The elongated guitar break in '*Reno, Nevada*' is something else again, far shorter than the band sometimes managed away from the camera's glare, but extraordinary all the same, with the intensity, jazz inflections and rhythmical subtlety of the best of the West Coast, Quicksilver or the Dead. Everything builds from the melodic bass riff, like a second lead guitar, but deeper.

Hutchings works closely with the drums and Nicol's strict rhythm, against which the young Thompson plays with a sense of determination which has flickered only intermittently since he has lacked Ashley's stern gaze on him, urging him upward. Here Hutchings rolls the bass like a ship on the ocean, suppling a low sonic rumble, a firm foundation for Richard to pierce with occasional shrieks of musical anguish.

There is not much joy in this music, more like a bleeding intensity, a soul on its way to hell (or indeed the gaming tables of the American desert). The video evidence is almost comical in contrast, with the two singers looking redundant, Thompson lost in his fretboard. Iain Matthews has round dark glasses just like Jefferson Airplane bassist, Jack Casady, Simon looks absurdly young and loutish, while Ashley is intense

MIDDLE EARTH

43 KING STREET
COVENT GARDEN
240 1327

FRI. - SAT.
10.30 - DAWN

Friday, May 3rd   10.30 - Dawn

CAPTAIN BEEFHEART
AND HIS MAGIC BAND

TANGERINE SLYDE • URIEL
LIGHTS • FILMS • JENNY DEXTER
MEMBERS 15/6d.   GUESTS 25/6d.

Saturday, May 4th   10.30 - Dawn

FAIRPORT CONVENTION
THE DEVIANTS

GINGER JOHNSON AND THE AFRICAN DRUMMERS
LIGHT SHOWS • FILMS • EVENTS
MEMBERS 10/6d.   GUESTS 20/6d.

NEXT WEEK: Friday, May 10th

THE FAMILY

Saturday, May 11th — Direct from U.S.A.

THE BYRDS
SPIDER JOHN KOERNER

THE FUGS' TOUR HAS BEEN PUT BACK TO A LATER DATE

Middle Earth, Covent Garden. 4th May 1968

in a full beard and moustache. The studio lights are too bright: it's like an alchemical mystery brought to shocking light, and all the band look as if they would be happier in the dark. All similar (colour) footage held by the BBC has been wiped, for which the managers responsible deserve to rot in hell.

Archivist Ian Maun was responsible for locating this priceless archive footage. "I got in touch with Judy Dyble through Dave Pegg, and she lent me her scrapbook. In the scrapbook was a reference to Fairport appearing on French TV. I found out where the archives were in Paris and wrote to them. They replied: "Yes we have got a video tape, but no, you can't have it!" So there were long exchanges over the telephone with France. In the end, I wrote them a letter saying that we'd got all the band's permission for it, we'd got Martin Lamble's parents' permission to get it out, and then one day, it just turned up with these three wonderful tracks on. I went off to work that morning floating on a cloud, having listened to that guitar solo on '*Morning Glory*'. All members of the band were given a copy, and the understanding was that it wouldn't be circulated, but Iain chose to put '*Reno, Nevada*' on his *Chart & Compass* video anthology. The remaining unreleased track is Tim Buckley's '*Morning Glory*', which I think is the best of the three performances."

On May 5th, they left for Rome, and the International Pop Festival at the Palazzo Del Sport. Roger Simpson gave pride of place in his review, though, to "Crouch End blues favourites Dr K's Blues Band". Meanwhile, "on the other side of the city, Fairport Convention were battling against the odds, trying to save the much publicised festival from dying. Bad amplification, "far worse than the Royal Albert Hall", and the lack of any real audience to play to, made the Festival a non-event. "Fairport's bass guitarist Simon Nicholl" [*sic*] commented that "it was a tribute to the Italian mentality. For in their bureaucratic fashion they messed it up. There were so many police and riot police, even some of the army turned out, that they were all tripping over themselves. After all, there were only about 1,500 people attending throughout the festival". Fairport enjoyed many of the foreign groups, "especially those from Japan", but as a commercial effort they considered it a flop. "We enjoyed it, but it was all a joke" Nicol concluded.

Some of Fairport – Hutchings included – encountered the Byrds at the Piper Club in Rome. Then under the tutelage of Gram Parsons, a rich young kid from the South, the Byrds were exploring the kind of country music largely despised by their peers – and which in turn found "long-hairs" to be some form of alien life form. It was the sort of music which the rednecks who kill the two 'heroes' in *Easy Rider* would listen to, before torching a mixed-race school. It was Parsons' gift to find an underlying nobility to the best of this music, and a form of homecoming for those marooned by psychedelic drugs and revolutionary politics.

Ashley: "Well, I've always liked the sound of country music from way back when I was a youngster listening to Bluegrass and Doc Watson. I've seen Doc Watson and Clarence Ashley. And then of course the Byrds, who by far and away my favourite group, went to Country Music. I was witness to the unveiling of this at the Piper Club. I was sat in the packed audience in this club and heard this fantastic mixture of Country and Rock, coming from the stage. Gram Parsons was there, electric banjo from Doug Dillard, and interspersed with their hits like '*Mr Tambourine Man*' and '*Turn Turn Turn*' was this amazing fresh Country Music.

"I spoke to Gram Parsons after the gig. We flowed out into the street after the gig and Parsons being fresh-faced and very enthusiastic, came out into the street as well, unlike long-in-the-tooth McGuinn, who probably hid away from the crowds until they'd subsided. I talked to Gram along with a couple of other people, and was struck by his enthusiasm, his humbleness and his excitement at being part of it all. It's sad to think how it ended so soon. Within a short number of years, this very young, very enthusiastic caring person, changed into this extravagant character dependent on drugs. For me it was a key moment.

"From 1967 onwards I realised it was possible to be hip and like Country Music. Another of my other favourite groups were the Flying Burrito Brothers. *The Guilded Palace Of Sin* and *Sweetheart Of The Rodeo* are both wonderful, wonderful albums that stand the test of time. But rather than slavishly follow their lead by suggesting to the band that we perform '*Hickory Wind*', I sought out some interesting and maybe obscure songs. Johnny Cash's '*I Still Miss Someone*' was on the *Heyday* album, and some very obscure things like '*Don't Make It 54*', a song about John Wesley Hardin. And of course we did a few of Dylan's things like '*Open The Door Richard*' which was originally '*Open the Door Homer*'. So Country Music snuck in occasionally with Fairport. And then carried on because Richard to this day, still sneaks in the odd Hank Williams' song."

Back on English soil, key members of the band again caught the Byrds' appearance at Middle Earth, later in May, with the now legendary Gram Parsons during his brief membership of the band. It was one of those gigs to tell your grandchildren about.

Kingsley Abbott: "I was lucky enough to get in round the back, bringing in the PA for the Byrds to use, because theirs had either disappeared or wasn't working. We had our PA in the van, so together with their roadie Jim Seiter, and Fairport roadie Harvey Bramham, we carried it in and set it up. That meant I didn't have to go down into the throng. I just watched the whole thing from the side of the stage. Ashley had got in down the front. He'd been let in because he always played there. It was jammed packed and he was stuck in the middle, centre stage about six to eight feet back from the Byrds. He was open-mouthed when Gram Parsons started to lead the country stuff. They played for a very long time that night, something like two-and-a-half hours, with a slight break. The first bit was traditional Byrds fare, and then they went into the totally different sounding traditional American country style. Ashley was gob-smacked. How they were presenting both the full-on electric folk rock, and this wonderful roots stuff that was stripped bare of the electrics…the 12-string didn't figure. It was real back-to-basics stuff. To my mind it fits very well that he may have seen that as a route for Fairport's direction."

Fairport's journey, though, had yet to really begin. The unenviable task of asking Judy Dyble to leave the band fell to Hutchings. Dyble later confided to *Hokey Pokey*, "I'd had this very weird feeling about the band for a little while because they were all males and I'd often find myself on my own after a gig. Eventually I had a phone call from Ashley saying 'Meet me at the bench where the buses stop at Muswell Hill.' He sat at one end and I sat at the other and he just said something like "the band think you ought to leave". I was absolutely stunned. It was like your friends saying "goodbye" …but in fairness it must have been hard for him as well". It had not been his decision alone, just him – as band leader – who had to carry it out.

Ashley: "I took her for a walk and told her. It was very difficult, and very sad. I think the band was getting stronger, heavier, and Judy's voice, which has always been light, was suffering because of it". Judy: "All they said was that I was singing out of tune for a lot of the time. I suppose I should have cut it dead there". At the end of the Rome show, "I threw down my hat in this dramatic exit and waltzed out saying 'goodbye'. When I got back to England it was snowing, and there was no-one there to meet me. They asked me to leave Fairport and it was Ashley's job to tell me. He was very brave about it, but he obviously hated doing it. I hated hearing it. Floods of tears on a park bench. It appeared to be, as far as I knew, a band decision. I had thought that it was Iain who wanted me out. He thought that I was being opportune when actually, he was more opportune than I was.

"It was really horrible. I felt like I was like being thrown out by my bunch of friends who didn't like me any more. I did try to go and see them, but it was very strained, and so I stopped. That's primarily why I didn't want to stay in any bands after that – I didn't want them to throw me out again!"

Judy didn't bear a grudge however and was on good terms with Ashley: "He was a great giggler and that's not his normal image, it has to be said! He was good fun and very serious. But he was a very good leader of the band, because he'd get everybody back to doing what they're supposed to be doing, possibly because he'd been out in the world and had a job. I had forgotten what an excellent bass player he is. Ashley's a very subtle bass player, less is more. He was fiercely passionate about what he was doing then and was so enthusiastic about things. "You've got to listen to this. It's fantastic!" "We've got to do this!" Yes."

Dyble maintains that "Fairport were a family who looked after each other. It was only after I left Fairport, there'd always be some guy saying "I'll be your agent. Just come and meet this guy and wear something…" I wouldn't go to those sort of interviews. There was never anything like that with Fairport. Fairport never left their friends. They didn't grow out of them, which was nice."

Kingsley: "Her departure was quick and painful. It was down to Ashley. It fell to him to actually do the deed. Obviously it was very reluctantly done. Richard and Judy were close for a while. Joe had a ruthless streak and still does. I personally never took to him. He had all the American charm but there was a steely edge as well."

Judy lost contact with the band, but her friend Roberta started to go out with Simon Nicol, so Dyble would hear "bits that were happening." As to her successor…

HARMONIES IN A MAELSTROM

The photographer Ray Stevenson also lived in Finchley. "One night at Middle Earth I offered them photos of the gig in return for a lift home," he remembers. "On the way I was raving on to Iain about how good Sandy Denny had been at Les Cousins the night before. A month later she replaced Judy Dyble. Then Sandy felt that she couldn't sing with Iain, so he was out". The nine months between these two happenings saw some of the finest gigs in Fairport's history.

Auditions for the new singer were held at the Eight Feathers Boys' Club in Parsons Green: about a dozen girls were auditioned, but Sandy stood out, in the words of Simon Nicol, like "a clean glass in a sinkful of dirty dishes". Even if Iain Matthews now reckons Joe Boyd to be a Svengali figure who hired and fired band members, and pushed new songs at them, Joe claims that he had advised Ashley "very strongly" against asking Judy to leave. He wanted the band to retain a female lead singer, to keep its individual selling point. He considered that Sandy's extrovert personality might clash with such "shy and diffident people", but "I think I underestimated the stubborness of Richard and Ashley." Ashley himself told journalist Pamela Winters that "I think we tempered her garrulousness. It also challenged her, vocally, in a new way. The electric maelstrom was a proving ground for her voice".

"I can remember seeing Sandy Denny at a very early concert, singing with the band," says Kay Hutchings. "And every time they finished a song, Sandy came over and sat with her mother and put her head on her shoulder. I don't know what on earth happened with poor Sandy." The tragedy of Sandy Denny's life has been explored by Clinton Heylin in his *No More Sad Refrains* biography. A singer without parallel and a loyal friend and colleague to those around her, there seems to have been a self-destructive streak which was to draw her life to a premature close. She is still sadly and fondly remembered. But at that point, all of this was in the future.

Simon: "There's little doubt that when Sandy joined Fairport, the band took a stellar leap forward in terms of music and art, repertoire, technique, personality... everything."

Sandy had established herself on the acoustic folk circuit, then briefly joined the Strawbs. The 'Youth News' section of a local paper, dated June 21st, has a picture of Sandy sitting in the middle of her new band. "Sandy Derry [as she is misspelt in the caption] lives in Earls Court and has been with Fairport for a month, but before she can go full time, still has outstanding dates to complete, including 'My Kind of Folk' for the BBC."

In a *Melody Maker* interview a month later, Sandy reckoned Fairport "does a mixture of country and western, folk adaptations, blues – but not like John Mayall, of course": musically they are "flexible but not self-satisfied". "We've all got our own ideas. There's not much conflict inside the group. They're all easygoing, I'm the one who tends to get uptight. They let me blow up then cool down". With a band, there is "no more standing alone with your thoughts on draughty railway stations. In the group van there's always someone to talk to or at – even if they are asleep".

Abbott noticed an immediate change with the recruitment of Sandy into the band. "You were immediately aware of her voice. She was another bubbly, humorous person who loved to laugh. I know there are things said about her shyness, but I wouldn't characterise her like that. She was a very definite person to be in a room with. She obviously was very keen on Richard initially. And was crucial in that interlocking with the band. There's no doubt that she took them to a higher level. Judy is a lovely person but she didn't have a strong voice and it tended to wander off key. With Sandy, it was like somebody putting a super V8 engine in a Ford Anglia. Although it was on similar numbers, there was now that assuredness that a really strong lead singer gives a band. It gave the rest of them something to really work with. She had the power and the intensity and the stage presence.

"Sandy wasn't a bad influence on us. If we'd have anything, we'd have a beer. We certainly weren't a spirits band until Sandy came along. I know that Joe indicated he was concerned about this hellraiser, but I think it went both ways actually. Joe underestimated the quiet strength and even-footedness that all the band had. If nothing else, we were all pretty sensible. It wouldn't have been easy to divert. We were able to resist. Things were around but everybody resisted.

"There was a tremendous strength of character in the band which is why I think they survived later traumas. There was probably a lot more strength of character in the band than Joe ever realised. He perceived young, naïve, nice boys, but in fact it went a lot deeper than he realised."

Ashley: "When Sandy joined the band, I suppose it was because I was the oldest

Fairport Convention. l-r: Ashley Hutchings, Simon Nicol, Richard Thompson, Martin Lamble, Iain Matthews and Sandy Denny. 1968

of the boys in the band, she looked to me, and I looked out for her. When we would get in to the van to travel anywhere, she always sat next to me, and there was always my shoulder to lean on when she was feeling tired, or indeed, slept as we often did on the way back from a gig late at night. That was a ritual we went through in the early days. She would always sit next to me and always lean on me if she needed to. Physically as well as psychologically. Which was a nice thought. I slept with her once, but that was for comfort. That wasn't for sexual reasons. That was for bodily comfort one time at her place."

Beat Instrumental for August 1968 saw Fairport as taking up the ebbing impetus of US psychedelia. The band slouch sullen on city steps, Simon in dark shades looking like John Cale, Ashley crouching on his heels. Thompson considers that the West Coast bands "all seem to be doing a sort of cross between rock and soul – look at Big Brother, Country Joe and Jefferson Airplane – it's not all that far from the sock-it-to me thing, and very American. We think of ourselves as a folk-based band. This is even more pronounced now that Sandy Denny is with us".

This suggests that the move towards traditional folk music came 18 months before the release of *Liege & Lief* and was consciously prepared for, perhaps as a result of those unforgettable concerts by Gram Parsons and the Byrds. Thompson told the magazine that Denny, unlike Dyble, "really knows what the folk tradition is all about, and the group as a whole are drawing from English roots. The fact that we're electric doesn't make any difference". As Sandy was moving from traditional folk towards rock, Fairport were going in the other direction. For a year and a half the conjunction would prove musically explosive. It would then be Sandy writing new songs, and Hutchings pursuing his experiments in traditional folk music with single-minded determination, and a brave recklessness. For the moment, he was still part of the 'new breed'.

The magazine continued its member profile: "the most immediately outstanding member is Sandy Denny, a girl with a strong Judy Collins-like voice. On lead guitar is Richard Thompson, whose sleepy-looking face belies the complexity and inventiveness of his work. Simon tends to keep in the background until he lets loose with his wild, eccentric electric violin. Providing a solid framework for the fireworks is Tyger Hutchings on bass. Together with Richard, he writes a lot of the group's material". The circle is made complete by Martin Lamble, "a sensitive, unobtrusive drummer yet firmly in tune with the rest of the group".

Beat Instrumental concluded that Fairport in full cry is among "the most exciting musical experiences available to a live audience in Britain. The songs are generally sophisticated folk songs, ideal jumping-off points for highly progressive journeys into driving improvisation". They also show a taste for C&W, "in many ways similar to the Byrds' current scene". What really sets the band apart, though, is "their extraordinary ability in setting a powerful mood and building it to a climax, and then subtly setting off in a different direction. The mind as well as the eardrum is given an overwhelming workout by Fairport Convention". A template that all of Ashley's greatest achievements, as yet in the future, were to follow.

Meanwhile, Fairport had moved on, at least in terms of their living quarters. Following Hutchings' lead, the younger members of the band were starting to flee their family nests. In Summer 1968 Ashley was still at Fairport, with Richard, Simon and Ian sharing the top floor of a smaller property in Brent, where "social gatherings occurred" and new music was rehearsed. Ashley was a frequent visitor, but one feels that a certain distance was emerging between him and the rest, geographically if nothing else.

As Kingsley Abbott writes "Simon Nicol exuded confidence and humour. He appeared way beyond his years in his dealing with the world, a good balance to Tyger's quieter persona, without being loud". He sees Fairport's fans in his own image, "jolly college boys with scarves".

Over the years, Richard, Simon and Ashley have all expressed their admiration for, and influence of The Band. Richard: "I've always thought that within their songs there was a kind of shared feeling about the compositions, and that the band members contributed more than their names to the credits. They are terrific ensemble songs. They are comprehensible to everybody in the band and there's a real spirit when they're played. I always thought that's indescribable. And I certainly fell short of that a lot of the time."

Kingsley: "Richard was the one who really led Fairport's appreciation of The Band. They were going back to roots in some ways, but within a rock context, whilst The Byrds were going in a more country direction. It took a little bit of time for *Music From Big Pink* to really dig into people's consciousness. I've still got Richard's copy of their second album. It had just come out over there, then Richard went and got an import copy, only to have somebody drop the needle on to the first track. It made a slight noise that lasted for a few seconds, but he just didn't want it any more. He wanted a clean, fresh copy. So he gave that one to me, which I've still got. It clicked about perhaps twice the way round, but it was an audible click. It was enough."

"You were only aware of their image with the second album. It was like when I first saw a picture of the Rolling Stones. They seemed to be a cohesive, foreboding look about them. Looking back it was a particularly clever cover for that second album. And they did look markedly good, the Band. Garth Hudson's beard, and the foxy, slightly untrustworthy look that Robbie Robertson used to have. They were a wonderful arresting bunch of guys who seemed out of place when I saw them at The Albert Hall. We should have really seen them in a low, old barn."

Fairport had played a handful of gigs without a female lead singer. Fan Chris Heasman remembers Sandy's appearance with her new band at the 'Dance of Words' at Portsmouth Guildhall. "All of the seats downstairs had been taken out, and poets were reading in rooms adjacent to the main stage, where the likes of Brian Patten and Pete Brown & His Battered Ornaments were appearing. Ashley announced that "this is the first time she has sung with us". She was wearing an old fringed suede coat, and a mini-dress. Her hair was all over the place, and I wondered who the hell this was, and then she started singing, and I forgot everything else".

Within a week, Sandy was the featured vocalist on Fairport's next 'Top Gear'. New songs included Eric Andersen's '*Close The Door Lightly When You Go*', Felice and Boudleaux Bryants' C&W song '*Some Sweet Day*' and '*Nottamun Town*'. This was of particular importance, the first purely traditional song to be performed by Fairport.

Hutchings describes it as probably "an old magic song using the device of riddles". The 'back-handed awk'ard talk' resembles the language of Mummers' plays. As one old chap told the Appalachian singer Jean Ritchie, "if 'twas understood, then the good luck and the magic was lost". Fairport took their version from traditional singer Shirley Collins – a signpost to Ashley's future – who learnt it from Ritchie, but cut some verses. By then, the song had crossed the Atlantic. Twice. Of what is left, Hutchings wonders if "sat down on a hot, hot, cold, frozen stone" might refer to a cemetery. In the same clubs, Procol Harum were coincidentally playing their sonorous settings of the lyrics of Keith Reid, death obsessed and jokey in just the same way. In '*Something Following Me*', the singer is pursued by his own tombstone, tripping over it, breaking his teeth on it etc. It is all part of the psychedelic brew.

Fairport played their second gig with their new female singer at Whittlesey Barn Barbecue, on Whit Sunday, June 2nd 1968, third down the bill to Donovan and John Mayall's Blues Breakers.

Fairport Convention on stage at the Whittlesey Barn Barbecue, near Peterborough. 2nd June 1968

Photo: Anders Folke

A stunning set of photographs by Anders Folke, who came over specially from Sweden, shows Sandy in a long black dress and looking either serious or scared. She plays electric rhythm guitar, staring into the middle distance, then stands ramrod straight at the microphone, hands down at her waist. Next to her, Iain looks casual in a denim jacket, open mouthed with folded arms and eyes tight shut, mid chorus. Richard, long haired and in a buckskin jacket, turns back towards Lamble or bends over his Les Paul, sinister in shades, like an errant member of the Velvet Underground. In another shot, he is sitting down and playing what looks like an electric dulcimer across his knees. Simon comes across as intensely serious and workmanlike, dressed in a polka dot shirt, with sleeves rolled up to the elbow.

Ashley appears in a separate photo, alone, his hands clasped over his electric bass, as if in prayer. He looks down at the floor, as if lost in his thoughts, the epitome of cool – chiselled face, frizzed hair down to his collar, white shirt, black waistcoat. He looks vulnerable and slightly sulky, but also determined as hell. Nothing in life is ever wholly coincidental, and five years down the track this high priest of the underground would be resurrecting obscure rites and rituals from this same area, Cambridgeshire, for his first solo album, the truly extraordinary *Rattlebone & Ploughjack*. This in turn led to the annual reappearance of the Whittlesey Straw bear, recreated from old photographs. This superb photograph seems to capture Hutchings at the exact moment of transition, from hippie visionary to arcane scholar of the English psyche.

As to the music, the twenty minutes or so that survive give a good indication of a typical Festival set. The material is far closer to *Heyday* than *What We Did On Our Holidays*, with songs drawn almost entirely from contemporary American singer-songwriters.

'*Reno, Nevada*' cuts off just as Richard gets going on his marathon guitar solo. What survives is still massively exciting, with pounding drums and truly vicious, intense lead guitar. Dylan's '*It Takes A Lot To Laugh, It Takes A Train To Cry*' has Iain taking the lead vocal and Sandy singing harmonies, while Ashley clunks out the bass lines of this standard blues. The band have a total command of dynamics, adding tension where necessary, then relaxing back into the song.

With Joni Mitchell's '*I Don't Know Where I Stand*', Sandy takes over a song previously sung by Judy and makes it her own, full voiced, with a heartbreaking sense of pleading. She gives way to a perfect and shivery lead break from Richard, and then the whole band join in on the riff. Sudden silence, just guitar embroidery and sandy singing, then drums and bass come in thrillingly. The whole thing crests to a climax, then quietens down again with just electric guitar and Ashley's bass, playing a stately gavotte. The dance years start here.

Next up is '*You Never Wanted Me*'. Sandy brings a Jackson Frank song into the band's repertoire, and again her voice is chilling in its intensity and sense of hurt. Pounding tom-toms from Martin, and subdued backing from the rest, giving Denny full rein. It is as if she is communicating solely to each listener, then and now. Uncanny.

There follows an unknown song which some thirty years on, Ashley simply can't remember. "It's probably one of those short-lived concoctions, written by Richard and myself in the style of '*If It Feels Good*', that we used to throw in to rock up the set." It starts off like Chuck Berry's '*Nadine*', with a shuffle beat, and Ashley answering Iain's opening vocal in his (then) trademark fake American accent. Simon too plays at being a deep voiced Statesider, and Sandy wails like a banshee. The music is a deliberate pastiche, more Lovin' Spoonful than Byrds. Good time music, delivered with a slightly superior North London smirk. It ends almost like cabaret, with a final vocal flourish.

'*Some Sweet Day*' boasts country style guitar from Ricard, and features Iain on lead vocals, as does Eric Andersen's '*Close The Door Lightly*', a sad lyric, but music which brings a smile to your eyes. We hear the opening to another Dylan related song, '*Jack O'Diamonds*', but then, cruelly, the tape runs out for good.

Anders Folke: "I had chosen to do a photo and sound documentation of

Photo: Anders Folke

Fairport Convention on stage at the Whittlesey Barn Barbecue, near Peterborough. 2nd June 1968

Speakers Corner in London as my "special-work" in school. I got a grant to buy a Telefunken portable tape recorder which had those special kind of cassettes and needed lots of batteries. I therefore had to always be careful not to record anything over fifteen minutes. That's the reason I never let it run through the whole concert. Sadly I had to change the batteries and missed Richard's unbelievable solos."

As Pamela Longfellow wrote, "so began Fairport's creamy days. They had one year left in which to produce that intense bitter-sweet, one-of-a-kind music that floats freely, if ever so rarely, from a chance blending of individuals". *Melody Maker* announced that "Fairport Convention, with new singer Sandy Denny, record their second single '*Some Sweet Day*' this week for July release". Wiser counsels prevailed. The release of another composition by outside songwriters would have proved counter-productive. For their next single A-side – and their first for Island records – Fairport would instead look to itself.

Dreamlike is just the word to describe the creative reverie which Ashley was currently inhabiting, and it was even more appropriate when he witnessed a 'Top Gear' session by one of his long-term musical idols, Leonard Cohen. Cohen had been a well respected poet before he ever picked up a guitar, and groaned his first lyric. John Peel had expected Cohen "to come in and sit in the corner in denims and be rather sombre", instead of which he appeared in rather a nice suit, and really took charge of everything. "I want the singers over there where I can maintain eye contact, and if we could have those screens over there please. He was just a very organised guy". Does this remind you of anyone?

Hutchings "just sat there enthralled at the back of the stalls. Cohen walked out for a break and I had a word with him." One month later the Fairport would do their only recording of '*Suzanne*' in the same studio. Cohen's set that day included '*Bird On A Wire*', also quickly appropriated by Ashley for his own band, and swiftly rearranged for two voices, male and female.

Fairport continued to barnstorm around the country, a "shattering live experience" as *Beat Instrumental* described them. They played many small London venues such as the Country Club, Haverstock Hill and the Fishmongers Arms, Wood Green. Not quite the Royal Albert Hall, but appropriate, as fan Bernie Doherty remembers the band at this time being "very sloppy" with much onstage drunkenness and with Simon the front man, "because he had long straight hair and looked like one of the Byrds". The poor sound systems of the time did not help, muffling everything except the guitar solos.

Doherty does recall favourably Nicol's "dry wit" and Thompson's ironic asides. The studied sloppiness of clothing – Ashley excepted – and lack of stage flash did not extend to the music, which was always honed to perfection. Hutchings hovered in the background to the audience's left, but omni-present, watching everything like a hawk, and tweaking the primitive sound balance. The overall sense of the band onstage was one of exuberance, a zest for life that was infectious.

Melody Maker reviewed a gig at the Wood Green Jazz Club, with "new singer Sandy Denny in top form". No mention of drunkenness, but Thompson's extended break on '*Reno, Nevada*' "brought the crowd to their feet and him to his knees". A letter to the same paper from R.E. Browne complained that "a neo-pop group called Fairport Convention" had ruined a 'Folk Concert' at the Central Hall, Westminster, with Julie Felix headlining. They "gave us twenty minutes of just noise. I do hope that next time the Committee organise a folk concert, they will exclude pop groups, as people who come to hear folk singing expect folk singing".

This review alone could have been the spur for the whole of Ashley's subsequent career! A riposte two weeks later points out that "I have seen Fairport perform many times and I have never seen them folkier than they were at Westminster. Although they have a contemporary image they did their best to forget this, and their normal electric guitar and drums format was only used in their final number. All their songs were gentle and volume was kept to a minimum".

Fairport played the National Jazz Pop Ballads & Blues Festival at Kempton Park Racecourse. Their afternoon performance was billed as 'Al Stewart & Fairport Convention', but the band was featured on only three songs. The evening show was billed solely as Fairport Convention. It gave journalists a chance to compare them with Eclection, operating in much the same musical area. For *Record Mirror*, "Fairport came out slightly ahead. There's more to them". For Tony Wilson in *MM*, despite Sandy's fine singing, the band "must tighten up on instrument changing, because of time waste".

Next up was a Free Concert at Hyde Park, and a 48-hour Middle Earth 'Freak Out' titled 'The Magical Mystery Tour', with all the usual suspects.

In August, Fairport recorded another 'Top Gear' session. The hilarious '*If You Feel Good, You Know It Can't Be Wrong*' – an extremely politically incorrect sentiment nowadays – is a Thompson/Hutchings song in which Richard and Sandy (as 'George' and 'Ethel') exchange smutty lines which turn out to be about limbo dancing. Next their marvellous take on '*Suzanne*', all tom-toms and shivery harmonies. Sandy Denny unleashes her ghostly song '*Fotheringay*', an acoustic tapestry underpinned by Hutchings' fluid electric bass.

In Ken Garner's *In Session Tonight* reference book, Ashley recounted the care and attention the BBC put into laying the radio tracks down: they shine all the brighter with hindsight. "On '*If You Feel Good*', I remember recording a kazoo and speeding it up on tape, just to get the right ragtime effect. And we took ages to record one tiny insert that was a musical joke. This involved breaking a cup, which wasn't as easy as it sounds, because it had to be just the right kind of smash, and then inserting it into the song after the line "put down your coffee mug"."

The whole operation took about an hour, and several BBC cups of coffee. Ashley: "We never recorded a lot of those tracks we did for radio sessions. We'd put down things we liked to do on stage, and we were doing a lot of cover versions, then. '*Suzanne*' was a stage favourite, and audiences would cheer the moment we announced it; but that BBC session was the only recording we made of it. The arrangement was all based on rhythm. Martin was going round the kit with beaters, and the two guitars, drums and bass were all doing different patterns. It was a masterpiece of rhythmic interplay, and Bernie did a good job on the production".

A few days later, the band played live on British TV for the first time, performing '*Morning Glory*' on BBC 1's *How It Is*. The tapes have long since been wiped, of course. Not so easily wiped from the memory is their performance at the first Isle of Wight Festival in 1968, held in a field of stubble. Joint headliners were the Jefferson Airplane, with whom Fairport had so long been compared, bringing with them their magnificent light show. Fairport went one better.

NME described the huddled audience of sleeping bags as a "musical refugee camp". Fairport finally tottered onstage – or rather onto a tarpaulin stage stretched over two flat-bed trucks – just before dawn. A strong easterly gale was blowing, with the tiny figure of Martin Lamble "crouched over his drums" and generating "a spark of heat that could not be dulled". Fairport had the difficult job of following Arthur Brown, whose flaming helmet failed to ignite in the windy conditions. Their set was "majestic". Iain Matthews always sang with his eyes closed. "I started Leonard

Cohen's '*Suzanne*' in darkness; when I opened my eyes at the end of the song, it was dawn".

A few days later, Fairport – joined late onstage by Sandy – again appeared on the same bill as the Airplane, this time at Parliament Hill Fields in London, playing to a tiny but ecstatic crowd. Mark Cooper, now producer of BBC's *Later* still describes this gig as the best he has ever seen.

The band now set off for a short tour of Holland, and recorded a show for Dutch radio. First up is Johnny Cash's '*I Still Miss Someone*', with a rambling countryish solo from Richard, and Ashley his unique self on bass. He is like a kid's swing rocking to and fro during Thompson's break. His playing can take on a life of its own, at times mirroring the lead, then counterpointing it. The band sound like a cross between the Parsons-led Byrds and the Lovin' Spoonful. The combination of Iain's ethereal voice and Sandy's warmer tones is richer than the Matthews/Dyble duets of old.

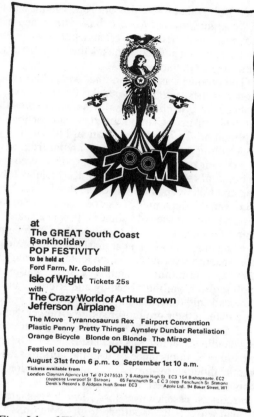

at
The GREAT South Coast
Bankholiday
POP FESTIVITY
to be held at
Ford Farm, Nr. Godshill

Isle of Wight Tickets 25s
with
The Crazy World of Arthur Brown
Jefferson Airplane

The Move Tyrannosaurus Rex Fairport Convention
Plastic Penny Pretty Things Aynsley Dunbar Retaliation
Orange Bicycle Blonde on Blonde The Mirage

Festival compered by **JOHN PEEL**

August 31st from 6 p.m. to September 1st 10 a.m.
Tickets available from
London Clayman Agency Ltd Tel 01 2475531 7 8 Aldgate High St   EC3 154 Bishopsgate EC2
(opposite Liverpool St Station)   65 Fenchurch St   E C 3 (opp Fenchurch St Station)
Derek's Record s 8 Aldgate High Street EC3   Apple Ltd   94 Baker Street W1

First Isle of Wight Pop Festival. 31st August 1968

Good time music, with a core of inner sadness.

Gentle applause, and Hutchings asks for his mike to be plugged in. His voice is refined, slightly haughty, seemingly slightly stoned. It is Amsterdam, after all. "That's a bit of country and western, you know, yeah, and it's intentionally very loose. Do you know Leonard Cohen?" Someone shouts in Dutch, suggesting this is not a good idea. "Don't you like Leonard Cohen? I like Leonard Cohen, so we're going to do a Leonard Cohen song, it's called '*Bird On A Wire*'." Iain comes in first, then Sandy as well, with the bass high in the mix, the lead instrument here. Sandy comes in alone for the next verse, and the effect is heartbreaking. At the end, the two guitars weave a stately pattern.

A bit of tuning up, then "this is a song which we're all supposed to be very happy to. It's a shame, it has a story and some of you might miss the story, but never mind … if you can join in the spirit of the thing. It's called '*If You Feel Good, You Know It Can't Be Wrong*'". He emphasises the word 'can't'. Another Spoonfully intro, then a youthful Richard on loutish vocals, with Sandy evoking exasperation. The music rocks and rolls, with bass flourishes.

Ashley is like a professor, stern but kindly, talking to his slightly dim students. "Thank you very much. We've got one more in this set, and we're going to be back later. Bob Dylan wrote this one, but you may not know it , because he didn't record it". Straight into '*I'll Keep It With Mine*', as serious as your life. Sandy's stretched out notes and fierceness of attack brings a new dimension to Fairport, a high intensity which suddenly makes them totally unique, and Thompson replies in kind with filigree guitar.

The producer asks for another song. Ashley: "Can you bear one more? This is a modern blues, we hope you like this anyway" – to the band, "Try Lacey, OK"". Notice who is in charge. Ashley's own composition '*Mr Lacey*' of course, and we're suddenly in Eric Clapton territory, slower than the 'live on Stuart Henry' version captured on *Guitar, Vocal*. Standard blues fare, with bass that shakes the floor, and high trilling guitar, but the words are far from any delta known to man. Then silence.

On their return to England, Fairport played the 'Festival of Contemporary Song' at London's Royal Festival Hall. Karl Dallas found a whole neglected area between pop and folk opened up. "The real thrill of the evening were the Fairport Convention who wed the dynamics of a good beat group to the meaningful lyrics that are usually the province of the solo singer". It was a shame that the venue's acoustic "was not able to compete with the guitar amps". Nevertheless, '*Suzanne*' "with the words sung against a continual percussive ostinato run on guitars, gave it a completely new dimension". A rough audience tape which survives confirms the strength of Lamble's drumming, matched beat for beat by Hutchings' bass, and anchoring the high register wailing of Sandy and Richard, on vocals and lead guitar respectively. After all this time, it still sounds exciting, grace under fire, and this is never more true than in their ground-breaking arrangement of the Leonard Cohen song.

A letter to *Melody Maker* by David Oliver complained that the only blemish on an outstanding evening was this last number. "In announcing it, a member of the group stressed the importance of it in the current scene, and then proceeded to destroy its gentle thought by gross over-instrumentation. The thumping guitar work almost completely masked the singing and in so doing the flowing poetry which is '*Suzanne*'s' essence, was lost". Two weeks later, T Walker's reply was good enough to win a free LP. "Contrary to his opinion, I find the rhythmic drumming in their arrangement creates a suitable hypnotic effect which is complementary to the poetry of '*Suzanne*' and I must say I find their version more enjoyable than the original".

The accompanying publicity shot is heavily posed in the studio, emphasising the group's separateness, with everyone looking in different directions, and not a smile among them. Ashley is in a pullover and has laid his right hand on his left shoulder. He's clean shaven again, with frizzy hair. Matthews is in a suit, dark tie and scowl, like a funeral director or an early role model for a character from *Reservoir Dogs*. Sandy is seemingly falling out of the picture at the bottom, like a disembodied head. Simon wears cowboy hat and a fringed suede jacket. Martin looks like Number 6 in *The Prisoner*, with his long scarf. Thompson has his hands hooked around his belt, and also wears a suede jacket, like a surly young gunslinger.

Fairport inflicted more thumping guitars, drums and bass on a willing audience at the Fairfield Hall, Croydon the following evening. Mick Sherrington remembers a gig from autumn 1968 at Leeds University, as if from yesterday. "They wander on stage, making excuses about an eight hour transit trip up the motorway. Despite a nervous start, the band are clearly something special: different material, some brilliant lead guitar, and an adventurous rhythm section. On bass, providing the introductions plus some slightly dodgy vocals, but pulling the whole thing together – Ashley Hutchings".

Ashley: "I think when you're young, you're not afraid to do things. Many things were done in the early days, particularly with Fairport, that I blanch to think about nowadays. I remember we drove all the way up from London to Stoke for a Fairport gig in 1968. A journey that wasn't easy in those days, and when we turned up at the club there were people out on the pavement, hippies who said: "They won't let us in because of our hair and our dress!" So we talked with them on the pavement and we left. We didn't do the gig as a mark of solidarity, we drove all the way back to London. Now good for us say I, but I can't imagine us doing that nowadays."

Late November saw the release of the band's new single. Both sides were Fairport compositions this time, with Richard Thompson's mysterious '*Meet On The Ledge*' – an anthem in the making – backed with the Hutchings/Thompson composition '*Throwaway Street Puzzle*', which was even more gnomic. "Come now Mister, step right inside and see the show" could be a calling on song for the band, or a threat. We need you, "just like a hurricane needs a tree": shades of '*It's All Right Ma, It's Only Witchcraft*', with the same typhoon of sound: Ashley's bass makes the earth move.

The *NME* for 23rd November reviewed the 'a' side as a "a folk flavoured track from the group's new LP. A song brimful of youthful awareness and expression. Beautiful vocal texture, introspective lyrics, throbbing acoustic guitars". The band were massively dejected when the single failed to chart, though *Disc* wisely commented that "it could get lost in the Christmas chart rush". Also, the lyrics were hardly boy meets girl. Chris Welch got it about right. "A stand out performance by a most under-rated group". '*Meet On The Ledge*' is a song of the ages, and has resonated throughout the strange twists and turns of all those musicians who played on its original release.

They were back almost straight away in the BBC studios, for the Stuart Henry Show. '*Mr Lacey*' is particularly crunchy, with cascading bass and Thompson at his spine-tingling best. His break plays off Ashley's rock solid riffs, like a man in freefall depending on his parachute.

A week later, Fairport returned to record a 'Top Gear' session. One gives praise to Radio 1 for their faith, and to the band for the width of their repertoire, fitting in songs which were never to appear on vinyl, despite the release of three separate new albums in the following year.

There is a parody of the Doors' '*Light My Fire*', while '*I'll Keep It With Mine*' is taken straight. The festive nature of the proceedings is captured in the mock Victorian ballad '*Billy the Orphan Boy's Lonely Christmas*', with friend Marc Ellington on vocals. A genuine Statesider in the band at last!

They were back yet again at the BBC on December 27th, recording four songs for the David Symonds show.

Sandy was bringing a new repertoire to the band. Other songs played in 1968 included Dylan's '*Dear Landlord*' and '*Open The Door Homer*' – respectively from his post-crash album *John Wesley Harding* and the basement tapes – and '*Percy's Song*', then unavailable as performed by its composer.

Sandy brought her old stage favourite, Jackson C. Frank's '*You Never Wanted Me*', and dipped it afresh in a sombre Fairport arrangement.

There is a set list, in Hutchings' handwriting, which he ascribes to late 1968 – an era when a band would customarily play two short sets, rather than one long one. Set one opens with '*Suzanne*' – any other band's set-closer – and goes on to '*Witchcraft*', '*I'll Keep It With Mine*', and '*Jack O'Diamonds*'. Only one band-composed song so far, and the same applies to set two. '*Sailor's Life*' first, then '*Gonna Need My Help*', '*I'll Keep It With Mine*' and '*Meet On The Ledge*'.

Had this line-up of Fairport played the States, or more frequently in Europe, then surely so exciting a band would have been deemed worthy of capture on tape. It would be only the palest reflection of the excitement of watching them live, but better that than silence.

1:7
HOLIDAYS

Fairport Convention's first album for Island, *What We Did On Our Holidays*, although reviewed in December 1968 emerged early in 1969. *Disc* praised "a bewildering and splendid mixture of folk, blues, rock and ballads. The album is literally about the sort of holiday we all enjoyed when very young, those feelings of bitter-sweet nostalgia – and the songs themselves are near perfect".

So is the way tracks are sequenced. An early test-pressing originally transposed the two traditional songs. Sandy explained that "we were sitting in a dressing room before doing a gig somewhere, and we thought, 'What can we do that is different? So I sang them some songs". The rest is history. Simon Nicol tells the story slightly differently: "We asked Sandy to sing some of her favourite songs, and we tried to follow her".

Traditional folk was, as yet, one musical style among equals. As the *Melody Maker* review pointed out, "A very together group, the Fairport are distilling the best elements into their overall musical pattern". Pete Frame in the first issue of Britain's finest fanzine, *Zigzag* used the album as a jumping-off point of a description of Fairport at this time, written in language to match. "Fairport Convention always impress. They're like a growing city – absorbing adjacent styles, but allowing them to retain their own identity. They just stand there – no frenetic cavorting – but they seem to be haloed by an air of precise infallibility. Denny waits reticently, hands clasped coyly, but when she starts to sing, her personality and vocal succulence ooze over the song like melted chocolate".

Any other band attempting such variety "would find themselves stumbling through a musical minefield. But the Fairport, an eclectic group (their stage act ranges from traditional English folksongs to Muddy Waters and way beyond), come through with almost unparalleled magnificence. Joe Boyd, who turns up treasures like a beachcomber finds shells, in the meticulous production of this record, has yielded his masterpiece".

As to individual players, Frame saves his highest praise for Ashley, "'*Book Song*' pinpoints Tyger Hutchings' bass technique. I have never heard such imaginative, inventive and lyrical bass playing anywhere – I found myself literally gurgling with delight on each track as I listened through the phones to the way he slid the riding embellishments and bubbling patterns into the music".

Frame's customary humour cannot be kept dormant for too long. "American listeners may be forgiven for misinterpreting '*Mr Lacey*', written by Hutchings, as thinly disguised pornography. All conveyed in a cascading blues form". Frame singles out Fairport's musical subtlety. "Everything is steeped in imagination from the vocals to the tasteful appropriate drumming of Martin Lamble. They don't put a foot wrong – lavishing care on each song (with a particular attention to introductions and closes) so that each is a superbly arranged and polished entity, and yet an integral part of a most satisfying whole". Follow that.

The article is surrounded by Rod Yallop's dramatic black and white photos, in which Ashley is a dark shadow in a hat, wears dark glasses, and holds his bass guitar like a terrorist cradling a machine gun.

Thompson is wrapped in a scarf like Rupert Bear, and Sandy flutters her hands around the microphone as if delivering a prayer. In another photograph taken around this time, and published in the first edition of the Fairport Convention biography *Meet On The Ledge*, Ashley is intent on his music, slightly bending forward in shoulder length frizzy hair, dark glasses and tie-dye shirt, like a fisherman waiting for the trout to rise. Sandy is blurred in the background, in a floor-length dress.

The album was recorded at Kingsway Recorders and Olympic and Morgan Studios, in the summer and autumn of 1968. There is one outtake, '*Dear Landlord*', a stately reading of one of the impenetrable songs from *John Wesley Harding*. The front cover features a cartoon of the band, by themselves. It is drawn on chalk on a blackboard, a reference to the favourite school essay of the title. Fairport are playing outside the anything-but-ivory towers of Essex University. Hutchings' glasses have shattered, due to the "noticeably worse sound": the band are straining the resources of the electricity pylon behind them, while a van splurting petrol is labelled "Fairport's triumphal arrival at yet another gig".

The cover has an extraordinary story to it. Ashley: "The reality is that we were playing one of our many University gigs at Essex University. We were given a classroom as a dressing room, which was quite common in those days. While we were waiting to go on, some members, probably Martin and Sandy started to do a caricature of the band and then it grew and grew. It's quite elaborate. All the knobs on the amps, the names, the voltage wires. So we must have been waiting to go on stage for some time. And we left it and went on stage. Very shortly after that, we were talking about the need to come up with a cover for our new album, and someone said "Why don't we have that thing on the blackboard?" And so hastily, Essex University, was rung, and asked, "Is the blackboard drawing still in place? Has anyone wiped it off yet?" We were told "No" and Joe Boyd rushed a photographer down there and it was photographed. Although you'd think that it was planned by a committee, it was literally an organic creation, done on the spur of the moment. It was just like '*A Sailor's Life*'."

Simon: "Ashley, ever the puritan, took the dog shit drawing away. He took the blackboard rubber and erased the dog turds. Poor little Bradford." Richard: "If he'd left the dog turds in we could have got an Arts Council Grant." On the back is a photo of the real band onstage – with Thompson and Hutchings having swapped places. Iain Matthews is standing behind his congas: Harvey's dog 'Bradford' is asleep at Ashley's feet, as the man in black wields a massive red Fender. Lamble's face is a blur, while roadie Harvey Branham has his back to us, as he adjusts an amplifier. The band are on stage at Wolverhampton Poly, with Sandy's face haloed in light.

The American sleeve, on A&M, is different, though equally evocative. The band are outside in a park, half covered in autumn leaves, with Martin Lamble in an upturned rubbish basket. Ashley stands above him, looking haughty. Richard looks like a wood-sprite, and Simon sits strumming a guitar, a Byrd perched on the ground. The autumnal theme is taken up in John Hurford's pencil drawing for the album as advertised in the underground press of the time. Leaves fall from the branches, a last butterfly emerges. There is something elegaic captured here, as on the album itself: the summer holiday is over, and winter draws on.

Hampstead Heath. 1968

There is another photo from the same shoot, used on the front cover of *Meet On The Ledge: The Classic Years.* Richard: "I liked the picture because you couldn't really tell where the band ends and the rest continues. It was taken up the back of Hampstead Heath, where they were burning the leaves. There's also that wonderful photograph of Martin in a waste paper basket, that was the American cover. I think that was the same session. I'm sure that was at Dollis Hill."

Rolling Stone was particularly excited about Sandy Denny: "her unthinkably beautiful soprano makes what would have been a merely superb folk-based sometimes rock group extraordinary". Her song '*Fotheringay*' "also features lovely acoustic guitars and Tyger Hutchings' perfect bass framing almost celestial echoed harmonies".

The first thing you hear on the album is acoustic guitar, then electric bass, then a second acoustic guitar and Sandy's voice, soft and luxuriant, singing of a tragic heroine, about to meet her end. The band sing gently in the background, like monks, and Matthews plays finger cymbals rather than drums. Radically different from the first album, with only the electric bass weaving through the mesh of strummed guitars – and the quality of Sandy's voice – differentiating it from the likes of Pentangle. Against the ethereal purity of Pentangle's Jacqui McShee's voice, Sandy is more earthy and 'in your face'. Even so this is as far from the Jefferson Airplane as could be imagined. Next up, though, what could almost be Hot Tuna: electric guitar, bass and heavy drums starting in unison, a shock to the system after the gentility of the opening song. Folk to blues.

Ashley's only solo composition for Fairport, '*Mr Lacey*' had been written about three years before, for his Durnsford Road neighbour. Humphries notes drily that worldwide fame eluded the professor, even after he played the Beatles' indoor gardener in *Help*, and he returned to his life-sized stuffed camel in North London. Matthews recalls that "Tyger said 'I'm bringing him down to play the solo'. And it turned out that the solo was three robots walking about making that noise. Oh, and he wore a space suit too."

Ashley: "'*Mr Lacey*' was a simple blues, and that's made me a bit of money down the years. Bruce Lacey of Muswell Hill, lived in the same street, only about five doors along from me. I knew him well and asked him to come along to the studio. He set his machines going." Richard: "It's a tribute to the mad professor who came into the Morgan Number 1 studio with his machines. I wish we had that on film."

Kingsley: "I picture Bruce in a duffle coat. You tend to associate those with the fifties. He's still around and looks pretty much the same, except greyer. Basically he had two women on the go. He had six kids by Pat who lived at Durnsford Road and there was another woman who wasn't allowed in the house, although Pat knew all about her. He eventually had three kids by her as well. And they've all sprogged. He's got this huge Lacey dynasty. One of his daughters, married an American so that he could avoid the Draft. She just met him at a party and they got married the next day. That's the sort of thing his kids would do. There was that broad anti-war thing. It wasn't political parties. It was reflecting the concerns of the day."

John Wood comments that the song "really illustrates that the Fairports have never been ones to take themselves too seriously. Roger Ruskin Spear of the Bonzo Dog band carried on this tradition, acting as support act for later incarnations of Fairport live, with huge robots which walked the stage, and never quite obeyed his instructions."

The Thompson/Hutchings collaboration '*The Lord Is In This Place, How Dreadful Is This Place*' later takes on an added poignancy after the premature deaths of Sandy and Martin, whose departing footsteps can be heard at the end. The tune is a reworking of Delta bluesman Blind Willie Johnson's '*Dark was the Night, Cold was the Ground*', and recorded at St Peter's, Westbourne Grove.

Ashley: "'The Lord is in this place. How dreadful is this place" now that's a quote from the Bible. I came up with it. I know I found it. It's "How full of dread" of course, not "How dreadful". We were just fiddling around. It's just odd. One had a licence to be odd in those days." And Martin Lamble was throwing coins like "the money lenders in church. It's very confused. What we were trying to say is very confused, and I couldn't begin to be coherent about what it was. It's Appalachian in a way. There's slide guitar. But what you get on that album really for the first time is mature writing from Richard, which you don't get on the first album. A lot of people commented on that when that album came out. The fact that Richard was a songwriter."

Of the traditional songs, '*Nottamun Town*' was known to the band before Sandy joined: Shirley Collins and Davy Graham performed it to a different arrangement on their groundbreaking 1964 folk/jazz album *Folk Roots, New Routes*. As to '*She*

Moves Through The Fair', based on a poem by Padraic Colum, itself a tidying up of a traditional Gaelic poem, and learnt (on record) from the great Irish traditional singer Margaret Barry, it was already in Denny's repertoire, and had been suggested during a group brain-storming session.

The album contains the first flowerings of the band's traditional side, '*Nottamun Town*' and '*She Moves Through The Fair*'. Ashley: "People thought that '*A Sailor's Life*' was our first traditional song, but it wasn't. We were slowly working towards it. The first time that we played an English traditional folk song was when Sandy joined and brought in her folk club repertoire that she had been doing. So gradually, literally just one, then another. Then we decided that we would put in the traditional songs. She wasn't pushing them, but she would play them. '*She Moves Through The Fair*' for example is, if you stripped away, if you had the soundboard in front of you and pulled down all the other faders, pulled down the bass slide, and pulled down the autoharp, and you just left Sandy up, that was exactly how she would do it in a folk club. So you've got Sandy singing and playing guitar, with us just literally busking around her arrangement."

With '*Nottamun Town*' it's a totally different approach. There's a sheer eeriness and strangeness to it. There's that edge of chill and terror to Fairport – a lovely, friendly group, but always that element of sinister edginess. Ashley: "People say: "Oh '*Nottamun Town*', Davy Graham did that, you obviously took that version." Our version if you listen to Davy and Shirley, is nothing like that at all. It's more probably coming via Dylan. And they're all riddles. Each verse is a riddle. So in microcosm, the two traditional tracks on that album show us two totally different ways of tackling the music. And that then carries on. We were doing '*Nottanum Town*' on stage a few times. We didn't do it an awful lot though."

Simon: "As soon as Sandy joined we were more or less thrust in to the recording, and so we were finding our feet with each other, and a natural shortcut, rather than just to thrust our repertoire upon her, and make her change everything she did, was just to find some middle ground. So that she was used to performing on her own, some of these straight forward traditional songs, and we thought: "You lead, and we'll just tinkle along behind. Individually, we had been exposed to this music, thanks to Cecil Sharp House. But that was it. There was no really defined musical policy. We had to create middle ground."

Richard: "We would fill in around her. It wasn't until the next LP that we could work on material like '*A Sailor's Life*'. It was a more fulfilled bridge between ourselves and Sandy, and between rock music and folk music."

Dylan's "*I'll Keep It With Mine*' was not even available on bootleg at the time. Joe Boyd took the whole band to Feldman's music to listen to some unreleased Dylan songs, and also found them Joni Mitchell's '*Eastern Rain*', which its own writer has yet to record.

The band's performance of Ian Matthews' '*Book Song*', weaves around Clare Lowther's cello and underneath Thompson's bell-like solo, suddenly leaping up high in the register at the end of the song.

For many, '*Meet On The Ledge*' has now become Fairport's most cherished song, though its exact meaning is still unclear, even after all these years. Certainly, its sense of impending tragedy and yet of a matching determination to survive was to prove prophetic. A way of living. Kingsley Abbott comes closest. "It's a Fairport family song, and as such is right to have its anthemic place in the group history".

1:8
HEYDAYS

1969 opened with a gig at Fishmonger's Hall, Wood Green. Then a return to Van Dike's (spellings vary) – Greg Vandike, the son of the club's proprietor, is now a well known record dealer – and, closer to home, the Country Club in North London. *Dark Star's* Steve Burgess remembers waiting outside the gig, with the rest of the band larking around, but Richard lost in his own head, with pain in his eyes.

Back to the BBC again, this time for 'Symonds on Sunday'. Simon Nicol's *'Shattering Live Experience'* is about yearning for love, and the life of a rock musician: "missed the morning, slept the afternoon. Half the day's gone, still I laze on, got no silver spoon". One presumes that this is not a reference to cocaine abuse, but rather part of the fairy-tale atmosphere of the song. Thompson's lead follows every twist and turn of Iain Matthews' vocal, underpinned by Hutchings' chunky bass riff. The thumping blues of Muddy Waters' *'You're Gonna Need My Help'* is led in by Thompson on slide guitar, before Hutchings leads in the rest of the band in a thumping, Spoonfully rumble. Sandy's voice cuts in like a knife. Last, but far from least, *'Fotheringay'* is close to the recorded version, again led by the bass, twisting and turning like a river.

Fairport's reputation was spreading. An issue of the US *Teenset* magazine, recounts a visit to (still) swinging London by two of its girlish correspondents. After sharing a box at a Ravi Shankar concert with Brian Jones, they "went to the Marquee club and heard Fairport

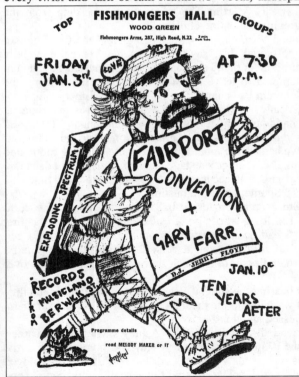

Fishmongers Hall, Wood Green. 3rd January 1969

Convention, a good group that hasn't had a record released in the States yet".
Redbrick, the Birmingham University newspaper, for February 12th carries a picture
shot from below of Ashley in glasses and a cowboy hat, plucking his bass with rapt
concentration. Brian Hinton caught them at the Adam and Eve Club in downtown
Southampton on February 26th: his schoolmate David Harris – who had to force
Brian to part with the 15 bob admission – remembers them starting with '*A Sailor's
Life*'.

"What an opening, twelve minutes plus of '*The Sailor Song*' as my diary
recorded it. The opening bars were heard by little more than eighty people, whilst
the closing interplay between Ashley, Simon and Richard was witnessed by more
than double that number as the small club room jammed to uncomfortable
capacity".

What followed was "astonishing, spellbinding stuff, including greatly extended
versions of '*Jack O'Diamonds*' – which closed the first set, and '*Reno, Nevada*',
which opened the second. Two and a quarter hours of music punctuated only by a
15 minute break between sets, and by several minutes as Sandy used her nursing
skills to tend some poor sod hit on the head by a falling speaker. Real concern
throughout the audience that the show would be prematurely halted (we Sotonians
are a sympathetic bunch)."

"Happily the magical proceedings continued, Ashley the ringmaster, the driver,
the essential catalyst of this motley crew was magnificent, as was the shy, youthful
Richard who spent most of the night skulking at the back of the stage in the shadows
to the left of a memorably sweaty Martin! The guitar work emerging from the
shadows was without compare, literally spine-chilling."

Someone on stage announced '*Bird On A Wire*' as being from the first Leonard
Cohen album, but Ashley corrected this, saying it was not yet commercially
released. He must have heard it first at the 'Top Gear' Cohen session he attended in
London. When the band attempted to leave the stage after their first encore, the
audience would simply not let them leave until they had played another song.

As to the opening song, Ashley remembers "we were in a dressing room at
Southampton" – where they had played in late '68, and again in January '69 – "and
Sandy picked up the guitar and played and sang '*A Sailor's Life*'. We picked up our
instruments and joined in – we had a little tuner amplifier in the dressing room, and
we busked along. Then the time came to go on stage. We made an instant decision,
I mean, we were all buzzing with that because we enjoyed doing it so much …
'Let's get out there and at it'." Spontaneous combustion.

'*A Sailor's Life*' is an 18th century broadside ballad, which Sandy had learnt
from singer and folklorist A.L. Lloyd, whose book *Folk Song In England* was first
published in 1967. Ashley: "I had been burrowing around in the library of Cecil
Sharp House, and had come up with subsequent verses". Having thus acquired a
taste, Hutchings was to return endlessly to this rich bran-tub of folk deposits over
the next thirty years.

Joe Boyd remembers first hearing the song at Bristol's Colston Hall (which they
played in Winter '68) "and it was clear to me that this was a new departure for them.
I remember being quite impressed and amazed by it."

This song, and what it portended – the direction for Ashley's whole future career,
for a start – was to sound the death knell for Iain Matthews' involvement in the
band. He thinks this gig was one of his very last with the band. "I never enjoyed
going into that traditional stuff. I didn't have any traditional roots, unlike Sandy, and
I didn't have any traditional sense, unlike Richard or Ashley. I had never worked

something up in the dressing room in my life, it had always been done at rehearsal. That was my first foray into it, and it didn't appeal to me at all. There was really no place for me in a band playing that type of music. The next thing I knew, Joe Boyd told me they wanted me to leave the band."

It is now Boyd, rather than Ashley, who has to do the dirty work. Certainly at the Adam and Eve, Matthews was still a major creative force, and though he was hardly a visual focus, his absence robbed the band of some of its musical dimensions. Conversely it drew the spotlight much more obviously onto Sandy, and onto the folk roots that the band was now in the process of rediscovering.

Iain: "My most vivid memory of Ashley is an unpleasant one. The day that I was fired from the band, we were going to a gig. We all used to meet up at Witchseason and were given times to meet there. So I got there at the given time to find I was the only one there. And Joe took me into his office and said: "Da-de-da-de-da-de-da...the band wants you to leave." He did that and there was still half an hour before everyone else came, so I sat around waiting for them. They all slowly arrived, we got in the van to go to the gig and Ashley, who was sitting in front, turned around and said: "Where are you going?" I thought Sandy was going to kill him! Sandy was so pissed off with him. I said: "I'm going to the gig aren't I?" He said: "No. You're out!" I'll never forget that. I don't judge him for it, I don't hate him for it. It's just that's my most vivid memory of Ashley.

"It's just a choice of direction. It was heart-wrenching at the time. But in retrospect, if I'd stayed with Fairport I'd would never have had a number one single with Matthews Southern Comfort." And possibly be dead! "Absolutely! You're damn right! Yes."

There's no doubt that when Iain departed, something left that band. A whole dimension vanished. Iain: "They immediately were done with the contemporary aspect. They went off chasing electric folk. That was why I didn't fit in. I did not want to do the trad thing. I wanted to pursue all these great songwriters that Ashley had turned me on to. Ashley played bass on the Matthews Southern Comfort sessions. He was responsible for turning me on to that stuff, and the least I could do was to ask him to play on my first album."

"Outsider is too stronger way of putting it," says Kingsley Abbott of Iain's status in the band, "but it never sat completely right, I think. It was a lack of reference points in a way. He had his own sense of humour but it was coming from a different place to ours. And if he'd been a North Londoner that would have been fine. But he did have a more focused individual direction. He always said this thing to me that he saw his musical career in steps. Each thing he leaves behind, the next thing takes him further. That would fit why he very suddenly left Southern Comfort. I don't think he ever saw himself staying with Fairport for ever and ever. Had they got to be a huge, huge band, it might have been different of course, but they got to that level and stopped basically. He was also very interested in contemporary song writing."

There is no mention of Iain in *Disc* in a review of a 12-hour concert at Oxford Poly on March 15th. A photo shows Sandy in a mid-length kaftan, playing electric guitar, with Simon behind her cradling an autoharp – and looking like a saint about to be martyred – and Richard in the shadows and in baseball boots, staring down at his fretboard. They "can play folky songs like '*Suzanne*' and out-and-out rockers like '*Meet On The Ledge*' (!) with equal excitement and authority. Their most surprising number is the closing version of '*Jack of Diamonds*' "which starts as hard rock and ends with amplified violin from Simon sounding like nothing as much as jazzman John Handy's '*Blues for a High-Strung Guitar*' which is a complete, utter

Photo: Neil Wayne

Brunel University poster. 7rd March 1969

gas".

Nine days later, they were headlining an evening at the Royal Festival Hall entitled 'Folk Meets Pop'. The words are almost unreadable on the poster due to their curlicues, with a cartoon of two long haired guitarists facing each other, one with an acoustic guitar, the other with an electric. Both are smiling. Also on the bill were the Sallyangie – with a very young Mike Oldfield – and compere John Peel.

This is the source for a poor quality audience tape. Peel's voice can clearly be heard introducing the band, Matthews is already gone, and the band launch into a splendid, driving version of '*A Sailor's Life*'. They leave lots of space, Sandy sings as if close to tears, and Ashley and Martin mesh forces like a ship starting to pick up full sail.

Then Thompson's guitar starts screaming like something out of *Psycho*, and the bass guitar stabs repeatedly in emphasis. Sinister as a soul being dragged down into hell. Folk-rock with the accent on rock. When it is all over, Ashley's very polite, posh English voice adds the information "that was basically an English traditional song".

Robin Denselow's review described Fairport as "a highly amplified outfit, who treat traditional English songs (and new ones) to the full electronic onslaught. In their moments of moderation, they almost succeed". This is largely down to Sandy Denny, who rescues the songs from "a totally unnecessary and unsuitable backing". So far so bad, but "when they don't try to play folk, they are a sensationally good pop group".

The tape next captures a fine version of '*Autopsy*', which Hutchings prefaces by suggesting that "you're not going to dance, I presume you're not going to dance, this is in 5/4, 3/4 and 2/4 time". Sandy giggles in turn. The bass guitar booms around the hall as it dances a gavotte, then underpins Richard's jazzy, strict tempo solo, clear as a bell. Sandy is about to launch into "the funniest joke in the whole world", but instead breaks your heart as she sings '*She Moves Through The Fair*'. Her voice loops around the hall, almost Arabic, in an arrangement as light as air. The whole thing is so beautiful and restrained that this is what you imagine the celestial music heard only by the dying sounds like.

Back to her babyish speaking tone, and the joke. A man enters a bar, and asks the barman, "do you serve lemons with little legs on?" "No, of course we don't". "Then I've just squeezed your canary Into my drink". She giggles and claims her mother told her the joke. Simon says "Hello, world", and reckons that no-one will give him a microphone. Guitars chime, and the tape runs out on a boomy '*I'll Keep It With Mine*'. Ashley's bass is like a heart beat.

The band went into the BBC on 18th March to record yet another set of songs for 'Top Gear'. An intense take of '*Percy's Song*' closes *Heyday*, while '*Si Tu Dois Partir*', '*Autopsy*' and '*Cajun Woman*' look towards the future.

For those in the provinces, it was Radio 1 that kept them abreast of what was going on. Ashley: "We'd start playing '*Suzanne*' or whatever, and there would be cheers of recognition because they'd heard that stuff on John Peel, or been passed around on tape. The folk tradition again. It was great. When it came to the second album, we actually had moderate success. It got into the lower reaches of the charts, and a certain amount of play on the radio. It was much more akin to what we did on stage. We still clung to the singer/songwriters, it was still at the time when we were doing Joni Mitchell and others.

"Something like '*Tale In Hard Time*' was so good. God knows why we didn't do it. It wasn't for commercial reasons that we clung onto doing other people's material as well as some of our own. Again, maybe with a firmer hand, someone saying "Listen, what you really should do is forget covers now, you've done them for a year. Let's have all of Richard's songs in there". We just continued doing what we fancied doing. By the time we reached the next album we are then doing stuff that we did on stage. All of it."

Modern bands would not be offered such luxury. Richard: "It's a much bigger music business now. Whereas labels used to have ten acts they've now got two or three hundred. At some point record companies decided that signing one act and promoting it, spending £100,000 promoting them, whereas spending £10,000 on ten acts each, they could get two acts to break. Two acts would stick to the wall. And whoever started it, they all copied. So everyone literally signed ten times the number of acts. The discard rate is phenomenal. So you have a situation where quite a talented band only get one shot to make a record, and if it doesn't work, they go back to the sticks. It's so totally demoralising. Thankfully we were given the chance to actually develop and sell pretty crappy numbers of records for the first three or four albums. And after that, five, six, seven, eight, nine, ten records."

Simon: "It was remarkable really that Island did stick by us. They stuck by us to the extent where we were the only act of our generation that hadn't actually carved out enough of a success to warrant a gold record. I mean Blodwyn Pig got maybe two albums, but we'd done maybe seven or eight, nine or ten for Island, and they felt so bad about this that they actually cobbled together the idea of a grand total, kind of long service award gold medal. It wasn't until 1974 that they got around to doing this. Such was the high regard in which the band as individuals were held by the upper levels of the organisation at that time. Because we'd been there a lot longer than many of them, and they could relate to us in a way that they couldn't to a lot of the younger bands that had just appeared. There wasn't anybody like Island founder Chris Blackwell. Blackwell was a one-off. The other guys who were doing that, were doing it from a different point of view. They were the Andrew Loog Oldhams who were doing it strictly from managerial or record production basis."

Richard: "It really does go through cycles. The business angle didn't understand the market. So we had about three years there where it was very, very loose, and we had all kinds of people – if Hapshash And The Coloured Coat could get a record deal, then we could!"

In many ways, what Richard and Simon have previously said about record labels was also reflected in the ever-changing venue environment. The small fish couldn't compete with the larger University and College predators swimming in the same pools. Richard: "The police closed down the Van Dike Club. They thought it was a place for young people to take drugs. It was a serious miscalculation. It was a lovely club run by really, really nice people. It was something for kids in Plymouth to do. If kids are going to smoke a bit of dope, who cares?"

Simon: "That's one thing about Fairport, I think you could easily interchange any member of the audience with any member of the band, and nobody would really notice. Richard's audience is different obviously, because they are much more refined and larger." Richard: "Quality and better taste. All judges and stockbrokers."

While much of the material from this part of the Fairport story was not deemed worthy of a contemporary official release, it did surface somewhat informally on *Heyday – BBC Radio Sessions 1968-69*. The album, along with its unofficial counterparts, is a fascinating part of the Fairport story.

The *Heyday* material – all in BBC mono – surfaced first on cassette in 1976, through the good offices of Ashley, very much the band's historian. The eclectic mixture of tracks included '*Gone Gone Gone*' (Everly Brothers), '*You Never Wanted Me*' (Jackson Browne), '*Some Sweet Day*' (Everly Brothers), '*Bird On A Wire*' (Leonard Cohen), '*I Still Miss Someone*' (Johnny & Roy Cash Jnr), '*You're Gonna Miss Me*' (Muddy Waters), '*Suzanne*' (Leonard Cohen), '*Reno, Nevada*' (Richard Fariña), '*I Don't Know Where I Stand*' (Joni Mitchell), '*Close The Door Lightly*' (Eric Andersen), '*Shattering Live Experience*' (Simon Nicol), '*If You Feel Good*' (Hutchings/ Thompson), '*Tried So Hard*' (Gene Clark), '*Meet On The Ledge*' (Thompson).

Artwork on the original cassette issue is minimal. The album of the same name which surfaced in 1987 on Joe Boyd's label Hannibal was beautifully packaged, though it re-ordered the tracks, shed '*You Never Wanted Me*', '*You're Gonna Need My Help*' and '*Meet on the Ledge*', and added '*Percy's Song*', perhaps the highlight of the whole set. The re-release on Boyd's own label was rather ironic, because, as he confesses in the 1987 re-issued album's sleeve note, he was the person who blocked the material's original release.

"As an American, my view was that Americans did these sort of songs in their sleep better than any English band could hope to". He pushed Fairport in the direction of developing their own song writing, and becoming as English as possible. Children of Albion, indeed. "Thus I discouraged committing most of the above songs to vinyl. Of course I am now forced to admit it is hard to find an American band who can do these songs equal justice".

Shirley Collins confirmed that their country life in Etchingham was responsible for the birth of the home-made record label through which they released the *Heyday* cassette from their house. "That was to try and make some money. We were very short of money, so it was for the best of intentions."

Simon: "Guess who managed to horn-swoggle tapes out of all the BBC engineers at the end of every session? And then they turned up later. That original cassette he brought out was like a personal bootleg. And who should be roped in to duplicate them but Judy Dyble's husband." He laughingly adds, "So keeping the circle for ever tightly sealed."

Geoff Wall recalls sending his postal order off for a copy, unaware that Hutchings himself was the vendor. In his accompanying letter, and ever hopeful, he asked whether a second volume would be forthcoming. His reward was a curt note to the effect that "you're bloody lucky to get this collection, let alone a second."

During those days, the BBC rigorously enforced a draconian Musician's Union edict that insisted all radio sessions be destroyed. Consequently very few of those early sessions have been retained within the BBC archives. In discussing 'lost' TV programmes, screenwriter Anthony Schaffer ruefully noted, the BBC in the 1950s and 1960s "wiped its best programmes like they'd wipe a dinner plate." It was a comment that applied equally to its priceless Radio archives.

Those hoping for a second volume of session recordings will therefore be disappointed to learn that all of the original reels that Ashley possessed were stolen

The extended Heyday CD sleeve. 2002

from Joe Boyd's car during the production of Hannibal's version of *Heyday*. So the prospect of a good quality follow-up is out of the question. Luckily we have the B-grade sounding bootleg CD *A Chronicle of Sorts* to sop our desire. But there are still a few missing tracks that no-one seems to have got, like '*Things You Gave Me*'.

In early 2002, as part of the Island Remasters programme, an extended version of the album was released as *Heyday – The BBC Sessions 1968-1969/Extended*. Ashley: "The original CD release featured songs recorded by the *What We Did On Our Holidays* line up. This re-release adds eight extra tracks from the *Unhalfbricking* and *Liege & Lief* groups. The later tracks recorded at the end of the sixties, feature the radical change of style to traditional British folk-rock."

Patrick Humphries has pointed out how Matthews' departure saw the visual focus move all the more to Sandy. "She offered a counterpoint to the scruffy oiks either side of her – Simon's long, straight hair framed his face, while Ashley stood stock still playing the bass, and rarely smiling."

Musically, though, Thompson began to take over the group dynamics from Hutchings. "Ashley may have laid the Fairport foundations, and Sandy may have provided the charisma, but it was Richard who was now powering the group. Singers and rhythm sections can be replaced, but the real power lies in the hands of the persons who write the songs".

Fairport were putting together a new repertoire in the first few months of 1969. It was a more uncluttered sound, and even Iain generously recognises that "the next two albums were amazing albums that I could never have taken part in. Fairport members were growing more confident in their own songwriting, though Ashley himself seemed to have temporarily given up as a budding Robert Zimmerman.

New material covered by the latest Fairport line-up included three obscure Dylan songs. '*Down In The Flood*' and '*Million Dollar Bash*' were from the Basement Tapes. '*Si Tu Dois Partir*' was more off-the-wall, a French translation of '*If You Gotta Go, Go Now*', a risqué song partly banned from the British airwaves when Manfred Mann recorded it. In French, censors would be too stupid to realise it was the same invitation to spend the night together. The audience, though, were in on the joke. It was a cunning idea, which was to give Fairport their first hit.

On air, Brian Matthew asked Sandy if she had acquired the new lyrics from Bob Dylan, at which she laughed: "No, you can't get near him". Fairport were at Middle Earth one night, waiting to go on at 3am, and "messing around in the dressing room. We thought it would be nice to give it a cajun beat, with accordion and violin and translated the words into this Americanised French, but of course we couldn't get that. So we announced over the PA that we desperately needed some French people who happened to be in the audience. They stormed in and spent about an hour translating the words into French, just as a joke really".

The song does not reflect their usual repertoire. Sandy: "I wonder what people who don't know our music think, they must think that we're some kind of joke Bonzo Dog Band type group, but we're quite serious really." For Ashley, "it was one of those things that was characteristic. Sitting in a dressing room thinking "what are we going to do now? Why don't we do it in French? Why don't we do it now? We were very impetuous, and we were very sparky, and I think there was a certain feeling with that band, of experimentation and energy."

The band is trying "to get a good sound onstage, we're really working towards that now". Fairport had a full gig sheet. April saw the slimmed-down band play gigs at Sunderland Tech, and the Alex Disco Club, Salisbury. Worthy venues, but hardly the Fillmore West or Royal Albert Hall.

Fairport were still basically a club band, going out for around £600 a night. With such a wealth of new songs, and with Denny's growing majesty onstage, they were about to move to a higher division. The loss of Matthews had sharpened the focus of the band, musically and visually – though the mixture was a little less rich for his loss. Those lucky enough to have seen Fairport in early 1969 knew immediately that they were onto something special, privy to a secret one-upmanship. The mass media are always a step or two behind. Such delights are what still drive people out to sweaty rock clubs, the chance of seeing something extraordinary. You will never be able to get so close – in every sense – again. By the same token, such attractions explode almost immediately out of the confinement that small venues impose.

There were two markers to the future, in retrospect almost like premonitions. Shirley and Dolly Collins supported Fairport at Liverpool Poly. Ashley: "I remember that Fairport really enjoyed their set. I said how much I enjoyed her singing and her music." And Fairport went down to see the Padstow Obby Oss on May Day.

For Martin Lamble, fame and success were things to be infinitely postponed.

1:9
CRASH

On 11th May, Fairport played Mother's Club in Birmingham. In the early morning of 12th, they set off for London in their Transit van. Harvey Bramham was driving: Ashley, Simon and Martin were in the back of the van, with Richard and his American girlfriend Jeannie Franklin seated up front. As they approached Mill Hill in North London tragedy struck. As Humphries puts it, "Bramham apparently fell asleep at the wheel, causing the van to drift." Richard grabbed at the wheel, but over-corrected and the van cartwheeled. As he told Pamela Longfellow, "I think I was the only person awake. I watched in a kind of daze as we swerved out into the middle of the motorway and I looked over at our roadie … God, he had his eyes closed. So I grabbed for the wheel to pull us back, and he woke up confused and grabbed the wheel back".

Simon Nicol had also been asleep: "I can remember waking up while the van was actually somersaulting. When I woke up, I was the only one in the vehicle – everyone else had gone through the windows and doors". As Humphries adds, with grim understatement, "Nicol survived because the equipment shot out through the doors at the back of the van, rather than forward, which would have crushed him to death".

Judy Dyble: "I was lucky. The seat that Jeannie The Tailor, whom I didn't know, had been sitting in, was the seat that I would have sat in. On the other hand, I was very good at keeping Harvey awake on those long drives." Iain said the same, when we spoke to him. He was grateful really that he wasn't there. He could have been.

The van hit the central reservation of the M1, then rebounded across the carriageway, before plunging 40 feet down an embankment, and ending up upside down on a golf course. In the circumstances, it is a near miracle that there were any survivors. Bramham had gone through the windscreen, Ashley and Richard were wandering around dazed, 90 feet away from the crashed van. Simon flagged down a lorry, and the driver called for an ambulance from the nearby Scratchwood service station. When it finally arrived, the dead – Martin and Jeannie – and injured were taken to the Royal Orthopaedic Hospital at Stanmore.

Kay Hutchings: "That was terrible. Simon had crawled out of the van, found a phone box and phoned his mother, who then phoned us. I think it was before 5am. We'd got the news before the police arrived. The police didn't call until 9 o'clock. They were taken to Stanmore Hospital and Ashley's face was terrible. He thought that he was blind when he came out because both eyes were shut. His nose was broken. It was very, very sad."

Nicol next remembered "hours and hours in casualty – Richard just looking at the wall, Hutch couldn't see because he had so much blood on his face". Ashley: "I had a broken nose, a broken cheek bone. I couldn't see immediately after the crash, both my eyes were closed up. When Iain Matthews came to visit us in hospital, the first time he saw my face, he fainted on the next bed." At least such surface wounds were to quickly heal.

The survivors seem never to have properly talked through with each other, however, the deep psychological scars which the crash left. Nothing would be the same again. It was an event which continues to bond together those who came through in a way no outsider will ever fully understand. Richard: "I lost something and I don't think I'll ever get it back". Yet he had to try. "I don't know what else to do with myself". Simon though reckoned that "what the crash did was to bring us very much more together as people. We found a greater understanding in each other through the tragedy and it made us more determined to succeed". It can be argued that the crash was the making of Richard as a songwriter – all the guilt and pain in '*Crazy Man Michael*' or regrets and loss in '*Sloth*'.

As the news spread, so did a sense of dull shock: for those who had seen so life-affirming a band onstage, it seemed to distance their memory to a lighted room. Almost the first question was 'would Fairport continue?' Any regrouping could not continue with the old repertoire, so closely tied to a line-up which could never now reconvene.

Dave Swarbrick and Martin Carthy had arrived in Newcastle, having just done a gig. Carthy: "It was midnight and there was an evening paper. It talked about a band smash. I thought "What band is this?" I looked and it said: "The band Fairport Convention had a smash". And I said: "I think you need to see this Dave", and Dave just looked and said "That's it then!". Then he got the phone call asking him to join, and got cold feet."

The Rolling Stones sent a large bouquet, and fans hitchhiked hundreds of miles from as far away as Cornwall. *The Evening Standard* reported that among those injured was "Ashley Hutchings (facial lacerations and concussion) of Donovan Avenue, Muswell Hill. The group were well known in the Underground pop world".

Sandy Denny had travelled back separately with her boyfriend Trevor Lucas. Witchseason's press officer, Anthea Joseph phoned Joe Boyd in the States. That same evening, Kingsley went to see the survivors. "Tyger's face was very bad, but he was making the best of things. Richard was very quiet. Harvey appeared mentally detached. Simon was around and was managing to rise above events as he kept himself busy with press enquiries. Ashley certainly wasn't the same after the crash. The crash just made time stand still. There was a strange sense of heaviness. It was like visiting separate little islands. It was quite a small ward, but they weren't all together. Simon being Simon, he had walked away from a wreck where two other people had died. At the time, everybody said: "That is typical of Simon". If anybody was going to survive that, he was. The others were very, very quiet. Like they had a protective bubble around them. Harvey was certainly away from the others. I don't know how purposeful that was. Maybe they already knew the real cause of it. Maybe it was arranged by the police or possibly Anthea. She might have fixed that. Harvey was right for the job, a modern road manager. Hardened, wizened, he was a character who you'd want on your side if there was trouble."

Kay Hutchings felt that the blackboard drawing on *What We Did On Our Holidays* was full of portents for the band's future, and that like The Beatles' *Abbey Road* sleeve, it contains various clues about the crash. Ashley: "Certainly there's a van breaking down going "Phut, phut" on the Motorway. And the fact that Harvey's in prison uniform with arrows on it. I suppose that it's things like that which are more than bizarre."

Kay Hutchings: "Ashley's really dedicated. He got over the crash, but I remember him when he came home, sitting there saying: "For the first time in my life – (and this was only when he was 25) – I don't know where I'm going!" He had a breakdown. We had to put a bed downstairs for him after the accident. That was when his American girlfriend, Ann turned up on the doorstep, married. The shock of this, immediately following the accident, is incalculable. He was on tablets during the whole of his later marriage to Shirley."

Ashley Hutchings: "I was oblivious to a lot of what was happening at that time because I was in hospital with severe facial injuries and other injuries to my ankle and pelvis. Harvey and I were the longest in hospital. In the meantime, while I was recuperating, the others were taken on a trip to America, and did a guest spot at The Troubadour. The *Unhalfbricking* album had come out, was selling and getting coverage. Charity concerts were being arranged that I didn't have much knowledge of. I knew they happened, one at The Roundhouse, one at the Van Dike Club and one at Mothers in Birmingham. I was recuperating and more concerned to get well again. I left hospital still having a very bad ankle and had to be helped out. I remember leaving hospital with my Dad on one side and my friend Richard Allen on the other helping me walk. I hadn't been living at home but I returned to my parents. I went to have extra recuperation and get my ankle better and everything else, back at home in Muswell Hill."

A benefit concert at the Roundhouse was announced in May, with the Pretty Things and Family. Old friends like Eclection. Blossom Toes, Martin Carthy and Dave Swarbrick, and the Pink Floyd were subsequently added to the bill. Mothers Club also announced plans for a benefit gig, while Van Dikes held one on May 29th, with John Peel, Yes and King Crimson. Judy Dyble made her musical reappearance,

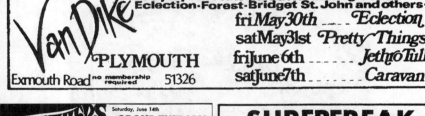

Benefit gigs

as one half of Trader Horne, with the Irish singer Jackie McAuley.

John Walters, producer of the Radio 1 John Peel Show, came to the hospital one night on his bike. "The two Johns had been very good friends to the band, championing their cause". Kingsley later joined Simon and Sandy on a visit to Peel's studio, for a live interview. "Sandy and I walked slowly down towards Oxford Circus, passing Margaret Street where they had so often played so beautifully. She gave me a kiss and a grin before she left."

Abbott also remembers going to Martin's parents' house in Harrow and being "struck by their strength in their great loss. I suggested for the funeral service the words from the *Book of Ecclesiastes* that Martin had enjoyed as they appeared in the Byrds' song '*Turn, Turn, Turn*'. The service was held at Golders Green crematorium on a bright and sunny day. There was a large turn-out. The simple beauty of '*I'll Keep It With Mine*' was played at the end of the service."

Judy sombrely recalls "I did go to Martin's funeral, but I felt very much an outsider. I went to see them in hospital but I didn't know what to say. If I'd still been their friend, I would have known what to say. But I didn't!"

Martin Lamble photographed in Harvey Bramham's flat.

Martin's parents bequeathed to Ashley their son's heavy signet ring, as a remembrance. He had worn it throughout Fairport. Its design is St George, fighting the dragon. Englishness personified. It is like a torch being passed...

In the *Melody Maker* for 24th May, Chris Welch paid his own tribute. "They were playing '*Meet On The Ledge*' at London clubs last week. Fairport were – and still are – one of the most liked, respected, even loved of those bands that spend their days and night hitting the road. They were the band we tended to take a little for granted. They never caused great sensations in public or uttered endless wise sayings in the press. They quietly improved and produced better and better music in two hard working years together."

Three letters to the same paper expressed much the same sentiments. They paid tribute to "a stunning group and beautiful people. I hope they get over this terrible shock and continue to do great things. Good luck, Fairports", as one letter put it. The accident had laid waste to a band in its prime, but from its ashes another wonderful line-up was set to arise. The reformed Fairport was now to take a conceptual leap, as a form of self-healing. The accident changed everything forever, and cemented a two way affection between the band and its audience, which continues to the present day.

If any song came to encapsulate this, it was '*Meet On The Ledge*', and its annual recitation at the Cropredy Festival has taken on a hymnal quality. If Ashley keeps his distance from this event most years – unwilling to be bogged down in nostalgia – the various incarnations of the Albion Band have interchanged personnel with the mother band, and there is a special charge in the air whenever Hutchings appears with the band he founded, most notably for their 30th anniversary in 1997.

Though not as publicly mourned as Martin Lamble, Jeannie Franklin's death was equally tragic. Jeannie had come to Los Angeles from New York in 1965, and opened two clothes shops, one near the Troubadour, the other inside the Whisky a Go Go. Very much part of the counter-culture, her customers included Jefferson Airplane, Them, Jimi Hendrix, and Jack Bruce, who was to dedicate his first solo album to her. She infused rock fashion, putting Paul Revere into tights and The Temptations into ruffles. She would categorise her clients, so that the Lovin' Spoonful were "Levi people with Bloomingdale tee-shirts with the stripe, dress down people". Like Martin Lamble or Nick Drake, she was one of those bright talents who burnt briefly at the end of the sixties, and can never be replaced.

Richard Thompson's songs '*Crazy Man Michael*' and '*Farewell, Farewell*', along with the later '*Never Again*', were partial attempts to come to terms – creatively, emotionally, psychologically – with what had happened. Writing such songs was a public but coded way to deal with subsequent feelings of guilt about the death of his girlfriend. So is the spine-freezing '*Bad News Is All The Wind Can Carry*', which Ashley rescued from a demo tape when he performed it with the Albion Band at the National Theatre in *Lark Rise To Candleford*.

There was one final personal tragedy associated with the crash. In a bitterly ironic replay of '*Percy's Song*' – Dylan's song about a man unjustly imprisoned for killing the passengers in his vehicle during a crash – already laid down on tape, but not yet released, Fairport's roadie Harvey Bramham, who had fallen asleep at the wheel, was banned from driving for five years, and given a six month prison sentence for the offence of "causing death by dangerous driving". He was released early on appeal. Lord Parker, the Lord Chief Justice, ruled that Bramham had "quite clearly expressed his remorse", and imposed a £100 fine in lieu of the rest of his sentence. In another bitter footnote, the band were visited in hospital as they recuperated by the drug squad.

Thirty years on, Ashley recalled: "Harvey suffered with a bad stomach ulcer and had that day been drinking milk in a effort to calm it. Members of the band were summoned to the hearing to give evidence, and were sympathetic to his plight. It came as an enormous shock when the Judge convicted him of manslaughter, and he was sent to jail. Upon his release, we did not keep in contact because we were then busy with *Liege & Lief.*"

In the meantime, the surviving members took a three month break. The *New Musical Express* for 17th May announced the cancellation of all of Fairport's engagements, including an appearance at the Royal Albert Hall in early July. They were at that time scheduled to take off for a six-week US tour for the group, including appearances at the Newport Festival and the Fillmore West. Ghost gigs, whose music will never be heard except in our imagination. Island announced it was to issue a "recently-completed album" in July.

A spokesman told the *Melody Maker* that "a big question mark hangs over their future at the moment, but they hope to carry on". The same magazine announced 'Fairport's Return' on 14th June: "Fairport Convention will start work again on their return from a holiday in America. They come back at the end of June and will spend July rehearsing and finding a replacement drummer". Richard, Sandy and Simon were flown out to Los Angeles to recuperate, and played the Troubadour as a trio one night. Ashley himself was the last to leave hospital.

1:10
MEMORIES

The title of 1969's *Unhalfbricking* is comfy and nonsensical, a private code. Simon Nicol told *Beat Instrumental* that "it came from a game we created in the van on one of the many times we ran out of petrol. We take it in turns to invent words. Sandy came up with this one, and we all thought it was so strange that it stuck in the memory".

The album's front cover shows a photograph of Sandy Denny's parents, and the group having tea in the extensive garden of the large house in which they lived, close to the tennis grounds in Wimbledon. Simon denies that it is a send-up: "Sandy's parents were far too hip to fall for anything like that." Fairport are seen through a wooden fence, and shaded by trees just coming into bud: a church spire stands mistily in the background. The contrast between the old couple, he in pressed slacks and neat pullover, she in a twinset, both neatly coiffed, contrasts humorously with the band, all flowing hair, jeans and baseball boots, but the underlying message is that of togetherness. The band might look like wild animals seen through the bars of a cage, but the gate is open, and the older couple look proud and hospitable.

Ashley: "The front cover was an idea of mine." It is a really provocative statement of inclusiveness and cool. Ashley deserves credit for the sheer panache of this portrait of Middle England, 1969 style. "This is the garden of Sandy's parents. The photographer Eric Hayes and the band go down to Sandy's parents' house in Wimbledon. We have a photo session in the house eating and then in the garden. Indeed a version of that picture is on the American cover. It was a conventional photo session in the garden and in the house. At one point I said to Eric: "Hey listen, this is a bit boring. Why don't you come out and why aren't we right in the background. It's far more interesting having to look into the picture to see us." So we persuaded them to pose, and Eric took the photo. We said "That's the one!" It's far more interesting. In fact we like it so much, don't put the title on the cover, because it ruins the picture. We thought that we were just going to end up with that. A lovely picture, an interesting picture. They agreed with us not to put the title on. It came out after the crash. Posthumously as it were. Maybe we picked up extra coverage and sales through the sympathy vote. But I won't feel guilty about that because the music is worth it."

On the back cover, Fairport are sitting together companionably, in the house in which the Dennys lived, eating a cooked meal. Two chairs are left empty but with full plates waiting: for Eric Hayes and his wife. Or is this too some kind of awful prescience. Ashley is caught in full verbal flow, a piece of bread half eaten in his hand: the rest listen. On the back cover he squats on the ground, a cup of tea raised to his lips. The American issue, on A&M, inexplicably features a series of dancing elephants, with a different picture of the band on the lawn, inset.

Dave Swarbrick guests on fiddle and mandolin, Iain Matthews makes a temporary return on *'Percy's Song'*. American folk singer Marc Ellington, a friend of Dylan who was over in Britain avoiding the draft, sings on '*Million Dollar Bash*', and "found" that song from a "collection of acetates made by Dylan purely as a guide to his songs for other artists". A third Dylan song, '*Si Tu Dois Partir*', joins '*Autopsy*' and '*Who Knows Where The Time Goes*' by Sandy and Richard's '*Genesis Hall*' and '*Cajun Woman*' – and the traditional '*A Sailor's Life*'. An alternative take, without Dave Swarbrick, later surfaced on an acetate. Suitably cleaned up, it later appeared, as if by miracle, on the Richard Thompson retrospective *Watching The Dark* in 1993.

The origin of this alternate take is taken up by Ian Maun. "That is one of two tracks off an acetate, the other being '*Autopsy*', and it's believed to have been recovered from a bin behind a recording studio in America. And the version of '*Autopsy*' begins with Sandy going "Again!" So it must have been quite a late take." The acetate had turned up at a garage sale – its flip side was an alternative earlier version of '*Autopsy*' – and was sent to the *Friends of Fairport* fan club, who arranged for it to be remastered at a West Country studio owned by DJ Simon Stable, by now married to Judy Dyble. Thus keeping things in the family. There is also a tape of slightly different mixes from *Unhalfbricking* and *Liege & Lief*. Less exciting than it sounds, the most interesting is an alternative mix of '*Crazy Man Michael*' with Sandy's vocals eerily unbalanced, as if in another room. Otherwise, anoraks only. The alternative '*A Sailor's Life*' is a different animal, with its own momentum and poise.

Ashley: "I wouldn't edit Richard during a twenty minute guitar break. I was a pain in the arse in terms of telling people what to do – but I wouldn't edit Richard's solos. Editing wasn't a word in use." Richard: "It wasn't an Olympic sport at that point. I think also you move with the audience expectation. The audience was really in tune to instrumental stuff and most bands were pretty rambling. And fairly free of substance in some cases. The audience wouldn't have that tolerance now. The audience wouldn't sit through a ten minute solo. We improvised round the traditional song '*A Sailor's Life*' for the first time onstage. And it was just a magical moment. And when we made the album on which that track appeared, the same thing happened. We just did one magical take. We went in and improvised '*A Sailor's Life*' with Dave Swarbrick on fiddle who we had never played with before, and it was just that magic moment. Silence when we'd finished. And everyone knew, the engineer, Joe Boyd the producer, we all knew what we'd done."

"That was the seed in the ground and then everything comes from that. We leapt in with both feet. We took a chance. The words 'Caution', 'Marketing' and 'Good career move' didn't apply. We just went for it. And there's a version without Swarbrick. I don't know where that came from. Maybe it was a soundcheck." Richard still says "I think that we're still scratching our heads about that take. We're not quite sure who played what. It was just a very nice take, a sort of happy accident."

For Simon: "The version which is on Richard's *Watching The Dark* compilation, without fiddle, was done within hours of the other one. It's got so many differences and they're not just points of detail. The whole atmosphere, the whole pace of it is just different. It's the innocence of youth, and a lack of technique." Richard adds: "A lack of technique works every time. And also it was musical worlds colliding. It is an interesting point. What do you do when Tin Pan Alley collides with R&B? What do you do when Folk collides with Rock? It's a kind of grey area and you invent it as you go along. When we started playing '*A Sailor's Life*', we really didn't know where the end was."

That said, it also throws into relief the alchemical change which Swarbrick's fiddle brings to proceedings, by turn jaunty, piercing, and a banshee cry. One can only compare it to the work of bands like King Crimson, where electic violin is used as a sound source all its own. Think, too, of the Velvet Underground, with John Cale's cello a harbinger of doom. Closest of all is Johnny Van Deryck's eerie punctuations to Michael Chapman's slowed down '*Aviator*' on *Fully Qualified Survivor*, another 1969 epic of flight and loss.

Oddly and chillingly prophetic, *Unhalfbricking* is a record of extreme joy and friendliness which deals with a road crash – '*Percy's Song*' – apocalypse – '*Million Dollar Bash*' – death by drowning and a song called '*Autopsy*'. Martin pushes over a stack of chairs on '*Si Tu Dois Partir*', and one thinks back to the sound effect of a pile-up on '*M1 Breakdown*', on an earlier album.

Writing in his column of *Disc* on June 28th, John Peel gave the record a rave preview. The review is tinged with hippie whimsy, sharpened by Peel's wit. "Early this week Simon Fairport brought for my ears a copy, battered in many ways, of the new Fairport LP, called after a Sandy word dreamed up during an extended game of 'Ghosts'. This group has brought me more joy during the past two years than any other I can think of. The things they have done for Radio 1 have brightened weeks, not hours. It is true, therefore, that any review I write will be coloured with love. The record made me feel warm and comfortable and part of them. It is an LP that you will want to hear daily for a very long time".

'*Genesis Hall*' was written after Richard had heard of attempts by 'squatters' to renovate a long-deserted hotel near the Arts Lab in London's Drury Lane. In '*Si Tu Dois Partir*', Sandy "doesn't sound altogether happy about singing in French, but you can chuckle a bit the way someone on the record does before the second chorus. It's that sort of a record. Trevor Lucas plays triangle (hoarse cries of 'supergroup') Martin couldn't find a washboard and plays instead plastic stacked chair backs and assorted debris. Sometimes Tyger and Simon and Richard aren't playing but when they do it's just right."

Peel continues: "The opening of '*A Sailor's Life*' is soft with breezes and sunshine and sea-guitar. Just gentle and stroked and so good. That's what those pedals should and can do. The wind builds and Dave Swarbrick is suddenly there on violin while Martin rolls the stones on the sea bed. Simon and Richard come and go as the sun does. Now we're being driven along by a fine wind and the bow cuts through the rolling sea on the edge of Richard's guitar and Dave's violin. Now Tyger is there on my right and the whole wondrous crew is sailing into calmer waters and a cymbal breeze. About eleven and a half minutes, among some islands and flying fish. Recorded in one take without overdubbing, Simon says, because you can't retake voyages like that. This is one of the best things I've ever heard".

Of the other tracks, '*Cajun Woman*' is the story of an incident from Greek tragedy transported into a Louisiana swamp setting. Joan Baez sang the opening of '*Percy's Song*' with Dylan in the film *Don't Look Back*, acapella. "There are strange wispy guitar sounds here like children sliding rusty nails on wire stretched between concrete posts. The song rocks back and forth, and [its chorus] builds the same mantric, mystic force that you found in '*Hey Jude*'. Finally the friendship and unselfconscious smiles of '*Million Dollar Bash*'. Marc Ellington sings the first verse. Unexpectedly Tyger, with a curious American accent speaks the second verse". This from a man who had previously had little confidence in his own voice. Peel finishes with a statement that it is impossible to imagine being written today, but which sums up a continuing truth. "Fairport, we love you very much".

His article is accompanied by a superb photo, in which Ashley sits in stripy rugby shirt, black waistcoat, circular shades and frizzy hair and a Zapata moustache. Of the rest, Richard looks like Rupert Bear, with a scarf knotted around his neck, and Sandy is in her kaftan.

Nick Logan's *NME* review was cooler, but is also spot-on. "It's not as much that they're such skilled musicians, but the almost indefinable quality that suggests youthfulness and vitality. Even on the sad songs the feel that permeates through is one of a joy of being alive". As another review put it, "should ever they seem too steeped in sadness, humour bubbles through".

International Times opines that the album rocks harder, with the vocals which open '*Cajun Woman*' "reminiscent of early Jordanaires doing Presley back-ups". US reviews were even more favourable. *Fusion* used the word "perfect", which *Rolling Stone* echoes in describing "Fairport's perfectly controlled attack", noting that Denny "never uses more than half of her power".

There is a kind of smooth intensity to the whole album, a musical self-confidence which has kept it fresh through the years. Nicol commented that "the record is much freer than the last one. There is far less overdubbing". Hutchings is the ring-leader, his see-saw bass underpins the foundations on '*Genesis Hall*', the opening track written much like a Scottish border ballad. He is a crucial component of the crunchy instrumental sound which defines this album as much as Denny's soaring vocals: knowing when not to play on '*Si Tu Dois Partir*', taking the musical lead on the complex '*Autopsy*', where half the power is from his precise and rhythmic bass counter-melody.

Not a note out of control, like a master watch-maker. The bass on '*A Sailor's Life*' is at the other end of the spectrum, impressionistic, gradually picking up speed and tension, with unexpected runs up and down the register, responding to every change of feeling in Sandy's emotional reading. Nobody has ever done this to folk music before, aeons away from Danny Thompson's acoustic jazz riffs for Pentangle. He thunders beneath the middle section, then comes to the fore as the music begins to slow down, a guide rail through the darkness, sticking to one note as the tension builds, then a gentle coda at the end, then silence.

The British Asian singer Sheila Chandra later wrote about how ahead of its time the track was, a precursor of 'world music' "using Indian structures within the framework of English folk". Guitar and violin first set out the notes of the scale, or "jog", they are to use, then the band weave around it, as does Sandy with the curlicues of her voice. "The track is actually a microcosm of 2,000 years of Indian music – it goes from Vedic chanting on two or three notes right through to full improvisations on a fixed note scale. All in one take! The band have realised that all folk music is based upon a drone, and shares a common root. For instance, the way the violin comes in with an insistent repeat of the drone note is reminiscent of the Indian wind instrument the shenai, and its distant relative the shawm in Irish music. It all connects."

A strange poem in *Fusion* reviews selected tracks:

> '*a sailor's life*'
> *– see-saw raga with sweeping*
> *generalizations and rolling*
> *rock-out ending.*

Back in the studio, as Ashley told Patrick Humphries, "they set the tape rolling and we did it, and the energy and adrenaline were incredible. When we finished, we knew what we had done. We went into the box to hear it. Joe and John were almost speechless. We knew we had done something different. We knew there was a path open to us that hadn't previously been clear". It was a path that led directly to *Liege & Lief*.

Nicol adds that the band came to realise "what an asset Sandy was, with her access to traditional material. I felt very honoured that Swarb came in – it lent folk authenticity". For Joe Boyd – who had already witnessed a musical form splitting itself down the middle when stage manager at the Newport Folk Festival in 1965, watching Dylan plug in – this track proved to be pivotal. In his case it was another example of being at the right place at the right time, and knowing exactly when not to interfere. "I was intrigued by what happened to '*A Sailor's Life*'. That take which you hear on *Unhalfbricking* is the first take, the first time Swarbrick ever played with an amp."

Martin Carthy: "Dave was asked to play on *Unhalfbricking*. We were gigging and he got this phone call from Joe Boyd. Joe had been pestering him to make an album all the time that he was in The Campbells. And he couldn't do it, because Transatlantic Records' owner Nat Joseph was jealous of all his people. Dave actually played a session on my first album, but he was still in The Campbells, and Nat Joseph fined him £5 which was one third of his wages. He fined him because he hadn't asked permission. We started working together in 1966 and Joe was immediately on the phone to him saying: "Do this *Rags, Reels & Airs* album."

At what point did Joe contact Dave about playing on '*A Sailor's Life*'? Martin: "We'd come back from Denmark and he got this phone call from Joe saying he wanted him to go and play on this album by Fairport Convention. His reaction was hilarious – "Oh, bloody rock & roll! I don't like bloody rock & rollers. You know me, I like jazz. What do I want to do that for?" I said: "Why don't you go and do it? It might be great!" "Oh well, I suppose. How much are they paying me? I'll go and do it". So he went and did it. I saw him a couple of days later. He was very quiet and said "No reflection on you, but I finished that session and felt that I wanted to play with that man for the rest of my life." He was talking about Richard Thompson. That's what he felt. So it was that good. "Oh. I can't tell you how good it was! It was fantastic!" Then he got the phone call asking if he wanted to join, very shortly after that. And he initially said 'yes' but he was worried about me, and I said: "Don't insult me. Don't worry about me, I'm a big boy now. I can manage. If you want to do it, do it." Then he got cold feet and didn't want to do it. Joe phoned him and he was never there. If Joe came to a gig he was playing, he would disappear. Finally Joe nailed him."

Was there any sense that you felt Dave had been poached? Martin: "Not for a second. I was pissed off with Dave, but I was pissed off because he kept messing about. And towards the end he was saying: "Oh you don't need me at this gig" and I was grabbing him by the shirt and lapels saying: "Yes I do. This is the last two weeks, let's just do it for Christ sake, just do it, finish it and have a good time!" And we did go out on a musical high."

Fairport must have been aware of Martin's work. After leaving the Three City Four, Carthy had brought a new seriousness and intensity to the folk tradition. Both Dylan and Paul Simon learnt his repertoire in the Soho folk clubs of the early sixties: Carthy's four year acoustic partnership with Dave Swarbrick produced a string of magnificent albums culminating in *Prince Heathen*, which came out the same year as *Liege & Lief*, and could be described as being the 'unplugged' version. Not just the songs, but the approach.

Ashley: "We knew Martin's work before we even started Fairport Convention. He was very special. I remember when we were talking about making *Unhalfbricking*, that we'd expressed an interest in having a fiddle on it. I recall Joe saying: "Do you want me to ring up Swarbrick and ask him?" And I can clearly remember our reaction which was shock. "Do you think Dave Swarbrick would do it? Do you think that he'd even play on our album?" Without question, Dave and Martin were heroes to us. We were still kids."

After his move to England for Elektra records, Boyd had immersed himself in the world of British folk traditionalists – more properly revivalists – like Carthy and Swarbrick, alongside singer-songwriters like John Martyn. These were artists who tended to work acoustically, at least when Boyd first met them. Once amped up, "it just all happened. But there was no thought at that time that it would lead anywhere else."

What had started as a one-off experiment, though, ended as a lifeline. Joe Boyd: "After the crash, the thought that they could take off from '*A Sailor's Life*' and become a truly British rock band gave them purpose in keeping the band together. It couldn't make up for the two lives lost in the accident, but it dignified the decision to carry on. I had nothing to do with any of that. Ashley was the one who went down to Cecil Sharp House and researched. I must say that I have so much admiration for Ashley in the single-mindedness of what he did".

None of the rest of *Unhalfbricking* had quite this sense of bridges being crossed – or burnt – but the album as a whole is greater than its parts, an extraordinary palette of musical colours which age and repeated plays still cannot stale. '*Cajun Woman*', for example, is a jolly romp (at least until you listen to Thompson's lyrics, which are oddly buried in the mix), with the bass intersecting nicely with Swarbrick's fiddle, dancing away underneath. Thompson later revealed that "I was always into cajun … all that Arhoolie stuff, you could actually find some of that in London in 1967. Ashley had a Rusty and Doug album, which was great".

On '*Who Knows Where The Time Goes*', Hutchings is more subdued, providing along with Nicol's acoustic guitar washes the groundwork over which Thompson can embroider phrases around Sandy's words, though he emerges from his musical hutch right at the end. '*Percy's Song*' opens with just voices, then acoustic guitar, then drums and bass: the lack of an instrumental break adds to the tension of the song, as the jail door slams on hope. The band suggested it as a single, "everyone will be whistling that in minutes. But they said it was six minutes and too long. So we lost".

'*Million Dollar Bash*', "a rocked up piece about an expensive happening", opens with strummed guitar, then bass and drums, "rather like a jolly barn dance, with each member taking a verse". Hutchings' first solo vocal is quizzical, laid-back, weirdly American (far more so than Marc Ellington, who procedes him). The whole thing rocks and rolls, a comic take on the sentiments of '*Meet On The Ledge*'. It all comes around again, or perhaps it's just the Apocalypse. Indeed, Hutchings was to update the lyrics for his two re-appearances with Fairport at Cropredy, in 1992 and 1997, and at Martin Carthy's 60 birthday concert in 2001, different each time.

Million Dollar Bash [Cropredy 1992 version]
Words: Ashley Hutchings
(with apologies to Mr Dylan)

Everybody from Muswell Hill to L.A. and back
They come every August, they come for the craic
Come one, and come all, and don't forget your cash
And we're all gonna meet at that Million Dollar Bash

Well the tents and the stalls come out of the barn
Danny Thompson was there, he spun us a yarn,
And along came Swarb picking his way through the trash,
Richard, open the door on that Million Dollar Bash

Well I've been hitting it too hard
Y'know my limbs they shake
I get up in the morning, it's too early to wake
First it's off to the soundcheck, but it's boom-boom, bang, crash,
DM's checking drums for that Million Dollar Bash

Well we looked at our watch, it was 25 years on
So we played an old tune, Vikki sang an old song
Now it's hats for the baldies, and pills for the rash
Who spent years on the road to that Million Dollar Bash

You can meet all your friends, you can meet on the ledge,
You can meet at the bar, you can meet Percy Sledge! –
Well, maybe not this year, but see the stars flash,
They're all gonna meet at that Million Dollar Bash

Million Dollar Bash [Cropredy 1997 version]
Words: Ashley Hutchings
Music: Bob Dylan

I got a note from Bob Dylan, He said to say "Hi",
He hoped that one day
maybe soon, he'll pop by.
Then he told me to leave off
His "Million Dollar Bash",
Or he'd see to my "partir",
et arrestez mon cash.

Well we still "Walk Awhile"
And it's thanks to the Peggs,
Matty's still getting caught
with his pants down his legs,
If you gotta go, sing,
While you queue for a slash,
And we still have a ball
on "Million Dollar Bash"
The Beer just gets better,
and just the right price,
The food just gets foodier,
MMM, hand me a slice,
Samosas and chillies,
Maybe sausage and mash –
Well, I can dream, can't I?
At that "Million Dollar Bash"

You can meet all your friends,
You can meet on the ledge,
Well it's five more years on,
Still there's no Percy Sledge:
But just keep on coming,
He's sure to gate-crash
One of these years
at that Million Dollar Bash

Well I looked at my watch,
It was 30 years on,
And here we all are again
singing this song.
The vocals are ragged,
The lyrics are trash,
But what d'you expect?
– Crosby Stills and Nash?

More to the immediate point, this is Martin Lamble's final appearance on vinyl, and suitably good-humoured and full of youthful *joie-de-vivre*. It calls eerily across the chasm of the crash to '*Come All Ye*' the opening song on *Liege & Lief*, which gives a roll call of the new band.

Ashley: "*Unhalfbricking* comes very quickly, after *What We Did On Our Holidays*, they come in quick succession. We're growing in leaps and bounds because this is a very unified album. The first album was very disparate, and then in quite a short space of time, we worked towards this, which I know some people still think is our best album. Probably Richard and Joe Boyd to this day think it's our best album. So it's quite an adult album and of course the jewel in the crown is '*A Sailor's Life*'. Which opens up the whole world before us. But still of course we consider that Dylan is a part of what we do. We're not able to exorcise him, and we don't want, and we don't need to. Because he, naturally for us, sits with the other music that we're playing, the traditional music. And of course Dave Swarbrick comes in as guest on the fiddle, and it's only then one middle-size step to the next album, *Liege & Lief* because we'd already made a start."

"THIS STRANGE LAND IN YOUR OWN BACK GARDEN"

Ashley: "Back at home in Muswell Hill the mind started to tick over, and I started to think what happens next? The others were doing other things. Obviously they came to visit me, but they were in America some of the time. The first decision was 'were we going to carry on?' And the second decision was, if the answer is 'yes', 'What are we going to do?' And I remember being very clear in my mind, that what I wanted to. And so at some point we met in Sandy's and her boyfriend Trevor Lucas's flat and we made those decisions. We would audition for another drummer, and we would pursue the direction that we'd started with 'Sailor's Life'. Consequently we would ask Dave Swarbrick to join on fiddle, who would help us in that direction. And that was at a meeting in a flat, no Joe. Just our own decision. And in fact if we'd have come out of that room, having decided not to carry on, Joe wouldn't have tried to talk each individual into changing their minds. He had the sensitivity to realise that we had to make that decision. All praise to him. So that's what we did. Again Joe organised the place at Farley Chamberlayne. And at a given time, we all went down there and started to work on *Liege & Lief.* We asked Swarbrick to join and he said "Yes" and that was great. He said that he was very excited. He fancied it."

Swarbrick was glad to escape the traditional scene, even if it was only to explore the same music with a radically different bunch of people. Quoted in the folk-rock compilation *The Electric Muse,* "I didn't like seven-eighths of the people involved with it, and was suddenly presented with the possibilities of exploring the dramatic content of the songs to the full". Aside of his famous acoustic partnership with Martin Carthy – later to join Ashley in both Steeleye Span and the Albion Country Band – Swarb had played with the Ian Campbell Folk Group, whose (then) acoustic bass player, one David Pegg, was subsequently to replace Hutchings in Fairport.

As Swarbrick told *Melody Maker,* "I think it was just hearing them that made me want to join the Fairport. They were a gas. They had this gorgeous sound".

Martin Carthy: "Swarb writes great tunes. The tunes he wrote for Richard's songs '*Now Be Thankful*' and '*Crazy Man Michael*' are fabulous. All his best tunes are slow tunes – without exception. He wrote one called '*The March Of The Hanged Man*' for that huge cantata arrangement of '*Jack Orion*' – an unbelievably good tune. The extraordinary thing about Swarb is he's been involved in folk music ever since he was that big. He's played the fiddle and learnt all those tunes since he was about fifteen, sixteen maybe. Not one of his tunes sounds like any other tune that you've heard. Everybody else writes a tune and you can pick up a little bit of that one there and a little bit of that over one – in the general feel of it. His tunes sound like nobody else. It's extraordinary, absolutely extraordinary."

Dave Swarbrick reckoned of his new band that "they were just kids, but they were bloody good". At Cropredy in 1997, Ashley proclaimed Swarb "the Maestro –

when he joined Fairport, it was an honour to have him in the group. The most influential fiddler, bar none, in this country – ever".

Ashley: "And then we auditioned for drummers in a room over a pub in Chiswick High Street. Palais drummer Dave Mattacks stood out head and shoulders above the rest. The key thing was '*Autopsy*'. What got Mattacks the gig was '*Autopsy*', because we said that we are going to play this tune that's in three different time signatures. It's in 4/4, 3/4 and 5/4, not in that particular order. See if you can play along with us. He seamlessly played the thing with us, and that was it as far as we were concerned. We were slightly concerned that he might not fit in personally – he was clean cut, well groomed, short back and sides – a gigging musician who played in big bands. It's surprising that he turned up for the audition as we'd almost expected a long-haired hippy. Indeed some of them were. Mattacks was best and we made the right decision because what he did on *Liege & Lief* was fantastic."

Dave Mattacks: "Simon said, "Do you want to come down to Winchester?" I did. After 24 hours, Ashley said "do you want to join the group?" I said "Yes, but I must tell you I haven't a fucking clue of what you're on about. I don't know anything about the music, I don't understand it. I can't tell one tune from another, they all sound the same, but if you want me to join, fine, because I really like it. I'm enjoying myself musically". This showed immediately in the results he achieved, bringing a fresh pair of ears to folk-rock, and matching the polyrhythms of traditional music with a light, jazzy style. He meshed immediately with Ashley's bass, and was to provide the percussive drive behind many of Hutchings' later projects. As Ashley later declared, "from the top of his double paradiddles to the bottom of his boom-chuck-a-chucks he is the King".

Ashley: "So then we all moved down to Farley Chamberlayne. We rehearsed there and brought it back to Sound Techniques to record."

Kingsley Abbott: "I think it was rather an odd decision that they left their normal North London homes and were whizzed off to the country. I suppose Joe had his reasons. I think that they might have returned to their London roots at that point, but they didn't. When things started to get themselves back together again, I was aware of a different feel."

Ashley: "Bob Pegg and I had become friends and he helped to augment my own research as a folklorist." Earnestly English, Bob Pegg is a controversial figure in the world of folk tradition. His book rightly argues that Rugby songs are just as valid as pastoral idylls, and he wrote an acerbic song about the Victorian song collector, Lucy Broadwood. As a performer he later forged his own very individual, and very English style, firmly based within his own locale. Ashley: "What we at came up with at Farley Chamberlayne was a complete package, music, album cover, image. It was seen through on stage. For the first time a coherent image – no wonder it took off. Before then it had been disparate – a bit of America, a bit of this and a bit of that, a bit of blues. Well I wore brown gaiters which I found in the loft at Farley Chamberlayne and am wearing them in the photographs. I remember for example, that Swarb had these trousers with fabric embroidered on the bottoms in a certain old-style design by Brigita, his wife, who's Danish. We thought that was great and so she did other trousers. I'm not saying that everyone wore them, but there was a certain uniformity of attitude. And we started to wear collarless shirts and things like that. So there was a kind of Britishness and historicalness, an English equivalent of The Band. You look at The Band's early albums and there's an image there. A rural, old time image that's totally organic. Never organised by designers or managers saying "What you should do is wear this and look like this". Saatchi & Saatchi were originally involved in Island. One of their first commissions was designing an Island logo, but we went our own way as usual."

Meanwhile, '*Si Tu Dois Partir*' was issued in August, and became the band's first – and only – top 30 hit. It reached number 21, helped on its way by Tony Blackburn making it his record of the week on Radio 1's 'Breakfast Show'. Some cynics said that this was only because he didn't understand the words. The record's success was part of a huge wave of sympathy towards the band. As one review put it "I hope everyone will rush out and buy the single, even though it wouldn't normally be considered as commercial".

The band mimed on 'Top of the Pops' with its two new members, and with roadie Steve Sparks on percussion, swathed in onions. A bearded Hutchings wore shades

Fairport Convention in the dressing room at BBC TV, prior to their Top Of The Pops appearance. 14th August 1969. l-r: Dave Swarbrick, Richard Thompson, Dave Mattacks, Ashley, Simon Nicol, Sandy Denny

and a French beret, and played an enormous acoustic double bass with a stick loaf.

Nick Logan interviewed Sandy two days later. "The accident taught me that I loved them all", she said. "The next album is going to be completely different. It will be based around traditional British folk music to which we may put new words if necessary". For material, they had been digging into the archives of the English Folk Dance & Song Society – the British Museum of Folk. "We're not making it pop though. In fact it will be almost straight, only electric". Logan asks her what it sounds like. "Heavy, traditional folk music."

A week earlier, Denny told *Disc* that "we've really been getting into traditional English music". She had briefly returned from Farley Chamberlayne, the "mammoth country estate" where the new line-up were rehearsing. "It may sound amazing, but we put old traditional music with electric instruments and our own words and it really sounds nice ... though it shouldn't. We're going along a completely different road now. It's really put a new breath of life into us".

As Swarbrick told *Melody Maker*: "it will be based on traditional music, not just an electric copy. It's just the Fairport sound, really. I think everyone is going to be surprised. Some of it will be fairly free, and some of it will be disciplined". Nicol added that "we want an essentially English approach. It needs thought and care, but we've had a lot of time recently – and the ideas are developing nicely". One can bet that Ashley was at the heart of this intellectual process. "You can call it an English electric sound, but the emphasis can switch around a lot, now that we can use Dave to the full". Swarbrick also brought an encyclopaedic knowledge of folk tunes and lyrics with him, to stir into the pot.

The band had decided on a completely new repertoire, drawing on the same traditional sources as· *'A Sailor's Life'*. As Humphries wisely points out, Lamble's death "effectively cut off the avenue of the past". In line with their early infatuation with American rock, their greatest musical influence at this time was The Band. The Grateful Dead were also taking the same route back into history and the solidity of traditional folk culture. As Thompson told Patrick Humphries, talking about The Band's second album, "it was *the* record for us – because it was so rootsy and unpretentious. They did it at home, it all just sounded great". The songs had been woodshedded at Big Pink, just as Traffic had put their own post-psychedelic music together in a country cottage in Berkshire.

Fairport attempted much the same when Joe Boyd moved them into the old Queen Anne rectory at Farley Chamberlayne, near Winchester, for three months in the summer of 1969. As Richard told Humphries, "it was the perfect place at the right time – it was a nice summer – a bit of football on the lawn and a bit of rehearsal, kite flying on Farley Mount. We'd be on the phone to Bert Lloyd saying "we've got to find a better 32nd verse for *'Tam Lin'*". This is how Lord Arnold turned into Lord Darnell on *'Matty Groves'*, misheard down the telephone. "There was stuff that Swarb knew that he wanted to do but we didn't realise that he'd pinched some of it off Martin Carthy".

Everyone got to know each other better in these commune-like living conditions. Their equipment was permanently set up in the large drawing room, overlooking the wide lawns. The band looked like dissident members of the nobility, setting their heartland to rights. As new boy Mattacks pointed out, "they went from being the English Jefferson Airplane to the English Fairport Convention".

Ashley was the keenest of the original members on this new direction, and remains proud of what was achieved that summer. As he told Humphries, "Fairport were the first band to make a success of British folk-rock" but equally important was the Fairport way of doing things, the "loose, relaxed, improvised, risk-taking, fun-loving way of setting about making music. We wouldn't have come up with the music if we had been a conventional band. We played everything from all over the world at all sorts of venues, and that was what led to *Liege & Lief*. It happened because we were willing to take chances". He added for the benefit of journalist Pamela Winters that "I became absolutely addicted to traditional music. By the time you've reached the rehearsals for *Liege & Lief*, you've got Sandy, an important cog in the wheel. You've got Swarbrick with his great knowledge of tunes. You've got me researching whenever I've got a second: going to Cecil Sharp House, looking in books, finding songs". For Trevor Lucas, Ashley "had been bitten by folk music like no one I had ever seen".

Ashley: "The excitement is that real sense of groundbreaking discovery of this strange land in your own back garden. We did discover traditional music and we took to it whole-heartedly. Of course we rocked it up, but it was like finding God. It was like finding religion. It was so exciting and we couldn't wait to do the next record or even the next concert. And show the people these wonderful songs and these wonderful tunes that we wanted to play. *Liege & Lief* was more pondered over than anything we had done previously. It was definitely planned. It was a conscious effort after the crash to go in a specific direction and make an album that we knew had to be made – a British Folk Rock Album."

Nicol remembered the debut album (all acoustic) by the Irish group Sweeney's Men as being constantly on the turntable, "folk music with the frills taken off". By mid-69, Sweeney's Men had gone electric, adding lead guitarist Henry McCullough: Hutchings was later to jam with them, and Terry Woods to become a founding member of Steeleye Span. At Farley Chamberlayne, it was Ashley, Richard and Simon who took the main role in adapting traditional material to a rock beat. Nicol remembers "three sets of Child books in the house. I'm sure the beetle-browed Hutchings had it all planned".

Rolling Stone carried a front page exclusive on Fairport, with another Eric Hayes photograph, this time of an apple cheeked Sandy brewing up a pot of tea. The middle class ambience of *Unhalfbricking* cover had given way to a bohemian jumble. There's no tablecloth, milk remains in its bottle, and a pack of 'Fruti-Fort' dominates the table, along with an advert for an Apollo 11 souvenir, and two American comics: 'Phantom Eagle' and 'Thor'. It could be Woodstock, not Winchester. Inside, Ashley is bearded, with a gypsy neckerchief, and in another shot is sitting down, in check trousers, bent over his bass and staring at the fretboard. Simon looks at him, and Richard at Simon.

Tyger Hutchings is named as bassist, and "chief disciplinarian". Thompson reveals that the band actively tried to withdraw '*Si Tu Dois Partir*', in case they

Photo: Eric Hayes

were mistaken for a "Frog jug band". They all seem oblivious to money, and still prefer playing clubs to appearing in concert. For Thompson, "The only time you're playing anything worthwhile is really when something comes out spontaneously and the only time it happens is in a club". In a concert hall, "you can't get anything back from the audience", but "in a club you can feel something really strong, all this energy: it feels to me like something to do with the life force itself if everyone's getting into it, and it's *going*". Even today Richard is usually at his best in solo gigs in intimate settings.

For relaxation, the band played two hours of football a day. They would also visit a local hostelry to watch the locals plays cribbage. Rehearsal sessions included two songs from the *Basement Tapes*, '*Open The Door Homer*' and '*Down In The Flood*', and two traditional songs not recorded till much later, '*Bonny Black Hare*' and '*Willow Day (Adieu Adieu)*'.

The *Rolling Stone* piece was not the only press coverage of Fairport's country sojourn. The band's tenure at Farley Chamberlayne was well documented. Ashley: "Joe Boyd was inviting people down, so it was probably down to management and marketing. Our van crash had been big national news and we were still in the public eye."

In 1999 the authors of this book returned with Ashley to the house at Farley Chamberlayne, almost thirty years to the day. Even now it is a hard place to find. You drive for some miles along a narrow road, turn into an almost secret entrance, and suddenly the place opens up in front of you with a large gravel drive, a paddock where horses graze contentedly, and a magnificent view. Ashley and Mike Fuller got lost trying to find it. When he did arrive, apologetic and rather flustered, Ashley was pleasantly surprised to see how very little the house had changed. Walking into the kitchen and looking at the aforementioned *Rolling Stone* feature was a quite unnerving experience for all of us. It exactly resembled the photos and we could almost see Sandy sitting at the kitchen table.

Ashley recalled the band's daily routine. "We'd drift down one by one and have breakfast casually, and then drift into the room, where all our equipment was lined

Photo: Eric Hayes

up permanently. It was just all set up ready to go. We'd start playing, working on the *Liege & Lief* material. I remember a sense of excitement coming down the stairs for breakfast thinking: "What are we going to do today? Oh, we're going to look at jigs and reels today, or we're going to tackle that ballad '*Tam Lin*', that we had a look at yesterday!" When Dave Mattacks came down here, we became complete. But it must have been pretty daunting for him to suddenly come in and invent Folk-Rock here in the wilds."

The bass has always been close to the drums – how did you find working with him as a newcomer? "It was both challenging and uplifting because he's such a good drummer. But also hard work, because you can imagine for Mattacks and me, the rhythm section, trying to find sympathetic rhythms to go with these old tunes and old songs, which of course hadn't been backed in that way. So it was a testing thing, but very exciting and very enjoyable. I simplified my bass playing from what it had been in early Fairport. Quite meandering and melodic. It was now much tighter and more solid. But it wasn't all work. We did relax, and I've got some nice photos of us in the garden. The weather was largely nice and we'd often go out and kick a ball around.

"*Liege & Lief* was a collective endeavour. Everyone contributed. Nothing's black and white in life, and specifically in relation to *Liege & Lief.* You couldn't say that just because Dave Swarbrick played more traditional music than us, that he was "the keenest", because I was pretty darn keen. You couldn't say that Sandy wasn't interested because she liked doing contemporary, because she was very excited about aspects of it as well. Richard, technically was really interested in getting to grips with the tunes, in particular, playing the fast jigs and reels. We all had enthusiasms and interests. And it kind of dovetailed."

So how did you find playing the jigs and reels, because they are so precise? After the largely improvised music that you had been playing before with Fairport? "I can't remember technically how, we just slotted them together. What I can remember is a very strong spiritual feeling of getting close to the people who had gone before – close to the tradition, close to the land. There were times when we sat in that room and we played magical ballads like '*Tam Lin*' or country songs where I really felt at

Photo: *Eric Hayes*

one with the music. Maybe that's indicative of the times in the sixties."

"I, personally, got a spiritual feeling from playing that music there, in the way that we did, and connecting with those songs. Really connecting, in way I haven't had since! I still appreciate traditional music but that was that first flowering of Folk-Rock where it really meant something special to me. Coming to Farley Chamberlayne after the crash was an almost religious experience. It played an integral part in that healing process."

Why come here in the first place? "I don't know! I was one of the people that took the longest to recuperate in hospital. By the time I emerged it had all been set up by Joe, Joe Boyd and his office. Joe said: "I've got this house. I've sorted this house out." In those days Management took on all of the organisation of things – nowadays it's very much a hands-on thing where I know how many we sell, what money we make, I'm on the phone talking to people about bookings and so forth. In those days, Managers did everything, took it off your shoulders. He just fixed it up. A big pat on the back to Joe, he found the right place for it all to come to fruition. I imagine Joe found an advert somewhere. In *The Lady* or *The Times* – "A large Queen Anne house for rent" Our Roadie, Robin Gee came down with the equipment, and looked after us. He probably did the shopping. Richard was probably a vegetarian by then. We just looked after ourselves."

The couple who owned the property actually lived in France for the summer, and rented the house out for the summer months.

"This place is nearer Braishfield than it is Winchester, and we used to refer to it as Braish – the local, nearby, slightly larger village. To refer to it in such a friendly and truncated way, we must have got used to it being local, so I would have thought that we must have been here for a couple of months. We didn't actually get out very much. I went to London once or twice to find some songs, but generally speaking we just enjoyed being here, being away from all the hurly burly – literally recuperating. Because we were at the same time getting our equilibrium back."

Ashley recalled: "Brigita had a lovely collie dog which features in some of the period photos. Quite a few people came down – Simon was married at the time to Roberta, but then you see how big the house is, it can hold all the families. A commune if you like in the language of the period. Swarbrick had a daughter as well. No drugs! Just music. Just the pure folk music. The best drug of all!

"We walked in to that Farley Chamberlayne rehearsal room with nothing more than a word sheet and Swarbrick saying: "The tune might go like this", or Sandy saying: "I know a tune and it goes like this", and singing it. Everything else, the drum patterns, the bass, the guitar parts were all made up and pieced together like jigsaw, there and then. All playing together.

"We played when the mood took us. Sometimes we'd all bound down and someone would have an idea and they'd start at breakfast saying: "I had this idea last night about such-and-such." Or Richard might say: "I've written a song". And so we'd come in and play in the morning. Sometimes we might not feel like playing until later. And sometimes we didn't want to stop which meant that we'd be playing into the evening. What a racket we must have made. It was a small room with quite a low ceiling. Lovely for rehearsal."

Were you taping any of this? Are there any 'work tapes' of what went down? "I don't think we thought about that." And yet there are a couple of 'private rehearsal tapes' of *'Come All Ye'* and *'Crazy Man Michael'* on Free Reed's mammoth *Fairport UnConventional* anthology.

So presumably then you decided what you wanted to put on to the new record

"All those decisions were made down here, and then we emerged into the world, by going to the studio in London and recording and by doing this 'showcase' concert in the Royal Festival Hall which was the big unveiling of Folk-Rock."

Was there one moment when you thought: "This is a different sort of music?" "No, not one moment. It was all exciting, it was all this is different. Minute to minute it was exciting because it wasn't just taking English country songs and rocking them up full stop. We're taking medieval ballads and tackling them, trying to make a 15 verse ballad interesting, and so: "So we'll change the rhythm on these bits, and we'll change the key, or change the emphasis, or bring in the fiddle on this bit to make it 15 verse ballad…" We're also trying jigs and reels in different time signatures. Everything's different, everything's an exciting journey. "How can we make this different? How does that work?"

Were you writing much? "We were actually. We were doing a bit of editing and writing of text. And of course add to all that some contemporary songs. *'Come All Ye'* which I co-wrote. It was basically Sandy's composition which I wrote a few verses for."

How about Morris music? "Not at this stage. It was all so new. The Englishness and Morris came later. This was a general kind of British folk-rock which included Scottish ballads, Irish tunes, fiddle tunes, as well as English."

"I remember very clearly coming out of the french windows, we'd spill out onto the lawn when we felt like it. There is a photo of Richard on that swing thirty years ago, with a cup of tea in his hands."

Does this make you want to come back? "Yes it does. As I walked out of the front door I thought: "When I win the Lottery I'll make the owner a handsome offer."

"I remember this tree so well. I remember standing by this small wooden shed with Swarb's Collie dog. It's such a beautiful and quiet place. I feel genuinely happy. Delighted that it's changed so little. It's almost feeling like a feeling of coming home. It was great standing in that rehearsal room. Not in any way did it feel spooky. There's no bad memories."

So you'd rehearsed the material, decided what you wanted to go onto the LP, and decamped to the studios and got stuck in. Was the excitement that you felt with the material carried on by Joe and the management? "They were very supportive and there was a feeling that everyone

Photo: Eric Hayes

knew. John Wood, the engineer, was also very important to us, he was very enthusiastic about it all. There was no problem. It was good."

This is your spell at University. "Well done! Absolutely right. We were messing around, studying really hard and then also kicking around. We had no responsibilities and were being well looked after. It was our time at University – the University of Farley Chamberlayne."

But in the current academic attitude, critics would say: "But look at these privileged upper middle class white youths. What do they know?" This is the thing that we now have to contest I'm afraid. People who themselves are privileged and rich. The fact that you felt yourself tapping into the 18th century Queen Anne House, tapping into that, not genteel but felt akin to Cecil Sharp hearing his gardener sing. "Absolutely, it's part of the same tree. It's continuous. And you know, we've never considered ourselves to be 'folk singers' – if we're anything, we're 'popular artists' who were consciously just making popular art. I say consciously as we're not pretending that we're of the soil."

If Ashley was a film maker, this could be his costume drama. Thinking that way – you've been through the sixties movie, the 'swinging sixties' and now its the costume drama, and then you went into your Wild West phase, the western. That's how we see you, an auteur. This place is responsible for spawning a musical genre. "It keeps selling. My royalty cheques prove it keeps selling. Thank God."

Liege & Lief was recorded at Sound Techniques in late summer and early autumn 1969, and hit the shops in December. The band had issued three albums in the calendar year, a release rate which would not be tolerated in today's corporate world. While recording, the band were so broke that "it brings considerable pain to Simon Nicol's heart that he cannot afford the cream cakes on sale in the shop next to their recording studios". Hungry, they worked on.

There was no single taken from the album, but there were three outtakes. '*Sir Patrick Spens*' could well be the source for the Denny-led version which appears on Ashley's *The Guv'nor Vol 2*, and has a different fifth verse to the words sung on *Full House*: "Last night I saw the new, new moon/With the old moon in her arm/And that is the sign since we were born/That means there'll be a deathly storm", an omen of coming disaster. '*The Ballad of Easy Rider*' appears on Richard Thompson's *Guitar, Vocal*. '*The Quiet Joys of Brotherhood*' is collected on Sandy Denny's box set *Who Knows Where The Time Goes*.

Reviewers of *Liege & Lief* were largely in awe of what they were hearing, though many asked, like whether this was a one-off project or a complete new direction. "Heaven knows, it would have been worth the money for the second side alone".

Lon Goddard in *Record Mirror* argues that though these songs have been sung for centuries, "these versions are the most magnetic yet conceived". '*Tam Lin*' "borders on a kind of folk-jazz: the whole thing occupies its own space in between trad folk and electric rock".

Friends directs the reader to "get your favourite elf on the phone. Now pack a pretty lunch with nut butties, boiled eggs and a little screw of newspaper full of salt, beg borrow or bludgeon a portable record player, take it out to the nearest piece of countryside, get your elf nice and high on Mead and play *Liege & Lief*"." As to Hutchings, his bass playing is so good "you won't even notice he's there, and that is rare". This is music that is "good for the soul". Even Mick Farren – the one time Social Deviant, admits that "English folk has previously left me cold", but Fairport give life to this material, "in a raunchy manner".

There are some dissenting voices, those who like John Platt feel that Fairport threw away too much when they plunged into traditional song. For their previous US champion, John Mendelsohn of *Rolling Stone*, those who want to get *moved* are directed back to previous albums. "Granted that the bass of Mr Hutchings and the drums of Mr Mattacks rescue it from dire Pentangle sterile folksiness, where are the exhilarating many-voiced harmonies, the sense of fun, and feeling of harnessed electricity?"

Lost on the M1, one feels bound to answer: it would be impossible for the band to have continued in that vein without Lamble, and a new seriousness has been visited upon them. Note that no-one on the front cover is smiling any more. *Disc* announces that "this is the last album before their reshuffle in personnel". The excitement of hippie days "has been replaced with the most traditional of traditional folk, which doesn't make for too much animation – they've over-simplified". The album is "nice, in a rather insipid olde worlde fashion".

Insipid is the last word with which to describe *Liege & Lief*: everyone concerned is singing and playing their socks off. If it is more demanding than their earlier albums, this is because of the magnitude of what is being attempted: this is certainly not just pop music. One advert from Witchseason headlines the album "The first (literally) British folk rock LP ever", and surrounds the album's title with what could either be a wreath or a floral tribute to May: beneath are the words "documenting a (very brief) era", and the band members, as were.

The album sleeve is tinted violet, and Eric Hayes' cover shots give the band a solemn, Victorian gravity: Sandy Denny could come straight out of a photograph by Julia Margaret Cameron, as could the grimly bearded Ashley. He is in profile, like a scientist or visionary poet. The CD reissue unpardonably features a picture inside of the pre-crash band, with Lamble on guitar and Simon playing violin. A clean shaven Ashley looks directly and quizzically at the camera, through dark shades.

The surrounding square of entwined leaves – into which stoned eyes could doubtless read all manner of horrors and secret meanings – is a drawing by Roberta Nicol, though this was mistakenly omitted from the credits at the time. Bob Pegg drew a strange cartoon of Ashley and Sandy attempting to revive Richard Thompson as he lies on the ground, like a scene from a Mummers' Play, reproduced in *A Little Music*.

On the back cover of the vinyl edition of *Liege & Lief* is a carved wooden totem owned by Dave Swarbrick, impossibly ancient – like a cross between a scarecrow and a human sacrifice, next to the Witchseason logo, and surrounded by a circle of flowers and leaves, a ribbon bow no less.

"Dave Swarbrick found that in a churchyard," Ashley explains. "He found it amongst leaves and things, and it was rotting away in some sacking, and it is quite clearly

Bob Pegg's unused Liege & Lief illustrations

some magical totem of some description. And we thought that it was just very suitable, and as you well know this and *Full House* are absolutely shot through with magic and mystery, both albums, and so we put it on the album. But Swarb found it."

Inside are portraits of folk song collectors Cecil Sharp (to whom Ashley will return) and Francis Child, the "rural songster" George Wyatt, and examples of surviving English folklore: the Padstow hobby-horse, morris dancers and the like. One can detect the precise hand of Hutchings in the scholarly descriptions of these rites.

Richard: "Very, very creepy. It was Brigita and Roberta basically, who thought it up. Certainly they presented the designs to the band and everybody said: "Fine or rubbish!" Simon: "This was all hand done. It's very beautifully drawn. Nowadays you'd just generate it on a computer."

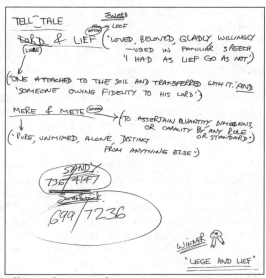

Album title voting slip

Richard Thompson's sleeve notes to *Full House* were to parody such mysteries, but by then Hutchings had left, taking his quest for British arcana in a different direction. There is a sense here of a ritual blessing, purging past tragedies. As Hutchings himself said, "there's a lot of magic on that cover. I think it was blessed, I think all that union was blessed. It was certainly a very magical period, also a very strange period. It wasn't simply us having a ball all the time, there was a lot of heart-searching going on. It was hard work to actually put those things into the rock format, but it was exhilarating and magical in the profound sense".

Ashley: "That's the Burry Man. The Pace-Eggers, an old fiddler, Jinky Wells and The Bampton Morris. There was a very nice corn dolly version of the name Fairport Convention, which didn't get onto the album sleeve – but it was a nice idea. And you've got those very Julia Margaret Cameron-like photos on the front. "That was Bert again. I always felt that the sleeve echoed the traditional folkyness of the music. It goes without saying that this is not pure chance. I organised the middle spread. I got everything. Each one of those, either from Cecil Sharp House, I found them or Bob Pegg drew them specially for me. I found this on a postcard in the loft at Farley Chamberlayne" – what we are looking at is the gravestone. "So I kind of got all this together and wrote captions and so on."

"We voted on the album title and I've still got the paper with the suggested titles. It got down to *Mere & Meet* or *Liege & Lief* in the end. The winner *Liege & Lief* was awarded a rosette."

When it came to choosing which songs to do, Ashley recalls that the band would just sit around and people would chip in: "We might say: "OK. We've done that one now, that was good that ballad. Got any other ballads?" And someone would say: "How about '*Matty Groves*'? How does that go? Well it goes like this" And we'd try and knock together some verses, or I'd got the *Child Book Of Ballads* here. We'd look up maybe compiled verses. I remember very clearly, just snippets, just flashes, one time with Dave Swarbrick getting on the phone to Ian Campbell and saying: "We need a tune for one of the ballads." So we had a lifeline to the world outside.

I was going to London and doing a bit of research in Cecil Sharp House – specifically '*The Deserter*'. I remember I found it and brought it back."

Richard Thompson says that he forcibly insisted that original material go on to the album and that he had rows with Ashley about that. Ashley wanted all traditional material. "That's fair enough" Ashley concedes. "But it's a better album for the mixture. But it could have gone dreadfully wrong. The great thing was that we knew what was happening at the time, so we could appreciate it at the time. Very often, when you're creating something, you cannot imagine what effect it's going to have, or how good it is even. We couldn't help realising that something very special was happening.

"Our heroes were The Band and The Byrds – to a large extent they were doing what we were doing over here. But if you actually analyse – we were getting far deeper into the tradition than those two bands did, and we were taking more risks, and we were doing more interesting things, technically speaking."

People forget Ashley's actual input as a bass player, because what he and Mattacks were doing was inventing how to put bass and drums to folk music.

Ashley: "Fairport were the first. The Byrds had put a general 4/4 beat, but you were actually going into quite difficult time signatures. The Byrds will admit that they were very influenced by The Beatles, their harmonies and so forth. Yes they did some folk songs, and they did some Bob Dylan songs. But it wasn't a million miles removed from pop music, and of course was very successful. They produced great pop music that will stand the test of time. But we were really going out on a limb, because it didn't equate with anything else that was happening. If you can imagine at that time, psychedelia and flower power and self-indulgent surreal lyrics – here we were going totally the other way. And trying things that didn't sound like anything that anyone was doing.

"The thing about *Liege & Lief*, you have got those two wonderful songs related to the crash – '*Farewell Farewell*' to Martin and Jeanie and '*Crazy Man Michael*' being about guilt, the feelings of someone who survives when their girlfriend dies. To actually put them with those wonderful traditional tunes, the whole things reads in a different way – the audience reaction was great sympathy and love, and here was an album that you had to read those emotions into it. It wasn't just, 'We're now going to do a folk album'. It transcended that."

Kay Hutchings perceptively commented "Without the crash they wouldn't have done *Liege & Lief*. Not that you could call it A Happy Accident."

Ashley: "Roxy Music, Marc Bolan. We're at odds with the world. In amongst the sea of all this colour, gloss and absurdity, comes over there The Band, and over here, Fairport. And later, Steeleye. So it's remarkable that we swim against the flood."

"The Band – their production values were outstanding. John Wood's engineering and production were excellent. Looking to most of Island's records they possessed a gloss almost. To be honest although I've played with all these other groups, and toured with them, I didn't possess many of their records. I was itinerant, as I've continued to be. I'm continually moving house and consequently I didn't build up a large record collection of these other acts – I saw them live."

"It's like John Tams once said, Joe Boyd layered it back. It's not 'in your face' or glossy literally, but that depth is actually there in the music, that's why on CD it sounds so good. It's why it stands the test of time, because if you listen to most of the other records, there are so many things that have dated on them. Be it the type of reverb, the style of music, the snare drum sound. I can almost date an album by the snare drums. The sound of our stuff really seems to hold up. Lamble's drums are so precise especially on '*A Sailor's Life*'. Extraordinary."

Ashley points out that *Liege & Lief* "wasn't made as anything other than a rock 'n' roll record". "Natural music" is how he now describes it, with properly thought out research coming later, after this musical bolt of lightning. "We were just picking songs out of the air – it was a natural rock record, the way that Americans like Ry Cooder make natural rock records drawing on a loose knowledge of traditional forms. Certainly not from an academic researcher, which I later became".

The whole project was a collective effort, shaped by the alchemy of that particular line-up. Force fields that came together, then exploded outwards, in less than six months.

Ashley: "All six of Fairport contributed to that record. It just seemed to happen. It's true that Dave Swarbrick had just joined us and brought a strong traditional influence, and also that Sandy brought a number of songs, and was the only singer on that record. But it's also true that without Mattacks we wouldn't have known where to start in putting it into a workable rock format – he was the right drummer in the right place at the right time! And Richard obviously had a very strong influence as he does on everybody – and I must have, because I get my finger in everywhere! And Simon probably kept us all sane: it was a team effort".

For a band who played at a club called Middle Earth, the writings of JRR Tolkien were a large part of the spell cast by the late 60s. The fantasy writings of this retiring Oxford don had suddenly achieved cult status. Ideally suited to stoned brains, *The Hobbit* and *Lord of the Rings* fuelled a taste for whimsy and folklore which became endemic to the scene, with restaurants called 'Gandalf's Garden' and would-be elves like Marc Bolan writing screeds of sub-Tolkien mythologies. *Liege & Lief* could almost be a pun on his non-fiction book *Tree and Leaf*, a study of fairy tale. Humphries reckons that 'lief' was what mediaeval serfs paid to the liege-lord of their manor. In fact it can be used as both an adjective and noun and according to the OED, originally comes from Anglo Saxon and was used in *Beowolf.*

Fairport, though, tapped in, not to Tolkien's whimsy, but the sense he can evoke of cosmic dread: the title suggests some kind of retribution, as if the sheer joy which the band's music exuded before the crash was something which called for payment. It is closest in spirit to Shirley and Dolly Collins' *Love, Death and the Lady*, their spookiest recording, and one said to have provided the soundtrack for many a pagan rite.

The opening track of *Liege & Lief*, '*Come All Ye*', is an update of the traditional Morris calling-on song, and sets the pattern for much of Ashley's future career. It is important for another reason, as the only Denny/Hutchings song in existence. Set to a jaunty trot, heavy on the bass, it is nothing if not ambitious – here is music to "rouse the spirit of the air/and move the rolling skies". The band is introduced in terms of their instruments, a fiddler whose violin is made out of solid wood. Ashley is "the man who plays the bass does make those low notes that you hear". No names, no packdrill.

Hutchings' bass is more restrained than before, buried deeper in the music with less chance for individual flashiness. Indeed, he is often distinguished here by what he chooses *not* to play. In '*Reynardine*' he plunges downward on each chord's root note, shaking the foundations. The note he plays as old foxy tempts the maiden to damnation is like a coffin lid slamming shut. After the jauntiness of the opening song, this is sombre and melancholic fare indeed, a view to a kill. Shades of Bluebeard's Castle, and a folk motif to which Bob and Carole Pegg gave a Yorkshire twist with their song, and band, '*Mr Fox*'.

Martin Carthy: "*Prince Heathen* was a very important album for me. It was then that I began to understand the depths of this stuff. The real, real depth of it. As much as I'm proud of anything, I could say I'm proud of that, 'cause I think that it actually marks something down. I suddenly found out how to play guitar. Funnily enough '*Reynardine*' is one of the songs that I'm not so bothered about. We did it because it was there, because Dave liked it. But '*Reynardine*' is a song that never convinced me. Too much Bert Lloyd! C'mon chaps, it's not the way these things work. Not literary, but too literal. And those songs are not like that. You get the creeps from the fact that this man is called *Reynardine*, he's got a fox's name. You don't underline it in red saying what big teeth he'd got. "Oh, what big eyes you've got Grandma!" – it's not like that. It's not appropriate."

'*Matty Groves*' starts cheerful – "a holiday" – and ends in a lovers' grave. Basically adultery, betrayal, a violent fight, murder, a husband spurned, a hint of necrophilia and a wife killed for her pains. Good fun for all the family. Ashley's bass leads in the jaunty riff, and drives it right through to the exuberant and lengthy finale, where he emphasises a very straight 4/4 beat under Thompson's dancing guitar. If this isn't rock and roll ...

Martin Carthy: "The Protestants went from Scotland, in fact they're Scottish really. They went to Ireland. The Irish didn't like them and they didn't like the Irish, so they went to Appalachia instead. The people who went to the Appalachians were Scots and English. If you look in the collections, you will find Scots tunes from Aberdeenshire falling over the feet of Appalachian tunes. Tunes like '*Shady Groves*' – you will find that exact tune in Aberdeenshire."

On '*Farewell Farewell*', Thompson has put bitter words to the traditional tune associated with '*Willie O'Winsbury*', also in the repertoire of Sweeney's Men. Hardly a break with Fairport's past, as Dylan too had been a keen 'borrower' of folk tunes, and '*Percy's Song*' both alludes to and uses a traditional air, '*The Wind and The Rain*'. Sandy sings this as if in a dream, almost in a whisper, a tense stillness. The words are unfathomable, using traditional motifs to summon up a tale in hard times. Even the line about one who "lies asleep alongside me" is ambiguous here, suggesting duplicity as well as one's true love.

All kinds of emotions swirl around this highly personal song. "Your bruised and beaten sons" alludes perhaps to those who survived the crash, condemned once again to roam the highways – "the winding road does call". While it would be impertinent to enquire too far, it is impossible given the line "will you never cut the cloth" not to trace the connection with Jeannie the Taylor, or not to see Martin possibly as "one who lies asleep alongside of me". These are resonances, not meanings. Thompson's words are moor-bleak, a testimony to life on the road, and his musical companions, "you lonely travellers all".

Hutchings comes in, almost subliminally, on the second verse, and plays a bass riff to break the heart. His instrumental throbs under '*The Deserter*', a song typical of the genre of the condemned man saved from the death cell. Hutchings later commented that "although we learnt this from a faded Victorian broadside, it is much older in origin". Thompson later parodied the happy ending on '*Poor Will and the Jolly Hangman*', where no such release occurs. The backing is careful never to speed up, and thus rob the song of its tension. Sandy's vocal begins melancholic, and ends gleeful: she sings it with relish, even the bit about surviving three hundred lashes. Victorian propaganda of the finest stripe.

Traditional musician John Kirkpatrick later worked with Ashley in the Albion Country Band: "My experience started with Morris Dancing and grew out from there, and anything that wasn't very traditional, just didn't speak to me at the time.

But then this band were playing traditional music on guitars. I remember the first time I heard it, what blew me away was that they were playing reels on guitar. I was a big fan of Dave Swarbrick who I'd seen with the Ian Campbell Group and then with Martin Carthy, and I'd loved everything he had done. Probably at the time, he was the biggest influence on my thinking about music, he was just so witty and funny, in his playing I mean. And clever and obviously a wonderful instrumentalist. And I thought: "That's a good way to be with an instrument!" And so what first attracted me to *Liege & Lief* was that Dave Swarbrick was playing fiddle in it, and then almost immediately, I thought: "FUCK ME! They're playing Irish reels on the guitar!" I just thought that it was astonishing. It's impossible! (laughs). I was more interested in instrumental music at that point as well. I sang a bit but I wasn't particularly interested in accompanying or arranging songs. Instrumentally it was just breathtaking, that record. I became interested in the band and what else they were doing and what else they had done. So that's how I sort of became aware of Ashley I suppose. And I loved *Liege & Lief*, I still do. I think it's one of the best records of interpreting folk music in a way that appeals to contemporary ears, that's ever been done. It's a record full of stories. The sleeve is wonderful. The whole thing is magical. What a good and memorable name."

The instrumental '*Medley*' fuelled a thousand imitators, but stands alone for the way it combines sawing violin with a rock rhythm section. Hutchings weaves through the instrumental medley, sticking close to Mattacks' strict beat, and keeping the whole thing musical. For those who accused English folk rock of 'pandering' to Irish jigs and reels, the rot sets in here, and the result is joyous. Healing music.

'*Tam Lin*' is mistitled 'Tim Lin' on the first CD reissue, laughable if it weren't so appalling on perhaps the most culturally important song Island released outside of Bob Marley. Here is a cut-down version of an extremely long and difficult song about the fairy kingdom, but fairies not from Victorian book illustrations but the dark roots of British folklore, who rape and dismember and kill. The words were collected at one point by Burns, and there is a Scottish brogue to words like "kirtle" and indeed "Carterhaugh".

Fairport's performance is a triumph of rhythm guitar from Simon – the bars mix 3/4 and 4/4, like 50s jazz, and their irregularity unsettles the listener. Mattacks later declared "I don't approve of jazz much: if it's at all jazzy, it was unintentional. We merely tried to play in an unobvious fashion. We broke up the backing and changed the tempo slightly". Hutchings plays an ominous riff low down, like depth charges laid at the bottom of the sea, though this version lacks the redemptive wildness which breaks out on the *Top Gear* version. After Sandy has finished her triumphant tale, the music seems to peter away.

'*Crazy Man Michael*' is the first songwriting collaboration between Thompson and Swarbrick, though the words are pure Thompson. As much a dismissal as the opening song is a welcome, it contains a huge sadness, and a resolution. The murdered lover has "flown into every flower grown", for him to tend forever. Again it is hard not to draw a comparison with Thompson's feelings of guilt after the crash, however unjustified.

It is also hard not to respond emotionally to a lyric which opens with the shock of great poetry. "Within the fire and out upon the sea" summons up vast vistas of loss and desolation. Sandy's remote vocal handles the transition from sadness to exultation with her customary subtlety. Hutchings plays gently under what is surely Thompson's finest and most restrained lead break, on a ghostly electric guitar.

Released on December 2nd, there was something very melancholy about its overall effect, a kind of requiem not just for the line-up that had produced it, but for Fairport's youth and the end of the decade which defined them. There is the same sense of a glory departing at the end of the movie *Withnail and I*. As Withnail walks in the park, to a Beatles soundtrack, the "greatest decade in the history of the world" is coming to an end.

British folk rock starts here, and amplification was crucial. As Swarbrick put it, crudely but with unarguable truth, "if you're singing about a bloke having his head chopped off, or a girl fucking her brother and having a baby, and the brother getting pissed and cutting her guts open and stamping on the baby and killing his sister ... having to work with a storyline like that with acoustic instruments wouldn't be half as potent dramatically as saying the same things electrically".

Hutchings himself remembers this as "a tremendously exciting and exhilarating time, during which we worked on many of the songs and tunes that were eventually to go on *Liege & Lief*. Nicol reckoned to Pamela Longfellow, "later I listened to *Liege & Lief*, and then to the album Swarb made with Carthy just before they split up" (*Prince Heathen*): "it was like listening to the same thing, but without the bass and drums."

Even for the ever self-critical Richard Thompson, "once we started we obviously had to keep going, there was no going back. I think it's also important to remember that around the time of *Liege & Lief* Fairport had a pan-British Isles repertoire. We were playing Celtic music, English music, Scottish, Irish, Northumbrian, South of England, it was all mixed in there, and Fairport had quite a big effect on Scotland and Ireland, on the traditional musics of Scotland and Ireland. In Europe there were bands in Holland, bands in Sweden, and other places who realised the possibilities. A band like Los Lobos picked up *Liege & Lief* and said: "Wow! We thought our tradition was corny, we'd been playing the blues. Let's start incorporating Mexican music into the tradition." You know The Chieftains opened for Fairport at the National Stadium in Dublin in 1969. That concert had a big influence on the popularity of traditional music in Ireland. Because at that time the Celtic traditions were very shaky. Very shaky indeed. In Scotland and Ireland. So *Liege & Lief* was a big re-invigoration of those traditions. I think that when you write for a band, the band has to comprehend it, and empathise with whatever you're writing. It's very difficult. I could really write some obscure lyrics."

Ashley: "Although we empathised, we often didn't comprehend, but were quite happy to go along."

Simon: "But the ones that didn't fall into that category have turned in to real keepers. Those are living songs which you got right first time!" Richard unsuredly responded: "Well I don't know you see. If you write stuff you get duffers. There's probably 200 great Cole Porter songs, and about 800 crappy Cole Porter songs. The keepers will survive and that's very nice."

Simon: "But it's the thousand that you have to tear up first, the ones that you did throw away, which have made you the song writer. You've got to get those cliches out of your head. It's an art form which requires a stick-to-itiveness, which is sadly lacking in my make-up. I don't want to be a creative artist. I decided a long time ago that I was just like a functionist-type person. I enjoy what I do, but I'm not a creator, I'm an interpreter. I'm very fortunate that I've got the job that you helped me get started in. I'm very fortunate that the hobby turned in to a job that turned in to a career, but it's still a hobby. And that's what Ashley's contribution to my life can really be summed up as, if you're looking for a snappy quote. A sound bite."

Ashley: "With a lot of the songs that we were doing in the early days, it was trusting you, trusting your good taste, but it's also something about like, a great poem, an obscure poem maybe, or a great work of art, that you give yourself to it, even though you don't fully understand it. As time goes by you might understand it a bit more. But you know quite early on if a poem is for you, or if a painting is for you, even though you don't fully comprehend it."

Richard: "With writing it's the same thing. I think you develop an instinct for what's a good song and you test it with an audience. If you're a band you test songs amongst the band. Then you know if something is communicated. Either something concrete or abstract. I think at the point that I left the band, I did feel frustrated. Somehow I wasn't writing stuff that could be shared amongst the band. It wasn't bad writing, it was quite personal. And I thought that I just had to get away and get through that wee bit there. The songs that The Band wrote – I think actually the other members contributed more than their names on the credits – I think they are terrific ensemble songs in that there is a real shared feeling about them. That they are comprehensible to everybody in the band. There's a real spirit when they're played. I always thought that's indescribable. And I certainly fell short of that a lot of the times."

Was 'Wheely Down' written during all this? Simon: "It was written afterwards. It was after Richard left. He was just like the gig fairy. We'd go off to a gig and come home and all the washing up would be done and everything would be put away. And it was Richard."

Richard: "I was still living with the chaps, in a Mole-Rat sort of way. I was the original house-husband, I suppose. I wrote it at the Angel. Wheely Down was near where the Bath Festival took place, near Shepton Mallet. We passed a road and I thought: "Hey, a nice name!" Simon: "Like 'Solisbury Hill', but without the royalties."

Richard: "I think that a lot of albums that get recorded are also quite conceptual because they're rooted in a time. Albums hang together more than they should sometimes, being recorded at the same time, the same place and with the same sound. The best ones have a certain resonance." Simon: "Liege & Lief probably would have been a different record had we not had the Farley Chamberlayne experience. Had we tried to record that in London, I can't imagine it would have worked out."

The most extraordinary public performance of the new material must have been when the band took a break from mind-twisting rehearsals at Farley Chamberlayne and busked the material, unplugged and unamped, in Winchester, in a mediaeval passageway which leads through to the Cathedral. The Pilgrim's Way, indeed. For those lucky enough to be passing, seeing the likes of Ashley, Swarb and Sandy beating out a musical revolution, for small change, must have been particularly apt at a place which had proved a wayfarer's shrine for a millennium. It must have been reminiscent of A Canterbury Tale, one of Ashley's favourite Powell and Pressburger movies.

Whilst walking around Winchester in 1998, Ashley recalled "I remember that we were underneath somewhere, in a mediaeval passageway. We busked the stuff from the LP, gave the first try outs to the Liege & Lief material – for fun. Acoustic guitars, probably a washboard or something, tambourine, fiddle. Unplugged, before it was fashionable! "It's definitely here because I remember it was the entrance to the Cathedral. So we set up and there was a big crowd. And as we played more and more people arrived. But the interesting thing is, we weren't just Fairport Convention the little-known folk-rock group busking for free in Winchester. At that point we'd just had our hit, 'Si Tu Dois Partir', so we're in the charts."

"We didn't really get set up for it. One day we woke up and thought: "Let's go busking. Let's try out some of these songs and a couple of the fiddle tunes!" We just

Photo: Eric Hayes

had fiddle, acoustic guitars, Sandy singing. Mattacks would have had a snare drum and I didn't have an acoustic bass, so I bashed a tambourine. That was the first airing of Folk-Rock in a busking situation. No advertising. I don't know if we took any money! I think in those days we were quite idealistic. We would have put it in the Poor Box at the Cathedral. Nowadays we might keep the money. It was a small crowd to start with, then a bigger and bigger crowd, which then extended right out into the street. No microphones. But just having fun. We didn't get moved on, which was nice."

There are various outtakes from *Unhalfbricking* and *Liege & Lief*, with the band running through new material in the studio, and these provide many of the bonus tracks collated over thirty years later on Free Reed's *Fairport UnConventional* 4-CD box set.

Ian Maun: "Tim Chacksfield and Ian Rennie went through Universal's vaults for the Island Remasters series and to say that these archives lack any order is something of an understatement. I know, I've been through them. Their records are notoriously inaccurate. There were a lot of part titles, working titles, mis-spellings, duplicates etc. Lots of it doesn't actually exist and others have not yet been checked for their presence. Teasingly, songs such as '*Go Go With Goldie*' and '*Soft Winds*' were listed among the sessions for the first album. The '*Wild Symbols*', also listed on the card index, is actually 'wild cymbals' – cymbals recorded alone. Other finds include a number of earlier versions from the early albums, such as eleven takes of '*End Of A Holiday*'."

The 2002 reissue of *Liege & Lief* contained lots of colour photographs of life at Farley Chamberlayne, plus a heartfelt reminiscence by Ashley. "There was also joy in the air. The joy of sailing along on instrumental patterns of sound and rhythm that lifted the soul. The joy in hearing a beautiful voice bringing the songs to life again."

The sumptuous package adds two outtakes from the sessions: '*Sir Patrick Spens*' is taken at a slower pace than the version which emerged a year later on *Full House*, with Sandy's voice clear and shiny as a bell.

Take 1 of '*Quiet Joys Of Brotherhood*' is strange as hell, with wah-wah electric dulcimer, Swarb's eerie fiddle and Mattacks' ominous, muffled tom toms. Sandy sings like the calm at the heart of a storm – Ashley and Simon are notable by their absence – and the whole thing is like a ghostly reprise of '*A Sailor's Life*' as if sung by the drowned sailor.

A minute's silence, and just as you forget that there is anything on the CD player, it springs back to life with studio chatter, and another take of the same song, which breaks down when Sandy gets the words wrong. Fade to silence...

Ashley: "Other items found included a long jazz improvisation featuring Dave Mattacks on piano, but the band vetoed its inclusion on the extended CD version as being out of character with the other material. It will certainly be released at a later date. Joe also gently vetoed the inclusion of '*The Ballad Of Easy Rider*' for similar reasons."

Joe Boyd: "*Liege & Lief* began in the summer of 1969 under the most inauspicious of circumstances. The group were poised to disband. No-one could imagine playing the same songs again without thinking of Martin Lamble. Slowly, painfully, they came around to the idea of re-forming, but the original members felt strongly that there had to be a new direction, a completely different repertoire, so that they would never have to revisit the songs and styles they had developed over the years with Martin. There were many reasons they turned to British traditional music for this new project, but there were two I recall thinking were the most important.

"Sandy had a habit of educating them on long trips and long waits in dressing rooms by playing traditional ballads. The group grew to love them, particularly Ashley. The other decisive factor was *Music from Big Pink*. They had always been enamoured of American roots music and singer-songwriters. The Band hit them hard. They couldn't stop playing the LP. They loved it, but they were shocked. It was so deeply American, so fully immersed in the roots of that culture, that Fairport felt that the goalposts may have been moved too far away. They could never inhabit the space occupied by The Band. But perhaps they could accomplish something parallel to *Big Pink* if they set their minds to it. Maybe they could create a repertoire as English as The Band were American. The challenge was exciting."

1:12
COME ALL YE

Fairport Convention made an emotional return to the stage on September 20th 1969, when they played a special gig at their West Country home-from-home, the Van Dike Club in Plymouth. The set was almost completely new, with numbers from their as yet unreleased album jogging along with traditional numbers like 'Sir Patrick Spens' and 'Mason's Apron'.

Three days later, the band entered BBC Studios to record five pieces for *Top Gear*. John Peel was clearly awed by what he heard, commenting that the band were sailing boldly into new and uncharted waters. '*Sir Patrick Spens*' is slower and more menacing than the version eventually recorded on *Full House*. Along with '*Tam Lin*' and '*Reynardine*', it is to be found on an Italian bootleg, the former with a looser feel and wilder guitar breaks than the recorded version, the latter more static. The instrumental '*Lark In The Morning*' circulates on tape. Most unexpected is Richard Thompson's vocal roughing up of '*Lady Is A Tramp*'. This deconstruction of the ultimate lounge singer Frank Sinatra chimes in with the Bonzo Dog's parody of Tony Bennett's '*San Francisco*'.

The *NME* for 23rd August had announced the "concert platform debut of the group's two new members" at the Royal Festival Hall, on Wednesday 24th September. It was obviously a late booking: one advert asked patrons to "please note the new arrangements" and that the showing of the film '*Swan Lake*' would now take place at the smaller Queen Elizabeth Hall. The event was announced as a "Folk concert" with more truthfulness than the advertisers realised. Tickets ranged from 8 to 25 shillings for the concert of a lifetime. The "And Friends" promised turned out to be first Nick Drake and then John & Beverley Martyn. Both, it should be noted, represented

Royal Festival Hall poster.

the kind of contemporary folk which Fairport were now fleeing. Drake wasn
projecting, "there was nothing coming over the footlights. He did four numbers an
then fled. He was shaking all over". Imagine, then, the even greater pressure on th
headliners that night, back as if from the dead.

When the audience returned to their seats, they were to witness a (continuous) se
which – without any warning – consisted almost entirely of traditional materia
David Harris, who had a seat in the front row, points out that the audience's mai
reaction was surprise, in that ALL the material played that night was new t
Fairport's repertoire, and as yet unrecorded.

A very rough tape has survived, and if you play it in another room – loud – yo
can recapture a little of the magic of that night. This is *wild* music, about as far from
the politeness of the likes of Pentangle as you can get. The sheer attack of the ban
is worthy of a jamming West Coast band like It's A Beautiful Day. The audienc
sound ecstatic, from the off.

A brief spot of tuning up, then we are into the measured stride of '*Come All Ye*
Sandy's voice echoing around the hall, while Ashley's bass booms underneath. Yo
can almost touch the emotion, and Swarbrick's electric violin wails like a banshee. Th
pace slows for '*Reynardine*' – lots of space between the notes – with Thompso
embroidering Sandy's melancholy rendition, and Mattacks making his mark wit
sombre drum rolls. The whole thing sounds like a lament after some dreadful massacre

As the band retune – there are obviously some problems up there – Sandy provide
an impromptu comic gloss on the next song, resolving any tension in a gale c
audience laughter. '*Sir Patrick Spens*' is played with brio, driven along by Mattack:
a tower of strength at the back. By now the elements of this new sound are becomin
clearer. Swarbrick seems to have taken over the role of lead instrument fro
Thompson, who embroiders around him. The old firm of Nicol and Hutching
provide the musical heart-beat. Ashley comes up to the mike for a few wise word:
Mattacks gives two taps on the cowbell, and we're off into the first instrumenta
medley. The sound here is definitely Irish, like a race with the various player
tumbling over each other. It's so exciting, and the applause seems to go on forever
"Thank you" says Sandy, "The next song is a traditional tune, but we've put moder
words to it. We've ruined it!" From the joyous mayhem of the jigs and reels, w
plunge down into '*Farewell, Farewell*'. Beautiful interplay between Swarb an
Thompson, then Denny at her bleakest, summoning ghosts. The song seems about t
break down after the first verse, as if with the emotion of it all, but picks up agai
after a heartbeat's silence. There's a nice little riff at the end, repeated as if to infinity

Sandy prefaces '*Matty Groves*' with a brief telling of the story, then a nervou
laugh which the audience gradually picks up. A self-confident strumming on th
guitar from Simon, and the band sail into the song, by now totally in control both c
themselves and the audience. Swarb's violin wails between verses, and Hutching
provides complex patterns underneath. Thompson seems strangely restrained – n
'*Reno, Nevada*' hereabouts – content mainly to play the tune, but he leads Fairpo
into an extended jam of '*The Fair Flower Of Serving Men*' at the end, making hi
guitar scream for the first time that night.

Again Hutchings' masterful juxtaposition of light and shade, as this near free forr
freak-out is followed in the set list with '*Quiet Joys Of Brotherhood*', to show that no
all is "folklore" as Sandy puts it, introducing the song with a brief tribute to Richar
Fariña. Electric dulcimer, bowed bass and beaters as Sandy seems to be singing onl
to herself. The band are like dreamers awake. Swarbrick's fiddle comes in with tha
uniquely shivery tone he can summon seemingly at will. Again, ghosts circle.

'*Crazy Man Michael*' after a false start is almost unbearably poignant. It sounds like a hymn, and is both played and sung with the utmost restraint. Once heard, never forgotten.

Perhaps the highlight of the whole evening is '*Tam Lin*', which opens abruptly with Mattacks violent on the drums, and the band tight as a Scotsman at Hogmany. Sandy is particularly majestic, effortlessly floating over the electric storm, then spitting out the Queen of Fairies' curses at the end. Thompson seems to stir himself into action, his guitar like an Exocet, targeted for mayhem. The musical restraints the band are now under only seem to make them wilder during the moments of release allowed them, and here the jam at the end seems to last forever. Folk rock, with the emphasis on rock. Compared to the eventual recorded version, this is a wild beast, prowling its cage. Or warfare, a mad charge on some distant machine gun post. Catharsis, or what?

Thunderous applause, then it is almost a relief to settle down with another medley of traditional tunes, played at breakneck pace and with no discernible emotion, but to huge applause at the end. Swarb's electric fiddle is piercing, balanced at the bottom of the sound scale by Ashley's rocking bass. Lacking the cultural purity of the album which followed, '*Ballad of Easy Rider*' again breaks the trad binding, and somehow taps into eternity, in the way Fairport sometimes could. Sandy's voice and Swarb's violin circle one another, and everyone comes in for the chorus, in a way that makes the hairs at the back of your neck prickle. Togetherness, in the face of adversity.

"The river flows to the sea", death and decay are a natural process of human life, but here lament turns into triumph over the odds, and a suffusing sense of love flows from band to audience and back again. "Flow river flow". The roar at the end says it all, like a home crowd whose team have just scored. Tension, and then release.

As if recognising this, the band encore with the country corn of '*Have You Had A Talk With Jesus*', (un)sung by Swarbrick. The Festival Hall turns into a country barn, solos get wild and ragged after all that technical precision, and we're all at the hoedown. Things end comically with the another country song, '*We Need A Lot More Of Jesus, (And A Lot Less Rock 'n' Roll)*'.

A first hand account of the band's fabled Festival Hall '69 gig was given us by Ian Maun. "Ashley was wearing his Country Squire look with gaiters. Always a very dapper man. I remember Ashley only too clearly. A somewhat severe face, I thought, framed now by the obligatory long hair and sporting a beard and moustache. Ashley said little, the introductions falling mainly to Sandy, but he introduced the medley of jigs and reels. I was surprised by the pleasant lightness of his voice – not such a severe character after all, it seemed.

"Sandy was wearing a flowery dress. Richard was in denim. Swarb in his white fiddler's shirt and he had his brand-new white electric fiddle that had been built for him by John Bailey. I remember just sitting there and this wash of sound, as they did '*Reynardine*', they played very loud, and it was absolutely stunning. And Sandy was very lively and bubbly. On '*Quiet Joys Of Brotherhood*', Richard was playing a dulcimer with a wah-wah pedal, and Ashley was bowing his bass with a cello bow. DM was playing on his cymbals and so on. I'm a great fan of Martin Lamble and so he was very much under my critical eye. He was a very different drummer. He was really good. At the end it sort of faded off into that strange thing, something like '*Have You Had A Talk With Jesus*'. That country sort of thing was strangely out of keeping with all the rest of it which was very pagan and folkie. When I came away, I was with a friend and I said: "I want to play that kind of music!" I went to a folk club, picked up a singer, and married her."

"I went down to Fairport's Festival Hall gig with Roy Guest and Chris Collins (Mike Waterson's sister in law)," Andy Irvine of Sweeney's Men recalled after consulting his diaries. "It seems that Roy had got me a ticket. I was evidently unimpressed by both Nick Drake and John & Beverley Martyn! When Fairport came on I found their music exciting. I seem to have been upset by not being able to make out the words and felt that the jigs and reels were their least strong point. However, over all it was a very new experience and I looked forward to hearing them again. This was praise indeed from the 27 year old A. Irvine! I was inclined to be unimpressed in those days. Roy, Chris and myself went back to Roy's place and found we all had the same difficulty in passing judgement as there was absolutely nothing to compare it to. It was felt that Richard was a little eclipsed by the addition of Swarb's fiddle. I had a safe house in Archway where lived one Trevor Crozier, who had been at Trinity College in Dublin. In the same house lived Tim Hart and Maddy Prior. We drank in a pub called the Dick Whittington. I met Ashley a few days later at Tim and Maddy's and he asked me where I had got the tune for '*Willy o' Winsbury*' – which, of course Richard had used for '*Farewell, Farewell*'. We all went down to The Peelers club together where Tim and Maddy were the guests. Mick Moloney, Paddy Finney and myself had rehearsed a set to do at the club, which apparently was a big success. I had been talking to Tyger during the evening and had the impression that he was: "A good straight bloke – a bit shy – but dead honest"."

"The concert Paul Brady and myself went to was a little later in Croydon, in the Fairfield Halls. I was more and more impressed by this time and felt the reels and jigs had been improved by Richard doing more in them. It was in the bar afterwards that Tyger raved on about The Band and their second album. We had never heard of them. Brady and me gave Sandy and her friend a lift back to Roy Guest's where they were evidently staying. Paul's driving coupled with the neurotic nervous energy of Sandy and Judy had me almost at screaming point".

"I liked [*Liege & Lief*] a lot. I also liked *Unhalfbricking* which I may have heard previously. One of the first things Ashley did, after we met, was to give me a copy of The Band's second album. He thought that was a breakthrough and I had to agree with him."

Ashley: "In any career you can put your finger on two or three key moments and that was one of them. Unveiling the *Liege & Lief* material to London, the press, the world, at the Festival Hall. And Swarbrick unveiling his solid electric fiddle, and playing that on stage for the first time. Having technical problems with it, but that just by the by. It must have been so strange being in the audience seeing it all."

The band were obviously aware that this was something new, but they were not looking over their collective shoulder to see if any of their contemporaries were going to pip them at the post. Ashley: "Never. Because there was no one doing what we were doing. No one within a million miles. Largely because we went completely against the flow, absolutely completely against what was going on, with the garish colours and the satin and the psychedelic. We went totally the other way."

Robin Denselow recalled the concert in *The Electric Muse*, a book which tried to follow the many musical paths leading away from this magical evening. "The old songs were made to crackle with a new vitality, and that vital element in each – the story – was not lost in the process". For Tony Wilson "the group as a whole had "that wood cottage look about it, and Sandy could probably bake one hell of a pie. It's cornbread music at its best … a lesson in British musical achievement". It would be interesting to record exactly who was in the audience that night. Martin Cartho was certainly there, for one. Denselow remembers how "the small, bearded and genial Swarbrick looked like a delighted weasel.

As to Nick Drake – whose career moved into darkness after the Festival Hall gig – in plucking him from obscurity, Ashley revealed an underrated side to his musical abilities, that of talent scout. Perhaps his use of Fairport, Steeleye and the many Albion bands to nurse promise into achievement has been equally undervalued – one simply expects Hutchings to continue to turn up musical gemstones from the car boot sale of public auditions. Watching Nick Drake's set that night was not of the utmost priority. Ashley was too busy fretting about how Fairport's set was going to go over to worry about the support acts.

Hutchings had been less preoccupied when he spotted Nick at the Roundhouse. "He was on a bill, a charity gig, with a friend, and I was playing with Fairport. I was in the audience wandering around before going on, and my eyes went to the stage. It was Nick the person, Nick the figure on-stage, which really registered".

It was a strong enough impression to make Ashley go away and recommend Drake to Joe Boyd, "I mean instantly. I recall him writing something down, a contact address or something. I definitely got a contact off him that night, otherwise he would just have vanished off into the underground of 1968".

Simon Nicol later described the next few months, playing the *Liege & Lief* material live in the clubs, as "the real magic period": In October, the full traditional monty was launched upon an unsuspecting Fairfield Halls, Croydon. Karl Dallas found Tyger Hutchings "one of the most up-front bass guitarists I've heard".

Next up were a 'Zigzag Benefit Gig' at Dunstable, a short Scottish tour, then Mothers, a particularly emotional occasion. Apart from the trad-folk, the set list included Dylan's '*Down In The Flood*' and '*Open The Door, Homer*', and two of Ashley's C&W favourites, performed tongue-in-cheek. '*Have You Had a Talk With Jesus?*' boasted vocals by Swarbrick, and Sandy on violin, while '*We Need A Whole Lot More Of Jesus (And A Whole Lot Less Rock 'n' Roll)*' was to become a staple

Zigzag Benefit, Dunstable Civic Hall. 4th October 1969

of Richard and Linda Thompson's live set.

An extremely rare recording of the *Liege & Lief* line-up circulates on a mono tape taken from Danish radio, and recorded in an empty cinema. The band open with '*The Deserter*' – sung with aching sadness – then go straight into a chilling version of '*Reynardine*', dead slow. Sandy sounds so vulnerable, you want to reach out and touch her. Ashley is subdued, playing the root notes, and Swarbrick's violin is very much in the musical driving seat. He also leads from the front in the '*Jigs and Reels*' medley, to Mattacks drum slaps: unless the tape is running slow, this is again sepulchral in the middle. '*Matty Groves*' is much jauntier, opening with creamy violin and thudding bass. Sandy begins perkily, and carries the song's emotional current through bravado, threats, violence and defiance to a final catharsis, when the band take over. Most precious is '*Crazy Man Michael*', with Swarbrick's violin matching Sandy's lament almost subconsciously, and the whole band throbbing in the background. Sandy again sounds close to tears, Hutchings runs up and down his fretboard, then Thompson comes in with a nimble but short guitar break. Sandy's singing in the last verse is almost unbearable, as tender as a mother laying her infant to rest.

But the endless string of one-nighters had begun to grate within the Fairport camp. For Thompson, "there's a feeling in your stomach and you're not sure what's going on, and you can't quite cope with things. You're going to bed at five in the morning, getting up in the afternoon, with nothing in between but playing the gig. I've never actually had a breakdown, but I've been close to it."

In late November, Sandy and Ashley quit the band. Faiport were about to implode. Gigs at Port Talbot and St George's Hall, York were cancelled. The crunch point had come when the band were due to fly to Copenhagen and record the Danish radio spot – no wonder it carries such a sense of dissolution and sadness.

Sandy was absent when the car arrived to take her to the airport. Anthea Joseph eventually tracked her down, and flew with her to Copenhagen. Meanwhile, the remaining members were discussing the future, amicably. As Simon told Patrick Humphries, "Ashley was as positive as anyone and between Fulham and the airport, suggested Bert (A.L.) Lloyd join, which was a concept I couldn't cope with". In fact, this was Swarb's idea, not Ashley's.

Martin Carthy: "Swarb asked me to join, in fact Ashley asked me to join, and then Dave asked me again after Ashley and Sandy had left. And I said: "No!" Ashley turned up at a gig and said: "Why don't you join too?", and I said: "No!" Because all I could have done at that time was play what I already played, LOUDER!"

For the moment, though, Ashley still saw his creative future with the band he had founded. During the flight to Denmark, Ashley decided that as Denny seemed about to leave Fairport, then "we would get a traditional singer, and push it further that way". When a phone call came through saying that Sandy would be on the next plane after all, something crystallised inside him. "I had a strange reaction to this, which I wasn't in total control of, and I think I decided within a day or two of that happening that I was going to leave the band".

On the flight back to England, the plane was rocked by a huge thunder storm. It seemed to symbolise something deeper. As he told Pamela Winters, "what I was clearly going through was some kind of delayed reaction to the crash. I vowed that if I ever got down to the ground again, I'd never go up in another airplane". Nor did he, for at least ten years. Hutchings had made another decision during the flight. "I said that I was leaving the band almost immediately".

One of Ashley's stranger ideas had been to expand Fairport to an eight-piece, bringing in the peerless singer Andy Irvine and Terry & Gay Woods from

Sweeney's Men, which Thompson found "totally impractical, fifteen guitar players or something." Richard: "Ashley wanted to bring more people into the band as I remember he wanted to bring in Gay and Terry Woods and Martin Carthy and Bert Lloyd. So Fairport was this huge 9-piece collective. And we thought: "Well, this is unworkable." Idealistically this might be fun, but I thought that it was important that we do more writing, that we were a contemporary band, upon the traditional principle. I think Ashley wanted to do more in the amplified traditional music."

Sandy was amused by Ashley's new folk evangelism. Bob Pegg also remembers how at the 1969 London Folk Music Festival, Tyger "had been appalled by a performance of the Tyneside song 'Keep Your Feet Still, Geordie, Hinny' saying what an incredible load of rubbish it was, and how it typifies the worst of the folk scene". Pegg's rejoinder was that this was typical of the Fairport approach, "basically an aesthetic response, which led them to choose a lot of Irish sounding material with flattened thirds and sevenths".

As Joe Boyd puts it: "He was discovering things with the zeal of a new convert that she had been familiar with for years. He would come back from Cecil Sharp House and say "I've just discovered this magnificent song" and she would say "Well, I was singing that when I was seventeen"." Sandy was trying to escape just such single-mindedness; purists had always thought of her as "a bit of a corrupter" because she sang with a guitar, and wrote her own songs. Now, Ashley "wanted to get deeper and deeper into the traditional music, folk rock, and she didn't. But I think the real reason I left was I was just kind of messed up and I didn't know exactly what I wanted.

"So then a very strange period for me, at the height of our success, with great reviews for Liege & Lief in general. The Royal Festival Hall concert, the world is our oyster, new music, at the height of all that, we fly to Denmark. I freak out on the plane coming back. I don't run up and down the aisles but I quietly, in a thunderstorm, flying back, think "I don't want to do this any more". Not really understanding why. Sandy's going through similar kind of feelings, and within a week of each other, we both leave. I leave and then she leaves a week later. Most unexpected from every standpoint. Can't be explained, it's just weird. Something in the air, something in us."

"I think it was a delayed reaction to the crash. A funny mood set in after we emerged into the world with Liege & Lief and it affected Sandy and myself more than anyone else. And it's no coincidence that it was Sandy and me who, as you say, who jumped ship, who left the band in a very short space of time, soon after we had done all this work. Popular belief is that we left for musical reasons, but the more I think about it, the more I think that it was just emotional. Strange kind of messed up emotional reasons emanating from the crash and not being sure where we stood. We didn't talk about it. We didn't talk about the horror and the sadness of it. And if we had sat and talked about it, we would have probably been all right I think. You just didn't in those days."

The euphoria experienced during the Farley Chamberlayne sojourn had evaporated quickly once the band had returned to the public platform.

"It's very sad," Ashley reflects, "But it's something, trying to understand why that great Liege & Lief line-up should suddenly break up when we'd achieved so much, and we'd had such a wonderful, uplifting time here. How? You can't! It's all creativity and emotions and things bouncing all over, and complicated people.

"Farley Chamberlayne was the high point. It was a place that possessed a healing spirit. We came together in adversity and then started falling to bits. A healing spirit but also the band were about to implode." A tomb and a womb!

The news hit the music press on November 22nd 1969, as if the two had left Fairport jointly, though it was Sandy's leaving which grabbed the headlines. *NME* gave the official explanation for Sandy's departure as "her unwillingness to travel", while Tyger "is anxious to concentrate on traditional folk music and, with a view to this, has been invited to join Sweeney's Men". Fairport themselves were "currently seeking a suitable singer-musician to fill the vacancy". *Disc* talks about two replacements, and that there were "several people in mind". It reports rumours that Sandy is to join Eclection – and shows a photograph of Sandy with Trevor Lucas, to prove the point. Ashley has by now left Fairport, "to form his own group".

Talking with Bob Pegg in early 1970, Simon Nicol reckoned the reason Tyger had split away was "not so much the sound as probably the attitude of the group. We're not all that serious a bunch". He gives Hutchings the most generous of leave-takings: from the very start "he's been a more serious listener than any of the rest of us. He has an amazing capacity to absorb things very quickly". Nicol rejected, with some vehemence, Bob Pegg's assertion that Fairport was taking folk to the masses. The band was playing to people who would otherwise be as likely to come across the words to '*Tam Lin*', say, as to win the football pools. As to the theory that playing such songs will convert the audience to more traditional fare, Richard Thompson added "that isn't how we think. I think that Tyger used to think like that, to an extent – in terms of pioneering".

Bob Pegg jumps in here. "At times I feel you're taking a conscious step backwards. I felt this mainly through my acquaintance with Tyger – whenever I talked to him about what he wanted to do with the Fairport, I got the impression it would be done". Richard agreed, "Tyger's always stuck by his ideals". Pegg fires back the question, "but did the group stick by Tyger?" After all, they could have fought harder for him to stay with the band. Thompson: " Let's say that often it was a case of Tyger dragging us along, because we were too slow. He tried to learn up his subject". This contradicts Hutchings' own contention that *Liege & Lief* was a "natural" record, based on a "loose knowledge" of traditional material, rather than rigorous research.

This latter was certainly to be true of his new project. The Fairport Convention of a year before had deconstructed itself, with Iain Matthews pursuing country music with Southern Comfort – on whose first album Hutchings plays bass – Sandy about to found Fotheringay, largely as a vehicle for her own songs, and Fairport retaining a trad-folk feel, but putting it to work on a whole new batch of Thompson-Swarbrick compositions. Their new bassist, Dave Pegg, had seen one of Ashley's last gigs, at Mothers, on his 21st birthday, and a month later was auditioning for the band. His own musical background included playing acoustic bass with the Ian Campbell Folk Group, alongside Dave Swarbrick.

Kingsley Abbott: "Peggy was definitely coming from a different tradition. Self-assured, pop orientated." At the 1997 Cropredy bash Ashley would describe Dave Pegg as "a ground breaking musician. He takes my breath away. He started the fashion for playing tunes – jigs and reels – on bass". He also, some years later, "started the fashion among folk-rock bass-players for baldness!"

Ashley remains full of praise for the next incarnation of Fairport. The surviving members had made a collective decision that "the particular direction which they had been going in – as a kind of English answer to American folk-rock – was what they were going to become." The band moved into a converted 18th century pub near Bishop Stortford, to rehearse new songs for *Full House*. Ashley: "It's one of my favourite Fairport albums. Mainly because of the songs. I don't think that the singing is very good, but the playing is great, and the songs are great. The ones that were emerging that should have been on it – '*Poor Will*' and '*Napoleon's Retreat*' were stunning. Of the Fairport albums that I'm not on, that is probably my favourite."

Ashley Hutchings was now off to pastures new, toying at first with British folk-rock, before rejecting that in turn for a more purely English model. By coincidence, in *Club Folk*, Bob Pegg and Simon Nicol spar verbally on this very point, with Pegg admitting "disquiet" at Fairport's own folk explorations following the Irish – "its infectious dance music and rambling modal tunes – rather than the English model. "They'd go down a whole lot better in Camden Town than at a barn dance in a Sussex village".

Simon responds with a simple "who cares where it comes from. We're not scholars". Ashley was, though. A few years down the line he would literally be playing at barn dances in Sussex with the Etchingham Steam Band. Simon is less trenchant. "I'm not deliberately trying to play 'folk music'. I'm just trying to play the music that is happening in the group at the moment".

For Pamela Longfellow, the *Full House* Fairport were "trying too hard, getting too flash". Thompson found, to his growing horror, that without Hutchings in control "all our numbers would start slowly, but after a minute or so everyone was hammering away as fast as they could. We were entertaining but it wasn't for me". He left within a year, then Nicol bowed out in San Antonio in late 1971, and Mattacks followed a year later. Both were to rejoin later incarnations of the band, but as Swarb led his own vision of electric rock into excess, Thompson – and doubtless Hutchings – felt for the time being that "it isn't Fairport anymore". Then he goes in deeper. "That name is almost dangerous. It's a Scorpio name with a life of its own. And its magic went out with Simon". There are many who still feel that the band is only true to its name when Simon is there centre-stage, as he has been now for many years (with musical holidays alongside, often with the Albion Band). Nicol is still the rock on which Fairport is built.

As to the chief architect of that band, Ashley had the last word on his own three years with Fairport, the band he so carefully put together, and which prepared him for all his future musical experiments. "We have always been anarchic, and this has continued into the Albions. This way of working, which I learned with Fairport – which Richard has learned, and continued with, and Sandy – which is a question of playing with anyone and everyone in a relaxed way, and from that way of working, coming up with new music".

As we have already seen, there is a darker side to all this. Talking to Jerry Gilbert in 1971, Ashley reveals that "at the time of leaving Fairport Convention there were a lot of thoughts flying around in my head, I can't pin it down to any one thing. It just ended up in me leaving and trying to form a new group".

Hutchings admits he left his own band "because the crash had finally caught up with me, and I couldn't do it anymore". He talks about the long-term effects of the M1 accident, and how the surviving members of Fairport never properly spoke to each other about how they felt, and to some extent still carry that night around with them, deep inside. Traditional music was something to bury oneself in, and its primal statements of fear and revenge, love and violence, death and birth, were a healing force.

"I felt we needed to throw ourselves into traditional music – it was far too soon to abandon it. After we started performing the *Liege & Lief* material, I got to know a number of folk musicians, and that gave me the confidence to form Steeleye

Span". With that album, he had pushed a door open into his own subconscious. There was nothing else he could do now but walk through it.

PART TWO
STEELEYE SPAN

"We were all pushing each other to make great records, and there was an innocence to it all, and an enthusiasm that I don't see so much anymore"

Steeleye Span 1 at Winterbourne Stoke. 1969. l-r: Terry Woods, Gay Woods, Ashley Hutchings, Tim Hart, Maddy Prior

2:1
CALLING ON SONG

Club Folk – Bob Pegg's Keele Retrospective Diary:

Friday night: *"Later that evening we have to perform in a concert compered by Packie Byrne. In the audience is Ashley Hutchings, the bass player of the Fairport Convention rock group. What's he doing at a folk music festival? Answer: He likes traditional music. He believes that many forms of music are going to come together in front of the young, eclectic audiences of the new pop. The following day Toni Arthur, relaxing on the grass, says that she is tired of being labelled 'Traditional', and wants to break out of the mould created for her and Dave by the club situation. Maybe Ashley Hutchings is on to something."*

Saturday evening: *"Talking 'til 4:30am on Sunday morning, with Ashley Hutchings, Dave and Toni [Arthur], Tim [Hart] and Maddy [Prior] and Tony Wales. Again the conversation is about the breaking down of the artificial barriers which appear to split music into distinct genres. There is hopeful talk of people like ourselves playing to sympathetic mass audiences at open-air concerts. The fantasy of the sound of melodeon, fiddle and concertina drifting out over the Hyde Park thousands is certainly an inspiring idea."*

The beginnings of Steeleye Span stem from this fabled summit meeting. Ashley explains. "It was the Summer of 1969, and I really started to get into traditional music. I went to Festivals even when Fairport weren't playing. I got involved and met Folkies for the first time, and just spent time and hung out with them. I got deeply in with the Peggs in particular, and the Irish contingent who were all good friends. I obviously learnt a lot from them but a lot of ideas start to form in my head. So you could almost pre-date the break-up of Fairport from before *Liege & Lief* started. You could say the seeds were sown because I was really getting deeply into the songs. We went to Padstow, and I can clearly remember a photograph of Martin Lamble with the Padstow Obby Oss, that would have been taken by either Eric Hayes or Keith Morris. We were recording *Unhalfbricking* then, so we were obviously getting very interested in the tradition. This is before the crash. We were interested enough to go right down to Cornwall on May Day in 1969, to see what it was all about."

"At the Summer Folk Festivals I talked to The Peggs, I talked to the Irish guys and The Dransfields. The person I was most drawn to was Terry Woods. Bob Pegg and I got on very well, and that was a very important, artistic relationship. But with Terry, it was a really good friendship as well as an artistic thing. I miss Terry to this day. So when I said that I would leave Fairport, the idea was that I'd get together with Terry and form a group that was more traditional. In many ways, it was me and Sweeney's Men."

"During the late Autumn of 1969, I started to form the embryonic Steeleye with

Terry Woods, Johnny Moynhan and Andy Irvine, all rehearsing at my house in Durnsford Road, which was still at the hub of it all!"

Mystery has long surrounded the legendary pre-Steeleye "rehearsal" band that comprised Gay and Terry Woods, Andy Irvine, Johnny Moynihan and Ashley. Andy tries to unravel the mystery: "My memory is that it was more of a meeting. I forget where it happened. I seem to remember that we all had to sit on the floor. I remember playing a song I had just written called '*Autumn Gold*'. Ashley was suitably impressed and just said: 'That's a minor masterpiece'. He was a man of few words! It was obvious to me from conversations with Johnny Moynihan that he was not going to get involved in another group with Terry Woods, with whom he had a pretty tense relationship. I felt with some regret at the time that my star was tied in with Johnny's, and if he wasn't going to join, I wasn't.

"Memory is a selective thing and I thank my lucky stars I kept a diary. It was sometime around 10th November 1969. There is reference to Sandy being kicked out of Fairport. Also, talk about our looking round for a record deal. It seems Nat Joseph had offered £2,000 and Harvest were supposed to be topping that to the tune of £3,000. This for van, equipment and initial wages.

"We were to meet in the Prince of Wales in Highgate: Johnny, Terry, Gay and myself arrived. Tyger didn't turn up and when I rang him, he said he had been waiting for a confirmation call from me. We finally met and had 'a bit of a rehearsal'. Tyger played some nice bass and Gay was good but 'there was an air of gloom' because of Johnny's reservations. 'Tyger and Terry sat there and tried hard to push us in with their enthusiasm'. I was definitely 'on' for it but only if Johnny agreed. My diary reports that 'Everybody was quelled by me singing '*Autumn Gold*'.

"Sweeney's Men had a gig in Ipswich the following day. Sweeney's were just Johnny and Terry at this point, but I played with them in the second half. It was when we got back to Liverpool Street and Terry and Gay had left that Johnny and myself had a long chat about the band.

"Johnny said that he wouldn't be able to join the group. His lack of empathy for Terry was the insuperable reason. It meant the end of the band for both of us. I was a bit depressed about this. Not only because of an opportunity going begging but because of the fact that Terry and Tyger had given it their all. Johnny promised to break the news to Tyger the next day. Tyger was upset and talked about going back into Fairport with Terry and Gay. I wondered why he had left Fairport before everything was settled? He said that my name had been suggested as a replacement for Sandy and he asked me if I would join. I said more or less certainly, "No!" I felt that I couldn't walk into a well established group, let alone into Sandy's shoes. Tim and Maddy knew all about what was going on and intimated that they would be interested in replacing Johnny and me. But Tyger was sold on Gay.

"I was depressed on account of both myself, Tyger and Terry who were so full of enthusiasm for the venture. I think I must have felt that Johnny was the only person who would have kept a link with traditional Irish music. Neither Terry nor Gay had ever shown that much interest in Irish music and I wouldn't have felt strong enough, alone, to combat any direction the three of them might take that I didn't like. Johnny and myself had a very similar attitude to music, at that time and I certainly felt that he was the man I wanted to be in a band with. Johnny was never going to be in the same band as Terry. Had their relationship been otherwise, I'm sure it would have been a huge success!"

Sweeney's Men had been experimenting with electric guitarist Henry McCullough, and at the 1968 Cambridge Folk Festival the band had been booed off by traditionalists. Some fans believe that Sweeney's Men provided the template for Steeleye Span, but Ashley discounts this theory. "I never saw Sweeney's Men in any form. I was given their two acoustic albums and I liked them very much, but I never saw the band perform. '*Willy o' Winsbury*' was one of the sources of '*Farewell Farewell*', so Richard would have known Andy Irvine's version. I don't think they can justifiably claim to have been the first electric folk rock band. It was merely the fact that Henry McCullough played with them, and that he played electric guitar. Retrospectively, after Fairport, Terry and Johnny told me about Henry and them playing electric. So the copyist accusation doesn't really come into it."

We had a long phone interview with Terry in Ireland, and his voice came over as being enthusiastic, friendly and emotional about what he had achieved. He recalled his first meeting with Ashley. "At the time I was in Sweeney's Men and Ashley was in Fairport. We met playing football behind the Prince Of Wales and got talking. He seemed to be unhappy with the direction Fairport were going in, and I was unhappy where we were going with Sweeney's Men. And that's how we started our conversation. We had an awful lot in common.

"There was a pre-Steeleye rehearsal band. We had a go with Johnny and Andy, but Johnny and myself had kind of reached the end. Andy still hadn't made up his mind whether he was going to travel to the Balkans or not. It didn't have the pizzazz that we needed. They weren't really interested and off they went. And then we tried Bob Pegg and his wife Carol. Then we asked the Dransfields. Tim and Maddy were interested. We went along and saw them, and things developed from that. Ashley and myself were trying to put together a band playing UK music and Irish music. We were going to use the format of Ireland but in the style of American music."

Gay Woods: "I came over to England to follow my husband Terry, and it was just purely coincidental that I was asked. It was a new kind of music. It was just like what I had been doing in Ireland, except that now it was in England and seemed kind of important. But we never knew at the time that it would go on for so long. Jesus! We used to go up to Ashley's house, Terry and myself, and we used to sit on a single bed in his bedroom, and I was amazed because it the first time that I'd ever seen anybody who had the bedroom downstairs. I always assumed that everybody slept upstairs. We used to go to his parent's house. I thought Ashley was just a grand guy."

Presumably the Woods were very steeped in the American tradition, more so than Irish traditional material? "When Terry and I used to sing, we would do Carter Family and Mike Seeger songs in Ireland, but the Irish stuff was always there. It was ever present."

Irish music went over to America, evolved and adapted in the Appalachians, and then returned. Terry and Gay were two of the prime movers who were reintroducing it to Ireland. Gay credits Terry with contributing to her musical evolution: "Terry's lovely rippling banjo goes through Steeleye's debut album. He's a great musician. He introduced me to the women singers, because they just had such great earthy voices."

"I was really into anything that was old for some reason. I think it was because my Grandmother lived with us for seven years. She was marvellous. She was from County Kildare, whereas my folks were brought up in the city. She was probably the very first person who put me on her knee and she'd '*Sing A Song Of Sixpence*' to me and *"Put on your old knee britches..."*

By December Ashley's new band was now expected "to consist of two girls, who will sing and play traditional British instruments such as autoharp and concertina, a bassist, a drummer and two others who will feature other traditional instruments such as mandolin and dulcimer, as well as guitar". A drummer is still on the agenda here, and the band is essentially electric folk with acoustic colouring.

Ashley was clear-sighted as to his new direction. "I want to develop along the same lines as Fairports did. They scratched the surface, now we want to take traditional British songs and adapt them to an electric setting, creating an unmistakable British sound".

Fairport were basically a rock group, but the new band would be "folk musicians going electric. We've already been practising", following the "aim" he had first sighted with *Liege & Lief*. "I hope we will be even more British, by virtue of the concertina, mandolin, dulcimer and so on. We are exploring, and it would be nice if other groups try it as well. There certainly seem to be rumblings in the folk scene at the moment".

It is interesting in view of the identification of early Fairport with Americana that Hutchings now wishes for a clean break. "I believe that virtually all rock music is based on American forms. We've got a number of fine bands, but they seem to end up taking American music back to America – it's the same with any music".

One wonders if this is a subconscious nod to Fairport, who had been set for their first American tour, before the crash put everything in abeyance. "What we are trying to do is to get people interested in British forms". British at this point, not specifically 'English'. He hopes that the new band will follow him in this quest, "by reverting back to the roots, and doing traditional material".

In *Melody Maker*, Steve Lake complains that Fairport "have abandoned sensitivity in favour of technique and become, perversely, a sort of folk-rock Ten Years After". Since Hutchings' departure, they now revolve "around the high-speed violin playing of Dave Swarbrick which is as meaningless as Alvin Lee's endless soloing". Paradoxically, the offshoots of the original band continue its "magical subtlety". Judy Dyble's Trader Horne, Sandy Denny's Fotheringay, Matthews Southern Comfort and Ashley Hutchings' new band Steeleye Span "all exhibit that type of exquisite, restrained understatement found only in the music of American bands like Love, Buffalo Springfield and the Youngbloods". British, or what?

A contradiction now occurs in our story in that Ashley recalls "At that time we were rudder-less, we were manager-less, we were cut adrift. So we were just getting on with it. The management and Sandy Roberton, the deals and RCA Records, that all came later." Terry Woods remembers things differently. "We'd already sold the idea of the band to Sandy Roberton. He was out for getting us a deal. I remember at the time he got us enough money for Gay and myself to go home to Ireland for Christmas. And then we just went to Winterbourne Stoke for rehearsals." Gay supports Terry's version. "I had a job as a typist. And when we got the deal with RCA Records, they phoned me and I was out of the office like a bullet to join the band."

Sandy got them a recording deal with RCA and this brought in enough money for them to buy a PA system and have electric versions made of normally acoustic instruments such as dulcimers. They also bought a Ford Transit van.

Ashley: "It was a hard time. And I found music to be a consolation and plunged into English folklore. It was a healing process. If you put it down on paper, it sounds very logical nowadays. I wasn't thinking at the time: "Oh, this is the logical thing to do"." Unconsciously or subconsciously you were looking for something, folklore is full of things about healing. "And the country is a healing place. Much later, I wrote a song, '*Kitty Come Down The Lane*' which is specifically my response to the healing properties of living in the countryside, being in the countryside and walking in the countryside. Years later the truth does come out, because people who were there, reminisce. You get the PR thing and then you have to dig deeper."

But something else was happening to Ashley which he has never revealed in public until now. "I was experiencing health problems that were a delayed reaction to the crash. Whilst walking down the road, I start to get a dizzy spell, and I'm panic stricken because I don't know what it is, and never had it before. It goes away and then it comes back. I go to the doctor and he gives me sleeping pills, and I still don't sleep. He then gives me stronger pills and I have more dizzy spells. Over a very short period of about two months, the lack of sleep, the increased strength of sleeping pills and the dizzy spells, and being told by the doctor: "There's nothing wrong with you!", I go on a big downward spiral. I lose all my hunger and am not eating. And so I go back home, I go back to the womb and sleep there for a period. Then in December of 1969 I wake up one morning at my parents' house, and I have in effect some kind of minor breakdown. I wake up in this desperate mood, feeling awful, as I haven't slept for days. I put on *Anthems In Eden* and upon hearing Shirley and that music, suddenly all the tears begin to come, and they won't stop. The doctor's called and he gives me sedation. He gives me pills to settle me. And very slowly I start to come back to a level.

"What happens during the rest of that winter is that we form Steeleye and go down to Wiltshire, to start the group with Terry and Gay, Tim and Maddy. While all that exciting stuff is happening, I have a permanent, piercing pain in my forehead, which stays with me about a year. And that's just the beginning. I'm then on sedatives for a few years, and I find it very hard to kick them. If you look at the photos of Steeleye, I've dark glasses and a white face. But there's a defining moment where I fell in love with Shirley, her music and that Englishness. It's my saviour from that moment on. That's the lowest that I've ever got in terms of health and spirit. I hadn't really got Steeleye started, and I couldn't sleep or eat. I simply didn't know where I was going. And I put on *Anthems In Eden* and the sun comes out, and within a year, I'm with Shirley, and then we marry. Eventually the dizzy spells and pain go, but I remain on pills right through meeting Shirley, getting engaged, getting married. I only come off the pills during the second year of our marriage. So, that's the personal story."

Was Ashley crying because of the beauty of the music or because of what has happened? "I think I was crying because of what that music has unlocked. It evokes the countryside and it evokes the healing. I just loved the naturalness of Shirley's voice. I imagine it defined the rest of my career. Only in retrospect can you say from that defining moment of listening to *Anthems In Eden* came my love of English music. But it wasn't from that moment on, "It's got to be England. I've got to form The Albion Band!" It was immediately just the spirit of the music. I saw nothing wrong with playing Irish tunes. I enjoyed it. That came later, when I was within Steeleye. That was when I discovered Morris Music and that's when I realised that I wanted to specifically play English music."

But things could have gone differently. "I remember immediately after I formed Steeleye, visiting the Fairport lads when they reformed at The Angel in Little Hadham, and having a quiet chat with Richard and Simon saying: "I really miss not being in the band anymore. I'd love to be involved. Can I rejoin Fairport? Is there still a place for me?" And that smacks of someone who made some kind of grand gesture out of an emotional expression. I had left the family, felt homesick and wanted to get back into it. They were very diplomatic, but they'd gone too far and had got their solid new group. I'd gone off with Steeleye. It was a mixed up emotional thing.

"The door was firmly shut. That was both fair and absolutely right. I had to stand on my own two feet. They'd got Dave Pegg in the group and there was certainly no room for me again. They'd moved on, and I'd moved on. I was saying: "I miss you and actually I'd like to be back again". Sandy would have probably said the same, and indeed a few years later did rejoin Fairport. I haven't felt it since. I felt that the gulf was too wide in recent years. I'm very happy with what I've been able to do with the Albions."

Neither Richard or Simon can remember Ashley asking to rejoin Fairport. Simon pondered, "Perhaps he asked Dave Pegg whether he could come back." Richard recalled "Ashley wanted to bring Terry and Gay into the band. We thought that this was unworkable."

Simon added, "Ashley was very charged up by the experience of the musical results of his experimentation with Steeleye. And he thought he'd really struck a rich seam of possibilities, and went on to pursue it. That wasn't the reason he left Fairport at the time, but it was one of the reasons we did go our separate ways. Traditional music will always be important to me, but it's not something that I'm prepared to bang a drum about. I'd rather have it subsumed into what I do than have it dictate what I do. The Albion Band are now doing what Richard did, about ten years later. Ashley's started subsuming folk motifs into contemporary songs. And he's done it very well."

2:2
WINTER IN WILTSHIRE

Like Maddy Prior, Tim Hart was part of the '60s folk revival, singing in local clubs, though he also played in a rock band, the Ratfinks. Maddy had begun by singing much the same repertoire as early Fairport until she met and roadied for the American duo Sandy and Jeannie Darlington, who asked her "why are you singing that re-cycled American stuff? Sing English stuff". So she did, hitching to play folk club gigs as a solo, unaccompanied singer – an oddity at the time. Some club patrons told her that her voice was too good to sing traditional music.

Prior and Hart turned professional in 1967, the same year as Fairport, but in the clubs "there was nowhere to go, once you got £25 at clubs and headline at occasional festivals, that's it. You either become a folk intellectual, or you become an alcoholic". He found the folk scene constricting: "it built its own limitations within itself". They did record two albums, now highly prized, which duplicate their club repertoire. Strictly acoustic.

Maddy Prior: "There was no question of career. You just muddled along until you did something else really. But I was terrified. I was absolutely the most frightened performer that ever lived.

"Tim started to get the business side of it a bit more organised. We moved to a house in North London's Whitehall Park, which became a communal house really, with Trevor Crozier living downstairs. We'd met Ashley at one of the folk clubs, and he was sort of insinuating himself into that world from Fairport. He was looking around for another band and found Sweeney's Men, who were in the process of splitting up, and finished up with Terry, Gay and himself. They were all staying around at our house. And then they said would we like to join? We went around to Ashley's house for a practice. So we thought fine, give it a whirl. We went to rehearse in the country for three months, got all the material together, made the album and split, as tends to happen when you spend three months with total strangers in the country."

Kay Hutchings remembers "Maddy Prior and Tim Hart came to Durnsford Road and Steeleye started in our front room. They came and drank all my cider out of our great big ornamental glass that was only for show." The duo jumped at Ashley's offer to join. As Maddy Prior put it "we just wanted to play with other people, and LOUD: we were on the edge of getting bored".

As to Terry and Gay Woods, they had both grown up in Dublin, and played the folk circuit as a duo before Terry joined Sweeney's Men. Like Tim, he was an multi-instrumentalist, and Gay had a softer voice than Maddy's – nicely complementing it – and played concertina. Unlike Tim and Maddy, both also wrote their own songs, though this facet of their talent was to remain mute in Steeleye Span. Gay Woods in person is extraordinary. A bolt of energy, highly voluble and still in love with the music, and has since made a deep study of Jungian psychology.

She left us breathless, and is now singing better than ever.

One of the more intriguing aspects of this fledgling band was the name itself. Martin Carthy explains its genesis: "Tim and Maddy had stayed with me down in Warminster, because they used to go down to the West Country a lot, and they'd come and stop off for the night, or on the way back. They turned up and said "We're forming an electric band – got any good names?" I'd just learned the song '*Horkstow Grange*' – with its chorus "pity them who see and suffer, pity poor old Steeleye Span." And I said I've heard this great name "Steeleye Span" and Tim went DING! Apparently he went and voted for it, and voted twice!"

Interestingly, Tyger wanted 'Middlemarch Waits' – referring to George Eliot's majestic novel of provincial life – while Terry and Gay preferred 'Iyubidan Waits".

The choice of the alliterative 'Steeleye Span' led to later confusion with the American band Steely Dan – chilly jazz-rockers named after a dildo, from a novel by William Burroughs. For a while they tried to insist that Steeleye change their identity. With Ashley, though, they were to meet their match in single-minded determination. The row was helpful to both bands in getting much-needed publicity. The band were also once named as The Steel Ice Band!

Unlike Fairport, Steeleye's given aim was "not to be a rock band but traditional musicians working with electric instruments". Although Terry Woods later proved himself a fine improvising guitarist, in Steeleye he was well reined in. None of Ashley's bands has ever allowed a solo instrumentalists to let rip, outside the space allotted. It's all a question of control…

As their new manager, Sandy Roberton recalled, "I met Ashley when he came to my office in St George Street in Mayfair. I had been running Chess Records and their publishing companies Jewel Music and Arc Music and decided to leave and join two friends Mike & Richard Vernon who were setting up a label and publishing company, Blue Horizon Records. I joined as a partner and ran the publishing side. I also started managing a few bands and producing them. Ashley said he'd left Fairport and was starting a new band, was I interested in getting involved?" When did Sandy and September Productions first become involved with Steeleye Span? "I got involved when they first started rehearsing."

Coming from the black music background of Chess and Blue Horizon, how did Sandy find the contrast between the blues and English folk-rock music? "I'd always been a big fan of Blues and some early country music so to end up working for Chess and the Chess publishing companies was a dream come true. There is a sort of purity about the early blues that somehow is connected to early folk music and I think I was attracted to folk singers in the same way. Although it's a bit of a stretch, what Elvis, Scotty and Bill did with Arthur Crudup is sort of what Steeleye and Fairport did with English Folk music. They just crossed the wires."

Terry Woods recalled: "Myself and Ashley walked the streets of London trying to sell this band, this idea of electric folk to various record companies. I remember I had to send home to my father to send over an overcoat because I was potless. We were lucky to meet up with Sandy Roberton. Who got what we were trying to do. He was the one who helped us get the deal. It seemed a very logical thing at the time. Ashley and myself were very into *Music From Big Pink* and we thought: "What a great idea. How sensible. Go off somewhere else and just work. Get away from London. Get away from all the things that you don't have to do". A friend, Andrew Preece, had this house in Winterbourne Stoke-Berwick St James, and he showed it to us. That's how it started." Today, Winterbourne Stoke is bisected by the A303, a busy road from Wincanton to Andover. When returning there with Ashley we could hardly hear ourselves speak, until we retreated to the quieter area near the ancient church. It was then sitting on an old wooden bench that Ashley talked about his breakdown. It was a very emotional moment.

The band moved to Winterbourne Stoke in the winter of 1969-70; wind whistled over Salisbury Plain, whistled past the house. The bitter cold led to enforced periods

Steeleye Span 1 at Winterbourne Stoke. 1969

inside, as Ashley recalls: "I remember very clearly going to bed with all my clothes on and an overcoat, and as many blankets as I could find on the bed. That's one of the enduring memories that I've got of it. And also of making the music in the house – it was all made exclusively in the house because it was wintertime. We couldn't go outside and play, which would have been nice. So we were in this cocoon, this womb-like house.

"At that time, we were in love with the music certainly, but we were also in love with the countryside and the history of England. With the exception of The Band in America, we were almost alone in wearing collar-less shirts, rough tweed type clothes and waistcoats and hats, big thick beards. We were immersing ourselves in the countryside and that made it easier somehow to play the music. There was a lot of snow and frost that winter. It's a very primeval landscape and it did help. Very, very shortly after that, I was involved with Bob Pegg and Mr Fox starting. There's a song on the debut *Mr Fox* album, '*Salisbury Plain*' which grew out of living in Wiltshire."

Gay: "There was lots of head-stuff going on, as we were all so young and all so mad. But unfortunately it all came to grief. And the daggers came out, and it was all terrible. But I always did enjoy my time with Ashley. And I still think he invented the folk-rock bass style and I love his bass playing. It's super.

"It's very fresh because everybody was just doing this spontaneously. Just coming from the different worlds that we were coming from. I didn't even know that if I played a wrong note, they could hear me in the studio. I was that innocent. It was a hard time. Everybody had no money. I don't know how we actually did it. It was terrific to move to the country, that was for me ideal. I think Ashley was caught up in Thomas Hardy novels at the time.

"We hired that bungalow, sadly it wasn't a cottage, but there was a cottage nearby and it was just like in *Return Of the Native* or *The Woodlanders*. We could just meander into it, and have a look around a thatched, old English building. It was just paradise for me. I had a great time and I used to drink Elderberry wine. Don't forget that Ashley was just getting over the traumatic car crash. But he was beautiful then. He was a grand fellow. I'd like to do something musically with him again. God we were terribly shy in those days."

Ashley remembers that "Stonehenge was only about five miles from where we lived and so we visited it. I'm a non-driver, so there were stretches of time when I was left without a car, and Tim and Maddy went off to do a couple of duo gigs, so we couldn't walk to anywhere like that."

Terry fondly recalled "One night Ashley, Gay and myself decided to visit Stonehenge. At that point in time there was very little stopping you approaching the stones. We were all pissed as newts. We hopped over the barbed wire and I tore the arse out of my trousers, and in we walked. And we were quite drunk, and this was three in the morning. It was very dark. And suddenly this blinding light. I thought I was dead. I thought: "That's it!" We stood there for what seemed like an age, but it was just a minute or two. The whole place just lit up. When we ran out of the circle the lights went off. It was obviously some type of sensor. And we got over the barbed wire and I remember thinking: "Jesus, the British Army will be out. We've had it. They'll throw away the key" And we walked down the road, on the far side. We didn't even wait for the car to drive us back to Winterbourne Stoke, whistling, pretending it wasn't us, you know. And out of the distance, this little man came up on a bicycle, with a sou'wester over his pyjamas. Under the road they had a little shed or some type of dwelling built for him. So he had a go at us but we ignored him. We just walked very smartly down the road where we were picked up."

Ashley: "It was so cold – the wind used to whistle over the Plains, and our house looked out and there was nothing to stop the wind and the snow coming across. We spent some two months at Winterbourne Stoke. It was a very important period. I'm by myself and I've got no income coming in. I'm saying: "I want to dig deep into traditional music and folk-rock, and find out what it's all about. I want to find out what the path is. And I'm not going to have any help from anyone – financially or in any way." But also we trust to nature. Steeleye was the start of my own individual road.

"A few months later, we made the first Steeleye album out of all the work that we'd done in the village. So there was a contract and there was management. But at that point, in the dead of Winter in 1970, there was no safety net. We were going by instinct and our own commitment."

Did Ashley feel that sense of a coming Ice Age? What had happened to the hippie dream? "Certain aspects of the doctrines had stayed with us, but we'd cut ourselves away from the peripheries – the clothing, and certainly the bright lights, the drugs and the lifestyle. And we weren't exactly living communally, but we were living and working as a band together. And it was very much a transitional period – the ending of the hippie thing and the beginning of an awareness of history and tradition of England and of Britain. Because we were playing more than English music. In fact, very much so. It was slanted towards the Celtic with Gay and Terry in the band. But it was a good period.

"We'd had all the fun, we'd had the bright lights in the late sixties. It was now time to roll up my sleeves, to get dirty and to dig deep, both musically and spiritually. And literally, because by then I'd started my great interest in gardening and plants. It was all part of it. You look at the old photos and you see me with a spade, digging. I've lived in the countryside for a number of years but this was just the beginning of it. This was my move from the city to the country. I got married to Shirley and moved down to Sussex. I then spent a lot of years living in the countryside of Gloucestershire, Oxfordshire and so forth. So this was the beginning of all that nomadic lifestyle."

Was it also part of the expected pop culture of 'getting it together' in the country? "I never felt part of the pop culture really. Even in the psychedelic days, Fairport were always on the edge of that world. I didn't feel that we were copying anyone else by coming to the countryside. It was a totally different thing really, because the groups who did move into houses to work together, did it for maybe two reasons: to play music and that's cool. Another reason was rock groups tended to get it together for communal reasons, like families get together, all those pictures of children and mothers, and home-made bread and so forth. LSD, and music. We came to the countryside to get close to tradition. To get close to the meat of the music that we were going to work with.

"There were times when I felt so close to the ancestors – the old singers, the old songs – by living in the countryside, by performing, by working, by editing the lyrics and so forth, just it was all one. It was all one. Thirty years later, the main arterial road goes through the middle of the hamlet. It's a bit like *Lark Rise*. All the houses are probably owned by bank managers. There's no room for the farm workers anymore. They probably live in Salisbury. There was an element of romanticism in what we were doing, and if we look at the photos, you can see how we were choosing to pose say, in front of that very picturesque cottage. Now that's not where we were living. So we went along with image, but it wasn't a shallow image."

Many artists and writers have followed the same path, among them, Robert Frost and Edward Thomas, who went to the small Gloucestershire village of Dymock to found a writing commune. Hutchings believes Steeleye were more in this tradition than say, the band Traffic in their Berkshire cottage: "We would have felt closer to Frost and Edward Thomas, than some of the rock groups. There were times when I was quite frightened by the fact that I was cut adrift. It wasn't so bad for some of the others. Tim and Maddy were continuing to gig as a duo in folk clubs and were established. But I'd cut everything off and was out in the darkness waiting to see what would happen. We never gigged and therefore weren't getting any feedback. But there is a plus to that – it's very exciting when you do appear. Like Fairport a few months earlier, appeared out of the countryside with *Liege & Lief* and everyone was knocked flat famously at the Royal Festival Hall concert when we unveiled the 'new' music. And I felt the same with Steeleye. It was quite nice to suddenly appear with this music that we had worked on."

Terry: "We'd get up and have breakfast. Kick a football around. And come in and then start to rehearse. Play music, learn the songs and work it out. Sometimes there were just the three of us. Sometimes there were Tim and Maddy. And a few other various people. Johnny Butler who was a friend of mine came in as the runner who'd get things for us. He was a big part of it all at that point. Sadly, I don't think there were any rehearsal tapes."

Fairport aficionado, Brian New recalled that when he used to live near Salisbury, he frequently visited the local pub at Winterbourne Stoke, where the landlord would recall how the band would always be in during most evenings to get

Steeleye Span 1 at Winterbourne Stoke. 1969

warm! Terry laughingly confirmed this story. "Yes, we did spend a lot of time in the pub. Pretending we weren't there."

We put it to Gay that we got a sense from going to Winterbourne Stoke of a monastic sort of determination to actually go and invent or reinvent old music. "Yes, just to live it. And of course, the countryside was such an influence. I had a drawing of the baker who used to come up the pathway with a basket on his arm." The band recorded five songs, "atrociously balanced", for *Top Gear* in April 1969. No drums, but Maddy provided five string banjo and step dancing. Maddy and Gay sang in unison, continuing Ashley's penchant for the female voice on from Fairport, but doubling it.

The *Melody Maker's* 'Folk News' page – to which Ashley was now self-exiled – on Valentine's Day 1970 carried a brief news item to the effect that Steeleye Span were now in business. "They are seeking a percussionist, and Sandy Roberton will be producing an album next month. The group will have an electric set up, and will feature guitar, concertina, mandolin, dulcimer, banjo and mandola: they have been featuring mainly traditional material with a few contemporary numbers". Perhaps these comprised some original songs by the Woods; certainly the trad-only policy which Steeleye were later to adopt seems not at the moment to be written in stone. Tyger, Terry and Gay "will be working together until Steeleye gets under way".

The full band were destined never to play together in public. They entered the Sound Techniques studio in Chelsea on March 31st, in the heart of south-west London, although *Folk News* carried a publicity shot of them as country bumpkins, standing outside a wooden country shack, akin to the Band landing in Wessex. Ashley resembles a 19th century farm worker who has wandered into the wrong photo: there is clear space between him and the others, literally in his shadow. In his black hat, waistcoat, rimless glasses and full beard Hutchings looks more American than English, the male partner in the much parodied painting of a pioneer couple, Grant Wood's "American Gothic'" he also seems to be playing gooseberry with the two couples besides him.

Gay outlines the difficulties facing the band during the recording of *Hark! The Village Wait*? "There was a load of shite going on, but I was just so naive that I thought it was fun. It comes across as a dream that album. I love it though. Apparently lots of people think it's the best one. It's just when it ended up so badly it took the good out of it." Gay laughingly added, "I sound like a little girl. It's a lovely record."

Hark! The Village Wait was recorded in a single week. Tim Hart remembers that "a few days before going into the studio we beat Fairport 8-2 at soccer". Hutchings had been granted the run of Ewan MacColl's folk archive; he also put many hours in at Cecil Sharp House. Interestingly, given the swerve he was soon to make towards a specifically English music, these sources – as with *Liege & Lief* – were mainly drawn from the more heavily ornamented Celtic tradition.

Richard Thompson: "I think that the work that Ashley did with the early Steeleye Span was very important as it kind of established the feel. The textures on the first album in particular are still beautiful, and still actually unexplored. Their first album is fantastic. Steeleye became a commercial entity later. Personally I was always hoping that folk-rock, British style, would be, without trying, a kind of commercial thing. Really a more acceptable thing to British people, but it almost seemed to be buried."

With hindsight, it is felt that the English folk movement was in a position where the movement had some major writers like Thompson himself, Steve Ashley, the Watersons, and the Dransfields, and it was on the cusp of mass acceptance. A potential audience was there and it could have gone forward, but didn't.

Richard: "It remained a cult, slightly off to the side of music, which is a shame. Steeleye certainly were commercially successful and had hits. I think there was a bit of soul selling you know. I felt that it was a bit showbizzy. Which is a shame because the music is so strong. But yes, it was nearly there. Perhaps we were fortunate only to be on the edge of the music business, considering what a hassle it really is."

An article on 'The Hart behind Steeleye Span', published on April 24th in *Melody Maker*, announced the shock news that Gay and Terry had already quit the band. Terry recalled "The unfortunate thing was that Tim and Maddy were committed to doing club tours which resulted in a lot of tension. At that point they weren't committed to the band. Not the way Ashley, myself and my ex-wife were. They expressed interest and they said they were, but it led to a lot of problems. That was the start of a lot of hassles that eventually surfaced during the recording of the first album.

"Things weren't really good at the time between Tim and Maddy, Gay and myself. We had differences which became clearer and clearer as the recording went on. There were definitely two camps in the recording and unfortunately Ashley found himself in the middle."

The Woods felt there was a hidden agenda in that Tim and Maddy wanted to get Martin Carthy into the band. Terry: "Well that was the case because when we actually put that band together we had decided amongst the five of us, if any of the five left, that was the end of the band. That was agreed. But then the shit hit the fan, and we left London in a lot of bad feeling. We went up to my sister's and I got a telephone call to tell me that Martin Carthy had joined Steeleye Span. It had very little to do with Ashley. He never struck me as that type of person, whereas Tim was very much that type of person. Now Ashley was not very mentally strong at that point because he was still getting over that crash. I had always thought that Tim took advantage of that. It's not really the 'band of friends' ethic that Ashley and I had started out with that. We had tried not to get into all the politics and ego tripping. It left a bad taste in our mouths. And we were very badly treated with all kind of legal threats. 'If you don't give us this or you don't sign that, you won't get this and you'll never see the light of day. You'll never work in this town again.' All that crap!"

And yet the record that came out of it was magnificent. Terry reflected: "To be honest with you I never listen to records that I made. But the band was very enjoyable and it should have been and could have been more enjoyable had people not tried to make political gains. I think it would have been a great live band. We would have had to get ourselves a drummer, but we would have been really, really good on stage."

The splitting of this band was apparently due to tension between the two couples with talks of "an absolutely monumental falling out." Carthy: "I know where my sympathies lie, quite frankly, with Terry and Gay. They didn't actually fall out with Tim and Maddy, they fell out with Tim. And suddenly they had no band". It was the English couple who stayed and the Irish duo who chose to leave. Whether by accident or intent, the band – and Ashley's future career – was a deliberate plunge into just such 'Englishness'. Was Terry surprised by Ashley's later move into English music? "No I wasn't, because he was always very studious and very interested in things like that and I wasn't. I followed him with keen interest. Ashley was very, very good for English music.

"English music was to a degree like some of the Irish music, it had become genteel. English music had been sanitised. From the time of the Industrial Revolution it moved away from the working class. The English middle class got incredibly worried about the period of the late 1790s. There was the rebellion of 1798. But they were extremely worried over *The Rights Of Man*, Thomas Paine's writings and what happened in France. They were terrified that it was going to happen in Britain, because their years and years of ruling would be ended if the proletariat would take it over. Ireland was very heavily put down at that point after the Rebellion, and I think they probably did a similar thing over in England except they didn't have to use as much physical force. They did it in social ways and some of that came through in folk music. You were left with love songs and the kind of "it's lovely to be in the country" type songs. But there were few biting songs of social comment. Which is surprising really considering that most of the population migrated from the country to the towns during the Industrial Revolution. It was a strange kind of phenomenon. I'm sure that there's an awful lot more to it, and I've had a conversation with Billy Bragg about this. Somewhere along the line someone will come out with a full analysis about it.

"I haven't followed Ashley's career in the way that I would be able to catalogue what he did. Our paths kind of went away after the Steeleye thing. Gay and myself didn't really want to know Steeleye for quite a while."

Gay: "There was a lot of silliness and bitterness that went on. And I didn't quite understand it. I was 19 going on 20. I just loved life. But their agenda was to get Martin Carthy in to the band. Actually, it was horrible. It was a very awful experience for me in my life. Terry and me went up to Nottingham because it was assumed that the band had broken up. And that Friday we saw in *Melody Maker* that Martin Carthy had joined the band. For me it was the first taste of real life and that kind of shit. What did we do? We went back home to Ireland and I got a job. I never wanted to know or see Steeleye Span or those people ever again. Tim Hart and Maddy Prior had an agenda that was their personal stuff. And all the rest of us could fuck off. We were just interested in the joy of life and being musicians. But they had some other agenda going on."

Terry: "In all the bullshit that occurred, I never ever held Ashley responsible. He was kind of dragged along with it. It was unfortunate because if the band had have been left to grow in its own way, we could have had a really good band and it would have lasted for a long time. Because at the time it was most unusual to have two females in a band like that."

As Maddy Prior told *Southern Rag*, "it was a most curious band, two couples and an arbitrator. We intended to do gigs, but in a mass melée everybody seemed to leave at the end of the recording – we hadn't actually finished the record."

Terry and Gay joined Dr Strangely Strange – Ireland's answer to the Incredible String Band – and then went fully electric (and contemporary, in terms of songwriting) in the Woods Band. Gay joined Ashley, Tim and Maddy 25 years later onstage at an all-day extravaganza in London to celebrate Steeleye's longevity: in 1996 she rejoined the band, as its lead singer. Only Terry Woods has refused any contact with the band he was so briefly part of – and against which his later band, the Pogues, were so obviously a reaction.

The journalist Karl Dallas worried that early Steeleye might be confining themselves to traditional material not because they happened to like it, "but because they feel that folk song is intrinsically superior to pop. This is a way that leads to cultural elitism of the most sterile sort." Rehearsals "placed the instruments in more of an accompanying role", but the flailing technique that Terry used on electric guitar "creates a new image (of) 19th Century County Durham in terms of the 20th Century. Probably the 'folkiest' of the post-Fairport electric bands, the blending of the four available voices plays a bigger part than the instruments". He notes "There are none of the "free-wheeling" dialogues between guitar and bass than one finds in Fairport or Trees, a band who had arisen to try to fill the gap which *Liege & Lief* had left. The use of session drummers means the band lack their own defined sense of rhythm: in turn some of the songs are "metronomic".

Hark! The Village Wait was a memento of months of hard rehearsal, and it is one of those magical albums which sounds fresher as it ages. Ashley had met its producer, Sandy Roberton, through Iain Matthews, and much of the credit for its clear, rocky sound accrues to him. The main difference from Fairport was the lack of a virtuouso lead guitarist: the band was there to support the voices, not outshine them. The album shows clearly Hutchings' interest in musical texture rather than virtuosity (though he demands that as well).

Ashley later described the album as revealing "unfulfilled potential, there is so much on that album that is nearly very good." It was one of the most hurried albums that he has ever been involved with, "and I think it shows. But it's full of smashing songs, and I love the sound of the two girls singing together. It could have been a very fine album."

Ashley: "Some of the performances we shouldn't have accepted. We should have said "Right do another two takes. We can get it better." Imperfect, but in essence, full of smashing stuff. At that time not like any other album because it was significantly different from *Liege & Lief* – apart from not having jigs and reels. Funnily enough, it was quite English in feel. More so than *Liege & Lief* which I always think of being very much a British album. The material was split. Gay and Terry brought stuff in. I found a few things. Tim and Maddy brought a few things. On balance, Terry brought more material than anyone else. But I don't think that's significant. That's just the way it is. That's part of being in a group. An album that many people are very fond of, and I think that I'm fond of it. It's that kind of album. I doesn't make you say "Wow, that's great". Your heart goes out to it. It's a very touching album because of those two lovely female voices – the way they interweave. And isn't it interesting that after so many years, Maddy and Steeleye ring up Gay and say "Why don't you come and perform again?" So you know there was a certain magic in those two girls singing together."

"We also had a different producer in Sandy Roberton, who was also our manager. September Production, was a different label, a different everything. Within a year or so people started to say that Steeleye were in opposition to Fairport. But we never felt that we were. Steeleye was a folk group that was electrified whereas Fairport was a rock group playing folk music. We were significantly better."

The album title takes its inspiration from Village Waites. Ashley: "Village Waites were groups of musicians and singers who went around in times gone by,

Steeleye Span 1 at Winterbourne Stoke. 1969

playing music. Now we mistakenly believed that the singular group would be called a Wait, not Waites. We got that wrong because Waites is still singular. So we called the album *Hark! The Village Wait*. What it should have said was "Hark! The Village Waites". Which still doesn't solve the problem, because if you have "Hark The Village Waites", the man in the street would think "The Village Waites for what?" Waites for the bus to come? Waites in this sense is bad, so we knock the "s" off, thinking we were doing it right, and totally screwed up any sense."

Was Andy Irvine surprised when Steeleye Span 'arrived' with their debut album? "I was very pleasantly surprised by that album. I had no real idea as to what the music was going to be like beforehand. I don't really think that Ashley brought any significant influence into Irish Traditional Music. Neither Terry nor Gay was particularly interested or well informed in Irish music at that time, their influences being almost entirely from the American Folk Traditions. Having said that, I loved the album and thought Gay's singing of '*The Dark Eyed Sailor*' and her other songs was quite beautiful. But then both Johnny [Moynihan] and myself had always been fans of Gay! Maddys's singing was very good too and I think the album succeeded in doing what it had set out to do. I wouldn't go so far as to say joining the two traditions but certainly bringing the 'urban revivals' of both countries together. Certainly, Ashley had only one tradition to follow and this he did with energy and success and, I'm sure great personal satisfaction."

The antique atmosphere conveyed by the LP title – like an extract from Thomas Hardy – carries over into the sleeve design. Steeleye seem cut from the same cloth as the old photos of a cross-dressing lady with three dogs on a country stile, a woman with a basket, and a grim faced man holding a lantern and the spokes of a cartwheel. The band stand grim-faced, on a bridge at Winterbourne Stoke: Ashley is in full beard, dark glasses and a fisherman's hat. An insert carries thanks to the likes of Ewan MacColl and Cyril Tawney, and "The Mad Sweeney for the tree to perch on". Ashley: "They're not ancient photographs. There was Johnny Butler, our roadie and the barn out back. You see that we're getting a very studied image of rural and old. An undertaker in my case. Which is in keeping with what we've said

Steeleye Span 1 at Winterbourne Stoke. 1969

– and an extension of what happened on *Liege & Lief*."

Each song is lovingly annotated, with scholarly flourishes. The Shanachie reissue carries a photo of a pub, Dickens' Old Pickwick Leather Bottle, which boasts "unsophisticated ales and stouts, good beds". The back cover is that priceless photo of the band, with Hart cradling a kitten, and Ashley a dead ringer for one of The Band. This band exude a cool otherness, apart from a smiling Maddy Prior. A recent CD release carries more, previously unseen, photos of the folk-rock five, standing in line on a village green, and by a five bar gate. Ashley is dressed in check trousers, with a walking stick and hat, bearded and smiling. The music inside these various packages has a freshness all its own.

The album opens with unaccompanied voices foretelling "many stories concerning our forefathers' times". '*A Calling On Song*' is the successor to '*Come Ye All*', an update of those "barking" up an audience for a long-sword dance. This song and album it introduces, once factory fresh, are themselves now part of the past and of history. Hutchings' lyrics, for which he adapted a sword-dance tune, assert that "there are no finer songs in this country, in Scotland or Ireland likewise" – of lords and peasants, love and work, to "drive out your troubles", then announces "we'll play on to the beat of the drum". Cue Gerry Conway.

Ashley's bass booms beneath '*The Blacksmith*', with Maddy's harsh tones backed by Gay's softer harmonies between verses, on this "collation of texts in the Folk Song Journal". The tune was recycled from the hymn '*To Be A Pilgrim*'. Electric dulcimer and banjo play the complex beat of '*Fisherman's Wife*', a song by Ewan MacColl taken from the Radio Ballad '*Singing the Fishing*'. Remember, Hutchings was given the run of MacColl's library while researching new material. Steeleye's rendition has much of the underlying joy which Fairport formerly exuded, again carried by a rich female vocal, from Gay Woods.

'*The Blackleg Miner*' was collected in County Durham, as late as 1949. Its savagery comes straight out of living history, and broke out again in the hatred of "scabs" during the 1984 Miners' Strike which saw Scargill pitched against Thatcher. Tim and Maddy sing in unison, then a clumping rhythm section thumps in – pure rock excitement – and words evoking violence, spine-breaking and wet clay rubbed in the face. From that, straight into the beauties of '*The Dark-Eyed Sailor*'.

Concertina and Ashley's bass at its most lyrical weave through the song like spun gold. The notes compare the song to '*John Riley*', covered by earlier folk-rockers the Byrds, but learnt here from Al O'Donnell, who remains perhaps the one great revivalist singer who has never had his proper due. The Albion Band perform this occasionally on stage, to this day: it has everything that one would expect of a folk song: pathos, tension, a happy ending and a lovely tune.

'*Copshawholme Fair*' was found in Cumberland County Library, recorded on a 78, and here on 33 rpm it comes to life through Ashley's percussive bass and Maddy's dreamy singing. All the fun of the fair. It ends with an odd, clattering instrumental coda, in 6/8 jig time, created by Gay and Maddy step-dancing in the studio. Ashley himself compares this with Ralph McTell's Hardy-esque song, '*The Hiring Fair*', which continues to be a stage highlight for Fairport, and its singer Simon Nicol.

Gay: "I did a lot of Irish dancing when young. It promotes good carriage. The Clog Dancing came on to the first album. Maddy interpreted it that way. I remember teaching her a few Irish steps in the kitchen in Winterbourne Stoke. I spent a lot of time in Holland, especially up in the north, and you get all that lovely rhythm in the music. That comes from the North of England because the Vikings were always coming over in their bloody boats."

Side two of the original vinyl release opens with '*All Things Are Quite Silent*', a song about press-ganging (not so distant when you remember the contemporary Draft in the USA). The song opens like early Fairport, weaving guitars rooted down by drums and bass, and a sad female voice on top. Indeed, it is the only song on the album to feature a conventional line up of guitar, bass and drums, and Tim describes it as the "most poppy track".

'*The Hills of Greenmore*' would not go down well with animal-rights activists, but this tale of hare coursing from Armagh in Northern Ireland, is given the full instrumental welly, and Terry Woods sings with passion. The tune has all the rich ornamentation of Celtic song, and Ashley hardly needs to point out that Terry Woods brought it to the band.

'*My Johnny Was A Shoemaker*' is also from Ireland, the two girls unaccompanied, one in each stereo channel. The decision to perform this song acappella "just happened". A long electric intro to '*Lowlands Of Holland*', then a bass thrum and the vocal over a lovely rolling rhythm. Rock and *roll*. The words are from Scotland, the tune comes via Andy Irvine, and Maddy is at her most passionate in this variant on '*A Sailor's Life*', with much the same naval lilt, but lacking Thompson or Swarbrick's soloing. Indeed, there are no solos as such here. This is the second song on the album to deal with press-gangs, but Ashley says that this is "no more than coincidence". If he press-ganged Terry and Gay into the band, then they soon jumped ship.

The Scots song '*Twa Corbies*' is sung and played as a lament, bass and drums like a death march. Two ravens on a battlefield discuss the pros and cons of eating a knight, freshly slain. Ashley: "This goes back to the 13th century at least, and was recorded at Tim's suggestion. Songs that go a long way back are usually about Lords and Ladies, possibly because they were a great source of interest to people, rich and poor".

The closing song, '*One Night As I Lay On My Bed*' comes from Dorset, and was learnt by Ashley from Ewan MacColl. It rounds the album off with nightfall and love-making, delicately (not) alluded to. It makes up for the perfidy of the Blacksmith, earlier. The musicians dance around the melody, so that drums, dulcimer, banjo and bass all join in.

Gay: "'*Noisy Johnny*' didn't get on to that first record. It was such a good tune that became a bone of contention between Terry and Tim, because Tim wanted that to go on. It was an instrumental dedicated to Johnny Butler, the man who's on the back, and who used to fart a lot. He used to drive us, so Terry Woods wrote a tune called '*Noisy Johnny*'. Tim Hart wanted it to go on, but we said: "No way!" So it didn't go on."

Steeleye Span 1 at Winterbourne Stoke. 1969

The album was advertised in *Melody Maker* on 13th June, announced as "out now", and with a photograph from around the turn of the century: Morris men in black face caper in front of an audience in caps and bonnets: children watch transfixed: behind the dancers a ritual chimney sweep stands stock-still, like something beyond time. The image is mysterious and slightly comic, making the viewer aware of the timelessness of these rituals, and his or her own brief mortality.

Sandy Roberton proudly said, "I think the first album sounded so fresh at the time simply because of the players and singers. They each had a unique style or sound and the combination was beautiful. On top of that you had great songs. Had that the original line-up continued I absolutely know they would have been successful. It's a pity that personalities clashed. Fleetwood Mac managed to survive years later with much more animosity going on. On *Hark! The Village Wait*, I'm not sure if the tensions between Gay and Terry, Tim and Maddy helped get a sort of electricity on the album but it could have."

Ashley: "Terry and Gay and myself were living at Winterbourne Stoke, whilst Tim and Maddy still with their flat in Archway. When they had a break, they would come and visit for a couple of days and we would rehearse. Then they'd go off and do gigs. So we weren't as a five piece, all sitting there, all working. There was a bit of a division from the outset. When the five of us were there, I think the business of the two couples plus me, and one couple being very English, and well behaved, and the Irish being barmy, difficult and cantankerous. We loved the music, but the seeds were sown. During the rehearsals, the friction was there. Just domestic in the kitchen, problems over the food and simple things like that." Robin Denselow commented that the band cooked in shifts because they seemed incapable of eating the same food. The Irish contingent allegedly preferred Guinness and cheese sandwiches, while the appalling English stuck out for coq-au-vin.

Ashley: "Once it got to the studio we were up against it. We had to deliver a bloody good album in a very short time. In a week. Exactly. That's all we had. We had a week. And we just snapped. No-one hit anyone. There were never any fisticuffs. There was just a lot of tension. I can't give you much dirt. It was just by the time the album was finished, we just wanted to sink back and say: "Phew. Let's not go through that again." And that was the end of the band. It was absolutely, fully understood. We don't want to meet again.

"The band broke up and I went to live briefly with the Peggs in Stevenage and that's where Mr Fox took shape. And then, Tim rang me and suggested we reformed Steeleye because Martin was interested. I remember that happening months later."

Ian Maun felt "There's always been a veil pulled over the demise of that first band. The record almost came out with blood on it." Over the years there has been enormous speculation as to why the band imploded, and one reason given is the perceived one-sidedness of the material's origin. Ashley: "I'd say that without question, everyone contributed. Terry Woods is a very, very strong personality, and he'll put his stamp upon any situation. He could have chosen not to put forward a number of songs if he'd didn't want to. But we were all throwing ourselves into it. That first album has a unity in that it's crammed full of really good, short songs, that only last three and four minutes songs. Some lovely tunes, some lovely lyrics. It was a significantly different album to *Liege & Lief* – which had a couple of long ballads, sets of exciting tunes. This album was different. I think that everyone is represented fairly on the album – I really do."

It's reminiscent of The Grateful Dead going from all those long jams to *American Beauty*. And Ashley's bass playing, rather than loping, is very cut back, very restrained. Almost religious, almost puritanical. "There's something in the air, you pick up on, very often simultaneously, artists at the same time, pick up a feeling. And of course over in America, The Band were happening. And we listened to their music, I don't know if they listened to ours.

"We were married to the music. There would have been three couples living together which could have been even more difficult. We were living in a small space, in a small house, and eventually the pressure, led to the break up of the group before we did any gigs. So we just made the album. We just about made the album, to put it more correctly."

September Productions were at the epicentre of those classic "Folk-rock" albums of the early seventies. Did Sandy Roberton see them developing into a genre that could have become as popular as today's "Celtic" music pigeonhole? "Funny, at the time I don't think any of us thought that we were in a special genre. I think we all just loved the music and it happened to be popular."

"I would never had been surprised by anything with Ashley, he was very driven and was always planning something new. I've lived in the States for fifteen years now and lost touch with everyone. Looking back on those days I do think lightning struck at that moment in time in English music, with Fairport, Steeleye, Sandy Denny, John Martyn, Nick Drake, Iain Matthews, Fotheringay, Carthy & Swarbrick, The String Band, Plainsong etc. What a time!"

The ancient and the modern. The one person who did not turn up at the 1995 Steeleye Reunion was Terry Woods. Ashley: "At this time, Dave Hill, the actor who was organising the whole thing, hadn't heard back from Terry. So we started rehearsals not knowing whether Terry would respond."

At one point Terry gave up music, put his instruments up on the wall, and worked in a factory. It was The Pogues who got him out of retirement. "All I can say about Terry is that when I knew him at the end of 1969 and the beginning of 1970, he was a great friend and we got on very well together. We weren't just musicians playing in the same group. I liked him an awful lot and I think he liked me a lot. It was a sad loss. He went off with the break up of Steeleye One and I haven't seen him again."

Having been in the Pogues, how does Terry look back upon that original Steeleye period of folk-rock? Was it too genteel? "No it wasn't. For the time it was really good. It was new music and we had all sorts of great ideas. The shame of it was that we never managed to fulfil them. When I think back...you have ideas when you're young, you think: 'Can I do that?' It's great to be able to say: 'Well I had a go! And we actually started it.' OK, things went wrong, but we did have a go."

2:3
PLEASE TO SEE THE KING

Unsure, lost and still on medication, Ashley found a retreat with Bob and Carole Pegg in Stevenage in the spring of 1970. "They, bless them, looked after me but I'm obviously on pills and still not feeling too wonderful." As his spirits improved and his energy returned, they discussed forming a band. They even thought of a name – Mr Fox. But their plans were thrown awry by a single phone conversation from Tim, as Ashley recalls: "Why don't we reform Steeleye Span? I've spoken to Martin Carthy and he thinks it's a great idea." I told Bob and Carole and they were very, very disappointed and bitter. It was the end of our friendship. I don't know whether I could have handled it differently, whether I could have carried on working with Bob, and helped him with Mr Fox. But I didn't. What we did do was reform Steeleye with Tim and Maddy and Martin, and we decided that we needed another member, so we got Peter in on fiddle. We went on to have great success."

Mr Fox was a band which would play a defiantly English music, based around contemporary songs and Yorkshire folklore. As Martin Carthy recalled, "so Ashley dumped Mr Fox and left poor Bob Pegg on his bum. Bob Pegg thought he had a bass player and suddenly Bob Pegg didn't have a bass player anymore. Mr Fox was Mr Fucked! I found this out a few years later from a really startled and offended Bob … he thought that they had something going." Ashley still feels 'rotten' about this. "There are a few moves that I made that I've felt in some way guilty about. But it was a move that had to be made."

It was Tim Hart who had acted as midwife for the second Steeleye. As Maddy puts it, "so Tim drummed up another band. He said 'Why don't we ask Martin?' I thought 'we can't ask *him*', but Tim said 'why not? He can only say no'. Martin was into the idea, so we were up and running". As Tim himself told John Tobler, "Maddy and I knew Martin and I got the feeling that he might be interested in joining". Carthy joined Ashley and Tim Hart when they visited the *Melody Maker* in late April. A few days later, it was officially announced that he had joined the band. The following week, a trade announcement was made that the new four-piece group – as it still was – was managed by Sandy Roberton, and could be booked through Chrysalis. Roberton had just about despaired of the Steeleye project, when "one day, Tyger walked in with Martin Carthy. It was a case of going down to Sound City to borrow an electric guitar for him. I don't think he'd ever played one before."

Steeleye worked out its "idiom", an "organic" process based on trial and error which resulted in "innumerable rehearsals in the front parlour of St Saviour's in St Albans where they are living with Tim Hart's father". For Hutchings, "Though our music was weird, it was traditional folk songs. The business of the harmony singing was what took it through and why people gave it a chance by listening to it. It was pretty well unique and was fabulous. 'Rave On' with the glitch was the speciality." Martin celebrated joining the new – electric – band by going out and buying a blue

Steeleye Span 2 in rehearsal at St Albans. April 1970. l-r: Peter Knight, Ashley Hutchings, Maddy Prior, Tim Hart, Martin Carthy

Telecaster, but "Then I had to try and figure it out. Less is quite definitely more. I did wonders for my acoustic playing, because it taught me about space. Ashley's bas playing got quite interesting! He was underpinning and actually becoming a lea instrument."

Ashley confesses that when he now listens to the bass playing on a track lik *'False Knight On The Road'* he thinks "God, what am I doing? I don't remembe playing that!" Carthy adds "'*A Cold Haily Windy Night*'. That was another one. Wha Ashley was doing in Fairport was much more filigree than what he was doing i Steeleye – he was the rhythm section. Basically drums and bass in one." Fo Hutchings, "it was a mixture of wandering around, trying to be interesting, but als underpinning. It was a unique sound, a unique band. There was that very hig interesting sound – a combination of Martin's Telecaster, and Pete's fiddle, which i quite trebley, sounding and the dulcimer. The blend of that together was just uniqu Very suitable for the Celtic stuff." Martin hates the very sound of the 'c' word. H says, more correctly, that "it was mostly *Irish* stuff that we did. I remember Ashle got quite upset because he thought that we were doing too much Irish stuff. Hutchings contradicts this. "That was really only towards the end." But Martin insist that this was the stuff that was most exciting to play. "It was what Peter knew, and was learning off Peter."

For someone as highly respected as Carthy to plug in with this experimental ban gave it instant respectability in the folk world. Ashley pointed out that "seven or eigh years ago I used to go to folk clubs a lot but then I started playing with an electri band, so I suppose you could say this was a second wave of interest". Steeleye woul not necessarily restrict themselves to traditional material: their vision – wa "producing a good English sound in the traditional idiom". Note the word 'English now that the Irish contingent had left.

It would certainly be hard to find a more English singer than Martin Carthy, a man seemingly unaffected by his own legend, and one justly awarded the MBE for his efforts 28 years later. When we met him backstage and between sets at a Folk Festival, what struck us first was the loneliness of the long distance folk professional, always on the road alone and far from home, meeting yet another bunch of well-wishers after the show, and then on to the next gig. No wonder that the camaraderie with Swarbrick, and then within Steeleye and subsequent bands like Brass Monkey proved so stimulating.

Carthy is as extraordinary offstage as on, with a face like an animated toby jug, a man of fierce passions and crackling intellect. He came back at our questions like a champion kick boxer, feisty and not afraid to say the unsayable. The chemistry between Martin and Ashley was warm and respectful, like two veteran gangland bosses comparing notes. At first, though, the two seemed almost nervous in each other's company; after all, they had not met properly for over twenty years, outside of brief encounters at folk events. Nostalgia was the *last* thing on the agenda: these were two men still in a hurry, creatively, both looking forward to their next experiment.

The similarities between these two doyens of 'English' traditional music are startling. Both left school relatively early, and both got turned on by skiffle. Ashley was acting in imaginary plays from an extremely young age, Martin went one step further, and worked for a time in rep. Like Hutchings, Carthy discovered English folk through American music, then "decided to get into that in more detail – you can speculate for hours on how songs arise in two different parts of the country and are the same". He does recognise, though, that "the image of folk singers – the weird eccentric image other people have of them – is justified. It's a defence of other people taking the mickey."

Speaking about those crowded few months on the cusp of the seventies, when life-long careers were still at the make or break stage, Carthy recalls: "I had no understanding of what was going on at that time. And I needed that breathing space between Dave (Swarbrick) and I stopping, and getting that phone call from Tim in April of 1970, just to organise the thoughts in my head. Dave and I had been 'married' for three-and-a-half years. I'd never done a solo gig – there were three occasions when he never turned up, when he was making Thomas Hardy's *Far From The Madding Crowd*. Flounder is not the word for it. God I was in such trouble. I literally could not work without him. And I had to make a couple of decisions like I was never going to play guitar with a plectrum again. Which is rubbish, I have done. But the decision was, that I wasn't going to play anything on the guitar unless I had something to play. I just wasn't going to go...dum, ching, ching, dum, ching, ching...like I'd been doing for years. So for a while my repertoire was 65-70 percent unaccompanied."

Ashley points out what is still not widely credited, the reconstruction job that Martin does on so much of what he performs. "So many people don't know that these wonderful ballads that Martin put back into the repertoire are 80 percent his own in many cases. He's got so deeply into the music and the language of it that he is almost the only person that you can trust to rewrite the ballads."

Martin: "It's a disgusting practice and I would trust no-one to do it but myself! As far as I'm concerned, I'm not doing anything that anybody hasn't done before. That's the process. Sometimes I've accelerated it, but all these things need to be handled. The problem is leaving them in the book, what I always refer to as "The Heritage Industry". There it is, the definitive version. And that's nonsense."

"The worst case of it is the worship of the Border Ballads. You may look but you must not touch. And their attitude was around when I first became involved with this in the late fifties. You carry this precious piece of crystal to a shelf and you put it down, and everybody goes "Ooooo". And if you don't maul it around, it doesn't come to life. There's nothing that you can do to songs that will spoil them. The only thing you can do to these songs that will spoil them, is not sing them. Because if somebody screws up the songs and you think "I hate the way that person does the song", you go and you find it, and you give it a go, and maybe you get it right. Or you find someone else who's got it right. I know that I felt that when I first heard 'Lord Franklin' being sung by Bert Lloyd. I remember this guy coming down to the Troubadour and singing it. I was incensed by the way he sang it, and I went straight back and got this Bert Lloyd record out, and Bert messed around with songs all the time. It's never cool for him to say so. Far too many Doctorates, far too many professorships hang on the authenticity of all that stuff. Ewan had the same problem. He gets his Doctor of Letters, but the idea that he is actually there with his hands, working on these things is not acceptable. And I think *that's* unacceptable."

Ashley admits to doing just the same with his source material: "Martin's influenced me greatly in that respect. Because, if we don't muck around with these things and sing them, and bring them into the vernacular, they will die. Or they'll freeze, which is equally as bad." Carthy agrees, vehemently. "I don't mind it dying if you're the only person who knows the song, and you die, that's tough! If you freeze the fucker – I could kill you!" Even Ashley seems a little taken aback by the force of this reply, which seems more than mere rhetoric, and hastily concurs. "You'd have a right to. What worries me very greatly now is that of all the youngsters growing up now and coming into the music, there are literally hundreds of wonderful musicians, fantastic instrumentalists of technical ability. But how many singers are there?"

Martin looks back to how he himself became first involved with the tradition, through the skiffle boom. It was largely a matter of chance, and good luck. "I happened to go to school with Bert Lloyd's son Joe. Joe always had the best songs in the skiffle groups. I wanted to know why. "I get them from my dad!" "What's your Dad do?" "My Dad's a singer!" Which was interesting. Not "My Dad's a folklorist." And I think that has always coloured my view of Bert. He was a terminally weird singer, but there was nobody who could electrify an audience the way Bert did. Ewan couldn't do it. I'll never forget the first time I heard Bert sing 'Tam Lin' – Jesus Christ! You could watch the whole audience when he said the line "We've won my love, we've won" – the whole audience basically went up like that – WOW! It was just that his later re-workings of songs are much, much better than his earlier ones."

This love of the music was to eventually lead him to Steeleye. For Carthy, it came at a fortuitous time: "My marriage had just broken up and I'd gone out on the road for about six months. I'd arrived back in Warminster to see our daughter and the phone rang. It was Tim and he said, "Hi, do you want to join Steeleye Span?" "All right!" I went up to London about four days later, and we met and talked about it." Carthy tried out some vocal harmonies with Hart and Prior. "We sang 'The Blacksmith' in the car. We did 'Lay Still My Fond Shepherd', just as an unaccompanied thing. There were a couple of things on *Please To See The King* that we did. And that's when they rang Ashley up." Ashley: "All credit to Tim and Maddy. They asked Martin, checked him out, and then rang me and said: "Hey, we can get the band together again!""

The two authors cannot have been alone in coming to Carthy's Fontana albums through Dylan and Fairport. The closest thing today would be buying one's first

African record after exposure to the Andy Kershaw show. Contemporary folk-rock was like a whisky blended for popular taste: here, it seemed, was the original malt. Carthy, like Swarbrick, was abandoning the purism of the clubs to electrify his unique guitar style – dramatising the words he accompanied with a rhythmic force all his own.

By getting him on board, Hutchings had hit paydirt: Carthy had found in Ashley a band leader who would allow him creative freedom. But a piece was still missing from the jigsaw. Hart recalls that "we rehearsed for a while, and decided we were singer-heavy and guitar-heavy, and we wanted another instrumentalist". They chose the violinist Peter Knight, who brought his own adventurous sense of harmonics.

The fiddle added extra textural depth, and could be seen as a counterpoint to Fairport, still with a rampant Swarb, though Knight was a quieter character, both on and off stage. Peter was classically trained, at the Royal Academy of Music, and was currently playing in a folk duo with Bob Johnson. For Martin, He was "a really thoughtful fiddle player. He came for a rehearsal, and just fitted in". Maddy remembered having done "a television thing with Leon Rosselson and Roy Bailey, which Peter was on, and Martin was on the session too. Peter had been playing around the Irish pubs and Ashley had seen him somewhere else". This Celtic edge would eventually prove the undoing of Steeleye Two, but for the moment it was a unifying force. For Maddy, "Martin was into Irish styles at the time, and I was into the Irish traditional singer, Bridget Tunney, it was all very Irish at that point".

The second incarnation of Steeleye Span was a weirder and bolder beast than the first, if less sweet on the ear. One of the first group decisions was not to have a drummer. For Prior, "I'd never worked with a drummer so it was no omission for me". For Hutchings, "I didn't notice there wasn't one! I used to bang the odd drum, shake a tambourine".

The Steeleye sound was a natural development of what Maddy and Tim had been doing as an acoustic duo. Maddy: "It was more complex, more developed, and *louder*. We had these enormous Fender Dual Showman amps and only a 400-watt P.A. – nobody could hear me sing! I thought they were all daft, must be deaf, because I didn't know about things like that". Martin rejected the idea that by going electric, the band had 'sold out'. Drummerless, "it's a lot more fluid, and avoids sounding like a folk group which have gone heavy". Carthy talked to *Music Now* shortly after he joined: the accompanying picture shows a four piece, wrapped up against bitter winds. Carthy's gaunt good looks match Tim and Maddy, who look like refugees from Woodstock, and a heavily bearded Hutchings. Steeleye were "starting from scratch again. We are concentrating on traditional material, simply because nobody has come up with a contemporary song! Tyger is a compulsive newcomer, but he has compressed a lot of learning into a couple of years. He has soaked himself in the music".

Fairport had always been a song-based band, and Hutchings' whole career could be seen as an attempt at taking the popular song into new areas, while retaining a love of well crafted words and good tunes. He was now relating the timelessness of folk music to electric instrumentation. Tony Norman points out that "for him the fusion of old songs with new sounds is natural: yet Steeleye Span is a very experimental band."

Carthy takes the long view. "Most people hear the end product, like a record, and don't think about the roots beneath it. When Eric Clapton does a concert, there is a vast knowledge of his field behind what he is playing. It's the same in folk. At one end you have unaccompanied songs, at the other, electric instruments. Mixing the two is just an extension, it just has to be done. It's all music." Steeleye plan to blend together all forms of folk music. "The only reason there has been no electric folk before is lack of finance."

Carthy intended to give only half his time to Steeleye, as did Hart and Prior. "The idea of living in a van may be a knockout when you are a kid of eighteen. I'm a little older now". This lack of full-time commitment to the band (other than by Hutchings) was to eventually lead to its downfall. Robin Denselow points out that, "on stage, they looked more like a collection of individuals than an integrated unit. As an extra problem, Martin played very loud, and the sound balance was sometimes extremely strange. The music Steeleye intend to play is not just entertainment. It's a question of give and take. The song speaks for itself and you sing it straight. You lay the song down and the audience pick it up. The musicians are simply "carriers". This central problem of how to play music that is essentially a communal experience to a paying audience is something which will exercise Ashley's imagination for the next twenty years! It is a theme around which he has played many variations.

Talking to the journalist Caroline Boucher, Ashley reveals that he spends a lot time researching for material – self-consciously all of British origin – at Cecil Sharp House. "Old songs are worth keeping, they have a lot to teach us. If you have no tradition or roots on which to base your music then it's a sorry state. Music today is getting away from the modes, and it would be nice to use them again". He is referring here to the modal scales used by English traditional singers, largely swept away by the 'standard' harmonies of the European classical tradition. Modal music is based on a set of scales long out of use except in the folk tradition, and so complex that scholars like Cecil Sharp could at first hardly believe that often illiterate and musically untrained ballad singers should take such things in their stride, singing as naturally as the birds of the air . Rescuing the old songs is hard work – the band has to sort out "the right tune and lyrics" from dozens of alternatives – but it is part of a "quiet revolution", with even the likes of Traffic and East of Eden now playing traditional material. Peter Knight, who from the start proved at ease on both acoustic and electric material, was a vital cog in this new machine.

Their first-ever public appearance took place on an ATV Birmingham television

Steeleye Span 2. 1970. l-r: Tim Hart, Peter Knight, Maddy Prior, Martin Carthy, Ashley Hutchings

programme called *Music Room*. The band performed in a studio next to the *Crossroads* set. Afterwards, the producer tried taking them to dinner at Birmingham's Midland Hotel, where all except the roadie were ejected for being unsuitably dressed.

The new band then recorded a *Top Gear* session on June 27th, reprising '*The Blacksmith*', the only song which survives from their old repertoire. '*Lark in the Morning*' is a different song to that used for the instrumental medley on *Liege & Lief*. There were three new numbers, all destined to become stage favourites. Two were traditional. One certainly wasn't. Buddy Holly's '*Rave On*' was perhaps the boldest thing they ever attempted, integrating a rock 'n' roll song into the tradition, just as a large part of the repertoire of field singers collected by the likes of Cecil Sharp consisted of parlour songs, learnt from sheet music. The acappella singers here were mimicking Holly's unique hiccuping style with nasal folk voices. There is an added musical joke, from before the CD age, so that the vocals imitate a needle sticking in the groove, in unison. The performance was a mixing together of doo-wop and traditional country singing, as radical in its time as later fusions like Edward II's joining together of dub reggae and primal folk. It was also very funny. Here was a band prepared to take risks, and not always take themselves too seriously (while the import of what they were doing was very serious indeed).

Tim Hart added banjo and dulcimer to his own and Carthy's amplified guitars, Knight's fiddle – not a virtuoso like Swarbrick, more tailored to the shape of the music – and Ashley's electric bass. Carthy and Prior's voices melded at once, though in a more angular way than Maddy had with Gay Woods, with Tim adding a third harmony.

Ashley joined in with his old colleagues in Fairport in late summer, at a benefit gig for the police dependents' fund at Little Hadham on 22th August 1970. 4,000 fans were lured to the depths of Hertfordshire to witness an hour-long jam session. A photo from this unique event shows Iain Matthews and Ashley complete with bass sharing one mike, Thompson on electric guitar, Swarbrick on mandolin and Dave Pegg on acoustic guitar. Thompson compares Fairport's sojourn in Little Hadham with the Band in Woodstock: "there is a feeling of shying away from the metropolis and getting back to the roots. But there's more to it than that, it's a complete feeling". What Thompson haltingly puts his finger on here is actually a sense of retreat. It was an inner search which characterised many post-hippies in the early 70s, as well as helping to fuel the movements for sexual and racial equality, long before they hardened into political correctness.

Iain Matthews: "I went to the Little Hadham fete with Marc Ellington and we both turned up and ended up onstage doing an hour-long jam of Fairport numbers. I don't think I was on stage for that long. I only did a couple of songs with them and that was a forerunner to the Cropredy thing. We're talking nine or ten years before they had the first Cropredy."

The band now hit the road. They made an impromptu, unaccompanied appearance at the Club Tent of the Cambridge Folk Festival in August 1970. They followed a traditional song with an unaccompanied harmony version of Buddy Holly's '*Rave On*'. Tim, Maddy and Martin had worked this out as a joke to surprise Ashley, who took his folk songs very seriously. To their surprise, he not only liked it but wanted it included in the band's repertoire.

The first advertised gig was at Salford University in September, and the current authors remember a wonderful, if squashed, appearance at Southampton University Freshers' Fair, with the capacity audience startled by the power and vocal intensity of the new music. The band now entered into a gentle regime of concerts, mostly at rock clubs or concert halls. Ashley remembers that "people wanted to continue to do solo things, so we only worked a specified number of gigs. We had a strict agreement on that."

Ashley: "We have to thank Sandy Roberton for enabling early Steeleye to function, because we would limit ourselves to what work we would do. We wouldn't just say: "Get work!" We would say: "We will not work more than eight gigs a month. That's it! Eight gigs a month. But fair play to him, he kept us going. He kept us financially afloat. We weren't cashing in on our then popularity." Many early rehearsals took place at Whitehall Park. "We did our first get together in that first floor flat of Tim and Maddy's. In some ways, it's as important as Fairport's Fairport. I lived in the ground floor front, Tim and Maddy were on the middle floor, Ashley lived on the first landing and Trevor Crozier was downstairs in the back."

In October, they guested on *Folk on One*. Aside from Dylan's '*Lay Down Your Weary Tune*', based on a modal folk tune – and remember that Carthy says his greatest ever musical experience was seeing Dylan live in 1964, when such songs were still in his repertoire – the set was again all traditional.

Melody Maker carried 'Spanning the pop-folk gap', the first major feature on the new band. Hutchings almost unrecognisable with neatly brushed, shortish hair and a flowing beard. He looks at the camera with a slight leer; the rest have that blank-eyed, refugee look so popular at the time. Hart in particular is a Che Guevara figure, like a wild man from the Brazilian jungle. As for their leader, "the quiet though terribly strong personality of Tyger still burns its own way through its own particular forests of the night". Of the others, "the way that Maddy slides her voice through intervals that lie between the black and white notes of a piano, using the same sort of glissandi that you hear from a good Irish piper is nothing short of phenomenal". Modal, too. It is no surprise that she and Tim continued to be booked by the ultra-purist Singers' Club, despite their involvement in electric music. Her expertise stems from "standing up alone in front of some of the most critical musical audiences in the world, many of whom not only know the songs in all their different variants but are familiar with the original traditional interpretation."

Again, visual style came to be an integral part of the band's identity. Ashley: "We had a very strong image, with the Union Collar shirts, the collarless shirts, the clogs – three of us wore clogs, and loon pants. Ashley insists that it was not a case of determining an image in advance, like – say – Roxy Music. "It was a natural thing that developed, but I think it probably helped to reinforce the music that we were playing. You've got to wind back the clock in your mind and remember that we're talking about the end of Flower Power and the beginning of all that gaudy early Seventies' Glitter. Suddenly we're going right against it. Yet we're still sharing the bill with people like Pete Brown's Piblokto. Somehow we sat uneasily in there – but we did sit in there."

Hutchings' arcane delvings into traditional music were also part of this plunge into the collective psyche. For Thompson, the nearest things nowadays to gatherings on the village green are pop festivals. "I'm very hung up on the ways words sound … and the ambiguity of them, particularly old words. Neither us nor the people who don't like us are anything to do with real folk music. You can't call it folk music, because in any sense it's a revival, or a taking, or a changing".

In October, Karl Dallas – politically, a veteran of the New Left – surveyed the electric folk scene, and put Steeleye at the top. "They have the strongest collection of vocal talents to be gathered together since the end of the Watersons and the Young

Tradition". Instrumentally, Martin Carthy's guitar playing is "tasteful and unobtrusive", Knight is "a very fine fiddler", and Hart "does beautiful things on the electric dulcimer". Unarguable, though – is Dallas's assertion that "for all this retiring nature, Tyger Hutchings has got to be one of the best bass guitarists in Britain". The band are set to debut at Cecil Sharp House in early October, with the brothers Robin and Barry Dransfield in support. Dallas finds Ashley "inscrutable". As to his new band, "it is only in their rare and enchanting unaccompanied songs that the voices get full attention".

Martin remembers how, to begin with, "gigging was difficult. I couldn't get a grip of the arrangements. I do remember the first gig when it started to make sense and we all came off stage and looked at each other and went "Yes!" was Manchester University. Suddenly the light dawned. Now I know what to do. Now I know how to do it. I remember, for instance a guy jumping on stage – a rock 'n' roll freak – and trying to grab the fiddle out of Peter's hands, because he was so angry. I think Peter quelled him with a look. The guy realised that this was a crazy man he was dealing with. Because Peter's a lot of things, including slightly bonkers! And Peter would have done quite unpleasant things to him I think. He was pretty tough."

Ashley: "Whilst we all lived at Whitehall Park, we took the full page advert for the house out in the EFDSS Folk Directory 1971. So you've Tim and Maddy. The opposite ad – Martin – you can book him at this number. Steeleye Span – you can book them. The photographer-designer Dick Painter was on the top floor and was advertised with one of his topless models. Andy Irvine and Johnny

Advert from EFDSS. 1971

Moynahan stayed there a lot when they were on tour. So their phone number and names were down. Martin would stay there quite a lot. When he was on tour he would stay there. Then there was a period when Linda Thompson and Martin became lovers. They were an item for a short period when we had Steeleye Two which was end of 1970 into 1971."

Martin reckons that what he most remembers about Peter Knight was his reliability. Steeleye's equivalent to Simon Nicol. "PA systems weren't wonderful in those day, but for us to all sing in tune all we had to do was listen out for Peter on the fiddle. Because his intonation was absolutely right. It didn't matter what key. I didn't realise how difficult we made life for him – we played '*Lay Still My Fond Shepherd*' in B – that's not easy for a

Gulbenkian Theatre,
University of Kent poster

fiddle player. There's only one worse and that's C sharp. Listening to Peter – you pitched to him."

Denselow recalled that "On stage the band found we had to stop for long periods between songs so that we could retune. To keep audiences amused other diversions had to be found. The band were delighted to find that Peter could juggle, while Maddy pre-dated Pam Ayres with her ability to recite extremely silly poems which were written for her by Tim. As these were never recorded, here is a sample:

> *On the wild domain of the African plain*
> *Lived a rare and quite unknown yak,*
> *Who had baleful eyes, horns twice his size,*
> *And a long woolly mane down his back.*
> *Now this African yak with the long woolly back*
> *Was subject to fainting and fits.*
> *But if while in a trance you should kill him by chance*
> *You should cut him up small into bits.*
> *And if these are stewed, a love potion is brewed –*
> *Once taken there's no turning back.*
> *'Tis a love potion famed, and the best is thus named*
> *The Afro-Dizzy-Yak.*

Groans – and the guitarist had hopefully finished tuning by the time that was over. Maddy would then get the audience on their feet by dancing across the stage to the jigs.

The band were still starting over, and on November 5th took the bottom of the bill spot at Friars, Aylesbury supporting Al Stewart and the Strawbs. They were also at the cutting edge. A stray press cutting from the 'Times' sees Philip Norman unleashed on a 'happening' at the Royal Court. "Music came courtesy of Jack Bruce and Lifetime, a brief explosion of talent which booted jazz-rock into altogether colder and more bracing climes. As to Steeleye Span , they are "agreeably scruffy, ear scratching people who include a fiddler and play jigs. Their great quality is relaxation, and spreading it about". Norman considers that one of the "purest sections of Pop is that occupied by folk groups with long-haired girls, now trying out amplification". The band certainly did not seem out of place in such a setting. The theatre years start here.

The project came about thanks to Keith Dewhurst, one of the presiding spirits behind a then revolutionary tendency in British theatre, that of bringing audience and performers into a closer relationship. When he moved to the National Theatre in London, this literally became the case, with actors and musicians weaving between the audience as they stood or sat on the floor. Dewhurst and Herbert Wise had produced a television play called *Men Of Iron*, which was about the building of the Woodhead railway tunnel; they wanted folk music with a difference for the soundtrack. Dewhurst: "Martin and Dave Swarbrick did the music. One of the things they did was that opening number on *Lark Rise*, 'Rise And Pick A Posy'." They used some of the recordings that Alan Lomax had done in Barra and Lewis. Dewhurst recalls that the director Bill Bryden was interested in an American version of that kind of music. "Bill had just set up with Bill Gaskall, a festival of alternative theatre at the Royal Court called *Come Together*. As part of this festival they organised a Sunday afternoon concert in the late autumn of 1970. Sandy Denny and Trevor Lucas played the first half of the concert and Steeleye did the second."

Dewhurst asked them to become involved in his new project, a rambling epic play called *Pirates* which would be staged on a Sunday night at the Royal Court, one of London's most innovative theatres. It was directed by Bill Bryden and the rehearsals ran for three or four weeks. Dewhurst recalls that "The rehearsal time was a fantastic, magical time. We were using a company of actors who included Jack Shepherd, Brian Glover and Derek Newark. That was what go us going. It was a seed-bed." Robin Denselow later reported that "Bryden and Dewhurst had originally asked Martin Carthy to provide the music for *Pirates* but at the last minute he was too busy. Maddy, Tim and Peter filled in, driving overnight from Sunderland to start rehearsing at the Royal Court the next morning."

Dewhurst remembers that "Bill and I had already discussed doing a play with this music in it. You couldn't have or afford a set for the Sunday night. All we'd done was

Friars, Watford Town Hall poster. 5th November 1970

draw on the stage the outline of a ship with just a white line. And Brian Glover did this wonderful thing speaking to the audience, where he confided to them by stepping over the white line and saying his line of dialogue: "We can't live like native fellas!" They sang '*General Taylor*', while they were burying this guy. They played a bit at half time and they played a bit at the end as people went out. I can remember Maddy sitting in the foyer with the spoons and Tim and Peter Knight acoustic. There was a single performance of *Pirates*: the writer got £20, the actors got £5 and there was £100 or so to spend on props and costumes."

Tim Hart reveals that Steeleye Two were formed specifically as a touring band, "mainly in universities, as we stipulate a sitting audience. Our music is intended to be listened to". There are no long solos, and the set usually lasts just over an hour. "I don't think you can ask an audience to listen quietly to a group for longer than that". Their particular trick is to create a folk club intimacy in bigger venues. "When we are on stage, this incredible 'oneness' happens. Nobody in the hall feels distant. We manage to get over the barrier of having to speak into mikes". Fotheringay tried much the same with their state of the art sound system, whose expense helped bankrupt them. "I think we endear people to us rather than WOW! them. It's like the Fairport thing – the audience just feel like their friends. The stage arrangements are tight – we are not an improvising band. I think it's nice to get what you do on stage down on record".

The band took time off from mixing the new album at Sound Techniques to talk to *Sounds*. They declared there would be no drums or free reeds: "it's difficult to make a concertina tight". It was Martin who had imposed the ban on drums: "I think that we would lean too much on the drummer, whereas we lean on each other, and you can hear what's happening internally. Also it's a lot more fluid; you shouldn't use the percussion like a club". Carthy does admit to putting some of his best songs into the group's repertoire, rather than his own. Though the unaccompanied songs tend to go down best on stage, all the band put a lot of energy into musical arrangements. "For instance, with '*The Female Drummer*' I suddenly thought of a little bass riff" – this is Martin, not Ashley – "but you can't just get an idea and just shove it into the middle of a song, because if its a definite idea you've got to have things built around it". The group's creativity comes from experimenting, "hitting things by chance". What works, you keep.

Karl Dallas wrote in early 1971 about the second generation of 'electric folk', exemplifying Steeleye and Mr Fox as the leading contenders. Ashley Hutchings, he believes, "exercises incredible self-restraint in keeping his bass playing so "subsidiary" to Steeleye's total sound, often restricting himself to a simple tonic-and-dominant alternating bass which prevents him from dominating the melody instruments and voices". For all that, this is still a rock group, most exciting when electric guitar and dulcimer play in unison. In '*Lovely On The Water*', "they take time off for a change of tempo and an instrumental interlude", generating the same excitement as Fairport did with '*Matty Groves*'. One problem is that Carthy and Prior sing in an 'acoustic' style, and have not yet "adapted themselves to the different techniques needed in a rock band". They are both influenced by Irish models, Maddy by the "superlative" Brigid Tunney, and Martin by "Irish Gaelic singers like Seamus Ennis".

Perversely, the band excel in "the sheer power of their massed vocal sound unaccompanied. This was apparent from the 'sneak preview' at the Cambridge Folk Festival. Their version of '*Lay Down Your Weary Tune*' brought out the power of Dylan's words far more than Byrds had on record. "I like the pleasant clashes of harmony caused by overlapping the end of the chorus with the beginning of the next verse".

On New Year's Eve, Steeleye played to a boisterous audience in Plymouth. David Harris reckoned that "Hutchings has infused much of his old group's English country jig sound". Their two hour gig was praiseworthy "not for instrumental adaptability but vocal brilliance". The voices of Prior, Hart and Carthy soared over "good solid British traditional folk music", with "some tight, precise work from Peter Knight on mandolin/fiddle and Tyger Hutchings". This was interlaced with three American spirituals, four or five unaccompanied harmony songs, and a "spot of 'poetry' from Miss Prior", and the inevitable '*Rave On*'. Hutchings' songbook includes the words and music to the unrecorded '*Beg Your Leave*', a four piece pace-egging song, "each one taking a character's part, virtually unaccompanied". This was originally sung by men known locally as 'jolly-boys', Easter-time mummers.

Steeleye might draw on ancient roots, but they flowered in rock strongholds like the misnamed Country Club in Belzise Park. Here they headlined over heavy-rockers Paladin, and in the same week as Uriah Heep. Ashley kept busy as a session man. On Iain Matthews' debut album, he joined Thompson and Nicol, alongside Dolly Collins on flute organ. Iain dedicates the album, perhaps ironically, to "Fairport Convention, who showed me new directions". The door for one.

On the first and eponymous Mr Fox album, Bob Pegg and Ashley are given co-writing credits on '*Mr Trill's Song*', another portrait of an eccentric, following the pattern established in '*Mr Lacey*'. Mr Trill is a folk dancer, and his band sounds suspiciously like Steeleye One: "two pairs to dance/two pairs to play". The song breaks into a joyous electric jig at the end. Ashley also wrote the words to '*Salisbury*

Plain', with funereal music by Carole. Based on traditional motifs, and with links to '*Farewell, Farewell*' – winds blow bleakly in both songs – this is a Hardyesque parable set near Stonehenge, at a time of war. Carole sings it with all the cold control which June Tabor would later command. Cannons fire, their "echoes shake the plain" – and seagulls chase the plough. Girls "once flocked to see the blues", soldiers in all their finery, but no more. The song ends with an ancient riddle: "when will there be a bull without a horn/and I say when there grows a rose without a prickly thorn". Co-incidentally, Shirley Collins sings the traditional song of the same title on her and Dolly's 1970 album *Love, Death and the Lady*, an album which is supposedly, much to her surprise, used as a primer for witchcraft.

Mr Fox also boasts one of the finest and most sinister front covers of the whole post-psychedelic era. Pegg's sleeve notes attribute the same atmosphere to the Yorkshire Dales, "innocent" fields which might swallow up a man whole. Hutchings also took part in another Sandy Roberton project, *49 Greek Street*. It was a nostalgic look back to the Soho folk scene, with songs from the likes of Andy Roberts and Mike Hart (both members of the Liverpool Scene) and Keith Christmas, with his drugs parable '*Robin Head*'. For no apparent reason, these solo performers are backed by a rock band, the hastily assembled '49 Greek Street Rhythm Section' in which Ashley is joined by the acoustic bass of Danny Thompson, guitar genius Martin Stone, and Tim Rice. The missing connection between *Lark Rise to Candleford* and *Evita*, perhaps.

Steeleye was a band full of inventiveness. The way the new line-up played only served to confirm Karl Dallas's later comment: "the whole direction of the band changed, becoming not only more 'folky' (in the sense that the Band are more folky than when they accompanied Ronnie Hawkins) but also heavier, more basic". March saw them on *Top Gear* storming through two reels, '*Prince Charlie Stuart*' and a sea-shanty medley of '*Bring 'Em Down/A Hundred Years Ago*', alongside another surprise, their new rock 'n' folk cover version of '*Let's Dance*'.

Martin Carthy was interviewed in *Disc* – beneath a photo of the band, with 'folkie' Martin in a black leather jacket, and 'rock star' Ashley in full beard and rustic hat, holding a long pipe, and kicking out his left leg. *A Hard Day's Night*, it isn't. Maddy, in what looks like a monk's habit, clings onto a sombre Tim, and laughs with eyes closed. He still, though, recalls their first gig with horror: "it was the country of one-eyed men, and no-one to hold onto. The PA was terrible". It does not now bother him that he is playing the same venues as, say, Emerson Lake & Palmer.

The archaic grammar of *Please To See The King* is matched by its hessian sleeve, with the 'S' of Steeleye twined around a drawing of a man ploughing the fields with two horses – *very* Thomas Hardy – and a photo of the band creased as if with age. "One of the finest logos ever to grace a roadie's T-shirt", as *Liquorice* put it. Released in Spring 1971, the album has certainly dated more quickly than its predecessor. Ashley is in his stripy trousers, clear glasses and rustic hat, clean shaven again. Sandy Roberton again produces, and the singers or collectors of the songs resurrected here are all carefully thanked.

Please To See The King was recorded in "bits and pieces" at the end of 1970. Tim Hart and Maddy Prior were concurrently recording their own album, *Summer Solstice*. A very stoned Bob Marley and the Wailers were recording in an adjacent studio. At that point, far from superstars, they were doing to reggae what Steeleye were doing to folk, retooling it with a rock beat and a contemporary attitude. Both bands were totally serious about what they were doing; just compare, though, Marley's political commitment, and the profound effect his music was to have not only on fellow West Indians, but on black culture worldwide with what in Steeleye's case remained a marginal eccentricity. Draw your own conclusions. Also around were members of fellow Island bands Free and Mott the Hoople, who "used to come in and ask us for smokes".

The resulting album was just as passionate and musically unique as anything that even Marley came up with, though Hutchings now reckons that "from the technical point of view, it's not good. The actual sound quality is poor, but it's a terrific watershed, it's just a very important album. When it appeared, there was nothing that had been like it before". Martin Carthy remembers that "the Leslie speaker produced a very distinctive organ sound". Mike Ratledge had been an early adherent, in his work with the Soft Machine. "It was one of the few sounds at the time, one of the few treatments you could give to an instrument. There was fuzzbox, there was wah-wah, and there was Leslie. I think flanging was just appearing, and people who flanged stuff were thought of as very weird".

Ashley: "I find it very, very difficult to listen to because of the recording quality. It's rough, it's very piercing. But people listen to it, because they can see through the technical drawbacks. It's part of its time. It was a combination of the high pitch sound of the electric dulcimer, the electric fiddle with a very unsophisticated pick-up, and Carthy's very staccato, very treble sounding guitar. Everything was quite high, there was very little down below. Only me. The bass playing is a bit different, a bit special, because no-one had done that before. No-one had tried to play British folk music in an electric context without a drummer, and so I was filling in lots of areas. That was fascinating. It was very unusual. I couldn't recreate that again, that's the interesting thing. I listen to those records and I think: "I couldn't play like that now!" I was able to concentrate on those bass patterns, because we were doing traditional song."

Hutchings explains the origins of the title *Please To See the King*. "This time we got it right. "*Please To See The King*" was spoken by the wren boys, when they came to the door to collect the money on St Stephen's Day – in other words, will you give us some money?" This album has on it '*The King*', the wonderful, wonderful wren song that Martin brought into our repertoire." Each of the group's members brought songs in, to varying degrees. Ashley: "I didn't bring a lot in as I was with the heavyweights: Martin, Maddy and Tim, all of whom had been leading the folk scene for some years. So '*Cold Haily*' was Martin, '*Prince Charlie Stuart*' was Maddy. I might have helped on finding that one. '*False Knight*' was Martin. '*Female Drummer*' came from The Watersons. '*Lovely On The Water*' might have come from me. '*Boys Of Bedlam*'. It was Martin who brought that in. During this period I'm doing a lot of study, a lot of research, building up my knowledge of the music, and coincidentally, stumble upon Morris Music.

"Steeleye Span had a totally unique sound. Augmented largely by the electric dulcimer. That was Tim Hart – a good dulcimer player. Angular. I always think of that album as being a sharp sound. You could cut yourself on it. It's too sharp really. I find the vinyl almost impossible to listen to. The CD is actually better. We were pretty loud on stage, even though we didn't have a drummer. We had big Fender stacks. We weren't afraid to push the volume up. Carthy played very loud on stage. We were all playing these interweaving lines. It was quite sophisticated and primitive music both at once." The band gigged prior to the recording of *Please To See The King*. "It was the longest album coming that I can remember. People were saying, "When's your album coming?" It felt like a year. It was finally released in March 1971."

Martin thinks that "Sandy Roberton had no idea how to produce it. There were no drums to stick in the middle. He had to think about painting a different kind of picture. And it's very innocent, quite boneheaded at times. But it's a very truthful album. It's got that excitement and magic." In a music weekly feature Sandy Roberton stated: "There are special problems with recording acoustic groups. It's difficult to record the guitar and voice. It just isn't because most folk artists need to play and sing at the same time and you get a lot of leak from the guitar onto the vocal track. An acoustic guitarist loses his feel if you put the voice on afterwards. It just sounds straight and lifeless." The sounds that Steeleye were pioneering here were as weird – and 'ethnic' – as anything which the Wailers were developing in the next studio. Dub folk-rock, anyone?

The album opens with a re-arrangement of '*The Blacksmith*', the first trad song on the previous album too, but here far more radical, with slashing electric guitar chords, no drums – bass carries out the percussive duties – and not as easy on the ears. Gone are the soft Irish vowels of Terry and Gay, and Gay's concertina, as is any sonic comparison with early Fairport. Here, Maddy sounds vengeful rather than sad, as before. It is a deliberate restatement of policy, a tougher and more radical take on electric folk rock. The folklorist Neil Philip has pointed out "how underrated the album was – Hutchings plays lead bass, and defines a sound that doesn't return to English traditional music until Eliza Carthy's *Red* – much praised for its mingling of trad with drum'n'bass, but, great as it is, it is rooted firmly in the sound of a record made by Hutchings and her father 25 years before".

Martin Carthy is the first voice on '*Cold Haily Windy Night*', then Prior comes in, and violin wails on this ghostly tale. Hutchings carries the melody, with the other instruments accenting the beat. The song has much the same story as '*One Night As I Lay On My Bed*', again told by the woman, but whereas that was joyful and tender, this is harsh and bitter. Next up are two jigs, '*Bryan O'Lynn*' and '*The Hag With The Money*', which sound odd and somewhat incomplete without drums. They do confirm, though, Hart's comments on Peter Knight, "he wasn't just a fiddle player, he was a trained musician … Martin and I wanted someone who was a bit more than an ear-playing fiddle player, someone who could read music and understand arrangements".

'*Prince Charlie Stuart*' has Prior at her most nasal, praising the Young Pretender, to a strummed backing, imitating the swirl and melody line (on fiddle here) of bagpipes. Of '*Boys of Bedlam*', the insert explains that the 13th Century Priory of St Mary became a famous lunatic asylum; this, hundreds of years before the British government's 'care in the community' policy released such inmates onto the streets. Carthy and Prior both sing into the back of a banjo, (like a primitive echo-chamber) set against simple percussion, then in comes bass like a bell tolling. The rhythm picks up, and sinister words about making mince-pies from men's thighs adds to the jollity. The whole thing has the gleeful gallows' humour of Alfred Hitchcock, tied to the riddling of '*Nottamun Town*'.

In '*False Knight On The Road*' a boy outwits the devil, and Carthy's low, sneaky vocals undercut a musical backing which seems to cut the air as it leaves the speakers, on vinyl at least. For a drummerless band, this is a very percussive track. '*The Lark in the Morning*' is the first truly gentle thing on the album, with nimble bass and Knight coming into his own on the instrumental passage, though with a musical pattern rather than a lead break. Something close to a rock riff opens '*Female Drummer*', though. Medieval cross-dressing, and both band and Maddy sound exuberant. A song for the women's movement, now on the ascendant: female empowerment in action.

The song turned up again, alongside '*Reels*' on the 'b'side of a single release of the stage favourite – and light relief – Buddy Holly's '*Rave On*', which could have been an off-centre hit, but wasn't. Ashley sang the number on-stage, but not on the single. As Tim Hart remembers, "Maddy, Martin and I spent a lot of time driving together at that time, and, being singers, sang for much of it. Our spontaneous in-car version of '*Rave On*' had made us laugh, so when we arrived we sang it to Ashley to make him laugh, and instead he solemnly said he thought it was very good, and we should record it". As a former rock and roller, now the "purest folkie of all of us", the rendition had originally been designed as "a joke for Tyger". Carthy adds that "If you listen very carefully at the end, you can hear two blokes talking, that was Dennis Jordan the roadie and I, walking down the stairs talking stupid stuff, we pretended to be a couple of delivery men talking about the group we'd just heard singing: "What a load of bloody rubbish"."

The single was launched with a full-page advert, supposedly with the pressing plant reporting a fault in the master copy. Sandy Roberton replies "it's meant to be like that ... it's a joke. That's how they do it on stage, as a finale number". Roberton visits the pressing plant, "somewhere in West Middlesex", and the entire department comes to a halt. As the Quality Controller comments, "we've had some queer ones in our time ..."

The CD reissue of *Please To See The King* now includes '*Rave On*'. '*The King*' yields the album's title. As Hutchings now asks, "how did they catch wrens, because they're very fast? But that's a great calling-on song". Carthy leads in a typhoon of a chorus, with the sharp edge of contemporary singing combos like the Watersons – whom he later joined – or the Young Tradition, one of whose members Ashley was later to snaffle for *his* next band. It now sounds one of the freshest thing on the album, especially on the toned-down CD mix. '*Lovely On The Water*' opens with mandolin, and Maddy's voice soars, though you can't hear all the words. The band suddenly change key, and the middle break is almost West Coast, with questing guitar, and raga-like in its rhythmic pattern. There are definite echoes here of '*A Sailor's Life*'. Maddy comes back sounding melancholy, and the album ends on a haunting note, with the cannon's roar and an unresolved final chord.

The musical line-up on the album is odder than before, Prior on spoons, tabor, and tambourine, Carthy on guitar, banjo and organ and Hart on guitar and dulcimer. Ashley plays electric bass, as does Knight, along with fiddle, mandolin and organ. All are credited with joining in on bells, an incorrect credit, as not one bell can be heard throughout the album. Looking back, Maddy Prior comments, "that was a very experimental album – we were trying things that hadn't been done".

Sandy Roberton remembers that at that point "we were all pushing each other to make great records and there was an innocence to it all as well and an enthusiasm that I don't see so much anymore. The business has crept into music so much now that it's more about marketing and style over substance. In those days as a manager I just did a bit of everything – get the bookings, press, deal with the label, tour manage – it was fun." *Please To See The King* was ignored by *New Musical Express* – still for pop kids – but received a rave review in *Melody Maker*, which made it their Folk Album of the month: "the uniqueness of Steeleye Span is that they unite British tradition and electric equipment in such a devastating union. The variety of the material heightens the effect".

Jerry Gilbert finds the way Carthy has been integrated "a joy". In '*Cold Haily, Windy Night*', "the familiar voice is projected by a thumping bass and fiddle swinging away in support. The highlight of '*False Knight On The Road*' is "the unusual metre and accentuation, and the way the voice is used as another instrument". He too notices the "repetitive Indian theme guitar riff" on '*Lovely on the Water*' which "suddenly changes key, and breaks into an echoed, nostalgic Shadows-style middle section". It is an album "full of subtleties and the unexpected". The lack of percussion gives it a flavour all its own.

Unlike Steeleye's debut, *Please To See The King* was a UK Top 50 hit in April 1971 and also topped *Melody Maker's* folk album chart. It set the pattern for Ashley's future ambitions. The feeling the album (still) evokes is best put by reviewer Pete Scrowther, "a perfect musical statement of an indefinable attachment I feel for this island, an awareness of some kind of tradition of Albion stretching back into the mists of time". It strikes a chord "which, like the album itself, is tuned to a sense of *place.*"

Sounds described Hutchings as a "quiet genius". "He has remained hidden behind conspicuous dark glasses and a front line focal point of ambassadors to the folk revival". The photograph beneath this interview is extraordinary: in clear glasses and under something close to a bowler hat, with long hair streaming behind, a clean-shaven Ashley looks like a music hall comedian. Hutchings points out that "I'm sure we've only just scraped the surface of what we can do". The main problem is the lack of practice time, due to the others' commitments – "the group isn't as tight as it should be".

Steeleye met noisy opposition from parts of the audience on some gigs supporting one-time blues band Jethro Tull, whose Ian Anderson osmosed his support band's style for later use (and was later to take over Fairport personnel wholesale). The March tour opened at the Gaumont State Theatre, and took in major venues like Brighton Dome and Blackpool Opera House. At the Empire, Edinburgh, the band were beseiged by fans who came crawling up the drainpipes looking for Tull. The reaction to Steeleye gained the band a new and wider audience. Ashley remains determined to carry his explorations further. So far, he has thought "purely along one line of traditional material" when choosing songs. "For instance, all the tunes we have played have been Irish, and the same goes for the Fairports. But English Morris dance tunes haven't been touched at all, and this is a major field that could be tackled by somebody". It turned out to be Ashley himself.

University of Essex poster. 6th May 1971

Liege & Lief had a "negligible" effect on rock music, but "it has turned the folk scene upside down, which is not what I expected". With typical honesty – this is *not* the thing to say when granted a precious slot to push new 'product' – he admits to preferring the first Steeleye album to the more technically ambitious *Please To See The King*. Maddy Prior found that touring as support to Jethro

Tull "was hard work, because we had to be a lot more organised, with a tighter act. Usually we go at our own speed ..." In April, they received a standing ovation at the Inverness Festival, on a bill which also featured Shirley Collins. Steve Sheldon remembers a less prestigious but equally musical gig at Trent Poly, where they were supported by Tir Na Nog. Admission was 50p on the door.

Robin Denselow recalled that Steeleye had agreed to appear in a special television show in which they would play alongside Fairport Convention, on Ainsdale beach, just north of Liverpool. It was arranged that a token crowd of 200 should come along as the audience. Unfortunately a Liverpool newspaper got the story totally wrong and announced that it was to be a free festival. The result was utter chaos when 5,000 people turned up. As more and more people kept arriving, the man operating the generator brought proceedings to an abrupt halt by driving the generator van away. It was then that the gallant Ainsdale police, all three of them, arrived to tell of another 5,000 people boarding trains in Liverpool. The resulting 10,000 furious fans first demolished the empty stage, then promptly set fire to it.

During the summer of 1971 the band were making another giant step in Ashley's career, providing the incidental music for a new play, Keith Dewhurst's *Corunna*, which opened for a week "upstairs" at the Royal Court. An announcement of this in the news pages of *Melody Maker* has a wonderful photo of Ashley seemingly wringing his hands in triumph, in collarless shirt and cufflinks. Tongue in cheek, he contributes to an *NME* musicians poll on his peers. He gives his three favourite bass players as Chris Hillman of the Byrds, Rick Danko of The Band, and Rose Simpson of the ISB! In the same spirit, Jack Bruce has only one choice, J.S.Bach. Steeleye and some of the actors from *Corunna* then embarked on a short provincial tour, performing extracts of the play, and accentuating the music.

Trent Polytechnic poster. 7th May 1971

Hutchings missed most of the play's rehearsals at the Irish Centre in London, suffering from severe food poisoning: "I got off my sick bed for the dress rehearsal having learned my lines in bed...luckily my main role, apart from playing the music, was narrator. We all had a role, and my role as Narrator didn't have moves to rehearse." Steeleye and some of the actors from *Corunna* then embarked on a short provincial tour, performing extracts of the play, and the music. Martin Carthy reminiscences that they travelled "in a coach with all the actors and all the gear, and did a tour of thirteen universities. We had to get there early every day and we had to rehearse it because each space was different. One

Corunna Tour Programme. June 1971

[stage] in Kent had an enormous long apron and a trap door; we tried to figure a way of using the trap door. It was just like a panto."

Carthy believes that Keith Dewhust was drawn to their musical expression of Englishness: "It was an English band playing English traditional music, which he liked, in a very dramatic way." Dewhurst had had the idea of *Corunna* when he saw the television version of *The Jolly Beggars* by Robert Burns, and decided to write: "I tried to sell it to Stella Richmond who was the Head of Drama at ATV. She asked if I could think of an idea for a play at Christmas. it must have been about 1964-65. I wrote a tiny bit of it, one lyric, the lyric that Martin Carthy sang in the show. ATV didn't want to know. And then when I met Bill, well, we're on! We rewrote it because we realised early on that Tim Hart was not as good an actor as the others, although his contribution to the music was considerable. I think that Tim had an inferiority complex in the presence of people who he knew were 'bigger' than him."

Keith Dewhurst had read English at Cambridge where he was inspired by the teaching of F.R. Leavis. Like Ashley, a football fanatic, he was for a time the travelling reporter with Manchester United after the Munich air crash, but found his real niche as a playwright. Martin Carthy: "Keith is very much for immediacy is Keith. I remember I did a play *The Battle of Waterloo* and he really wanted to do one thing, but didn't quite have the nerve to suggest it – he loves his alienation – he wanted somebody dressed up in the uniform of the particular Regiment, to be leaning on the camera, and to be talking to the cameraman. With his rifle and bayonet."

Dewhurst: "I was very interested in theatre outside of the proscenium arch. In every theatrical epoch the suspension of disbelief occupies a slightly different area. And the writers are always trying to nudge it. Of course a crucial way of nudging it was to have a band, as they address the audience directly. And the front man of a band actually speaks directly to the audience. So when I wrote *Corunna*, I wrote a very specific part for the front man who was Ashley.

"In *Corunna* we needed Ashley, but later he needed us. I cannot emphasise too much how at that stage in his life he merited the nickname Tyger. He was young, in his prime and bushy tailed. "Tyger, Tyger burning bright!" During the course of rehearsals, I made his part bigger. We had to do a costume change and needed time, so we gave him a much longer speech. He was acting the part of the host, but he wasn't acting. I mean, he was acting the persona of Tyger Hutchings and he did it awfully well. The first night of the tour in that beautiful theatre at Kent University, a lovely theatre that was absolutely packed. The show went fantastically. There's this thing in *Corunna* where the French cavalry come on hand-held horses, and they did the thing finely. They all went off and people chanting and clapping, and Ashley came on with one of these things and said "I've brought on a friend to say goodnight!

"At Harrogate, Jack Shepherd had a few drinks too many before he went on and started being a bit silly. And on stage, in full view of the audience, in a very good way that worked, Ashley came right down to the front of the stage with his guitar lead and got Jack together, as though it was all part of the play. He was very much in command of the evening and the whole event. He was *the* Captain. It did deliberately use the front man of the band to do that. I don't suppose Tim Hart could have done that. Ashley rose completely to the event.

"The band was integral to the action in *Corunna*. It was done at the Theatre Upstairs on a stage and a ramp going down through the middle of the audience. When we took it on tour, we had to re-rehearse it for the various venues. But if we could reproduce those conditions like in the Student Unions and in the Country Club at

The assembled cast of Corunna! line up for the French army scene. June 1971

Hampstead, we would create a space like that with the stage at the back.

"Canterbury was a theatre on the campus, Hornsey wasn't. We played Harrogate, Liverpool and Manchester. Those were three great gigs. We also played Canterbury, the Country Club at Hampstead, Croydon's Fairfield Hall, and Southampton University. Audience numbers went up and down.

"At that time Ashley was in the background. It was Sandy Roberton who ran the tour. If you look at the poster, it says September Management and the Royal Court present. The show was actually a huge underground hit. This is in response to the fact that posh papers didn't realise what it was. They did review it but didn't realise what it was either in terms of it as an artistic event in itself, or what is implied in trying to get the theatre outside.

"Besides the actors and band, the tour was run by a very small coterie. There was Di Seymour (Designer), Sally Crocker (Stage Manager) and Deborah Morris (Wardrobe), Dennis Jordan (Road Manager) and Gordon Grahame (Sound) and that was it. It was almost like a rock tour. In some places there was no stage at all. We had to move tables and everything and make a stage up. So the tour was a fantastic event. The production was obviously so ground breaking. But because it was on and off, who knew it was ground breaking?

"It was in Manchester that Jack Shepherd shouted at the man in the audience, who was desperate to go to the loo. Jack had this huge speech at the end when the man got up. Shepherd stopped the speech and said "BASTARD!" Then went on with his speech. Peter Knight played this guy that had his tongue cut out and could only speak on the violin, on the fiddle. Which was quite effective as he was a marvellous actor. But Mark McManus was a great actor. He was England's John Wayne except he never got the chance to be. The company that worked at the National Theatre was actually from the Royal Court. Glover and McManus were the midfield generals. And they were there right at the beginning, and they're sadly all dead now.

"*Corunna* was never recorded or filmed, although the band did record a Radio 1 "In Concert" show and some of the music was part of that broadcast. Parts were also on the band's *Please To See The King* and *Ten Man Mop* albums.

"The Royal Court then had an offer from Michael White, the producer of *The Rocky Horror Show* to transfer *Corunna* to the Young Vic, but the band wouldn't do it. I'm sure Michael could have covered his costs within that time. Our cause would have been immeasurably advanced if only the band would have given us six weeks. An audience could have gone and watched it again. There was a whole period of not being sure whether they were going to do it. Nobody quite understood the politics of who ran the band and who didn't. When Joe Lustig later managed Steeleye, all business dealings were done through him. If there was a refusal, Joe conveyed the refusal. If there was an acceptance, Joe conveyed the acceptance. You didn't get this at this time. Roger Croucher threw a tea-party at the Theatre Upstairs. We had a big cake and all the members of the band went, except for Ashley. It was his attempt to persuade them to go. I was amazed to read some eight years later that the band broke up over this issue. I was so pissed off with them I never discussed it. We assumed at the time that they didn't stay because they could make more money touring than we could pay them in the theatre."

Tim Hart believes that *Corunna* was one of the contributing factors to the demise of Steeleye in that the whole band wanted to do the Young Vic, with the exception of Ashley. And his views prevailed. Dewhurst: "I'm sure that is probably true. Was Sandy running the band? Was Tyger running the band? Was the band democratic? That was never confronted really because (a) we wanted to work with them again and (b) we wanted to stay friends with them personally. All those things should actually have been confronted."

When asked what did the band actually contribute to *Corunna*, Dewhurst replied "The music!" Surprisingly, he dictated what was included. "I said this is what tune you'll play here! The thing about musicals is, if you get the book right, if you get the narrative right, the music can then work its magic. That's why Wagner was no fool and called himself a music dramatist. He knew that if you got the story right then the music would take you into another world. If you don't get the story right, it's disaster.

They think the music will do it on its own, but it won't. So if you do a play and you
have a band in the arch and can play this stuff, you've got to finish on a big tune.
Because the tune will sum up all the emotions of the evening. And the first time that
I did it was in *Corunna*. At the end of the play, Jack Shepherd's character comes back
from the war and goes back to Manchester. And Manchester's completely changed.
He says "I can't remember what the England we fought for was like. What was it
like?" And the band answers the question with '*Lark In The Morning*' which was a
sensational piece of theatre."

"This is what all the source of friction between Ashley and the theatre is about.
If Ashley wants to write the play, let him write the play! But Ashley can't write a
play, unfortunately. We would say 'we should really have this song, and should
really have that song'. These were all key songs. In some places I had written lyrics
or left bits where I said they should write them. They should come up with
something. We'll listen. We'll audition the song. Tim said this is the song to do and
did '*The Wassail Song*'."

Corunna took as its subject the British Army's retreat during the Peninsular War.
Dewhurst's play reintroduces a link between traditional song and acting, ritual even.
A review in *Sounds* rejoices that "folk theatre lives. The rustic environment and the
willingness of actors and musicians to meet each other half way expedited its
success". The audience sat at trestle tables on both sides of a narrow platform. If
Steeleye's talent as actors was sometimes in doubt, "at least the roles were cast
perfectly, and the music lively and well executed". It was less a musical than a folk
opera, with '*Cold Haily Windy Night*', '*Gower Wassail*', '*The Female Drummer*' and
'*Lark in the Morning*' – "so nostalgic that it hurts" – all neatly integrated into the
action. Another highlight was '*The Mountains of Spain*', a new song. The play ends
back in an England laid waste by the Industrial Revolution. Ashley and Tim sing lead
vocals on '*Song of the Advertising Copywriter*', wearing shades, and delivering lines
like "In my polaroid glasses/I despise the masses".

Corunna! June 1971

The professional actors included Brian Glover as Blacker-Me-Boy, "the robust, rough-neck of a rifleman", and who confessed himself a convert to folk-rock after the run. The riflemen turn away from fighting to "lust, looting and drink": they return to an England rent apart by industrial change, but the play ends not in bloodshed but with a dance. The production shows the benefit of "taking the theatre to the people", an aim shared by contemporary troupes like Hull Truck and Welfare State International. Indeed, the programmed trumpeted how *Corunna* was "the first attempt to make such a play and then take it to the various halls in which a pop group normally appears".

One review reckoned that "the narrative was well carried by Tyger Hutchings". Peter Knight was excellent as Drummy, an "idiot fiddler", and one of the most moving scenes went to Martin Carthy, when he sang '*Johnny Trap's Lullabye*'. Mark McManus – later to find TV fame as Taggart – gave a dramatic rendition of the poem '*The Burial of Sir John Moore*': he also played Moore. Other actors included Jack Shepherd (whose distinguished TV credits include the lead part in *Wycliff*), and Juliet Ackroyd playing Mrs Hudson, "widowed, raped and insane". Mike D'Abo of Manfred Mann was in the audience, and during the finale "could restrain himself no more, and leapt on to the stage to join the dance".

The tour programme declares "that Steeleye Span should act and sing in a historical piece is appropriate because they are the foremost exponents of the folk music of a vanishing England". Interviewed by *InCant*, Ashley is asked if there is an "educative" purpose in his music? He replies, "Hmmm, down in the jungle" (does Tarzan impression with gargling noises and finger in mouth). "I suppose there is a tiny element of the missionary in there. But when I notice it, I get worried". Of Martin, "like me, he got disenchanted pretty quickly with rock bands". Ashley also expresses himself doubtful about his own songwriting. "It doesn't follow that if you're a good musician you can write well. Frequently the opposite".

Karl Dallas joined the tour bus to Southampton. At a Little Chef, Tyger and Brian Glover talk of *The Rank and File*, a TV play in which Glover appeared. They reach the university at 2pm to find the place in chaos, and with only 6 hours to build a stage, set up the gear, and rehearse. All is ready on time, and "Tyger's commentary is somewhat reminiscent of his dry, humorous chat between numbers at concerts". Afterwards, the Director Bill Bryden gives the cast a backstage slagging-off for "a lousy performance", although the band has been called back for two encores.

Also in June, Radio 1 recorded an hour of Steeleye in concert, compered by John Peel and featuring music from *Corunna*. Martin: "I remember we used to do some shanties, we did '*Bring 'em Down*' and there's that wonderful verse in there about "Liverpool born, Liverpool bred, strong in the arm and thick in the head." And when we finished: "I'm not sure that I approve of that!" A good chap was John. Peely and Whispering Bob were always using us a lot. It wasn't that unusual for us to do maybe three or four of Peel and three or four of Bob Harris sessions a year."

Steeleye also appeared at the 'Folk In', a six hour spectacular of song and dance put on at the Festival Hall by the EFDSS. They joined a bill which ranged from the Spinners to the Bampton Morris Men, the Copper family from Rottingdean to the High Level Ranters from Tyneside. The Monkseaton Sword Dancers performed a "riotous" mummers play. In a photo in the *NME*, Ashley sports a fine pair of flared trousers, while Carthy – similarly attired – holds his electric guitar like a machine gun. Hart sits down, studying his dulcimer. Ashley still evoked suspicion in some quarters. At the Festival Hall, his band was introduced with the words "and now we have Steeleye Span, because no one else could follow that loudly".

In July, Steeleye played what was officially described as 'A Concert of Contemporary and Traditional Folk Music' at Tupholme Manor Park, Lincoln. Sandy Denny was accompanied by Richard Thompson, Dave Pegg and Gerry Conway – as 'The Happy Blunderers' – and gave one of her greatest performances, largely of new self-written songs. It was a reminder of what Ashley had walked away from.

Martin: "Lincoln was the festival where Swarb and I did our "Reunion Hour" right at the end. They had us billed to close the festival. Buffy Sainte Marie was supposed to do a 25-minute set, and she stayed on for 50. Dave and I were waiting to go on, getting colder and colder and colder. And I thought the unthinkable: "Fucking Custer was right!" Sorry Buffy! We finally got on, with this huge crowd of some 50,000 people in front of us. I was looking out on the right hand side where these beautiful wooden toilets had been built. The audience were freezing and somebody torched them, whoosh, and set fire to the lot. We're standing there playing and this huge sheet of flame – a monster sheet of flame going across 50,000 people." Ashley: "It was great fun. You handle it because you're young and don't care. I went off big festivals when I did the 1979 Reading. They were throwing cans and everything. I didn't really want to ever do another massive festival again after that."

Headlining at Lincoln were the Byrds, albeit a radically different line-up to that which Hutchings had caught twice in early 1968, with Gram Parsons. "We were hit by hard rock, straight country and even gospel", with Clarence White shining on lead guitar. With a set which combined "early Byrds, middle Dylan and late McGuinn", *Friends* remarked that "the folk influence is ever-present, even in the later songs, for the Byrds owe more to folk music than probably any other American band". *Melody Maker* reckoned that coming straight after the "clarity" of a set by bluesmen Sonny Terry and Brownie McGhee, Steeleye's set was "a startling reminder that sound balance don't come easy. If any instrument suffers, it always seems to be the fiddle, and Peter Knight was no exception".

The band's appearance at the Keele Folk Festival was prefaced by a public debate, chaired by Ian Campbell, on whether amplification was necessary, or an impertinence. It was like a rerun of Newport in 1965.

Lincoln Festival poster. July 1971

Martin Carthy – pictured stern-faced, in black leather jacket and flowing hair – exploded "why can't we just accept that some people like electric folk music and some people don't?". The discussion became farcical when Bob Pegg declared that Mr Fox were really a pop group, and only came because they didn't want to turn the gig down.

Ashley recalls a "certain amount of ambivalence from some people in the folk scene to Steeleye Two. We're talking about very early seventies, we're not very many years past the heyday of the folk clubs with the Aran sweaters and the pewter tankards. It doesn't stop us from becoming very successful. We're talking about sales into six figures. And it culminates in an appearance by Steeleye at the Keele Folk Festival, where in a forum, Martin and I are taken to task over "doing it for the money". I can't remember who by. People, not just one person. Not fellow artists. Joe Public on the floor. They'd let Fairport do it, because Fairport were from Rock – and were dabbling. But once we started playing music, seducing the likes of Martin, Tim and Maddy from the folk scene, that's when some of the anti-reaction kicked in."

Martin remembers that "Bob Pegg was being quite sarky and deliberately mixing it – and talking about "Of course I'm doing it for the money!", which infuriated people and made it impossible to discuss. I don't remember any particular antipathy to the music." Ashley recalls things "getting so heated that people saying we were only in it for the money, I can remember you shouting: "I want to say something now. If you want bank Statements, I'LL SHOW YOU BANK STATEMENTS!!!" I remember that very clearly." Martin also clearly remembers the same incident, "but I never took it very seriously, because I never really got that much flak as far as the music was concerned. I remember us going up to Aberdeen and there was this guy named Claude – a great guy – a broad Aberdeen accent, coming up to me and saying: "It's absolutely immoral but I love it! He was the man who held the Guinness Book of Records' record for drinking a yard glass of Lyles Golden Syrup! People just thought that if there was money involved – which of course there was, because we couldn't have afforded all that gear – then we were necessarily sullied, besmirched. I think we were on £5 a week at that time, or £10 a week." Carthy told *Sounds* that "I've not had any misgivings about electric music, because I don't see it as a step or as progress in any way: I'm one of those animals who's anti-progress so I just have to adjust to it. The instruments don't make a ha'p'orth of difference, they're just a means to an end".

Steeleye played the 1971 Cambridge Folk Festival, alongside Jean Ritchie, the Dransfields and Anne Briggs. For *Melody Maker*, as compared to the "brash and grating" Mr Fox, Steeleye "have resolved the problems created by an electric music/traditional marriage by combining elements in a distinctive pattern of black and white, rather than a distilled grey".

The official history of the Festival describes how "where Ashley's band took material of traditional origins and made it contemporary, the Peggs tried to cut deeper into the essence of what tradition was all about – and especially the magical element – composing original songs that might have well been written a century ago". It was this latter direction which Ashley was to himself later follow. Another guest at Cambridge that year was American fiddle player Sue Draheim, who jammed with the Dransfields, and who was to play a part in Ashley's next musical step. The Festival history acknowledges that "musically Steeleye's more modest ambitions succeeded better than Mr Fox's – let's face it, they have better vocalists".

Also fine vocalists, the Fisher family had been part of the Scottish Revival. Now married to Colin Ross of the High Level Ranters, Ray Fisher had had to wait until

Steeleye Span 2 at Cambridge Folk Festival. 31st July-1st August 1971. l-r: Peter Knight, Maddy Prior, Tim Hart, Martin Carthy, Ashley Hutchings

the musicians she wanted were available. "It gives us a chance to do something we wouldn't do with Steeleye", Hutchings cuts in. Ray stresses that "she hasn't gone electric or anything absurd", and Ashley as usual puts the record straight. "Martin and I were with Ray in a cafeteria discussing music and we suggested to Ray that we play on her album, so in fact the original suggestion came from us".

Hutchings plays bass on the resulting album, *The Bonny Birdy*. The band on these tracks is essentially Steeleye, with Ray replacing Maddy Prior. Ashley also wrote the sleeve note. What, he asks, do you do when Fisher's torso wiggles in the middle of a recording. "You just have to do another take, that's what, for how can a person be expected to concentrate on a formless lump of wood when the best pair of shoulders in folk music are at work?". He also finds that he loses interest in eating a cheese sandwich when Ray – his "favourite Scottish singer and person" – starts gliding over the floor, lost in some glorious strathspey". By now, even the most casual record store browser must have realised that – despite her name – Ray is a woman. Eric Winter's review of *The Bonny Birdy* praised Fisher's "precise" singing, though he was surprised by the size of her backing band. In '*The Forfar Sodger*', "Carthy/Hart/Knight/Hutchings do the backing, so it's come back Old Steeleye, isn't it". By the time of the album's release, only two of the above mentioned were still in the group.

2:4
TEN MAN MOP

All looked well enough in September, when Diane Easby interviewed them all in the studio. The accompanying photo sees them all squatting down in a garden, as usual, though this time all are grinning. Perhaps the grins are, in retrospect, a little too forced. For Peter Knight, a former junior exhibitor at the Royal Academy of Music, "we're all fighting the same cause – to produce good electric music". Tim Hart's favourite band is the Flying Burrito Brothers: "they started without a drummer as well". He suggests that Steeleye might themselves add drums, soon. Ashley stresses how difficult it is for the other, acoustically trained members of the band to come to terms with electric instruments. "Steeleye is at a disadvantage, if that's the word, with other bands, there's so much retuning to be done". A sign of a growing discontent with his colleagues, perhaps.

Folk and Country carried a two page spread of photographs by Toni Arthur of the band in the studio. Ashley, headphones around his neck and in moustache and herringbone jacket, grins at Peter Knight, dapper in waistcoat and beret. The front cover is another outside shot, but this time Ashley – whose short hair and jacket make him a dead ringer for Cecil Sharp – is the only one not smiling.

On October 30th, shortly before he was to quit the band, *Melody Maker* published an interview. In one of the oddest photos ever taken of him, Ashley wears steel glasses and a floppy straw hat, eyes closed, plucking a Fender bass, with either a psychedelic light show or extremely garish wallpaper on the wall behind. Ashley corrects the idea that Steeleye are the first exponents of an "English sound". The music they play is British with a current predominance of Irish. "As far as traditional music goes, the first English traditional group is still to come. Probably Mr Fox were the first English electric group, though they didn't play traditional songs. I would have thought

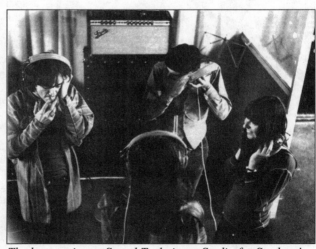

The last session at Sound Techniques Studio for Steeleye's "Ten Man Mop" album. 1971

Photo: Toni Arthur

that *Liege & Lief* was the start of it all". As to Steeleye, there wasn't a set plan. It wasn't a conscious effort to achieve a sound. It just happened". The only major decision taken in advance was to play traditional music with electric instruments: "I am continually astounded by what we have achieved by complete chance".

He says enigmatically that "I think other groups will form" with "more definite set ideas about what they're going to do". Unlike the rest of Steeleye, "I can take the music completely on its own terms without thinking of it in relation to the folk clubs". He lacks their "loyalty" to that circuit. Adding electricity makes folk music "something else", but "in any folk music you care to name you get the old and the development of it running side by side". What he is doing is part of an ageless process. His one major disappointment is that, both with Fairport and Steeleye, his music has not taken off in America: "I'm an idealist, I suppose. I really am surprised, knowing what the Americans are like about British things".

Back in September, Steeleye recorded a session for the Pete Drummond Show, playing a riotous '*Uncle Tom Cobley*'. The line up was missing Peter Knight, who was ill, and proved to be the final broadcast by Hutchings and Carthy as members of this incarnation of Steeleye Span. The writing was perhaps already on the wall. July had seen the release of Tim Hart and Maddy Prior's album *Summer Solstice*, advertised alongside *Please To See The King*. Terry and Gay Woods, too, had finally achieved their ambition, forming the Woods Band. Journalist Andrew Means pointed out that Pentangle and Fairport both had drummers who came from a jazz background, and thus lacked "the deceptively simple rock-solid drumming of Levon Helm, for instance". The Woods had taken the rhythm section of Granny's Intentions, so were really rocking. "Strangely, it is the band without a drummer, Steeleye Span, who manage to achieve that "cooking" rhythm we associate with rock, perhaps because they are anchored so firmly to the foundations of Tyger Hutchings' bass line".

Steeleye Span UK Tour poster. 1971

Steeleye released the *Rave On'* single. For Carthy, "it was very deadpan and we had to do it absolutely straight faced. As to the needle sticking, Ashley would come along and bang the mike – the timing was such that he'd bang the mike and we'd go back into it. The three of us singing. It was great – it was absolutely split second. We were singing it in rehearsal and just did it." The band then undertook a twenty two date UK tour. Geoff caught a Bournemouth Rag Concert and clearly remembers support act, Andy Roberts coming on during your set wearing a huge Afghan coat, plastic ping-pong eyes, and Usherette's ice cream tray chanting: "Drugs! Drugs! Get your soft drugs here!" Both the band and audience burst into hysterical laughter; it was a humorous counterpoint to Steeleye's serious image.

Roberts had only known Ashley "very peripherally from my work with Ian. And we were managed by the same person, Sandy Roberton. In 1971, immediately after I came back from doing an Ian

Steeleye Span 2 at Hastings. 1972. l-r: Martin Carthy, Peter Knight, Ashley, Tim Hart, Maddy Prior

Matthews tour in the States, which was the trio tour with Richard Thompson, Ian and myself, I came back to do a solo tour supporting Steeleye."

Jerry Gilbert of *Sounds* gave a track-by-track description of their new album, the weirdly named *Ten Man Mop or Mr Reservoir Butler Rides Again*. The first phrase was a Hutchings invention, Butler was a gypsy singer of old. Peter Knight's fiddle was now taking a more prominent role in the music, and overall "their spectrum appears to be broadening as the group continues to grow into a more resilient unit". The record sounds "less busy, and a good deal more spontaneous than the last". Ashley acknowledges that, compared to the previous Steeleye album, "the recording quality is better, but as we all know, something which is technically better is not necessarily a better album."

In *his* preview of the album, Andrew Means singled out Peter Knight's contribution to the album in a way that would worry any reader who was aware of Dave Swarbrick's similar impact on Fairport. On *'When I Was On Horseback'*, a song and tune related to *'The Streets Of Laredo'*, "his pizzicato and bowed instrumental passage relates to the song without being melodically contained by it".

Jerry Gilbert of *Sounds* interviewed Knight about the new record. "We decided to make it a good album, and not experiment too much". They wanted to record only numbers they could play live – on the previous record, *'Boys of Bedlam'* had been too difficult to perform on stage, despite many requests to play it. "There was no fighting for effect this time, and we weren't thinking of things to put on for the sake of it". Peter could see little chance of the band covering contemporary material, other than new tunes written to traditional words.

The new album was subtitled 'A Selection of Ballad Songs and Airs of the British Isles', and was packaged like a book, with endpapers and details of the 'publisher': Old Church Street, November 1971. Each band member is given their own page, and photograph, as if plying their trade. Carthy leans on a handcart, Knight is propped against a fishing boat and Ashley is in a walled garden, holding an agricultural implement. He wears a collarless shirt, shades, moustache and white hat. The good guy. They match the honest rustics pictured on the front and back cover, with the band and title picked out in gold. Ashley: "The second album is nicer and easier to listen to. It's much neater. But it didn't have the magic."

'*Gower Wassail*' is a mid-winter song, once sung around the houses, to summon up Spring. Its Welsh setting makes it stand out from what is largely an Irish repertoire. Certainly there is very little on this album sourced from the England in which all five of the band grew up. After sepulchral chords on electric guitar, adding a sinister note to proceedings, Tim Hart sings lead and the vocal ensemble echo him, like a church choir gone to the devil. The almost surrealistic notes to each track – much like Thompson's Goonish comments on *Full House* – are a series of in-jokes: here the mixing of old and new is alluded to in "a Telecaster, a Mustang and a Boosey & Hawkes tabor". Of two Knight-led jigs that follow, one was learnt from an Irish musician playing in London pubs, the other from a record by Sean Keane of the Chieftains. Peter Knight has found his feet with the band – no longer the new boy among more famous colleagues – and sets a sprightly pace, though one that is lightly amplified at most.

The theme of a husband fooled by his adulterous wife is as old as Chaucer's *Merchant's Tale*. '*Four Nights Drunk*' is a variant of the song which the Dubliners expanded by 72 hours and turned into a top twenty hit. "There's no horns on the Dubliners" is both a pun on session musicians and another reference to cuckolding, a joke which goes back to Shakespeare. Here, Carthy puts traditional words to a reel played by Knight, and stretches his voice alarmingly as he harmonises with a solo fiddle: the rest of the ensemble come in at the end, cheerily. Producer Sandy Roberton brought his dog, a Yorkshire terrier called Marcus into the studio. The band nicknamed the poor hound "the mechanised rat", "the mobile scrubbing brush" and "the clockwork mop". The dog's revenge can be heard towards the end of '*Four Nights Drunk*'. Perfectly on the beat there's a loud yelp from the control room.

An Irish setting again for '*When I Was On Horseback*', harsh words sung sweetly. The arrangement could almost be early Fairport. The notes allude in an inter-textual way to '*Sickness and Diseases*', which Thompson wrote for Fairport but never recorded with them. Maddy has perfected here the sexy sweep of her voice. Hutchings masters here, and on the album as a whole, the art of minimal bass-playing. Each note counts.

Of '*Marrowbones*', Knight comments that "it's much slower than a jig although it's a jig rhythm, and we had to consciously keep holding it back". There is a gamey quality, with Prior at her most vocally playful, and Carthy acting the wide boy as he tells this of a young woman who fails to trick her aged husband, the obverse of '*Four Nights Drunk*'.

'*Captain Coulston*' was learnt by Maddy from the singing of Brigid Tunney, and featured her voice at its most floaty, though the loss of consonants makes the words hard to follow. Derring-do on the high seas, with pirates out-manoeuvred, and the band sound fully integrated in a way they never quite were on *Please To See The King*. The three reels which follow were all learnt from Irish musicians, '*Dowd's Favourite/£10 Float/The Morning Dew*', and showcase Peter Knight, and a 'percussion section' consisting of Maddy Prior on spoons. There is a lightness of touch here which contrasts with the direction Fairport had taken since Ashley left. '*Wee Weaver*' was based on the drone of the pipes, with Maddy's voice sliding up the scale in their place. It lacks the harshness of the previous album, though the words are again difficult to make out. The notes tie it to the miser and George Eliot character Silas Marner.

'*Skewball*' ends the album on a touch of high drama, a horse race keenly contested. Tim is again on lead vocal and banjo, which opens proceedings, on a song learnt from A.L. Lloyd. 'Bert Lloyd' is given 7 points in the notes, above 'Peter,

Paul and Mary'. Carthy's electric guitar has real bite to it, and works excitingly in congress with Ashley's bass – the whole thing has a spirit and sense of adventure which augured well for a future never to take place, a career cut short in its prime.

Ten Man Mop is the sound of a band which has grown tight and lean, through heavy gigging. The players are far better integrated than on *Please To See The King*, with Carthy and Hutchings least featured of the five (though Hart subsequently was to claim otherwise). Maddy Prior plays spoons and tabor, Carthy guitars and organ, with Hart on dulcimer, guitars, organ, 5 string banjo and mandolin, and Knight on fiddle, tenor banjo and timpani. *Disc* reviewed *Ten Man Mop* as a requiem. "This album gives a true picture of what Steeleye have been doing onstage for the past few months and it's sad in a way because they may not be able to produce exactly this sound again". There is more space for Peter Knight, and "amplification only serves to add more drama".

Fred Woods is a dissenting voice to all this, discerning that the album is "very much the mixture as before, but with one new ingredient added: a sense of the routine. I can sense tiredness". Similarly, concert performances by this line-up "seemed to have gone as far as they could". Sandy Roberton's production fails to pull the voices forward enough. '*Gower Wassail*' is practically a dirge, while in '*Marrowbones*', "Tyger's bass plonks away in a positively elephantine way".

Melody Maker carried the shock news on November 27th that 'Tyger quits Steeleye'. He "will be replaced by another bass guitarist, as yet not named." Steeleye would be playing the remaining four concerts booked for 1971 as a four piece. The release date for *Ten Man Mop* had been put back to January, because of production difficulties with the sleeve, which reportedly was so expensive that each copy sold cost the band money! The band was set for a US tour in April.

It is almost the same story as before, Hutchings quitting a band he had founded, and masterminded, on the brink of some important American dates. Ashley himself had no certain plans, but was "involved in forming another group. I just thought it was time to go". His departure had been amicable, but "I would like to play more English songs as opposed to predominantly Irish, which was what we were playing. That was not the reason for my leaving, but it contributed.

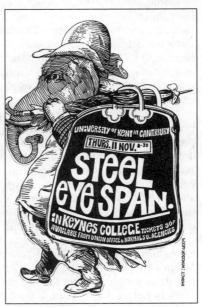

"There were two reasons why I left Steeleye Two. One was I'd found my path, which was hearing William Kimber playing Morris and realising that I wanted to concentrate upon making English music. And the other was the gulf between Tim and me was getting wider and wider, and I really didn't want to be in a band with him any more. It was quite a relief to leave Steeleye and not have to deal with Tim again. The band had a lot of love and a lot of support at that time. I was first to upset the applecart yet again when I left. Again, as with Fairport, my departure was followed very quickly, this time by Martin."

Keynes College, University of Kent.
11th November 1971

Ashley told the rest of the band that there was "too much Irish stuff and he wante to be more involved in English material!" During a gig with Lindisfarne he watche them on stage laughing and joking and then told Carthy "That's what a band' supposed to be like, not like what we're going through at the moment!" By now th atmosphere within Steeleye was very dour, with long periods of silence within th dressing room. He added "We were all mates in Fairport who had a good time."

Carthy: "When Ashley left, I wanted to ask John Kirkpatrick to join, then we ca be more English, but I was in a minority of one. I couldn't very well say: 'Oh wel you all leave and I'll be Steeleye Span!' I was the one who felt like that and so I left.

A year later, Ashley opened up to Karl Dallas. "People just see the tip of a iceberg when a band comes on stage. There's a lot of other contributing factor they're not aware of. I spent the last nine months playing with Steeleye Span agains my wishes". Since the release of *Please To See The King*, no less. "I would rathe have left, but I couldn't for economic reasons. It's very sordid, but there it is, that' the business". He had left when he received a cheque for £1,800, covering bac royalties from Fairport. Even so, financially, Ashley was going into the wildernes for a second time.

Robin Denselow reckons that the breaking points were Hutchings' refusal to g on the American tour, and his veto on *Corunna* moving in for a season at the Youn Vic. After he had quit, there was "a major policy disagreement" between Tim an Martin. After a experimental gig with Rick Kemp, who had previously playe electric bass with Mike Chapman, Carthy left too, to be replaced by Bob Johnsor Knight's previous musical partner. As Martin told Rosalind Russell, "I just didn't f in anywhere." Carthy was later to rejoin Steeleye in 1978, briefly, for a tour and it *Live At Last* album: he also later joined Ashley in a prototype Albion Country Band and at the National Theatre.

Commenting upon the departure of Hutchings and Carthy to *Melody Maker*, Tin Hart said "Tyger and Martin both had preconceptions about the music which Pet [Knight] and I didn't have. Because we didn't have any we followed their lead. think the rift was mainly musical. The thing about folk music is that you get terribl intellectual. Then you come out the other side and get folk music in perspective wit other music...It's almost like a folk puberty which you have to go through. I thin this is what Tyger is going through at the moment. He's got to come out the othe end and play non-specialised music again."

Martin: "I remember Tim saying when we were making *Ten Man Mop*, "This ha been too much like Martin Carthy's backing band!" "OK, so do it yourself." So h produced '*Skewball*' and '*A Gower Wassail*'. I felt, "Yes that's right, there's a lo of me on that first album", but I do remember those rehearsals when we were in S Albans, saying "Come on then Tim, you do something!" And he replied "Oh no, I'n perfectly happy sitting here playing the dulcimer!" Now I'm thinking "Who's got short memory. Why make war?" And there was definitely a feeling that I sort of blame is the wrong word – I look towards Tim. Tim does have a streak in him – h does have this idea running through his head of "You've done me wrong!"

Second raters often do! "You said that! None of it was felt, none of it was share by Ashley and me. At least I presume Ashley didn't share it because he just left When I say, I was in the minority of one, I thought we should go in this direction and three people thought that we should go in another direction. The answer is, an it really hurt, I didn't want to do it. I went to Sandy Roberton and said: "I'm goin to have to leave the band, and I fucking nearly cried. I was so upset. But immediately walked out of that place and I felt I was walking on air. I felt a whol load had been lifted from my shoulders."

Ashley: "The pressure had built up. The silences were just unbearable. It was such a shame, because it was a good band. We played well and we loved the music. Still, after all these years, and all these changes, people still talk about the early band." Carthy reveals that Tim wrote him a letter many years later, saying that the only two line-ups of Steeleye which were truly worthwhile was this line-up and what Martin himself terms the "All Around My Wallet band."

He also places on the record that "the person that I really want to salute is Maddy because she was under colossal pressure during that period from the rest of the band. She batted her way through, tense as things could be, and came and saw Norma and myself when we were in Hull. They had nothing to do with me because Ashley and I were the big bad wolf. And she just basically said "This is horseshit, these are my friends!" She put her head down and barged through, and just came to see us. It was an enormous thing to have done. And her presence at the door said "I'm fucking here. Hello. It's really nice to see you! Grrrr! I'm fed up with this shit." So thank you Maddy. It meant a lot."

Isn't there a crucial difference between seeing Martin in a folk club, a visceral and direct experience, and the barrier which a rock band with electric instruments automatically places between the audience and the musicians. Martin: "We were turning it into something else, and the music can survive perfectly happily doing that. But it is different, and then you have to make your choices. My personal choice is to do something like that every now and again because it's great. I love all that volume. Turn it up to 11! Only 11?"

Didn't live music also evolve at around that time from sweaty rock clubs to the University/College circuit? Martin points out , with not a trace of arrogance, that the band were already big time. "We were playing in the big hall. We weren't playing the University/College folk club. You don't have that immediacy you get from a folk club audience. It becomes something else. When it gets more and more and more, and becomes an arena then you're into events, and you're not into music at all." As Steeleye became after you both left. "Like I say – you make your decisions."

Melody Maker later made *Please To See The King* their Folk album of the year. Thirty years on, the album also made the top ten of the *Folk on Two* poll. Karl Dallas put his finger on the reason as to why Ashley left a band that were so hugely popular. Carthy's new approach was "marred by the same sort of Irishisms which crop up with such force on the new Steeleye album, exaggerated portmanteau slurs" up the scale. Maddy Prior was also "singing rather shrilly". Dallas warns that Irish folk is more exotic to the English tradition than Memphis rock n' roll," and for that reason it could be a more dangerous influence".

Hart told Andrew Means that Ashley's replacement Rick Kemp's "whole approach to bass playing is different. Tyger isn't a melodic player. He works around the chords. Tyger was a lot more compatible to Martin's music than he was to ours". Regarding the choice of material, "Tyger and Martin both had preconceptions about the music which Pete and I didn't have. We followed their lead". One of the aims of the new band was to create "a sound that doesn't owe an identifiable amount to any one member of the group". There are no hurt feelings, though. "I think the rift was mainly musical. There was nothing personal". Hart compares their future plans for Steeleye to Tyger's old favourites, the Byrds, with a "fluctuating membership": this has proved over the years to be far truer of Fairport, and Ashley's own projects.

As Hart later said, the reason for Ashley's leaving was "disillusionment upon finding that we were musicians first and folkies second that drove him to run off with the Morris Men". When he left, "a different energy came in." The new Steeleye became less doctrinaire, and it must be said, easier on the ear. They also changed manager and record company, became more commercially minded, playing baseball stadia and the like, and made a fortune. For some the introduction of Wombles mastermind Mike Batt as producer was a liberation, for others it was the final straw. Talking to Colin Irwin in *Melody Maker* about the frustration of repeatedly hearing people dismissing the current Steeleye with all the commercial success in comparison with the days when the revered Carthy and Hutchings were with them, Peter Knight commented "I enjoyed the band when they were in it. I thought it was as good as it is now, for the time it was occurring, the age I was then. But everything is changing. I've no idea what the band would be sounding like now if Ashley and Martin hadn't left. If people preferred us in the old days, that's cool. I can understand it. I can't say we're better or worse, we've just changed. It had to change because Bob, Ric and Nigel weren't particularly folkies, they were rockers." Commenting upon Ashley's rocking bass work on the jigs and reels, Rick Kemp said "Status Quo should have been influenced by that."

That was not quite the end of Ashley's involvement with Steeleye Span. Dave Hill had acted in *Corunna*, and "we'd sort of stayed in touch over the years". His work for the charity War Child led him to the mad idea of gathering all the different line-ups of the band to play on the same day. A phone call to Ashley produced "positive feedback". The Forum in London was booked for an one-off event now labelled *The Journey*, with all profits going to War Child. Simon Jones: "There was a queue round the block. Ashley had unselfishly offered to start with the Albion Band and played a corking set as the audience came in. And suddenly we all relaxed".

But Terry Woods was nowhere to be seen. "It was only three months of my life and I didn't want to revisit. There was no point, for me to get on stage and say 'How wonderful it is to be back in Steeleye!' I really didn't feel any obligation to revisit the experience.

"Gay said that some of the situations in and around Steeleye were as bad as they've ever been. And to be quite honest with you, I'm too old to be dealing with all that crap. I don't need it. I have a management company and do the odd thing for friends, but I don't play any longer as a muso. I kind of lost it after ten years with The Pogues. The music business takes its toll. It may have a lot of charisma, it may look wonderful, but it can destroy you I'm afraid. Nobody understands the sheer

"The Journey" War Child Charity flyer. The Forum, London. 2nd September 1995 tedium of life on the road. Even my present wife sees it as ten years spent partying with the Pogues. A lot of it was partying but all of the parties happened out of the sheer frustration – when you're travelling, when you're sitting in airports, when you're on a coach for ten hours. If there's one thing you learn from being in a successful band – you learn patience."

For Martin Carthy, though, the reunion was a great experience. He came off stage telling Ashley "We've got to do this again." Things at first had been chaotic. Martin: "John Eales did the mixing. He quietly took control. He went and commandeered the sound-board and just did it."

The resulting concert was indeed "mesmerising", and has received due tribute in *The Journey* double CD. Gay Woods, her hair now turned white, bangs a bodhran. Carthy sings without any of the affectations which began to afflict him first time around. Maddy dances, in a painted dress. Ashley is dignified in a collarless shirt, and as everyone assembles at the end grins like a gargoyle.

Tonight Gay joins Ashley, Maddy and Tim, with Martin Carthy on banjo and John Kirkpatrick's concertina filling in for the absent Terry. Ex-Albion drummer Michael Gregory sits in on drums, and suddenly the first line-up of Steeleye makes its live debut, a mere 25 years after their inception. And they sound just fine.

Six songs are resurrected from the album, with an unaccompanied '*Calling On Song*' acting as an overture for the whole shebang. "The beat of the drum" leads into '*Blacksmith*'", with a sinuous bass line from Ashley, high in the mix. The two female voices intertwine so lovingly that you wonder if this is where *Rumours* era Fleetwood Mac got their inspiration. The world depicted here is far tougher than 70s LA, or course, breaking spines with a cord, or men risking their lives out at sea. On a sultry '*Fisherman's Wife*', Ashley carries the melody on his bass, with concertina and acoustic guitar taking up the rhythm. '*Lowlands of Holland*' opens with Carthy's banjo picking out the tune, then Gay's voice almost breaking with emotion. On "hold your tongue", she lapses into speech. Then almost a country "yip", as the band power back in.

It is a road not taken, or perhaps one taken by others far outside the range of 'usual suspects'. This is what the Corrs are like, in their dreams. As Simon Jones puts it, "these softly constructed harmonic electric folk numbers proved that if Steeleye One had ever gigged, just how well that first album would have stood up on the road". An American woman at the front is reportedly close to tears at the emotion of it all. Truly, music brought back from the dead.

Simon Jones describes *Please To See The King* as "perhaps the most perfect electric folk album" and the selections played here bear that out, with Carthy's driven vocals, Ashley's driving bass and wailing violin on '*Cold, Haily Windy Night*'. Maddy sounds like she's in another room, but comes stage centre on '*Prince Charlie Stuart*', gliding her Rolls Royce of a voice up and down the scale, yet strangely intimate. The band play a drone, Eastern European almost. '*Gower Wassail*' is choral, led by Tim's almost out-of-control lead vocal. Ashley's bass is like a heartbeat. '*Lark in the Morning*' opens with Hart's percussive dulcimer, then Maddy floats in, Carthy adds a descant, and bass and fiddle complete the picture. No drums, of course. That said, this is fully electric music, as conceptually 'heavy' as Black Sabbath. It is music that takes no prisoners.

Perhaps the most unexpected words on the War Child gig came from Gay Woods during her public resignation from Steeleye, as recounted by *Record Collector*'s Colin Harper. *The Journey*, was an eye-opener: "If you fart in Steeleye Span it gets recorded! It was a fun day and it was a great idea but you should hear the real tapes

– they all went back in and re-did things. It stinks. I left my songs as they were: "This is live, this is how I am"." During Steeleye's spirited 2000 UK tour rebirth, Gay tellingly commented "You get disinterested if you're getting nothing from a personal evolutionary point of view out of your music, because that's the reason why you do it. It's just to stimulate the psyche – to kick start it!"

Martin Carthy: "There was talk of doing a thing with our Steeleye and the *All Around My Hat* version of the band. Tim's wanting to do that very much, but Maddy is less interested because she's only just got out from under. She may be interested in a few years down the line. But Tim has come to the conclusion that music is not for him. Then he said – these were his words, and not mine: "Of all the versions of Steeleye, the easiest one to work with was ours!" Which it was. Because it was just standing up and playing. It's strange really – there's two lots of musicians – there are those who are young and enthusiastic, but then they just stop and give up. And the second – the people who are the hard-core addicts, for whom it's for life.""

Meanwhile, back in 1971...

PART THREE
THE ALBION COUNTRY BAND

"There's no other music that I want to play, but I'll see if I can find some completely unknown musicians with a fresh approach."

Albion Country Band 1 in the garden of Simon's home in Northampton. 1972.
l-r: Steve Ashley, Simon Nicol, Royston Wood, Sue Draheim, Dave Mattacks, Ashley

3:1
NO ROSES

Ashley's musical journey into the folk traditions of his native England was only just beginning: it was to be as strange and incident-packed a trip as anything which had gone before, but Hutchings was moving out of the musical spotlight. This was to be just as 'underground' an experiment as anything which he had encountered at Middle Earth, a mere four years before.

Flower power had wilted, and people were retreating into themselves, as economic gloom descended. Like the ornery hero of one of John Ford's peerless westerns, Ashley was taking to the hills. Shirley Collins recalled "In November 1971, two months after we married, Ashley quit Steeleye. He said he wanted to play more English music and when that royalty statement came – he said: "I can actually do it now!"

When Ashley quit, that must have been quite hard from a financial and family point of view really. To suddenly leave a reasonably successful enterprise to start all over again. "You don't think about money. I mean it was wonderful. I remember he did get this huge £1,800 cheque and it was all about royalties for Fairport, finally coming through. I think I would have supported him in whatever. I remember him not being happy with a lot of things that were going on. He was interested in things becoming English."

Ashley finds it interesting Martin reminding him about the tense feelings within Steeleye as "I think that explains in some way, *Morris On*. It reinforces why such a fun, simple, devil-may-care album was made at that point. In many ways it was exactly the same as with Fairport and early Steeleye – going into the great unknown. It was still exciting. And it was never to happen again after those two groups. I did then marry Shirley and live in Etchingham in the countryside for seven years. But the band didn't get together there and rehearse. From then on it was never the same again."

Hutchings had begun to build up a genuine interest and knowledge of English music. Shirley Collins was the archetypal English Rose. "Encouraged by her, I make contact with John Kirkpatrick. I meet him in Tottenham where he's living with Sue. The first time I meet him we have this conversation and I say "How about making an album of Morris music?" And he says "You must be crazy! What do you want to do that for?" And I say "Listen. If I get Dave Mattacks, and Richard Thompson, we could make an electric morris album. Don't you think it would work?" And so he went along with the idea. And so while I'm still with Steeleye, we make *Morris On*."

How did the rest of Steeleye respond to your extra-curricular activities with *Morris On* and suchlike? "That was fine. I don't think that there was any objection to it. "No, it was just Ashley being eccentric", quote unquote. Doing something on the side, because I had a reputation in those days of being a bit unpredictable. So no, they allowed me the freedom to do it. *No Roses* was made for Sandy Roberton, *Morris On* wasn't. *Morris On* was made by John Wood and myself. John engineered, and John and I produced it. Joe Boyd didn't get involved in that which was quite unusual. But no, there was no animosity or anything like that."

Throughout that period the other members of the band had concurrent solo or duo careers, and Ashley was the one very much committed to Steeleye Span, more so than the rest were. "There was a period of a year or so when they were doing odds and ends with other people, duo or solo work, and I was just kicking my heels until the next Steeleye album. So it was strange that in the end, I was the one that made the big move. So I started to form Albion Country Band and, I was only aware much much later, that Shirley resented not being in the Albions to start with. But at the time I felt that it was a quest that she supported me on."

Albion is the earliest recorded name attached to the British Isles, and the name became attached to Brutus, who according to Tudor historians had escaped from the battle of Troy to found London. One writer of the time looks back to Henry V as "Protectour of Brute's Albions".

But if any one author has fixed the notion of Albion in the public mind, it is the same who wrote of a 'Tyger' burning bright. *Jerusalem, the Emanation of The Giant Albion* was William Blake's last great poem, completed in the late 1820s, and is centred on London, and the Thames, though there are multiple references to the names of English towns and counties. For Blake, the nation of Albion might be currently in deep slumber, but it is evoked in mythic terms.

Just as Ashley Hutchings learnt how to fuse words and music, William Blake's extraordinary gift was to bring together the disciplines of poet and artist: his great epic poems are literally Illustrated Books. There are other similarities. Both men have also been largely responsible for overseeing the production of their own work, keeping close control. Both are intellectual mavericks, stubbornly following a direction of their own devising.

Given Ashley's birthplace, there is a key line in *Jerusalem* "Hampstead, Highgate, Finchley, Hendon, Muswell Hill rage loud". Another phrase from the same poem could be said to describe Hutchings' whole *raison d'être* as a creative artist – to celebrate "a pleasant Shadow of Repose called Albion's lovely land".

For Ashley, such things came into proper focus with the formation of the Albion Country Band, and all its guises and line-ups, right up to the present day. Hutchings has attempted to carry through that same idea ever since, celebrating the country of his birth without ever letting this quest descend either into mere nostalgia or rancid jingoism. As the poet Jeremy Hooker wrote recently, it is not easy for any contemporary artist "who loves the things of these islands to lift them up as valid signs of a real unity". And even more difficult to continue to do so, year after year.

Of course, it would be fanciful to push the comparison between Hutchings and Blake too far. Even so, one illuminates the other. The commentary on 'Jerusalem' in W.H. Stevenson's edition of Blake – also first published in 1971 – points out that the giant Albion himself represents something far wider than a little England, "subsuming all Britons, present and past and future". Only Los – "the personification of the true artist" – remains faithful to Albion. In turn, whenever anyone sees "visions of eternity", and then translates them into the "vital forms" of art, then "the spirit of Los is awake". Which describes Ashley's whole musical career in a nutshell…

Come All Ye
Denny/Hutchings

To rouse the spirit of the earth,
And move the rolling sky.

Ashley: "You've got to remember that at this time I was literally falling in love with English music. *Morris On* was a crusade and *No Roses* was a labour of love. So I was only partially present. Round about 1971/72, I hear a recording of William Kimber playing concertina for the Headington Morris, on an album of Morris Dance music which was a limited edition EDFSS record. And I flip. I think that this is the most wonderful stuff. It's so English. I've never heard anything like it. It's not like what we did on *Liege & Lief*, it's not like these Irish tunes that Pete Knight's playing."

Even though *No Roses* and *Morris On* were conceived virtually concurrently , the latter was recorded a few months later, so it is best to separate the two projects, and deal with them chronologically. Both are deeply imbued with the English folk tradition. Both are tinged with genius.

As he prepared to leave Steeleye, Ashley was putting his latest theory into practice, masterminding and co-producing (with Sandy Roberton) an album of *English* traditional music, with full electric backing. Recording was completed in October, but the album had been announced back in June, and *Sounds* for 24th April 1971 was first to reveal that "Shirley will be featuring Richard Thompson, Simon Nicol and Dave Mattacks on her next album" She is planning an album with her sister Dolly. "I've got a lot of fresh songs that I want to do". Shirley Collins now adds that Dolly did an arrangement of Richard Thompson's '*Poor Will And The Jolly Hangman*'. "We sang it at a couple of concerts. It was quite hard for me to sing. The only successful Richard Thompson one I've ever done was '*Never Again*'.

Sandy Roberton opinioned that *"No Roses* was a classic record. Ashley was the mastermind of the whole thing. I just helped him reach his goal. He had planned the whole thing. We co-produced the album but his pre-production is what made the album." The album with Dolly will include "Morris tunes, which haven't been exploited". Shirley and Ashley also hope to "get a little band or our own going – almost an amateur band really. We are hoping to get a concertina player and a drummer, and run the band as a little sideline because we obviously won't be able to play much together otherwise. The idea is to make this band a Sussex band because the bulk of my material still comes from the South". From this idea would flow both the Albion Country Band and the Etchingham Steam Band: this prototype is clearly seen as an adjunct to Steeleye, not its replacement.

Hutchings has persuaded his wife-to-be to spend more time researching traditional material. "It's incredible the way new songs are emerging all the time. The one thing Ashley has done is drive me back to Cecil Sharp House to listen to tapes again". She had been "coasting along" on the material she had unearthed with Peter Kennedy while researching the Caedmon series.

The most extraordinary revelation, little remarked on at the time, is that Shirley has already laid down some tracks with the prototype electric band: Ashley, Richard, Simon and Dave Mattacks. "We just all got together in a recording studio one afternoon and did it from scratch and it turned out very well". She does worry that going electric might look like "jumping on the bandwagon, especially as it's the same musicians all the time". After a period of "quiet assessment", she is looking forward to singing with Dolly and "having a little band as well".

The English being an Island race have always tended to have more of an interest in what goes on around them. We're more outward looking I think. But why "Albion" rather than "The English Band" say? "That's easily answered. It's a more interesting name. It's a more historical, mythological and more elusive name. So that is exactly why we are not "The English Country Band"." *And yet it does conjure up an image...* "The Albion Band" "I think it does, yes. But it's very, very difficult nowadays talking specifically about what our music is and what English music is. It was easier in the early days. If you wind the clock back to the Seventies, there was kind of a conscious movement. It was almost akin to the Pre-Raphaelites: Richard Thompson's *Henry The Human Fly* album, *Morris On*, *No Roses*, the Albion Country Band album: we were consciously trying to commune with tradition, our background history, mythology, magic. The whole thing. But it was very conscious."

Meanwhile, back at *No Roses*, the collective name Ashley and Shirley gave to the session musicians he brought together for this one-off recording project was the Albion Country Band. Not only did it symbolise this new immersion in purely English models, but it would enjoy a weird and twisting history all its own. As Ashley later revealed that this was the very first time that the Albion Country Band name was put to use. "Shirley and I discussed it, we wanted a way of crediting all of the musicians. Later on, it was used as the name for a touring band. This is a good album, it's a bit heavy handed in places, it was very exciting to make".

No Roses was received very well. For Shirley, the reason that her existing fans liked this new direction was that "my singing never changed. I was singing in the same voice, which I've always sung in." Your speaking voice. "That's right. So although people might have got miffed by the rocky quality of it, they couldn't apply that to the singing. Karl Dallas said something about "Shirley sails serenely along like a ship chugging on the English Channel" or something crappy like that. But he was quite right of course – the Englishness of it was always there – it wasn't me attempting to be a rock singer. Well I couldn't ever be that anyway. That was great to do and because it was done in the studio, it was easier to do. Whereas reproducing the stuff on stage is a lot harder which is why I think Ashley possibly thinks that some of the first Albion gigs with Steve, Royston and Sue, were perhaps not so good."

One thing that was never explained was the title, *No Roses*. "It was a song from The Coppers' '*The Week Before Easter*'.

> *A week before Easter the day bright and clear*
> *The sun shone brightly clean blue the air*
> *I went down to the forest to gather fine flowers*
> *But the forest can yield me no roses.*

"And I thought that it was just perfect. It's a song that not many people would necessarily know. It's so important, again The Copper Family remain the epitome of English song writing and heritage. It just felt right the instant I quoted it. I said *No Roses* and there it was!" *No Roses* suggested that this would be no exercise in nostalgic fantasy in the vein of magazines like *This England*, which still evokes a country of rose-bedecked cottages. Even so, after their marriage, Ashley and Shirley had moved into a part-Tudor, tile hung house in an acre of land, on which they grew most of their vegetables. From 'Mock Tudor' to real Tudor. A house, too, which just happened to be called Red Rose Cottage.

It was a distillation of the post-hippie dream. The retreat into ruralism was a path which many of the original disciples of flower power and soft drugs had taken, away from a city environment decaying visibly. It was also the kind of rustic life which Dylan and the Band had lived up in Woodstock, and also tinged the lives of rock musicians as otherwise different as Van Morrison, Neil Young and the Byrds.

The garden boasted two swings (one broken), a seesaw, a badminton net and a heraldic sculpture which Ashley discovered was the insignia of the War Office. The house was called Red Rose, not because it had red roses round the door, but from its rent centuries before, one red rose a year. One of Shirley Collins' earlier albums was called *Sweet Primroses*, to which this was an electrified riposte.

No Roses seemed an odd title nevertheless for a newly married couple, pictured clasped together in rural bliss on the inside cover against a background of uncultivated fields, hedgerows and trees: no houses, motorways, or oil seed rape. Ashley is in antique gaiters and a rustic, collarless shirt, with dark glasses and moustache: Shirley wears a floor-length, neck high, blue dress. A full page advert added the words '*No Roses*', "the first electric English country music album, in which Shirley Collins and the Albion Country Band sing and play nine songs of love, death, transportation, ritual and custom from the English tradition".

The photographer was Keith Morris, preferred lensman to the folk rock aristocracy. The front cover is dominated by an carved heraldic beast, guarding a mullioned window. The back cover of the original LP shows a photograph by Cecil Sharp of a whiskered farm worker, proud as

Shirley Collins and Ashley at Red Rose, Etchingham. 1972

the lion on the front, his skin creased with hard work and the seasons. This fitted in with a back-to-the-land movement sweeping through many of the original hippies: even Ken Kesey, whose Merry Pranksters had once been pied pipers for LSD. Kesey had now retired to a farm in Oregon, and the original magic bus was now rusting forever amongst wheatfields. Hutchings' identification with Cecil Sharp was to surface more fully with his one-man show in the eighties.

Shirley was surely the most English singer to emerge from the Revival, retaining her charming, breathless Sussex burr. She and her sister "come from a big country family, which used to get together for monumental sing-songs". Dolly studied composition with Alan Bush, and kept herself in the meantime by working as a bus conductress. She then lived in a converted bus in an open field, "where she composed a children's opera at an upright piano installed on the lower deck". The female Bruce Lacey.

Shirley now lives in a quiet ground-floor apartment on the Sussex coast, from where she can easily walk to the South Downs. She was initially nervous about meeting us to talk about her ex-husband – there is still bitterness there, alongside a huge respect for his talent – but fellow musicians managed to persuade her that we were not so much hardened journos, sniffing out sleaze, as interested fans, who merely wanted to uncover an unjustly forgotten episode in British culture. First, we walked with her along the beach – talking politics, with the twin piers of Brighton just in sight – then she fed us lunch before the notebooks and tape recorders were unleashed. Her home is filled with exquisite framed memories, especially of her sister, plus some jewel-like paintings by David Suff, whose Fledgling record label has reissued most of her criminally, long deleted albums. Shirley found talking about the past an emotional experience: at one point Brian was sent out for low-tar cigarettes, even if she gave up years ago. She still has the luminous beauty of those early album covers, but is so down to earth at times you forget exactly what made her special in the first place until, to illustrate a point, she sang a few lines of a traditional song 'Under The Mistletoe Bough', and hearing that unique voice seemingly out of nowhere was one of the most spine-chilling moments of all.

Talking years before to Fred Woods, Shirley explained that "the old singers weren't just farmers or shepherds who happened to sing; they were special people, with *special* talents and special responsibilities – and a special place in the community. This is an attitude which goes back to the *makar* and beyond". Her own upbringing was rooted in romantic socialism. It also now sounds idyllic.

"Dolly and I used to sing close harmony, and we used to sit at the top of the stairs. There was a big empty space above with a super echo, and we'd get our voices really tight close so that they seemed to vibrate".

Shirley sees herself as a "revival singer". "I haven't sung it as my Grandad or my Mum would sing it, although of course I still sing with their accent". But they shared a common background, completely different to that of her new husband. "I was working class, I was country, and I didn't know much about the world, in a way, but I always knew that I had an understanding of what life was like for these people". Undaunted, Shirley began to sing at Labour club socials. Soon she was touring Poland and Russia, and Ewan MacColl told her to extend her repertoire beyond love songs, and not to use nail varnish.

When he was copy-editing this book, Julian Bell made an interesting political point. He finds "there is a more, sophisticated, more subtle, more grounded understanding of the whole nationality/folk tradition argument from Shirley, with her background in the rural working class intelligensia than you get from Ashley's obsessive, rather tunnel-vision Londoner's quest for Englishness". We would argue back that even if he doesn't seem prepared to fully verbalise his take on this debate, Ashley speaks far more subtly through the projects he has carried through. Trust the tale, not the teller.

Where Ashley and Shirley concur is on their view of where this folk tradition is currently going, or more accurately, it isn't! For Collins, "my criticism of modern singers is they're not looking for new stuff. They're relying on stuff they've learned from Nic Jones, from the standard repertoire. I was out there as a young singer and all I got was a handful of songs that I'd got from home, I knew The Coppers, I'd heard stuff on the radio, but I went looking for it because I loved it so much, I wanted to find out more about it. And I absolutely immersed myself in it. And I think anybody who claims to love traditional music should do the same thing. You've got to listen to the old singers, and they don't seem to be doing that."

"I listened to Jean Ritchie. She and her husband, photographer George Peacoe, came over here in 1961 or 62. He asked me to be an assistant to him while he was photographing London. We went into the Houses of Parliament. He'd got permission to photograph Big Ben, on the understanding that we didn't touch anything or move anything while we were in there. And while we were up there in the tower, George asked me to move a ladder because it was in the way of his shot, and I moved it, and what it actually did was stop the pendulum. So I actually stopped Big Ben!" Time stood still. "This is the essence of the tradition you see – it's actually making it timeless. Literally!"

Shirley repaid the compliment by travelling over to the States, with the American collector Alan Lomax. "I was born in 1935. I made *Sweet England* before I went. Alan went back in '58, and I joined him in '59." There you were in Appalachia, soaking up all this extraordinary back-porch music. "Well, funnily enough I'd soaked an awful lot of it up before I went because I was deeply enamoured of Appalachian music. The first two books of Folk Music I bought were Sharp's *Folk Songs of the Southern Appalachians*. Wonderful songs and wonderful ballads. And because I'd heard Lomax on the radio, I just thought that mountain music was wonderful, and is. So I knew a lot about it before I went. But being there, the reality of being in the South, was not the romantic…"

In the USA on a recording trip with Alan Lomax, Shirley recorded folk and blues performances in the field, even visiting Parchman Farm jail. Touring the Deep South made her drop American material from her repertoire, and fully find her own public persona. Englishness was the keynote. "I've got a mouldy and strange voice, but at least it's my own". As Fred Woods points out, "it is also one of the few unmistakably *personal* voices we have in this country today".

Commenting upon the English tradition and Englishness, which she exemplifies as an artist, Shirley said: "Where my generation was different was people before us, were regional people. I'm still regional. I think of myself as Sussex and I like to sing Southern music. There's no point me singing anything else really. With the occasional foray into something else, like Irish music. But then I've got Irish grandparents on one side."

Shirley returned to the recording studio with the legendary Soho guitarist Davey Graham for 1964's *Folk Roots, New Routes*, a largely unspoken influence behind Fairport. One of the songs they played together was '*Nottamun Town*'. She followed it with the ground breaking album, *Anthems in Eden*, a folk suite recorded for Radio One, and set in the times before the Great War. Arranged by the doomed genius David Munrow of Musica Reservata, it featured the likes of shawms, racketts, rebecs and crumhorns, besides Shirley's five string banjo and Dolly's pipe organ. It was a baton which Hutchings took up with the Albion Band of the late 1970s.

Shirley: "Because I knew them all from *Anthems In Eden*, I was able to give Ashley some sort of link into that as well. He'd have come to that eventually I'm sure. But he had a bit of a head start, a kick start really." For now, however different the route it took them to get there, Shirley Collins and Ashley were both a vital part of the English underground. Shirley and Dolly had links with the Incredible String Band, and were signed to Harvest, the 'progressive' label formed by EMI, alongside such hippie luminaries as Syd Barrett, Kevin Ayers and Pete Brown. Mediaeval music was just one of the many colours in the kaleidoscope of late 60s culture. As Shirley herself says, "it was a heady time!"

So how and when did Shirley first meet Ashley? "He phoned up one day when I was living at The Keep in Blackheath. He phoned up and wanted to talk about '*The Whitsun Dance*' and what it was I'd said, at the beginning of that song. That the song was written to commemorate the ladies of the English Folk Dance & Song Society who'd possibly lost their sweethearts and husbands in the First World War. As we know, almost a whole generation of country young men were wiped out and perhaps turned to Country Dancing as some form of solace. The village Maypole once the centre of so many village greens was replaced after that War by the memorial stones. And I said this to Ashley and he said: "Wow!" on the end of the phone. I was gigging at Cecil Sharp House a few nights later, and he turned up to see the Folk Club. And in the interval we popped along to the pub, and I never drank in those days, and I said: "I'll have a brandy." He brought me a brandy, handed it to me, put his hand on the back on my head, gave me a kiss, and that was it! That was just it. I knew from that moment that we were going to be together and get married. It was all lovely. What I didn't foresee was that it wasn't going to last that long."

"From when I first went to London in the fifties, I'd spent almost every waking moment that I could at Cecil Sharp House in the library looking for songs. We obviously then went back together to look for music and to look in the Cecil Sharp Archives – well, they weren't any archives then, they were just boxes gathering dust in the cellar. All the Maud Karpeles collection was there, all the Lucy Broadwood stuff – it was just there. It was wasting away, it was dusty, it was being destroyed. Not looked at all. And we investigated that, but that was later of course."

Kay Hutchings: "Shirley was ten years older than Ashley. She was lovely. She used to come here and I'd say: "Don't wait on me Shirley. Don't be a horse. If you act like a horse, you'll be treated like a horse." "OK, let me be a horse!" she'd say. Lovely she was. A lovely singer. She's a unique voice. I learnt a lot from Shirley – we used to talk a lot. But 25 and 35 is quite an age difference. And she had the two children, Robert and Polly. In his own way he was very good to the two children. He tried to do his best. But they were always so poor. They had a terrible struggle. Shirley always did everything. She was horrified that nothing was insured. And knowing about insurance she did everything."

Ashley points out that Fairport were aware of Shirley's music, early on. "There was one specific occasion where we were playing Liverpool Polytechnic. And Fairport were on and Shirley and Dolly were supporting us. It was the classic *Unhalfbricking* line up before the crash. And she said something in that concert which I remembered and have referred to a few times, which is in announcing '*Whitsun Dance*', which of course is a rewrite of the traditional '*Week Before Easter*'. Written by her first husband Austin John Marshall."

"A year later I rang her up and said 'will you just repeat that thing about how the centrepiece of any English village used to be the Maypole but after the Great War it was the War Memorial. It was so good an image and we're looking for an album cover idea."

"Then I met her in Cecil Sharp House, when I was with Steeleye. And she says, that I walked across the room towards her, and kissed her, and she then fell in love. Or she knew that I was going to be her husband. And obviously we fell in love. There was another occasion when we travelled up to Whitby for a folk festival, up on a train together. I think that was the beginning of our relationship. She was living in Blackheath at the time. I think she was divorced. And she had two children by Austin John Marshall. So I became her boyfriend and then within a relatively a short time I became her husband and stepfather to Polly and Rob. Which makes leaving them even worse, not that I'm going to start beating myself with birch twigs, but I wasn't just leaving her in 1977, but leaving two step-children. It was a betrayal of trust there. But we all do things that we regret. We don't all follow our hearts, but many of us do and find it difficult."

There's little doubt that had Ashley stayed with Shirley they'd have been the first family of folk music. They'd have been The Coppers, the electric Coppers. Kay Hutchings: "That's also one of the problems with Ashley and Shirley, they had such a public separation – their break up was so public and you can't just ignore it. She came here for a month to stay when the break up was on. He said to her: "Go home to my mother.""

Kay Hutchings remembers that Shirley had a pearl ring, "and she said to me that all the pearls had fallen off, in front of Ashley on the table. She said: 'I knew it would break up!' Well, I don't suppose that they would have been compatible now. Shirley must be 65 now. Still as beautiful as ever though. A natural beauty with her golden hair." Shirley was already aware of *Liege & Lief*, "and thought that it was wonderful. And I think he's a lovely bass player. But I had no thought of meeting him. We were married in 1971." When it all went wrong, she threw away their marriage certificate. "I chucked an awful lot of stuff out fairly soon after Ashley left – it was too painful to hang on to. I didn't want it. It's stupid now, but you don't look to the future too much...you don't realise..." It's remarkable that despite the trauma, Shirley remains very positive about what they achieved together. She was very proud, and quite rightly of *No Roses*.

Recalling the story about her pearl ring, Shirley said: "That was extraordinary. And Kay's got the ring. I gave it to her after we split. Ashley and I were in Charing Cross Road looking for an engagement ring, and I wanted an old one. There was this lovely little gold band with flowers engraved on it and seed pearls entwined around it. I said to Ashley: That's the ring I want!" And we went inside and it fitted perfectly and we bought it. The jeweller asked "Would you like the original box it came in?" We said: "Yes, of course!", and it had ASH initials on the box. Ashley Stephen Hutchings. It was Ashley's initials. It gives me goose-pimples now when I think about it. It was only a coincidence of course, but it felt much more significant than that. And after we broke up, I remember saying to Mary Miller – one of his lovers – that: "I thought it meant that we would always be together", because I was still terribly upset that he'd left, and she said: "Oh that was then, this is now!" I thought: "Oh well yes. I expect you're right!" It was yet another little way of learning to cope with it all.

"Ashley was still playing with Steeleye and we went down to that wonderful outdoor theatre in Cornwall. They were playing there, and we went down for our honeymoon, we had about two days. We married not in London but after we'd been in Etchingham for a while. I know Ashley was going up to the Royal Court to play in *Corunna*.

"As regards our move back to Sussex, I remember Ashley was at my house in Blackheath the day that my Decree Absolute came through. And I had a gig at Exeter University that night. Ashley stayed behind to look after Polly and Rob for me. I had to sell the house in Blackheath because John needed his half. I'd found this lovely cottage called 'Red Rose', and both Ashley and the kids took it sight-unseen. I said: "This is it. I've rented it, it's lovely." We packed up everything in London, got the delivery van, got the cat on our laps, and off we drove down to Sussex. Happy ever after! But we were very happy there for quite a long time. I remember we moved down and the second night he had to go off to do a Steeleye gig."

Returning to the sleeve of *No Roses*. Album sleeves are like the cover of a book – they actually do give you clues. Especially that extraordinary gatefold photo of Shirley and Ashley wandering through a corn field in Sussex. Ashley: "This is just out back, literally just behind our cottage. That was the view we had. But that was literally out the back of the garden. But at that stage I'm still wearing dark glasses, and I'm looking very pale." It almost looks like Shirley is holding you up. "Well to give her credit, she nursed me through."

Shirley: "Well, he had been ill. Because when he left Fairport after the crash, he did need a lot of looking after. He needed care really as he was in a such bad way.

It was I suppose our equivalent to the Great War, him being in a car crash. It did us all good down there. It was wonderful for the children, and it was wonderful for me, I loved being down there, and it was good, up to a point, for Ashley. It gave birth to a band later on. In fact it led to two."

It has that feeling of the First World War veteran coming back from the front. Ashley: "I think that's a brilliant description of it. Coming back from the fields of Flanders." Or the fields of psychedelia. "I'm wearing gaiters that I found at Farley Chamberlayne. It was a massive project as you can imagine. This did capture the imagination of people. It immediately was received very well."

Shirley: "The photograph on the front is Eltham Palace and Ashley and I used to go there from Blackheath when the kids were at school. I remember, I spotted it and said: "Wouldn't that make a lovely picture!" Another piece of the jigsaw solved. "Well, I think it's lovely." Everything about it, right down to the artwork. And it is so much more of an English record – it is a stranger record than *Liege & Lief* – *'The Poor Murdered Woman'*... "I think that's one of the greatest ever songs. But yes, you're right, in many ways it's quite exotic stuff. It is so English but it's not English music as people know it, or think about it.

Shirley Collins and Ashley at Red Rose, Etchingham. 1972

"This was the first time that I sang with a rock rhythm section and a band, but thankfully in the studio you can build it up. I remember talking to Martin when he first joined Steeleye and watching him, and watching him when he joined the Albion Band. He just loved it. That turning up LOUD. He went absolutely potty. I remember he couldn't sing in tune for a bit, he'd everything so loud. There's so much excitement there and so much energy. It wasn't as if it was rock music for the sake of it being rocky. I think that all of the arrangements work really well – possibly a bit heavy on the drums from time to time."

Ashley: "Shirley wanted to make an album. We were married by now and were thinking along the same lines. Almost like a gift to her, I said 'I'll produce the album and we'll make this really good. We'll get as many good people as we can find. You pick your favourite songs. We're really go to town on it.' Which is what we did. We ended up with a massive roll-call of guests, and thought that we've got to find a way of crediting these people, we can't call it a solo album. So I remember it as both of us, jointly coming up with this. But I thought that we both came up with the title – the Albion Country Band – as a way of crediting all the people. So it was Shirley Collins and this big umbrella of the Albion Country Band. In a way it was a homage to English music and all these English musicians, and English singers."

Shirley: "It was done for Sandy Roberton, so it must have been Ashley's suggestion to Sandy, because I never approach people to do anything. But we went into the studio and it just sort of built every day. You know, people would come in and play on the song that they were supposed to play on, and then say: "Can I stay!"

It didn't feel like a responsibility. It also didn't feel like you were breaking ground. You don't set out with the idea of "I'm going to make a seminal album!" It just grew in the studio and it worked. It was fortuitous really. Everything conspired to make it work well. That's how it was. It growed and growed!

"Of course he was diving in and out of Steeleye Span, then forming the Albion Country Band, and we were whizzing off to places like Northamptonshire to have rehearsals at Simon Nicol's house". Some of the musicians used were, to her taste, "unreliable and unsuitable. Good music, but a bit precarious. But then one learns that Ashley's lifestyle is a bit precarious, the way he opts in and out of various things and has a different line-up every week. I'm surprised we were married for as long as we did".

Ashley's creative restlessness is both a glory, and yet deeply aggravating for those closely associated with him. As to *No Roses*, the first fruit of his post-Steeleye energy surge, "the band actually grew in the studio. By then I had come to like electric music – it was so alive and energetic. It really got to the heart of things in a wonderfully gutsy way. And the power was wonderful: when you hear it and certainly when we were in the middle of making it, it was just incredible". Hutchings masterminded the choice of musicians. Arrangements were "very spur of the moment, a lot of it wasn't rehearsed".

At this point, annoyance breaks through, "I think I'm a little peeved that Ashley has held on to The Albion Band, especially as I got ousted out of the band, and then got ditched". Such feelings were a long way away from an album whose overwhelming impression of is that of a singer in love, however bleak some of the songs she sings. Richard Thompson might now consider the record "lumpy", but for us an underlying buoyancy and happiness infuse every groove.

No Roses begins where *Anthems In Eden* left off. Its musical palette fuses medievalists like Francis Baines on hurdy-gurdy, Greg Butler on serpent and Dave Bland on hammer dulcimer with full-blown musical eccentrics like Trevor Crozier on Jew's harp and free-jazzman Lol Coxhill playing alto sax. Hutchings called up revivalist singers like Royston Wood and Mike and Lal Waterson, alongside Maddy Prior and Nic Jones.

As Shirley told avant-garde musician David Tibet – a long time admirer – what "started out as an ordinary album, one or two accompanists, just snowballed. We kept on getting more and more musicians in and they kept staying and playing on other tracks. I just kept on thinking of other things to do, and everybody was enthusiastic and kept suggesting other things: it was a big sort of group thing really". The resulting album carries across the organic sense of musicians bending themselves round the chosen songs.

It was certainly an eclectic mix. The whole of the later *Morris On* team were present, alongside Simon Nicol from the old firm and Quiver's Tim Renwick. Hutchings' electric bass is at the musical epicentre, alongside Roger Powell and Ian Whiteman from Mighty Baby. Powell in particular gives it a good rock wallop. His previous band was the Action, arch mods and cockney musicians schooled in Tamla and Stax rather than Folkways.

Despite the presence of Van Dieman's Land and the River Bann – one of the glories of traditional music is, after all, its width – these songs are noted as being collected in Sussex, Hereford, Lincolnshire, Cornwall and Surrey. In the heart of rural Albion, each one. It could be argued that the long-term influence of this album, not least on Ashley's own subsequent career, has outweighed that of *Liege & Lief*, though this remains an album which has been cruelly underrated, except by those who know it. The fan-club worked both ways: Shirley admitted that *Liege & Lief* was "my favourite record even *before* I met Ashley". She also admitted that "it's difficult to know whether I just love electric folk, or whether I love electric folk because I love Ashley. I know it makes me feel great – all that sound wrapping around all round you. It really feels gorgeous, standing there soaking it all up".

An unsigned review on the folk page of *Melody Maker* focuses on what has been visited on *'Maria Marten'*, "an extreme extension of the album's spirit". There is a huge sense of "self-sufficiency" here, though as with another band – Sergeant Pepper's Lonely Hearts Club – this is not music which could be reproduced live. Conversely, it overcomes the usual objection to most records of folk music, that they "lack the atmosphere of live performances". Fred Woods points out that the electric backing has given her voice "more edge, more pressure, a crisper attack. There is also less of the apparent artlessness that characterises her singing". She has had to "sing out" more, simply to make herself heard.

Karl Dallas points out that "this is Tyger's album as much as it is Shirley's, although he appears officially only as a bass playing member of the Albion Country Band. I've been waiting for a long time for the electric folkers to discover the remarkable tone colours available in the instruments of the English tradition, and it's finally happened".

It ranks alongside *Liege & Lief* as the great English folk-rock album. Ashley: "It wasn't like anything else. It wasn't anything like *Liege & Lief* nor was it like Steeleye Span. It was very English. The man on the back cover was one of Cecil Sharp's singers. And why he was chosen is because we thought he looked like a lion. He's got a mane and whiskers. So the lion on both sides. He's magnificent and so is the lion."

And then we have maybe the most controversial track that you've ever been associated with – *'The Murder of Maria Marten'*. Ashley: "Many of the things on the album naturally happened by bringing the good musicians together. But *'The Murder of Maria Marten'* was very much my idea. It grew this way. There is a fragment of it sung by the wonderful, and my favourite male singer Joseph Taylor of Lincolnshire, that Percy Grainger recorded. And the fragment is what we hear at the beginning. The fragment is really from the middle of the song – that's all he remembered. So I went back and found the original broadsheet. And so what we get is Shirley singing this fragment and then it's like a flashback in time. Then, we go back to the beginning of the story." The way that the electric folk band wails behind Shirley's voice is one of the closest things on tape to the 'shattering live experience' that was early Fairport, here joined by Nic Jones on violin. And of course Maddy Prior appears – so the Steeleye connection was still there." Even so, this was something radically different. As Hutchings himself puts it, "the Englishness was building up." Ashley is at great pains to explain whose vision was behind the album: "Shirley and I both conceived of it. I think it's fair if we both take credit for the album."

The whole album is very eerie, the packaging and the music. Again part of the late sixties, your mindset coming out of that, looking for the strange aspect. "Absolutely. When you live in the countryside for a long time, as we did, you realised how much mystery and pain is there, dog eat dog. We had all that. A weird place the countryside."

In responding to *No Roses*, Martin Carthy commented: "I thought it was fabulous. *'Maria Marten'* sticks in my mind for all sorts of reasons – for its theatricality, for the hurdy gurdy, for Shirley and Nic Jones singing unison to together. Nic having the wit to sing in unison with her, and not trying to sing harmony. Nic was always a very, very clever musician. As soon as he got to grips with his technique, by God he used his imagination."

Richard Thompson's initial observation is that "Mighty Baby are in there. Everybody and the kitchen sink are in there." Far from the faded hippie outfit that their name suggests, Mighty Baby were one of the most subtle bands on the late 60s circuit, devoting 40 minute improvisations to the memory of John Coltrane , and effortlessly melding together country, jazz and Eastern musics. Ashley had played in a session band with their lead guitarist Martin Stone on the extremely obscure album *49 Greek Street*.

Indeed, Stone was Ashley's equal as a questing intellect, formidably well read and latterly a rare book dealer of almost legendary status. The band's rhythm section help fuel the underlying thrust of *No Roses*, giving it the 'welly' one would expect of the original spine of English mod pioneers the Action, whose repertoire was 90 percent black soul music. They later joined Thompson on his 1977 tour, reinvigorating sacred Islamic texts with just the same polyrhythmic excitement. Even so. Richard now finds *No Roses* to be "a messy record." But it's very "English". I think sometimes the musical styles don't gell because the players aren't used to playing with each other. Nice clash, but there's also a lack of ease about it. When you put musicians together from different genres. There's a very exciting thing happens. So that happens on this record but sometimes for me it doesn't quite sit. But I can say that because I was there. And I must also say that I think it's a great album. I'm not belittling it." We think it's an album whose time is yet to come actually.

Simon Nicol reveals his three rules of what makes a great rock album. "Good songs, good performance, good production. The three R's. Without the good songs, you have style without substance!" Richard adds that "On here you've got some crackers, because they've stood the test of time. '*Claudy Banks*' is a classic. But also Ashley is messing about with the tradition on '*Maria Marten*'. He's taking great risks and it coming off." Simon butts in. "You must remember that it just wasn't a song, it was a very popular Victorian melodrama. He didn't really break any new ground, he just transformed it as a forgotten idea from a pre-Vaudeville stage to a different medium." But aren't such transformations the very stuff of art, reinvigorating contemporary experience with a dose of the past, but twisted to a new mind-set. Just look at James Joyce or T.S. Eliot: they did it all the time. It is always the same old ground, it's just that every generation someone comes along and digs it up with a new spade.

No Roses was released in October 1971. The opening track is learnt from the Copper family of Rottingdean – near neighbours of Rudyard Kipling – and strikes a new note in electric folk. '*Claudy Banks*' kicks in with bass, drums and the twin electric guitars of Nicol and Thompson, the old firm reunited. Shirley's voice floats over the band like a waking dream. Ashley's bass is far freer than with Steeleye, and there is a relaxed quality here, no sharper edges. A song of love fulfilled, on an English shoreline. Alto sax and bassoon intersect at the end.

'*The Little Gypsy Girl*' is jauntier, the tale of a young girl at large in the big city, seeking fortune and fortune-telling. There is lots of melodeon and a nice sticks break from Mattacks, with Ashley's bass alone enough to bring a smile to your lips. Richard Thompson later used this song as the basis for his own '*Poor Little Beggar Girl*'.

'*Banks of the Bann*' opens with Dolly's precise piano, and Ashley running up and down the fretboard, as if released by the music and ensemble. Shirley sounds

pensive and sad, her voice warm honey spiked with Librium. A very Irish song for
an Albion collection. John Kirkpatrick remembers playing on what he describes as
"a lovely flowing thing. I just did some smooth accordion, kind of chordy stuff. I
remember it because it was the first time that I'd ever done an overdub. My first time
in a big studio, because I'd recorded in Bill Leader's front room...that was all I
knew.. I thought: "God, what do I do?" I heard this fantastic band in my head, and
they said: "Play along!" I was shitting myself. Ashley kept saying: "Can you play a
bit louder?" "My god, they're going to hear it soon!". It was just all so new. It was
so frightening. So I did 'Banks Of the Bann', I'd finally got it together enough to be
audible. Then Ashley requested: Could I play a Jew's Harp solo on 'Little Gypsy
Girl'? So I thought: "Wow! I'm in this big rock studio. I'll be like Jimi Hendrix." I
went out to Mars on the Jews Harp. There was a sea of puzzled faces. And on the
record it was Dave Bland just playing the tune."

On 'Murder of Maria Marten', Shirley's voice coasts over the full storm of an
electric band, then the whole thing fades into silence, made all the more absolute by a
bass run which does not quite reach a conclusion. Now we are alone with Francis
Baines' hurdy-gurdy, and Collins' voice takes on "a macabre echo" as she goes back
to the start of the original song, and declares how the murder was planned. Silence,
again. Mattacks crashes in with perfect timing, and the electric band are back as
Shirley relates how foul murder was done, as if recounting a dream. There is a guitar
solo – surely from Thompson – which unostensibly but beautifully follows the melody
line, and then Nic Jones joins in on vocals, telling all the grisly details of the parents
finding the body. The old song's psychological details are worthy of Ruth Rendell at
her most obsessive. Hurdy-gurdy again, and a distracted Shirley as the murderer,
repenting his wrongs, about "to be hung upon a tree". Then a bit of street theatre.

In Folk and Country, Karl Dallas describes how "the tumbril rumbles its way
across the stereo like one of those old demonstration records that they used to play
in hi-fi shops, presumably on its way to the gallows". Shirley's vocal style varies
from "her usual uninvolved, uncommitted posture, to a wilder, more passionate
voice than has ever been heard from her". The original ballad, learnt from Joseph
Taylor, has been "cut-up into several parts, each of which has been given a different
type of accompaniment. By upsetting the chronological order of the events related,
she focuses our attention even closer to its horror, in much the same way that a
contemporary film-maker will flash forward or back. One is forced to admit that,
like Charles Marowitz's cut up Hamlet, it works very well indeed. I only hope there
are no imitations".

The 'red barn' murder was the subject of a popular Victorian melodrama, and the
arrangement here picks up on that actorly quality, its chronological cross-cutting
distancing it from simple emotion. It is as if the singer and musicians are acting out
a stage play, an impression added to by the sound effects at the end. To complete the
text, Mr and Mrs Hutchings added verses from a contemporary broadsheet to Joseph
Taylor's "tune and the few verses he could remember". In his book A Little Music,
Ashley adds two more verses, which he has subsequently come across in a version
of the song collected by George B. Gardiner, which "I suspect Shirley would have
included had I found them earlier", and which deal with the discovery of the body.

"The very first stroke that they struck,
They howked up the mould.
Her apron, bonnet and spencer
And furbelows we did behold.

> *They dug full eighteen inches deep*
> *And then her body found*
> *Tied in a sack and mangled*
> *With many a ghastly wound".*

'*Van Diemen's Land*' was collated by Hutchings, and subtly blends a rock band with acoustic folk instruments – concertina and small pipes – as well as the unclassifiable ophlicleide. There is a lovely swaying quality to this warning to poachers, lest they end up as new Australians, and missing their sweethearts. Ian Whiteman's piano has a jazzy quality, and drives the song along, though Shirley seems to plough on regardless of her backing. She lacks the ability of Sandy Denny to mould her voice to an electric band, or of June Tabor to dramatise her material. Yet Shirley sounds – as indeed she is – far closer to the folk tradition, like a force of nature which her musicians can frame but not control.

'*Just As The Tide Was A'Flowing*' comes from her aunt Grace, and Shirley decorates it with relish: the vocal duet with Maddy Prior is reminiscent of the first Steeleye album. Natural music. Hutchings' use of phasing on the instrumental bridge is an interesting take on a technique more readily associated with psychedelia, and the likes of '*Itchycoo Park*'. Here it sounds like the waves slapping on the shore. Karl Dallas compares the Beach Boys' '*Lookin' at Tomorrow*' on *Surf's Up*, "which is also a folk melody".

'*The White Hare*' opens like ritual music, with a wonderfully English folk choir of Mike and Lal Waterson and Royston Wood. Hutchings is on percussion at the beginning, on a single drum and what could almost be jingle bells. It evokes the determination of the hunt, whipping on the hounds. The wicked glint in his eyes with which Mike Waterson (metaphorically) always sings dominates here, so that Shirley becomes a backing singer on her own album, both on the acoustic opening, and the electric conclusion. '*Hal-An-Tow*' goes back to the roots of English myth, originally sung as part of the May ritual in Helston, with shards of the Mummers' Play, St George and all that. It is sung with the kind of passion which would have perfectly fitted the very British horror movie *The Wicker Man*. One can imagine Christopher Lee and his fellow pagans singing this at the end of the film, as Edward Woodward burns alive in his straw coffin. Jews harp gives a bushwacker quality to the song, with Thompson on slide electric guitar.

'*Poor Murdered Woman*' is indeed about a kind of sacrifice, a mysterious song replete with sadness, which Collins picks up intuitively, so that her voice is both distant and committed. The band is vintage Fairport, with a beautifully liquid quality to the guitars: tubular bells, or something very much like them, clang a death knell. Ashley's notes in *A Little Music* recount that the words were written by a brickmaker named Mr Fairs, according to its publisher Iolo Williams, who cited it as "a song of very poor poetical quality".

Ashley finds value in it as "a direct statement of concern by one member of the community for another. Buried a little is the same feeling of desolation one gets from a Thomas Hardy tragedy – the particular melancholy one experiences when wandering through a country churchyard reading inscriptions on neglected tombstones".

Karl Dallas concludes that "despite the eclectic instrumentation, the sound is closest to that elusive English country band that Shirley has been striving for since *Sweet Primeroses*". Hutchings's arrangements are "constant encounters with joy, exciting with their exquisite rightness". Her voice coasts along "like a Hastings fishing boat sailing up the English Channel on a sunshiny day, untroubled by the cross currents and errant breezes of differing musical traditions which seem to have strayed into the studio". *No Roses* is an album whose impact only deepens with the years.

There's just not the amount of record company money to actually make a project like that anymore. Shirley: "We were jolly lucky to get it in the first place. Because if you weren't a big name, or managed by Jo Lustig or somebody, you stood very little chance. I remember going along to a prospective record label with Ashley, when *The Power of The True Love Knot* was made. I had this interview sitting next to Ashley with this A&R man at Polydor Records. Ashley was talking about Shirley Collins wants to do this album, we've got the titles, we've got the musicians, you know we're going to use the Incredible String Band, and we sat there for about fifteen minutes talking, and this chap leaned forward and said: "And who is this Shirley Collins?" And I was sitting next to him! Anyway, Joe Boyd sorted that one out and got it, and he produced it luckily. But it's always been a struggle to get albums made. *"No Roses* – That was worth seven years!"* Has it had an influence? "I don't think so. It sounds vain, but I don't think anybody else could do it really. What's the point of copying it? And people didn't copy it. It's still selling though. The funny thing is I think my influences were early with the Davy Graham stuff, that influenced Fairport."

On the same page as the album review, the *MM Folk Forum* gives an interesting cross-section of live gigs of the time. Fifty pence to see Sandy Denny supported by John St Field (the wonderful Jackie Leven under another name) at Exeter University, while Mr Fox – now with a rhythm section from the disbanded Trees – play the Pied Bull pub. Andy Irvine has a solo gig at Peelers. Tim Hart and Maddy Prior are playing the Leyton Assembly Hall. The Coppers are singing in Hampstead, and John Kirkpatrick is at the Troubadour, with Nic Jones at a pub in the East End. The whole scene is thriving but far from show biz, and like a little world all to itself.

Both Fairport and Steeleye were fish out of water here, too big and expensive to play the clubs and pubs of the semi-amateur folk world. Not singers themselves, except in the bath, your two authors found themselves alienated at the time by some club singers, who would expect total silence for their aran-sweatered renditions of over-familiar songs, then talk loudly through the guest's set, as if their professionalism was somehow an intrusion on the comfy, cliquish world of the club regulars. There would always be a raffle. Conversely, a really good club could engender an intimacy and warmth outside the bounds of concert hall or rock club; the feeling that the audience were all in it together. Some of the most intense evenings put on by the acoustic duo of Richard Thompson and Linda Peters a year or so later were in the clubs.

Thompson – somewhat at a loss since he had left Fairport – also joined in the latest of Ashley's inspired wheezes. As he later told *Liquorice*, "Shirley Collins had these gigs outstanding, they book up a long time ahead, and she sort of stopped working, and she had about three of these, a little tour left over. So we got a little band together. There was me and Tyger, John Kirkpatrick and Royston Wood who was our roadie, he sang a bit as well". This mini-tour could be viewed as being the origins of the gigging Albion Country Band. Shirley says, only half jokingly, that "we were a country band and I'm sure that some people would have yelled out "Judas" like they did to Bob Dylan. It was a great lark. Because it was always such a pleasure to be in Royston's company. Royston Wood was one of the loveliest people there's ever been. He was just a real treasure of a man. He was so funny and so grave at the same time. He had a wonderful dignity and this wonderful gravity, and this lovely voice. He was just sweetness personified. I think everybody truly loved Royston – you couldn't do anything else. I remember it being great fun, but I was very nervous as well, because it did seem like something different from what I'd done when I'd went gigging before.

"It was a continuation of *No Roses*. But then, as I've said, doing it in the studio is easy because you get several cracks at the thing. You can just do it as many times as you want, and you haven't necessarily got all the instruments there. Nor have you got an audience in front of you that you're feeling responsible towards."

When asked if Shirley could still remember which songs she performed with this pick-up folk rock supergroup: "It would have been my repertoire. '*Claudy Banks*', '*Gypsy Girl*', '*Banks Of The Bann*'." '*Maria Marten*' might have been a difficult one to do? "Well, that's true. It was initially a tour with Dolly, who became ill, so we obviously cobbled together a set pretty sharpish? I remember that it was full of energy. It was an adventure really and it worked well. It was electric bass, electric guitars, squeeze-box and no drums. Just as well really because we couldn't have fitted in drums. No, it was a lark. We weren't called the Albion Band. It was Shirley Collins and Friends on that jaunt"

John Kirkpatrick recalls that "it was three days and I couldn't do the third one because I was playing for a dance, somewhere. As regards material – I was already doing '*I'll Go And 'List for A Sailor*', which got onto *Morris On* because I sang that and everyone joined in. It was mainly Shirley singing". The tour is now wreathed in mystery. Nobody seems to remember. "One of the reasons is that on one of the nights, we were fed this sensational drink!" Ashley: "Hot gin and molasses. The place was jumping! It was what the local sailors used, which is probably why there are so many shipwrecks on the rocks."

Richard Thompson remembers things too through an alcoholic haze. "They had this amazing drink called Mahogany. There was one show about which I have no recollection at all. It totally blasted the brain cells. "It was very relaxed." Even here, things were not quite as they seemed. Simon Nicol pays tribute. "Well Shirley was one of those immensely appealing people on stage. You couldn't help but have a nice time on stage with Shirley, it's like going to see Ralph McTell, he's like a bundle of nerves, but walks on stage and everybody goes: 'Aaaa. How nice!' It's like everybody relaxes, and they get comfortable."

On successive nights in early December 1971, the ensemble played three dates in Devon: the George Inn, South Molton, the Lobster Pot, Instow and Plymouth Polytechnic. Karl Dallas was lucky enough to see lightning strike, twice. "So there we were, 50 to 100 local hairy freaks and maiden ladies with EFDSS badges pinned into their tweed jackets, suspiciously eyeing the big Sound City loudspeaker columns on either side of the room". Shirley first played solo, accompanied by her 5-string banjo, which she intended to pension off after the tour. When her band appeared, after all Shirley's experiments with exotic medieval instruments, here she was with musicians who looked forward rather than back, "playing Fender Mustang and Rickenbacker rather than hautboy and viol". Collins had found her rightful environment, "leading a country band, playing music to move your body to rather than rack your brains about". *No Roses* had been too structured for such abandon. "It was the looser ensemble in that pub room, the very occasional fluffs and mis-starts, which took the whole business closer to the traditional".

Dallas compares it to New Orleans jazz, the way someone will start, the rest suddenly pay attention, then join in at first tentatively until "by the end of the first chorus the band is stomping away like mad". When Shirley comes in, her voice is less perfect than once it was, though still with "the sexiest glottal stop in the business", and this gives it life, the way she will "break into a lower octave here and there". Royston Wood and John Kirkpatrick both took over on a couple of songs: "you could imagine the thing developing, with a couple of dances perhaps, a tale or two, the Shirley Collins revue and road show". Replace her name with Ashley's here, and Karl Dallas has clearly been given prophetic powers.

Shirley is worried that he is going to over-egg the pudding (not that a major article in a national music weekly is something which most pick-up bands playing a North Devon pub out of season receive). "You're not going to write this up as the beginnings of something much bigger, are you? They've just come along with me in place of Dolly". Royston adds, between humping gear, "it's really just a bit of giggle, that's all". Not to the hundred or so patrons the next night, standing on their chairs at the Lobster Pot. Dallas comments that it is a shame the band has to split up the following night. "Oh Karl", she said, her eyes alight with the memory of having finished the best two performances of her entire life, probably, "I agree".

Shirley says regretfully that "we didn't record anything with the pick-up band subsequent to the tour."

Dallas points out to the reader, by now jealous beyond sanity, that "this is a game where I suspect replays are impossible". With virtuoso performers like Thompson, Hutchings and Kirkpatrick, "you wouldn't play 50-seater gigs in the wilds of the west country, would you?" A booking at the Royal Festival or Royal Albert Hall – where such a line-up really *should* perform – could never be quite as spontaneous.

3:2
MORRIS ON

No Roses and the Shirley Collins' mini-tour were signposts of a reunion of elements of the original Fairport. Thompson had left the band in late 1970. Simon Nicol followed in December 1971, after the *Babbacombe Lee* tour, culminating in an emotional concert at the Rainbow on November 27th which saw Thompson and Denny rejoin the band for extended encores, including a *Liege & Lief* medley. The spontaneous rock 'n' roll material which Thompson led that night, with lead guitar like "an electric wasp sting" supposedly gave Trevor Lucas the idea for the *Bunch* album. It also led to journalistic speculation.

The original members of Fairport – including Ashley, their organising genius – were foot-loose, and set to recombine. As Karl Dallas wrote in early December, "the whole electric folk scene is in a tremendous state of flux": any predictions as to what would happen now "is just whistling in the dark, because the people concerned don't know themselves". Ashley was half-way through his stint as "member (and leader?) of Shirley Collins' Albion Country Band", Iain Matthews had moved to the States, while Simon Nicol "is said officially to be thinking of leaving Fairport, and he's been working on a new instrument – drums". Then there is Royston Wood, currently roadie for the Albion Country Band, who "has already announced his intention of forming an electric band. Various permutations of musicians have been jamming with Royston to see what develops".

Elsewhere, the Woods Band – with two of Steeleye One on board – are recording a debut album, Mr Fox is on the road, and Trees have reformed, with a fiddle player. Electric folk has grown organically, "more of a rambling rose than the careful category cultivators would like". Indeed, were it not for the needs of record companies and booking agencies, "the whole idea of a 'band' as something hard and fast and immutable would be completely unnecessary". Prophetic words, as the Albion Band and its offshoots were set for just such constant, organic change, more akin to an acting company than a rock band.

Also in December, *Disc* explained how "Fairport Convention minus Steeleye Span could add up to Fairport Convention mark two". The feature considers that these first two bands have done more for folk in the past four years "than anyone else has in forty. It's possible that traditional music as such will die out, leaving a style which is directly attributable to Fairport". The architect of all this is "the self effacing Ashley Hutchings. No doubt there will be plenty of people to inform us that they thought of doing electric folk first, but it stands that Tyger was the first to make it work, not just once, but among a combined force of associates who must number around thirty and who shift around from group to group". Such freelancers have produced an "inbreeding of albums", which in this context is all to the good.

Hutchings is the "organising mind behind the projects", though "a modest man and the last to admit to being a leader": it is those who have worked with him who describe him as "a man with the ideas". Through all the changes to Fairport, he was "organising, quietly and unobtrusively", acting as a musical director. As such, "he has never forced his ideas on any of the groups he was worked with, but has lent them as guidelines that have ultimately been accepted".

Now Nicol had made the same decision: "we've just had too much work and we need a holiday. I've been with the band since the start, and I need a rest. I won't deny that Richard and Tyger and I have talked about working together again". Ashley admits that all the original Fairport – or at least himself, Richard, Simon, Sandy and Ian Matthews – are "on the loose now", though denies there is any firm plan to reform. "Nothing is settled. I have been working with Richard for a couple of weeks and I will inevitably be involved in another electric folk band. But we wouldn't call ourselves Fairport. The style will be similar, but we don't want to duplicate what we've done already".

Between leaving Steeleye and forming a full-time Albion Country Band, Ashley was involved in various side-projects, alongside others who had escaped the mother ship of Fairport. January 1972 saw a straggle of Fairport members past, present and future arriving for a week's residential stay at Virgin's manor house near Oxford. They were there to test out the new recording studio built into an old barn, which was later to earn its weight in gold with Michael Oldfield's *Tubular Bells*. The project in hand was to record an "all British rock album": though planned contributions from Dave Swarbrick and members of Traffic never materialised. Ashley made a cameo vocal appearance on Chuck Berry's '*Nadine*', capturing the foxiness of the original. Pat Donaldson plays bass throughout here, even on '*Nadine*'.

Despite talk of recording some new songs, the musicians restricted themselves to cover versions of American rock n'roll songs from the 1950s and early 60s, from Presley to the dawn of the Beatles. It was the kind of music which fuelled the tender years of those present, and the young Ashley's record collection. The resulting album was titled *Rock On* – with a front cover modelled on an old auto-change record player (strictly mono) and a flexi single of Sandy Nelson's '*Let There Be Drums*', reinterpreted by Gerry Conway. Biographical notes are given on each participant. As to Tyger Hutchings, "Fairport again of course. Then a highly exciting and productive stay with Steeleye Span. He can play with the best and shine. For some reason, he wanted to be known as Ron Smith for this album. But the real Ron Smith objected". The photos hardly support the project – Thompson in a Rupert Bear t-shirt, Mattacks suggestively sniffing a coke bottle – and only Ashley looks the part, in dark shades, cascading hair, and an ornate tie, a Southern gentleman cut out of the same cloth as Jerry Lee Lewis. Possibly carrying a knife...

This musical collective titled itself anonymously as 'The Bunch' – a kind of down market Band. Dave Pegg couldn't take part: he had mumps. In *Sounds*, Steve Peacock reported back from the Manor. The studio was strewn with gaudy sheet music – "it looked like the perfect setting for a band of Neasden rockers making demo tapes". It was the kind of day when something was always on the verge of happening, but never quite did. Sandy Denny threw paper darts at any photographer present. Thompson plays "some astonishing guitar, finely balanced between being tasteful and really ripping things apart", while Sandy "sings dirtier than I'd been expecting". There is a certain amount of "self indulgence" present, but also good healthy fun, as signified in the working title of the album, *Banana*. Not so much unplugged as unpeeled.

Recent record label archaeology has discovered a large cache of unreleased material from these sessions but fuller details remain vague. Perhaps Universal may be tempted to reappraise these recordings as part of their ongoing Island Remasters series.

Trevor Lucas had been inspired by the impromptu jam with which Fairport ended a concert at the Rainbow. He and Thompson then sat down and listened to 60 or so rock'n'roll albums, to find songs that had been bone-fide hits, but which had "died naturally". The selection lacked the sureness of touch which Ashley would have brought to the same exercise. Ashley was to wait a further twenty-two years to record the far more authentic *Twangin' 'N A-Traddin*, which recreated Memphis rock n' roll as it was re-interpreted by British youth club bands. On the sleeve, he and his fellow 'twangers' even dressed the part, with collarless Beatles jackets and flash shoes. This was a deliberately provocative title, suggesting that Sun retreads were another form of the tradition. It could be argued that rock'n'roll 45s fulfilled the same musical function in the life of the infant Hutchings as, say, traditional ballads in a 19th century farm labourer's cottage. Both could provide material for sing-songs or playground chants, and thus carried on the oral tradition.

Fred Woods took no such hostages with The Bunch. "There's a curiously mechanical air. There's no gut in the sound, they remind me of those anonymous cover versions of hit songs. I *hope* it's a spoof. These talented musicians could delude themselves thinking that this was a good record". For Patrick Humphries, "the concept of a group of serious, intense musicians rocking out to old Chuck Berry songs was unsettling to say the least". Richard Thompson himself found it "fun, but terribly indulgent. It was a bit of a throwaway in a sense. Conceptually Ashley and Fairport and myself and Sandy – we were developing this fairly fragile style of music that no-one else was particularly interested in, it was this British Folk Rock thing – that was the path we were going down, and *The Bunch* was rather a retro-step. It wasn't really what we should have been doing at the time. *Morris On* was the kind of record we should have been doing. The Bunch was just a bunch of folkies doing old rock'n'roll songs". He now thinks it would have been more valid to have redone '*Sally Racket*' in the style of Led Zeppelin, or "a rockabilly version of '*Blue Bonnets Over The Border*'". *Morris On*, in fact. For Humphries, though, the record still retains a "ramshackle integrity".

Rock On proved a blind alley, though one worth a brief visit. Hutchings' quizzical vocal on '*Nadine*' – particularly upset when he cannot unlatch her safety belt – was one of the album's highlights, revealing the comic side of the stern visionary. As this book is beginning to show, there are always creative sparks when he and Thompson meet onstage or in the studio. Both were to be next involved in two albums, the aforementioned *Morris On* and *Henry the Human Fly*, cornerstones in their attempt to create a genuine English rock music.

John Kirkpatrick's album *Jump at the Sun*, on the specialist folk label Trailer, includes 'Humphray De Echyngham' on bass guitar and 'Agnes Mirren' on twelve string. There is a cryptic thank you to "Agnes and Humphrey for being such a jolly couple". The former is Ashley, in the first reference to the name of a future, all acoustic band. The latter, as can be guessed from its hint of Scots, is Richard Thompson. All three also collaborated concurrently on putting a rock beat behind the ancient weirdness – and bawdiness – of the English Morris tradition. Kirkpatrick remembers that "either side of recording *Morris On*, I was doing my first album. And so, because we'd done it on this little tour, I forced these two innocent bystanders to come and play."

One of the many reasons why *Morris On* was so surprisingly successful was that it came out on a budget label, and only cost £1.35, around half of a full price release.

Island advert for Morris On.

Ashley: "There's no question that it has sold thousands upon thousands. For an album of Morris Dance music, regardless of whether it's got drums on it, to sell 40-50,000, it's just incredible. Generally sales have fallen off a lot nowadays, but people tend to forget what massive sales we had in the late-sixties, early-seventies." Barry Dransfield and Dave Mattacks also took part. The album is credited to the five musicians under their individual names. Shirley Hutchings, as she now is, sings on two songs, the solidly named Bert Cleaver plays pipe and tabor, and Ray Worman dances a jig, in stereo. Most importantly, the Chingford Morris Men – though Norman Tebbitt is not represented – perform two stick dances. It is a long way from Middle Earth. *Morris On* appeared on Island's budget label Help, alongside such esoterica as Henry Wolff's Tibetan bells, and the Habibya's Sufi meditations. File under hippie conceits, though this was a far earthier enterprise. A full page advert featured a cartoon from Bill Tidy's strip 'The Cloggies' – which bolted together morris dancing and the more violent aspects of rugby league – in which our six cloth-capped heroes were served their pints by a dancing barmaid. "If you thought Morris music was high in energy-level and low on melody content, lend a jaundiced ear", it trumpeted, "make every day a personal first day of spring. At £1.35 you can afford to dance all day, every day. It's out on June 9th". A bit late for spring, but that's record company schedules for you.

Hutchings recalls that "I heard a recording by William Kimber, the concertina player for the Headington Morris, from whom Cecil Sharp collected at the turn of the century". Maud Karpeles wrote of "his perfect carriage, the dignity of his bearing, his loose-limbed yet controlled movements, and, above all, the sparkle of his step, which is one of the glories of the Morris Dance". Ashley was with Steeleye at the time, and getting "deeper and deeper" into traditional music. The recording of Kimber was made sometime in the 1950s, but what immediately appealed to Hutchings was the way it was "so thoroughly English, the tunes, the harmonies that were employed. It became clear to me that really I'd only tackled half the story, the Irish and Scottish stuff that we'd done with Fairport and Steeleye". Martin Carthy reckons that there is somebody else equally important to this project, and one considerably younger than Kimber. "And he's been there like a little beacon all of the time, John Kirkpatrick. There's certain records that Ashley could not have made had it not been for John." Ashley: "Certainly *Complete Dancing Master.* Certainly *Morris On.*" Martin: "John was so bewildered about *Morris On*, – "What the fuck are we doing this stuff for? I've been playing this for years! All right, you want to play that one? Well here we go!""

Ashley very quickly became obsessed with exploring specifically English music. The first foray into this was to invite the various musicians who made *Morris On*. "It was my brainchild, although it was very very important for John Kirkpatrick to be involved, his stamp is on the whole album*"*. If Ashley was new to this traditional culture, it was in Kirkpatrick's blood. As he later told Patrick Humphries, "I started morris dancing when I was twelve. Then I began playing it as a teenager. It had been my life really; instead of beating up old ladies and squeezing my spots all day, I was learning how to play my accordion". He used to sing in the church choir, and "the morris team was an off-shoot of the church originally". A odd combination, rather like those church buildings – usually ruined – that one sometimes finds built on pre-Christian earthworks.

For Cecil Sharp, "out of the debris of ancient faith and cult have issued three forms of folk-art. In the Morris Dance proper we have a dance of grace and dignity, instinct with emotion gravely restrained in a manner not unsuggestive of its older significance, full of complex co-ordinated rhythms of hand and foot, demanding the perfection of restrained muscular control". Sharp rejected the common idea that the Morris Dance was of Moorish origin, and thought this misapprehension had come about from the fact that many dancers would black their faces, as one man told him "so that no one shan't know you, sir". Dancers would also disguise themselves as women – the 'moll'.

For Patrick Humphries – and presumably for the musicians on the clattering, ecstatic *Morris On* – "the popularity of the dance and its accompanying seasonal rituals owe much to its flamboyant energy". Cecil Sharp is more puritanical. "To dance the Morris ungracefully is to destroy it. It is true that the dance is vigorous or nothing; but vigour and grace are not incompatible. The impression (it leaves) is first of beauty, solemnity and high restraint, then of vigour". As a Morris dancer of Sharp's time put it, "plenty of brisk but no excitement".

Ashley remembers reading that "some of the movements of Morris dancing were designed to draw a power from the atmosphere, and the ground beneath them, and their bodies. Some of the movements were specifically worked out, much as the mystical teacher Gurdjieff would instruct his followers. Our ancestors who did these dances, did these rituals, knew far more about what they were doing than we imagine."

Martin counters this with "I remember seeing a team of Morris Dancers who were bikers on TV's late-night James Whale Radio Show. Every time they finished their dance, they'd drop down into a squat, and rev their bikes. Fantastic! They were great dancers too. That's the sort of thing you do. You have people taking a hold of it, taking control of it."

And that's what Martin and Ashley have done as musicians. They've put back that forcefulness.

Martin: "I call them Biker Morris. We know there are other Morris dancers, John's lot, The Shropshire Bedlams, they do it, frighten the life out of you. Great stuff. It's what it's supposed to do. Garstang used to be like that. Probably still are now. When Garstang first appeared – Clog Morris – same sort of thing. Bampton – same sort of thing. Feet into the ground."

Someone once commented that they were concerned about the Germanic undertones to Morris dancing. Martin: "Concerned about them? It's appalling. What are the Germanic undertones?" They felt uncomfortable about the militaristic nature of all those blokes together in their uniforms, and all that shouting…Ashley: "Probably the simple, kind of basic nature of the march, into the ground, the earthiness of it. It doesn't make any sense." Martin: "There's definitely a 'four legs good, two legs bad' attitude towards English music – It's just an Englishness or whatever you want to call it, an English identity. It's really very discomforting. I worry about the people who say things like that!"

We met John Kirkpatrick in the upstairs room of a pub in east Oxford, a mile or so from where Cecil Sharp collected Morris tunes from William Kimber, and where John himself was later to play a solo gig. Large and affable, offstage as well as on, he proved more patient than we did when Ashley was delayed for some hours on a Virgin train, as we sweltered in the car park, and tried fruitlessly to get any info about what was happening. Conversely, Ashley and John delved into the past with relish, and there was a lovely chemistry between the two collaborators, even if their musical directions had diverged since. Kirkpatrick told us that, in the hurly burly of a busy life's gigging, he rarely had the chance to look back on what he had achieved. Here, in this dusty room next to a busy road, he did just that. John had first met Ashley when he was running a folk club in Tottenham Court Road in London, called The Roebuck. "And I didn't run it for very long. It was on Wednesday nights and I decided to ask the librarian at Cecil Sharp House, the Vaughan Williams Memorial Library, a guy called David Bland, to come and show some archive films. There's masses of films there that you just never see. So I thought, instead of having a guest singing and playing at this folk club, let's have something a bit different. It was a disastrous idea because only a few people came. One of them was Ashley, because he'd been spending a lot of time in the Library, and he knew Dave Bland. And we just sort of said "Hello!" And then I thought: 'Wow! Ashley Hutchings!!!' I told all my friends. Then Ashley wrote to me saying he'd enjoyed the evening. It was a kind of ceilidh club and I was playing in a country dance band, and we sort of played a few tunes at the beginning, and there was a bit of dancing, and the main thrust of the evening was singing. He wrote me a letter saying he'd enjoyed the evening and enjoyed the band, and would I be interested in doing a tour with Shirley Collins, with a small backing band. Which would be Ashley and me, and some bloke called Richard Thompson on guitar, and thirdly, would I be interested in making a record of Morris Dance music with a folk-rock ensemble? So I thought: 'I'm glad he liked the band. That's very nice!' And I thought: 'Wow, playing with Shirley Collins, you know, that's fantastic with Ashley and Richard. That would be fantastic.' And then I thought: 'Well, he's raving mad if he wants to make a record of Morris Dance music. Nobody in their right mind would buy a record of Morris Dance music!' And my reasons for thinking that, were mainly because I'd been involved in making Morris music since I was 12. I thought: 'Well, everybody I knew was into Morris Dance music, they either did it or knew about it, so what's the point of making a record because they all know the stuff? It turned out to be quite a good idea!' Ashley recalls that John was then living in Tottenham, near the Seven Sisters Road. "That's right. We actually rehearsed some of the *Morris On* stuff in my house. Ashley came with Richard and Barry and we actually did it in my front room."

Kirkpatrick had first become aware of Fairport with *Liege & Lief.* "I didn't know about the band before that, because I was up my arse with traditional folk music. Anything that wasn't traditional, I wasn't interested in. At that time there were

Traditional Folk Clubs and Contemporary Folk Clubs as they were then called. You just went to either one or the other. And so I wasn't interested in song writing or the more American tradition of singer-songwriters stuff. I didn't like it, I thought it was stupid."

For Dave Mattacks, *Morris On* provided an escape route from the kind of crowd-pleasing monster which the Swarbrick-led Fairport was turning into. "I was very struck with the whole idea of this album, with the simplicity and the beauty of a lot of those songs. I was going through a phase where I'd had it with jigs and reels at a million miles an hour. I loved doing the album, it was a great joy. It was done very quickly and very cheaply. I'm very proud of it, it stands up and still sounds good".

Presumably the *Morris On* title was chosen because of *Rock On*? Ashley: "No. 'Morris On' was a correct phrase. You'd dance on to a 'Morris On' and dance off to a 'Morris Off'. So it's a traditional title, but there are connotations such as 'Rock on', so I'm using a two edge thing really."

Barry Dransfield told R.M. Bancroft that recording "took about a week, and was done very early '72. Some of it was done before Christmas, and some of it afterwards". Sound Techniques, where it was recorded, has now been knocked down, "turned into a supermarket or something". The record "was done live, the occasional vocal overdub, but it was a live session". Morris dancers were brought into the studio, for that final touch of authenticity. Barry found the Fairport crowd "nice people", but felt a little in awe of them, and subsequently his playing could be a little constrained. "Which is where Tyger Hutchings comes in, 'cause he doesn't make you feel like that – you feel OK with Ashley". When Bancroft brings up the thorny topic of nationalism, he is equally upfront. "The upside is that everybody has the right to come from somewhere and belong to a certain culture": the downside is prejudice against others. You "have got to be very careful not to try to exclude other people from it". The English folk tradition is "timeless and universal", like Shakespeare.

On this particular updating of English folk rituals, John Kirkpatrick contributes button accordion, anglo-concertina and harmonium to the project, while Dransfield adds acoustic guitar to his peerless fiddle playing. Everybody other than Mattacks sings. On the album cover – some copies of which appear to be in 3D – the band appear photographed by Keith Morris as if in in a woodland setting, actually the garden of 'Red Rose', Ashley's home in Etchingham. One thinks back to the cover of *Unhalfbricking* and to Fairport's first ever publcity photo, both also taken in a garden, where Nature is luxuriant but managed, safe and under human restraint. Eden, reborn.

Ashley: "The *Morris On* cover was my idea. It's a satirical updating of the attendant figures to Morris Dancing in it's traditional form. Morris and Mummers. So we've got Richard dressed as Robin Hood but with a modern stainless steel crossbow. We've got Barry Dransfield looking ravishing as a Moll with a fantastic bosom." In Morris, it's not a transvestite role is it? "Yes, oh yes, most definitely. Holding a very symbolic balloon. That would have been a pig's bladder, but in this case it's a high tech coloured balloon. You get the picture, don't you? So we've got John Kirkpatrick as a chimney sweep, which was again very often an attendant figure in the Morris and the processions. With a kind of vacuum cleaner. He's got one tooth blacked out there, which is great. Me, as a Morris musician, and I'm actually modelled on Jinky Wells, who was a great fiddler for the Bampton Morris many years ago during the forties into the fifties. Modelled on photographs of Jinky Wells who had these very short trousers which flapped around his calves. I went a bit extreme there. So I went as a Morris musician, but playing a Flying V guitar, which was the most outrageous guitar that I could find. For the modern element, with ribbons on the thing, like he might have ribbons on his fiddle. Then we have Mattacks as the hobby horse man, and his hobby horse, instead of having a hobby horse frame around him, he's on a modern bicycle. He's on a Chopper with the handles."

It's one foot in the past and one foot in the present, striding the two worlds. Archetypal of what Ashley is still doing. "I'm playing new variations. It is again a perfect cover for the music that's within. It's not a designer imposing an outside idea into the thing." So *Morris On* reinvigorated the whole tradition? Richard: "I believe so." Simon: "Gave it quite a kick in the arse." Richard: "Yes and the cover's a terrific picture. A bit of a blurry picture but a very clever picture." JK said that he was particularly annoyed to have lost the Robin Hood costume to Richard. Simon: "Richard was an accomplished Toxopholite at the time." Richard: "As I used to do a bit of archery I thought: "I've got to have that, you know"". Simon: "And you liked the boots!" Richard: "It was the tights actually. The tights were just great. I didn't want to take them off. It's a great concept. The album updated and contemporised traditional music. And some people have never looked better really! Barry looked fantastic."

Shirley says that her daughter Polly still remembers vividly Barry using her bedroom as a dressing room. Richard: "I broke Shirley's window. I think that we were playing cricket and I put a cricket ball through her window. I wasn't very popular at all." As to the cover, the overall impression now is to make Captain Beefheart and his Magic Band look normal, these are people acting half-seriously, half in jest: it is certainly a weird outcrop of the hippie dream, but something which has grown naturally from the Middle Earth/*International Times* subculture, a form of English pranksterism.

Patrick Humphries grasps the essential nature of the album, as "an ensemble piece, with Hutchings' resonant bass guitar and Kirkpatrick's jaunty vocals and multi-instrumental abilities shining through". There is something very comradely about *Morris On*. The sense of naughtiness is most pronounced on 'Cuckoo's Nest', but there is a rough and ready charm here, an ease with the Tradition about as far from *Liege & Lief* as could be imagined. For Humphries, though, "the album rings false. The artifice extends to cod 'rural' accents and a wishful-thinking, rose-tinted view of Eden before The Fall". Not to these ears, mate. There is certainly a drunken charm about proceedings, closer to the Faces than to the more po-faced proponents of 'folk-rock'. Such raucousness is part itself of the Morris tradition, as it is now enacted outside village pubs on summer evenings, all loudly thwacked sticks and a fool beating spectators around the backside with his balloon. Even without its matching dance steps, the album itself proved to be a godsend for drunken post-pub sing-alongs, thus returning things back to the oral tradition.

The album opens with '*Morris Call*', a solo violin piece, like a cry from some lost age, which then cheers and speeds up, slows down again into plangency, but the ensemble crash in, led by Mattacks' stern drums. The sound is rich beyond compare the electric crunch which Ashley has always managed to summon up. A touch o flanging – *à la* '*Itchycoo Park*' – Morris bells and stamping feet for '*Greensleeves*' almost unrecognisable from the school standard, with Ray Worman dancing the bacca pipes jig. Thompson ends with a shuddering chord, a touch of psychedelia For '*The Nutting Girl*', Kirkpatrick comes in all plain English yeoman, and the res on a cappella singing, with lots of innuendo on 'nuts' and the like, the odd whoop and some ironic harmonies in the chorus. The band come in again, sweet as a nut

Their casual mixture of the natural – concertina, fiddle – and the electrically enhanced is beautifully played and recorded, with melody foremost, a sprightly pace and a sprung rhythm. Next up, a bit of studio banter – "is that Jerry Fieldmouse?", then Barry Dransfield's Yorkshire vowels recite a piece of ancient doggerel about sweeping cobwebs beyond the sky, introducing the medley of '*Old Woman Tossed Up in a Blanket/Shepherd's Hey/Trunkles*'.

There is an underlying stateliness, which belies the revolutionary character of what is going on, ancient and revered Morris tunes being rocked up. An enterprise which makes *Rock On* look the pale caricature it really is. This album is far closer to the rhythmic punch and ensemble work of primal rock n'roll. There were no reports of Teds setting fire to their quiffs in protest, but various folk purists began to revolve in their graves, or on a spit of their own devising. Brian Hinton remembers one archetype, all short back and sides, beard and pewter mug, telling him in all seriousness that Ashley Hutchings was the "enemy", the man who had single-handedly destroyed English folk music. But oh so tunefully …

'*Staines Morris*' has two ominous guitar chords, then Shirley Hutchings on vocals, and rough male voices urging us all to the Maypole. Shirley sounds come-hitherish, but Mattacks' percussion has a touch of brutality to it, and the music goes wobblily off-key for one sinister moment. The contrast between Shirley's mellifluousness and the shouted male chorus gives a certain tension, with shaken bells for emphasis. Even rougher voices usher in the Chingford Morris Men for two stick dances – '*Lads A'Bunchum/Young Collins*' – with good cinema-verite sound effects (lots of different ways of hitting sticks) and an accordion-led accompaniment. The only electric instrument in sight is Ashley's bass. Music and actions which it is generally better to perform than to listen to, but this is odd enough to work (thank God its not a whole album, though) with some backchat as the Morris men relax at the end, most likely with a beer or three.

Time for a natural break. Side Two opens with '*Vandals of Hammerwich*', on which Bert Cleaver plays pipe and tabor. This sounds like a dry run for one of Ashley's later theatrical excursions, as the musician approaches the microphone from afar, like a stray musician from *Sharpe*. Shirley again for '*Willow Tree/Bean Setting/Shooting*', a tale of seduction. She sings solo, then the band crash in for emphasis, change down a gear, then speed up for the final dance.

'*I'll Go And 'List For A Sailor*' opens as a Kirkpatrick solo piece, a tailor's farewell to his trade, then solo fiddle comes in as embroidery. A counted in 1-2-3-4 – a false start and laughter, then the electric band are back for the stately '*Princess Royal*'. The pace slows further at the end, alternating with more sprightly passages, ideal to lead on dancers. One can feel the sure-footedness of the rhythm section (which, on this album, has Thompson in the Simon Nicol role of chords rather than lead runs), born of long experience.

Next up is a bit of rural filth, with Barry Dransfield leading a country saga, in every sense. The timing of Hutchings and Thompson's musical interjections is split-second. The band's strict tempo bouys up the roguish lead vocal. The band lead out from the song with a sprightly tune, which undoes the forward-moving tension of the song's rendition, with the same trick as before of slowing down and then speeding up the music. Ashley: "I can remember some significant occasions when we have been heckled. One was when we did '*The Cuckoos Nest*' from *Morris On*, a traditional folk song obviously, an erotic song, about a man wanting to clap his hand on the cuckoo's nest…the female parts…and a man stood up in the auditorium where we were playing and said: 'I find this song sexist and offensive!' It took the wind out of our sails. We were doing just what came naturally. We were singing a folk song in an electric context. To be honest we hadn't thought about that. But subsequently when we did the song a number of times, we referred to the problem of it being out of step with the time. We said: 'Yes, you may find it offensive. But it's a folk song and actually as most rock & roll is sexist and offensive, what's wrong with doing this?'"

'*Morris Off*' brings the album to a humorous close, with the injunction to "go get pissed" bleeped out, ironic after the far more direct smut of '*Cuckoo's Nest*'. A final accordion flourish, and the "incapable Morris" – or should that read Maurice – has staggered away up the road.

Shirley: "*Morris On* – that's one of Ashley's real achievements actually. That and *Rattlebone & Ploughjack*, which was strange and absolutely wonderful. It was absolutely magical. I had so much respect for him, because he was really digging for stuff, and then re-presenting it in a truly remarkable way. I was steeped in traditional music. I had been listening to it since I was a child really. And listening to it really intensely from my 18th birthday on. I was knocked out by a lot of it. He really had got the feel of it, he understood it, he plumbed its depths. And I suppose that what disappoints me is that he didn't continue in that vein. But then of course it's very difficult to continue to do remarkable things.

"He brought an audience with him. And it was wonderful, because Celtic music had this stronghold, and everything was Irish, everything was Scottish, nothing was English, and it was such a hard battle to fight a lot of the time. You hadn't got the media with you, for instance. You hadn't really got an audience with you. You had to really win them. I think there were a few people out there who thought about English music and liked it, but on the whole, we were blitzed by Celtic music... American music, even more so nowadays. And the very fact of calling it the Albion Band was an absolute sign of intent. So, when he did *Morris On*, he was giving Morris music back to people, shaking it off and saying: This is the dynamism of it, the energy, sort of secular erotic, sexy. It was fabulous. It was such a lark. Life just seemed so lovely. It was just such fun. It refers to the different characters. It was really inventive, and really properly thought out and beautifully executed."

One person actually said: 'I see Ashley Hutchings as being a parvenu'...an outsider coming in from another discipline. "But I have to say that I think his association with me helped him in that regard, because my credentials were absolutely sound. All I remember is the happy people at gigs – who just loved it." Can we ask what Dolly thought? "I don't think we ever discussed it. She was married to Dave Busby who was one of the Chingford, later became the Albion Morris Men. I'm sure she loved it because she loved Morris tunes anyway. I think it's a lovely record. I think it still works. It still holds up."

How was the Morris tradition at that time? Was it on its last legs? "No, I don't think so. What it did do was to give it a wide audience. It opened people's eyes as to what English music could be. We were all used to Cecil Sharp House and the English Folk & Dance Society, prim and oh it was so bloodless, you know. And Ashley gave it blood back, filled it with life and beauty as well. The glory of those Morris tunes – suddenly you hear them and you think..."What have I been missing all this time?" I think that was wonderful."

Ashley adds that "If John had said: "Sod off!" to me, "I don't want to do electric instruments with Morris music, what do you think I am?" that might have been the end of it. Thank god he said "Yes! Thank God for the royalties as well." John: "It was absolutely Ashley's idea. He wrote this letter to me. I've been steeped in Morris

Dancing since before I'd adolesced. I knew all the tunes. I knew the meat of the stuff. My experience was so narrow at that time. But I loved *Liege & Lief* and I loved the early Steeleye stuff as well. *Please To See The King* is only just second on my favourite-ever list of folk music records. To have the chance to play with those people, I thought: "Wow! This is going to be amazing!" And so there we all were in my front room in Tottenham, with me teaching Ashley and Richard Thompson the chords."

Ashley found one of the most difficult new disciplines that of learning how to play 'capers'. "Because on a technical point, it's strange stuff. If you've just come to it and you're in rock music and you suddenly go into half time. The feel of all the capers, in illogical places as well. If you're new to it, they're in illogical places" John comments that "the music really is out to Mars isn't it?" Ashley agrees. That was fascinating for Richard and Barry and Mattacks, to get to grips with. John was cruising through and we were concentrating. You've got to remember the background to it – Morris was an old man's occupation. There was Hammersmith and there were some young Sides, but generally speaking, it was slowly dying. I'm not talking about the old people that Sharp collected from. I'm just saying that people in the Sixties who were removed from reality in many cases, it was going with them, and that illustrates just how radical *Morris On* was. Thirty years on, we're used to all kinds of music being rocked-up and sampled and whatever. But then it was pretty drastic stuff that we were doing."

Kirkpatrick is in agreement. It was a brilliant idea "to apply all that formula to English music with this fantastic weird native stuff. It was a masterstroke. And I thought Ashley was bonkers! It was a terrific idea and it was very successful. It tied in with a new look at native English dancing. And I knew a few people who thought: "This Morris dancing is OK after all!" And somebody I play with a lot now, Martin Brinsford, he'd never seen Morris Dancing, but he went and got some hankies and danced around his garden. That was his first contact with folk music."

For Ashley, "a whole pack of cards started to fall down then, because over the next half dozen years or so there was a radical rethink by many people, with regard to English Dance music. It didn't just end with the Morris. Obviously we went on to make *Compleat Dancing Master*, but then we went on in our different forms to work with ceilidh band music, which again was locked into the old way of doing things. I always think of the Seventies as a parallel journey that John and I took, sometimes meeting along the way, popularising English Dance music. It wasn't just the Morris, it then moved on to social dancing." John: "A whole lot of things were bubbling under at that time and the resources were becoming available to find what English music actually was. Recordings were coming out, field recordings, for the first time. I think that *Morris On* was probably a very massive beacon to say: "Look, there's this other path that you can go down!" As Ashley says, lots of strands pull together for a long time in the wake of that. It made it socially acceptable to like English music for a while. It was cool. It was an incredibly popular record – everybody we knew had a copy. Everyone used to get back from the pub when we were drunk and listen to the '*Cuckoo's Nest*'. It is filthy. Ashley: "It's allowed to be filthy."

Suddenly, such music has proved to be hugely influential on a new generation of young players. It is also highly fashionable. According to *Mojo*, "no other genre seems to excite collectors as much as '70s folk rock – or acid folk, as it's usually referred to". The first album to be listed, alongside the likes Trader Horne, Forest and the soundtrack to *The Wicker Man,* is *Morris On*. "The idea was to finish off the job started by *Liege & Lief* and celebrate a bucolic English idyll of the mind".

Shirley is "beguiling" and Kirkpatrick "bestows a sense of glee", while "men bang sticks". Overall, this is music "best enjoyed pickled".

Even thirty years on, Richard Thompson still regards it as a terrific album "We recorded fairly quickly. But it was quite successfully recorded." Simon Nicol remembers John Wood as being "right behind it." For Richard: "And it's nicely put together, leading from track to track." So is it true what John Kirkpatrick reckoned, that the 'progressive' rockers seemed very interested in half-beats and all the other technically strange elements to this ancient music? Richard: "There are these rhythmical anomalies in Morris music. I'm not sure that we really cracked it. There's a funny kind of surge to Morris music if you hear it played properly. I think a lot of it comes from the concertina and the melodeon. If you listen to the guitar playing of Martin Carthy, he's got that kind of a surge or lilt, which you hear a lot in the concertina playing of someone like William Kimber. I don't know what you'd call it. It's not 6/8. Drummer Ian Maun reckons it is triplets played against a 4/4 rhythm. You get a classic folk-rock band playing a shuffle, or your British Blues bands playing a blues shuffle. It very rarely is that." Simon sees these rhythms as very definitely coming "from the feet". It echoes John Kirkpatrick's practice in going back to dancing whenever he felt he was getting into a musical rut. Richard: "That's absolutely right."

After a few years you made *Son Of Morris On* (which John wasn't on), and John made *Plain Capers*. Ashley: "We went in different directions. I made the follow up with other people to *Morris On*, which took the show element one step further. It wasn't a less relaxed album, it was a more developed album. And John went the other way. I didn't feel I was doing the right thing and that John was doing the wrong thing. I admired everything he did about the Morris and I know why he didn't want to be on *Son Of Morris On* and wanted to take the other route."

John Kirkpatrick found that the folk-rock approach "slightly bludgeoned some of the music, because Morris Music is very, very subtle. Any sort of dance music, any British Dance music, there's very, very subtle rhythmical and dynamic things going on. And it's a kind of rippling, like the way a wave goes or a body moves. Somebody asked me to make another record of Morris tunes, and I thought: "I've done *Morris On*. We couldn't have done it any better but I was keen to explore these subtleties, and have an acoustic band, rather than a folk-rock band. It was just something that I had to do to satisfy myself that it was possible. Ashley in fact phoned me up and asked me if I wanted to be on *Son Of Morris On*." Ashley: "I understand why you said 'No!'" John: "It was right in the middle of my working out what became *Plain Capers*. I thought it would be too confusing for me and for anybody choosing between the records. *Plain Capers* was very agonisingly thought through and worked out. I think that it was quite good that they came out at about the same time." Ashley: "What's just flashed into my head was how civilised everything that we've just said was compared with the attitudes of Sharp against Mary Neal, when in the early days they were almost at fisticuffs with each other, over how steps should be done, nuances of tunes, and how more healthy our attitudes are."

Because *Plain Capers* was extremely influential on that acoustic English Country music. And yet funnily enough The Etchingham Steam Band in some ways followed on. Karl Dallas has winced for years at "the maidenly fol-de-rol which is your average EFDSS country dance band": here at last is "music with balls", fit for a "tough *machismo* music" in which male dancers leap, as sympathetic magic to stimulate the crops to grow. He can compare the spirit here to the oldest surviving traditional Morris team in the country, at Bampton in Oxfordshire: the whole record "really dances along".

Interestingly, Ashley found that his music was popular with non-white audiences. "I could name a lot of places where our music has gone down well. An old dear friend of mine, the actress Mary Miller, went to South Africa. She took *Morris On* and when she returned said that it was being played in this broken down record store in Soweto or somewhere down in the township, and that they all were jumping up and down to it, just loving this Morris music. It was just fantastic, they reacted to it in the way we would hope. I'm sure that it's purely a question of marketing. I'm sure that the music that we make, British music, English music...is so accessible. The tunes are strong tunes. The songs, many of them are beautiful or exciting. There's a lot that is accessible."

On the same page, Dallas of *Folk Review* discusses a record which is close in spirit to *Morris On*, sharing some of the same personnel, and much the same raison d'etre. This is Richard Thompson's first solo album *Henry, the Human Fly*, again from Island, with contemporary words but a sound and approach which could be timeless. Hutchings has again been edged out on bass by Pat Donaldson, and supplies backing vocals only, though his influence casts a long shadow.

It is to the detriment to both men's careers, that they have worked so rarely together since Fairport. Hutchings' on-stage intensity refuses to allow Thompson ever to become sloppy, while Richard's virtuouso musical skills prompt Ashley to find the conceptual frameworks in which best to display them. Thompson's finest improvisations rely on a strong bassist. In turn, Hutchings has long sought just that kind of sparky lead guitarist ever since Fairport: Graeme Taylor, Phil Beer and Ken Nicol. When, at the occasional Cropredy, the old firm is reunited, one can almost literally see the musical electricity set loose.

Thompson later recorded a five song, acoustic demo for Ashley to use in later incarnations of the Albion Band. They share the surrealistic wit and mystery of the *Henry* material. '*Rainbow Over The Hill*' (on CD only) and '*Time To Ring Some Changes*' – recorded on *Rise Up Like The Sun* are songs of hope and determination. '*Bad News Is All The Wind Can Carry*' is a song of terror and self-recrimination. The Albions performed it at a climactic moment of the '*Lark Rise*' production. Even more intriguing are two songs never performed by Thompson, '*You Got What You Wanted*' – played live by the Albions circa 1992 – and '*Someone Else's Fancy*', a weird song about a horse race, a theme which for some reason obsessed Thompson at the time. The songs on this demo, like those on his debut album, inhabit a timeless space, a dream world which just could be the here and now.

For Dallas, *Henry* is the other side of *Morris On*. Thompson is "pursuing his own personal vision of what could be a contemporary analogue of the old tradition", one which Thompson himself continues to visit in songs like '*1952 Vincent Black Lightning*'. Dallas's one complaint was that Thompson's voice is shyly hidden so far down in the mix that it is hard to hear the words. In interviews, though, his relationship to the folk tradition came over loud and clear. "'I'm no folkie' says Thompson" was the headline for an interview in *Disc*, in June 1972. The music he is now playing is "not necessarily folk, it's British music with a bit of rock thrown in". He admits that "the Morris album was really enjoyable to do" but reckons if he had to play such music "all the time, I'd go bananas". "Doing Joseph Taylor songs is fine, but it's revivalist music … traditional music doesn't satisfy my soul".

Thompson does wax lyrical about an album he and Ashley have been recording with Mike and Lal Waterson. "I think there's a bit of hope that there will be a revival in English music. The Watersons' music is not at all antiquated, although it is derived from traditional English music". *Bright Phoebus* remains one of the oddest and most brilliant albums of original songs to evolve from the English Tradition. Ashley plays electric bass, Dave Mattacks drums, Martin Carthy acoustic guitar, and Maddy Prior and Tim Hart help swell the chorus. Fledgling have recently put together a tribute album in which singers reinterpret these strange songs, and others recorded at the time only as rough demos, and never publicly released. A review in *Melody Maker* sees the album as wedding the "emotional fire" of the Watersons on stage – Norma is also present as a singer, but not songwriter – to "alarming" songs which evoke "many imaginative moods". Both words and tunes sound traditional, but with "surrealistic twists, the lyrical form is impressionistic rather than narrative". This is exactly the direction in which Ashley is himself now travelling, thirty years on.

Mojo also lists *Bright Phoebus*, describing it as the reverse of easy listening. "The siblings' weatherbeaten Yorkshire tones suggest a wintry agrarian world that scratches intangibly at the listener's unconscious, and where beauty and hardship are intertwined." One can only speculate as to what would have happened if the *Bright Phoebus* band had gigged in public, or if the album had been released on a mainstream label – with advertising budget to match – rather than on the trad-based Trailer. Although the record sleeve credits the album as being produced by Bill Leader, Trailer's boss and guiding spirit, Ashley is sure that it was actually co-produced by himself and Martin Carthy. *"We very much made it happen".*

Things were certainly set to move fast. In December, Island released their carefully packaged double album *A History of Fairport Convention*, "being a compleat history of the musick of those notable and distinguished players, together with a planne, various pictures and a booke containing descriptions of the songs". Talking about Ashley, recording engineer John Wood reckons "Tyger really is a great eccentric. Of course, now, Tyger is one of the leading champions of a real contemporary English folk music".

3:3
ALBION RISES

We need to break off to consider some of the wider issues which Hutchings' music must of necessity address. Ashley's work is, suddenly at the centre of a national debate. One in part sparked off by Lord Bhikhu Parekh's report for the Runnymede Trust into the "Future of Multi-Ethnic Britain'. In the main valiant and sensible, it was not only right-wing zealots who were troubled by one short section of this 400 page door-stopper.

"To be English, as the term is in practice used, is to be white. Racial and cultural 'differences' – have been "symbolically written out of the national story". In fact, what Ashley Hutchings has achieved in over 30 years of music is just this kind of inclusiveness, and a view of the mongrel English race as – at their best – tolerant and welcoming. Just as they were to his own Huguenot forbears, the asylum seekers of their day.

The kind of thinking which prompts poet Jo Shapcott to write about the "complicated shame of Englishness" simply as a given fact is totally missing from Ashley's world-view. Look at his dissection of our national psyche in *Ridgeriders*. His lyrics – by turn comic, tart and ironic – are at heart generous of spirit in a tradition stretching back to Chaucer.

What Ashley totally lacks is the contemporary equivalent, a kind of snooty finger-pointing. Look at his one man show portraying Cecil Sharp – warts and all – as a fussy Edwardian gentleman, but one who also transcended his class and time through a genuine love of English traditional music. Then read Georgina Boyes' one-sided portrait in *The Imagined Village*, which sees *only* the snobbery and distortions of the man. Then guess which of the two won the 'Katherine Briggs Folklore Award'. Victorian biographers tried to cover up their subject's feet of clay. Some contemporary academics focus on the clay to the exclusion of everything else. Hutchings has always been an artist who tries to show us the full picture.

So how does this all connect to Ashley's increasingly focused search for a specifically *English* folk culture? Maybe the place to start is Cecil Sharp's *English Folk Songs, Some Conclusions*, first published in 1907. Sharp identifies the term 'folk song' as having come from the German. Even so, Carl Engel instead uses the term 'national music' in a set of articles published in the *Musical Times* in 1878. The word 'Folklore' was first recorded in English in 1846, and defined by the learned Society which bears the same name as "the science which treats of the survivals of archaic belief and customs".

Survival is a key term. At much the same time as Sharp was writing his masterpiece, Vaughan Williams and Percy Grainger were beginning their quest to save and preserve a folk tradition seen to be in terminal decline by incorporating its tunes into high art. It was the same work of seeking to preserve a dying 'peasant' tradition as WB Yeats and Lady Gregory were attempting over in rural Ireland. Ashley later claims, surely rightly, that he was to do much the same with Morris music, some fifty years later.

Sharp sees English folk tunes as cast almost entirely in the ionian, mixolydian, dorian and aeolian modes. Minor scales are notable by their almost total absence. Cultural diversity, even within Great Britain, is a bonus, not a barrier. "English children may at first experience some difficulty in grasping the peculiar scales and intervals of Keltic tunes; but what Scotch, Welsh and Irish children can sing naturally, English children can acquire, and the trouble will be amply repaid by the widening of their musical horizon, and by the more deeply poetical influence which Keltic music will exert upon the young mind". *Liege & Lief*, anybody?

So is there a specifically English Sound? in his novel *English Music*, Peter Ackroyd traces this back to the 16th century. "The cadences. The clear harmonies. The sweet melodies." He takes this up to Elgar and Vaughan Williams. "It was a line of light. A line that moved among phrases and melodies of music just as it did within the colours of painting. It was the light that brought all things into harmony – and yes, it was present too in the curving and bounding line of the landscape which surrounded me as I sat in the music-room through this late afternoon."

Musically this means a very straightforward, four-square, no nonsense, straight-ahead feel (in 2/3 and 4/4 time) as opposed to the very diddly-diddly flourishy curlicued (9/8 in particular) favoured by the Irish. Morris stomps while jigs twist and flail. English music doesn't fight shy of chucking in a bar of 5/4 in the middle of a 4/4 song. As Ian Maun puts it: "that's pure English bloody-mindedness."

Cecil Sharp also deals with a very English characteristic, "the habit of self-deprecation, and the ingrained belief that nothing of musical value can come out of England". Nothing much has changed. "We must remember that for centuries past it has been the fashion in England to honour the foreign and decry the native-born musician". Sharp argues that "the natural idiom of a nation will be found in its purest and most unadulterated form in its folk music".

True, this begs the question as to what exactly a 'nation' is. 'People' would perhaps be a more acceptable term.

Ashley defines himself within his 1991 BBC Radio Scotland broadcast *The English – A Beginners Guide* as: "I'm English. I'm also a musician. A writer of songs, poetry and sundry media programmes. A dancer. A folklorist. Romantic and appreciater of good food. A gardener. A natty dresser. Lover of the countryside, yet a town dweller. And a sports enthusiast."

In Dorothy L. Sayers' essay *The Mysterious English* she describes the English as a mongrel nation who have picked up bits of cultures as they've gone around the world. The Englishman or woman's one wish in life is to be left alone and not interfered with by governments, bureaucrats or foreign powers. The English are patient in the extreme, but if their tail is twisted too much they will break off relations without a word.

The name 'Albion' which has become so dear to Hutchings is largely an invention of Tudor historians. They imagined a land inhabited only by giants until Brutus – an escapee from the Trojan Wars – discovered it, and renamed it Britain. As Jennifer Westwood puts it in *Albion, a Guide to Legendary Britain*, it is both a "storied land" and a "fabled inheritance". A myth, composed of fictions. There is a constant sense of England as an ancient landscape which suddenly connects – if seen from the right vantage point – to reveal a hidden meaning.

Time and time again, writers think they have caught a brief glimpse of this mystical heritage, just as it disappears. John Aubrey wrote back in the 17th century of how "Bookes, and variety of Turnes of Affairs, have putt all the old Fables out of doors. Printing and Gunpowder have frigted away Robinn Good-fellow and the Fayries". Such fables – along with the literary heritage supposed by Aubrey to have undermined them – were deeply entrenched in the concept of nationhood which helped build an Empire, and of which Kipling is the greatest exemplar. His stories and poems for children dealt direct with native spirits. So too do Ashley's lyrics for *Ridgeriders*', building up a ballad history of Southern England.

Fearless TV interrogator Jeremy Paxman concluded in his study *The English, a Portrait of a People* that the English are "simultaneously rediscovering the past that was buried when 'Britain' was created, and inventing a new future". He could be writing directly about Ashley's own musical voyage of discovery. "The new nationalism is less likely to be based on flags and anthems". It is by nature "modest, individualistic, ironic, solipsistic, concerned as much with cities and regions as countries". Every word of which applies to Mr Hutchings too. "In an age of decaying nation states it might be the nationalism of the future".

The most emotive recent musical statement of just this undemonstrative pride in one's place, is June Tabor's rendition of Maggie Holland's song, '*A Place Called England*': in a land now characterised by "prairie field and factory farm", the heroines are called Meeta and Eileen. The lyrics celebrate pride in one's back garden, literally. Patriotism now takes the form of cultural resistance. England is a melange of King Arthur, come back to life, and a robin perched on your spade, "and English earth beneath your nails". It comes as no surprise to read Maggie's sleeve notes: "It took me a long time to finish this song – and I probably would never have started it if I hadn't emigrated to Scotland about six years ago... I could not have written it without the inspiration of Christoper Hill's book *The World Turned Upside-Down*, Leon Rosselson's song of the same name, Naomi Mitchison's *Sea-Green Ribbons*, William Cobbett's *Cottage Industry*, Hamish Henderson's *Freedom Come-All-Ye*, Jean Giono's *The Man Who Planted Trees*, animated discussions with (rightly) proud and passionate Scots like Dick Gaughan ("the first place to be colonised by the British Empire was England")...

In *The Isles, a History* Norman Davies redrafts the English-centric view of British history as espoused by the likes of the earlier historian Arthur Bryant. In doing so, he opens up our past, and gives it back afresh. He takes a passage from George Orwell, as misquoted by John Major, which stresses diversity, and sidesteps nostalgia. "The clatter of clogs in the Lancashire mill towns, the to-and-fro of the Great North Road, the queues outside the Labour Exchanges, the rattle of pin tables in the Soho pubs." This, far more than "old maids biking to Holy Communion through the mists of the autumn morning" is the landscape which Ashley Hutchings the songwriter has more recently made his own.

A more aggressively Anglophile message came from Antonia Byatt's introduction to the *Oxford Book of English Short Stories*. She saw English literature as currently sinking beneath something called 'British Cultural Studies', and determined "to be strict about Englishness". As a literature, and a nation, it is "mongrel rich". Byatt identifies three characteristics of the English race. "Solidity", a "preoccupation with wickedness", and "the shiftingness, the twisting I have come to think of as English". No wonder, therefore, that Ashley's latest project deals with English criminals down through the ages.

All this might seem a long way away from Muswell Hill in the mid to late '60s, as the first rays of hippie-dom (a creed which preached racial inclusiveness, even if its view of sexual politics might now look a touch primeval) lit the settled slopes of North London. Kingsley Abbott explains that "The fifties had a feel where we were still very much emerging from the War. There was still a pride in Englishness. It was there in a form of humour. It was there in the conversations. I wasn't at all surprised by Ashley's future direction, because it does fit. It was the honourable thing for an intelligent Englishman to do. To go back and really discover roots and get to be an expert in something. That's a very English fifties thing to do. There was a great interest in becoming experts on things. I don't know whether he'd see it in those sort of terms but that idea certainly fits." Revealingly, the globe-trotting Richard Thompson revealed to *Mojo's* Colin Irwin: "What I miss about England are the bits that aren't there any more that I grew up with. The greyness. The pride people had in being working class, in their country and their street. People would wear uniforms and be proud of it. It's all gone."

Newspaper writer Allan Brown looked at it from another perspective: "Fans are fascinating. Buffs is perhaps a better description. In Britain buffery follows a benign model. Town planning created a race with little fondness for command activities; at heart Britons are loners and loners require pastimes, whether keeping bees, insisting that the earth is flat or archiving films and television programmes. It is a country with a curatorial tradition, where the past is cherished and attended to. Hence its reputation for breeding eccentrics, mavericks, devotees who follow instructions only they can hear."

The question of what exactly *"Englishness"* means now was the subject of a discussion between Billy Bragg and three leading politicians – New Labour's Chris Smith, Liberal Democrate Lembit Opik and Conservative Michael Ancram – published in the May 2001 edition of *FRoots*. Despite his thirty year struggle to engage in such a national debate, the name of Ashley Hutchings is not mentioned, as surely Christy Moore or Paddy Maloney would be in an Irish context, or Dougie Maclean or maybe Aly Bain or Dick Gaughan in a Scottish one.

First up is Billy Bragg's proposal that the government should create a study centre for English folk music, bringing together material at present spread over a wide range of collections. He argues that "a centre for English folklore wouldn't only be about England, it would be lifting the lid on England and seeing the way that our culture is wired up. It would be a multicultural project rather than a narrowing one. It can only break down barriers". Opik throught that "one of the things that holds us back is a certain fear of English nationalism. The damage that the National Front did to the whole business of *"Englishness"* has made people still a bit wary of it. They think that an English tradition risks being symbolised by the British bulldog and skinheads". There is a greater desire in Scotland and Wales to prove their own separate identity. "Nationalism is a product of oppression. England maybe hasn't been threatened enough in a long time to feel that requirement".

He goes on to argue that 'Celtic' music has entered the mainstream of popular music in a way that English music simply hasn't. "But I think it's not cultural prejudice in England, it's cultural apathy. It's not that people are against it, they just don't register it". *FRoots* editor Ian Anderson interjects here that if there is one fight that the English have lost, it is that against the steady march of American cultural imperialism. Early Fairport could be seen as a case in point, at least up to the point where they began to write their own material. So what is the nature of *"Englishness"* today? Bragg thinks that "people don't know how they feel about it. Because of that ambiguity, a vacuum has been created that has been filled by very narrow-minded xenophobic people. We have to get to a place where we feel at least comfortable with being English."

Chris Smith considers that "one of the glories of English culture is that it combines so many traditions". This is much the same argument as when the then Foreign Secretary Robin Cook argued that the English national dish is now chicken tikka masala. Billy Bragg points out that there is a long history of such multi-culturalism in England. "We have the hyphen in Anglo-Saxon to fly in the face of anybody who tries to suggest that this never was an island of many different types". We must repossess our own history, and "use the fact that the folk music of our country was influenced by being a maritime nation, and that people came here from all over the world". Chris Smith gets political, and attacks the way that in his view the Tories now see England "as being in glorious isolation from the rest of the world".

The discussion moves on to education, and Billy points out how music in schools is currently underlining English multiculturalism. "I live in Dorset now, and my son goes to the village school. The headmaster has brought in a guy called Roger Watson and his TAPS artists. Roger is from the English tradition, and begins talking about local songs. And then he shows how the rhythm that he's playing on his melodeon translates to this tabla player from India, then to the guy who plays the drums from Gambia and then to Mauricio from Chile."

TAPS (Traditional Arts Projects) also runs the 'Public Domain' scheme, with which Ashley Hutchings has himself been closely associated, alongside Roger Watson. It is a development of what he has done ever since '*A Sailor's Life*', taking on an old song and making it new. As Bragg puts it, "it's the idea of using the wealth of English folk culture to get the kids to be creative".

Ashley: "I dipped my toe in the water in the late 1970s and late 1980s with a few compositions which were based on folk-songs, but it wasn't until I found Roger Watson (musician, singer and head of TAPS) was similarly fascinated that something approaching cohesive order was instigated. Together we formed "Public Domain", which attempted to encourage writers to look again at the old songs and perhaps create new songs out of them. Our success was muted, but it has led, a half-dozen years later, to my *Street Cries* album."

Working with schoolkids, Ashley has given them the benefit of his own knowledge, while in turn being energised by their inventiveness and their refusal to be intimidated by the past. "In recent years I've done quite a bit of work in schools, in between touring and recording. I find it very rewarding passing on what I've learned about folk-music and dance. They have invariably enjoyed the work too. On occasions I've worked with young teenagers, and the common problematical thread that links all these young people, whatever their ages, is that they find it hard to connect with the language of the songs. Not the timeless tales but the style in which they are presented."

"'*These Cold Lips*' on the album was composed in a song writing session by two 14-year old girls, with my assistance. We chose to set the story in an area which the girls were familiar with, and we visualised a tragic situation with which they could identify. Thus the Press-gang of the original song is replaced by a drunken gang of youngsters coming out of a pub."

"Of course what I'm doing is nothing that the tradition wouldn't naturally have done to its' songs. The difference is that I am speeding up the process, and doing it "consciously". Well that's my take on it."

The notion of *"Englishness"* is now a matter of lively discussion. For Martin Carthy, *"Englishness"* has to be a shifting thing because who ever comes into the picture, you have to adjust the focus very slightly. Pre 1952, you could talk about "England", and I mean England, (I'm not talking about Britain-England interchangeable) as being a white nation. But 1947-48, you had an influx of people from India and Pakistan. And then you had the Empire Windrush bringing the first wave of West Indian migrants to Britain. And they changed the picture and their children alter it dramatically."

They're only the latest wave. Ashley comes from Huguenot stock – originally we all came from somewhere else. "Exactly! I'm Irish. My great, great grandfather came from Ballybunyon, County Kerry. But he came and changed his name, and became George Carthy. He wanted to hide. And he became a Protestant as well. He was a Catholic. At least I assume that, because the rest of the family, who I found in New Jersey, are all Catholics." What's your original name? "McCarthy. These days McCarthy is a big deal. At that time in 1850, Carthy and McCarthy were interchangeable. Yes, Son of Carthy. He would have been known as Tim Carthy. But then would have been known as John's Peter's Paddy's Tim's Tim, 'cause they do that still in the countryside. So everybody had at least three or four names."

But the whole point of "Englishness" is that it's like a soup, and different ingredients spice it up. The soup keeps on bubbling away. "That's true. It's also true that its identity has been under attack for at least 300 years. You know, what culturally it meant to be "English" has been the subject of ridicule for a very long time. A lot of the things we assume to be our traditions are nothing to do with us."

Like St George who's Spanish. "Well even that. What I'm talking about is the Tower Of London, I'm talking about Trooping Of The Colour, Changing The Guard. It's rubbish. The little things that are left like the Padstow Obby Oss, or The Green Man. Ceremonies that actually define people because they say it defines them! Something that I really admire is a number of Scots lads these days because they wear the kilt. They know it's Sir Walter Scott. They know it's phoney, but they say: "We say it means THIS! We want to define ourselves like this! Take it or leave it!

"I won't have anything to do with the Cross of St George. Because I think, apart from anything else, the Cross has caused so many bloody deaths, "bloody" deaths. So much mayhem over the years, that I want nothing to do with it. Some of those things define *"Englishness"* like the various kinds of Morris Dancing. Talk about those to your 'average English person' and you will have people falling in the aisles with laughter. And you'll get supposedly intelligent people saying: "Yes, George Bernard Shaw said that everybody should try incest and Morris Dancing – but only once [*sic*]." Stuff him! He also said, he was "a better playwright than Shakespeare", and we know that's bullshit too! But he was Irish, so what the hell does he know?

"The Irish want to claim everything. The Irish would claim Cuban music. "Hey Fidel, get your fucking arse over here!" The Irish want to be everywhere. Hooray! I love the attitude so I'll do the same. And no one believes me. The Irish are great. It's great music but it's in danger of becoming as all consuming and Fascist as Rock and Roll.

"The Irish went everywhere. The Irish got driven everywhere. The people who went to the Appalachians were Scots and English. You will find, if you look in the collections, you will find Scots tunes from Aberdeenshire falling over the feet of Appalachian tunes. Like, the tune Ashley used for '*Matty Groves*'. '*Shady Grove*' you will find that exact tune in Aberdeenshire. The Irish want to be everywhere. The Irish want to be in Quebec. Quebec music is English. Quebec music has a thing called a Brandig in 3/2. Quebec you'd think was French music, but the French don't have 3/2 tunes. They don't have these kinds of tunes. The Irish don't have them. The people who have them are the English – they call them double hornpipes and they were around in the 18th century."

So let's approach *"Englishness"* through the musical metaphor of folk-rock. Imitators of Fairport were largely leaden-footed…Richard Thompson: "There were legions of those! Never quite enough technique. Also, if you listen to most British blues band at the time, what was wrong was probably 'the feel'. Particularly the rhythmic feel. I think that was true of English people…British people learning their own culture as well. They didn't have the right feel for folk-rock. Because they didn't do the dancing or know the dance tunes, so you know there was a real lack of…an intuitive feel. What was lost was rock and "roll". The fact that rock music had the roll as well. The Swing was missing. You know, all good rock and roll had Swing to it. That's why I hate Techno. There's no Swing at all in there. It's essentially white music on the beat. It's kind of effete really. It's got no balls to it. It's got no grit to it. Some of those classic rock and roll records – like a Chuck Berry record…you probably had two jazz guys and two rocks guys, colliding in the middle. And the jazz guys are feeling everything in triplets, and the rock guys are feeling in eights, and it just works together. And miraculously it just bounces and you think: "Where the hell did that come from?" And I think there are subtleties in playing amplified versions of British traditional music that we are still exploring." Back to Ashley Hutchings…

3:4
ALBION COUNTRY BAND

The clearest account of what happened next is that given by John Kirkpatrick. "Ashley and Royston suggested having a band which was basically *Morris On* on wheels. They asked me just before Christmas 1971 if I was interested in being in the Albion Country Band. It wasn't an existing band – it was just a bunch of people who'd played on *No Roses*. We had one day's rehearsal in Cecil Sharp House." Joining him were Simon Nicol on drums, Richard Thompson on guitar, Ashley on bass, Royston singing, and Sue Draheim on fiddle.

Sue Draheim had been featured in *Melody Maker* six months before, as an unknown, jamming with Packie Byrne at the Loughborough Festival. She had "rapidly acquired a fan club who weren't sure how to take old-time country music from a West coast blonde". She had only just arrived from California, and – if visa problems could be sorted – would be recording with John Renbourn and on Royston Wood's "much anticipated solo album", never to be released. Draheim had been a member of the New Tranquility String Band, and had appeared on Janet Kerr's album *The Blue Ridge Mountain Field Trip*. She was just what Ashley was looking for, another musician who was already in complete control of their instrument, and a traditional style, but who wanted to break through into something else. Ashley: "When my music is good, it's not when I'm playing it, it's when it's playing itself. It's got a life of its own".

Sue Draheim was born in Oakland California and first played at age eight, having been influenced by her father's RCD Red Label 78s of Fritz Kreisler. Her later influences included Michael Coleman, the great Irish fiddler, the very English Dave Swarbrick, and the very "Old Time" Tommy Jarrell. She'd learned a lot playing in various bands in Berkeley and had met Joe Cooley, the great Irish accordion player from County Galway, who was then living in San Francisco: "Joe had taken a few of us lucky musicians under his wing. Those were wonderful times. I was left a bit of money from my grandmother and I determined to travel. Yugoslavia was a possible destination as I had also become quite enamoured of Balkan music! I met Janet Kerr in North Carolina – she was making a field recording for Bill Leader at the time – and she gave me an open invitation to stay with her if ever I should come to England. So London was my first stop on this adventure of mine and I never did make it to Yugoslavia."

Despite her American origins, Draheim had no trouble adjusting to the specifically English music of the Albion Country Band: "The music wasn't really so different to what I had been playing. After all, all of the American Fiddle tunes had their roots in the British Isles. So it seemed a natural progression or regression perhaps. One of our tunes, '*Babylon*' was a Shaker Shape Note Hymn. American as apple pie. I brought a few fiddle tunes and I like to think my own inimitable style. No one else sounds or did sound like me! I loved the band. I wish we had had a bit more time to create. I loved Richard Thompson's songs and I wish I could have worked with him more. He had so much feeling in his music."

The other new face was Royston Wood, a founder member of the Young Tradition, largely unaccompanied, and led – in terms of lung power at least – by the extraordinary bleating of the late, great Peter Bellamy. To hear them, you would think you were in the presence of three rustic ancients, probably related to the Copper family of Rottingdean, but to see them was to be transported to an episode of *Adam Adamant*. Victorian chic, as reflected through the prism of the late 60s. Royston sported a frock coat and William Morris trousers: the "self-styled daddy of the group", he was a long distance lorry driver when not singing. The group's third and final album was *Galleries*, an ambitious folk-suite with a backing band of Dolly Collins and David Munrow's Early Music Consort: it was recorded at much the same time, and with much the same aims and musicians, as Shirley and Dolly Collins' *Anthems In Eden*.

Following in that tradition, Royston had sung on *No Roses*. With his Victorian side-whiskers and taste for dark, formal clothing, he looked like a 19th Century undertaker, and sang bass, the vocal equivalent of Ashley's chosen instrument. He was also looking to form his own electric band. At this point, neither Steve Ashley nor Dave Mattacks were involved in this prototype line-up. Shirley Collins was also exiled from what had originally been her backing band, and one she had helped name. Talking to David Tibet, some 25 years on, she still could not understand why. "I was pretty cut up about not being included in the first Albion line-up. I think Ashley thought, probably quite rightly, that I wasn't a good front singer for an electric band, but then I don't think that Royston Wood was either, or Steve Ashley, they weren't experienced at singing with electric instruments either".

Shirley: "I did it for some time, but I think I wasn't reliable like Sandy. She could always sing well. But there was a sort of fragility that I had, that Sandy also sounded as if she had, but she didn't. She had an incredible strength in her singing that I didn't really have. What I minded was when the band first formed after *No Roses*, and it was my name…we were a partnership. He wanted to form a band called the Albion Country Band. I wanted to be in it but he didn't.

Albion Country Band 1 at Northampton. 1972. l-r: Dave Mattacks, Steve Ashley, Ashley Hutchings, Sue Draheim, Simon Nicol, Royston Wood

"We used to go up and rehearse at the Nicols' place in Northamptonshire. I remember Simon's wife 'Bert, spent all the advance money on duvets for everybody, so that they could stay up there and sleep." Shirley jokingly added, "I was just being a groupie really!"

Even without Shirley, rehearsals for the prototype line-up went well: for Kirkpatrick, "it was very nice, but Sue

Harris, to whom I was then married, had just packed in her full-time job so we could work as a duo just before Christmas 1971. So the timing was appalling. I was committed to working with Sue, so I said no …" *Disc* reported in January that "Tyger is still working on getting his own group together, but hasn't been able to finalise things. He's been working with Richard Thompson and Royston Wood, but would like to have John Kirkpatrick join them. As John had a full diary of bookings he wants to fulfil, this seems to be some way off".

On the same day as the *Disc* report, *Melody Maker* excitedly headlined an article 'Reunited Fairports?' "The future of Royston Wood's new group is once again in the air following the withdrawal of John Kirkpatrick in order to work in a duo with his wife. The group was not to have started serious rehearsal until April, but a tentative line-up had been worked out". The *MM* piece is topped with a picture of Thompson, lost in full flow, so it is no surprise to read that "Simon Nicol was to have played drums and other instruments alongside bassist Ashley Hutchings and guitarist Richard Thompson – thus giving some ground to the recent 'original Fairports reformed' prophecies". Sue Draheim was to have completed this line-up, doubling on fiddle and banjo. The new band were to have drawn material "from traditional sources and also probably from songs written by Mike and Lal Waterson and Steve Ashley". Royston Wood had indicated in an interview published in *Sounds* in mid December that he was "fulfilling his dream of the ideal band", though this turns out to describe the pick-up band for *No Roses*.

Royston confirms exactly who the creative mastermind is here. "I went to Tyger and said 'help me make a band', expecting him to get me a drummer, bass player and guitarist. Two or three days later he returned with a list which included myself. I felt very flattered". He is not sure now if he should have been. "He questioned me very closely about my motives, as Tyger will, and from then on he took on the band building". As to Hutchings' brand of man management, "he tries to squash you and if you succumb to that you're not worth working with from his point of view. If you block that, then he will work with you".

Royston Wood's idea of the new band becoming "the nucleus of a travelling circus with a changing periphery of other performers" was not to be realised, except perhaps in the idea of taking along its own Morris dance team to gigs. The same was to apply to his dreams of a solo career: it already seems implicit in the way that he admits to being "really afraid of making an ass of myself, and it's taken a lot of good friends to nag me into dropping that point of view – like Martin Carthy and Ashley Hutchings used to get at me in nagging, subtle ways". Successful people are never troubled by such self doubt, certainly not at the start of their careers. Such things usually come later. Nothing has ever emerged of the solo album he describes here, involving many "jamming sessions" in the studio. One of these sessions, for '*Bold William Taylor*', involved Ashley Hutchings and Clive Woolf, and the electric amplification they brought to it decided him on his new direction.

Royston has met Sue Draheim in August and spent a couple of days working things out. "This gave me the idea of a band and Sue was the first person I asked to join. I'm not the governor of the band anymore – there are three governors". This has to be the first reference in print to Tyger's later nickname. Despite some confusion at the time, Ashley's new band was a quite separate entity to Royston's planned combo. Ashley explains that "Royston wanted to form a band at the same time as I was wanting to form the Albion Country Band. I think that we just made it one, instead of two separate bands. Bless him, had he been alive today, well I'm sure, he would agree that that's a false impression that those articles may have given."

Ashley believes that these first sessions for a Royston Wood solo album came to nothing, supplanted his plan and the Albion Country Band blossomed instead, although "he did make an album later with Heather, not then, *No Relation*, and I'm on that".

Prospective members of the new band met to decide their future. When the Albion Country Band finally emerged into the open, it was with Steve Ashley on vocals, Simon Nicol back on guitar and Dave Mattacks on drums. Richard Thompson was nowhere to be seen, off recording *Henry* and then embarking with girlfriend Linda Peters taking his original songs around the folk circuit, in an acoustic setting. Both would help Ashley out, some nine months later, in his hour of musical need. Simon Nicol has weaved through Ashley's working life, even more so than Richard. Simon jokes that "I'm cheaper, and I'm much more available." Richard joshes back, "You're damned right!"

It was not the best time to plan a new band playing 'electric folk'. Karl Dallas, who claims to have coined the term, asked whether now was the time to "pull the plug out?" He sees the next step as a fusion of folk club culture and the wider rock world. "My biggest hope for 1972? To hear Ewan MacColl recording with Ashley Hutchings and Richard Thompson and Carol Pegg and Terry Cox". Fairport meets Mr Fox and Pentangle, and sings Radio Ballads!

It was a brave experiment from the start for Hutchings to attempt to keep a six piece electric English folk band going and solvent. Ian Campbell had earlier taken an acoustic folk band on the road with, among many others, Dave Swarbrick and Dave Pegg, but the costs were exorbitant. "We travel with all our instruments in a Ford Zephyr. An electric band needs more ampage, a van, roadies, and a ton and a half of equipment. They can't perform in the clubs, so have to concentrate on making records to appeal to a bigger audience. Then they have to water down the music to make it more like pop music so that it will sell". This sounds like just the path that Steeleye Span took after Ashley's defection. "A lot of traditional singers don't resent the electric groups, they envy their financial success."

After a long hiatus away from the music business, in which Steve Ashley was working as an administrator for an international charity, he released an album, *Everyday Lives*, whose Englishness is the reverse of tub thumping, but is central. When interviewed, Steve himself seems little changed from his Albion Country Band days, but came across as determined but nervous, terrified in case he should offend anyone. Privately, we wondered if anyone so obviously genuine and gifted, but also a man easily deflected by critical brickbats, should venture again into the shark filled waters of the music biz. He looked back with genuine affection, but also something approaching anger, that so important an initiative should have run onto the rocks. It was certainly not the fault of Island Records, who gave them a generous advance with which "we all got some exotic instruments. I had a crumhorn, Sue had a bass viol, and Simon had a hurdy gurdy. When we sat down together we drew up a shopping list of what we were going to need."

Steve was the final addition, having been auditioned alongside the melodeon players Doug Sheriff and Tony Hall. Steve: "Sheriff was a melodeon player who worked at Cecil Sharp House. He and I both went together to have a try out for the band. We went up on the train together and I had half an hour with the band and Doug had half an hour with the band. Then we had a game of ping-pong between us, literally. Once the weekend came to its conclusion, the band had decided to invite me to join, which was very nice, but very disappointing for Doug. I remember Ashley calling us in to say what they had decided, and I said: "Sod it, we've decided to form our own band!" sitting in the ping-pong room waiting for their decision."

It was Steve Ashley's ability as a singer/songwriter – and his extra skills on a harmonica – which tipped the balance. Like Hutchings, Steve began his career playing in a teenage blues-band, but changed direction in 1962, after seeing Anne Briggs perform at the Centre 42 festival in Southall. He immersed himself in traditional music, at places like the Singers Club, though, as he told Karl Dallas, "I began to feel a bit castrated singing only traditional songs. It is more of a craft than an art – once you've learned to do it well, it becomes rather limited. The idea of traditional and contemporary music being separate things became quite a hang-up". Anne Briggs herself had covered Steve's '*Fire and Wine*', and a demo tape of his songs – recorded by Austin John Marshall – was in the hands of the cognoscenti. "Not only that. He has an incredible voice, a cross between Pete Bellamy's power and a more intense version of Bert Jansch's near conversational style". His work makes "little attempt to sound like folk song", but deals with the "great elemental subjects of love, life and death". Dallas can imagine Steve's "very English material being appreciated in America and Europe simply because of his Englishness." He takes that background and "universalises it". Who better to join the *Albion* Country Band?

Early in 1972, the *NME* announced that "a new seven-piece group is currently engaged in rehearsals, prior to taking the road in June. The line-up includes Tyger Hutchings on bass and Shirley Collins on dulcimer, guitar, keyboards and vocals. Other players comprise Royston Woods (sic) on vocals, Simon Nicol back on guitar, Dave Mattacks on drums, Steve Ashley on guitar, penny whistle, harmonica and vocals. Violin comes courtesy of "a girl named Sue" – which sounds like a Johnny Cash outtake. "The *NME* understands that the band's policy will be dedicated to English traditional music".

When the band started gigging, though, Shirley was back home in Etchingham. Ashley: "I was only aware much much later, that Shirley resented not being in the Albions to start with. But at the time I felt that it was a quest that she supported me on. It grew out of this legendary mini-tour that was done in the West Country. And out of that grew, in a very similar way to the beginning of Steeleye, sessions and rehearsals and boxing around trying to get a line-up for the first Albion Country Band. And the people that we went through, in no particular order, were Tony Hall, the melodeon player; Richard Thompson; Simon Nicol on drums, not on guitar, and then eventually we settled on the first line-up. So we had a band with three ex-Fairport members and concurrently there was a band running, with no original Fairport members in it. Here were two originals and one very important *Liege & Lief* member in another group – The Albion Country Band."

"Well, we started right at the beginning of 1972. So we started fresh, a new leaf. We very often took the Albion Morris Men with us, because having made the *Morris On* album, guys broke away from the Chingford Morris and formed The Albion Morris Men. And they were magnificent, and still are to this day. They were always the most athletic, the most exciting, the most maverick dancers. So they were ideally suited to being with a folk-rock group."

Two weeks later, under the headine 'Tyger-Nicol album', *NME* provided an update. Island will be releasing their debut album in the autumn. This (mythical) album is also predicted in the *Melody Maker* of 8th April 1972, under a weirdly posed photo. Just like Steeleye One, the band half sit, half stand outside a house, and Sue Draheim cuddles a cat. Hutchings stands enigmatic as ever, hands in pockets, check-trousered legs slightly apart, clean shaven and in shades. His piped blazer could be that worn by Patrick McGoohan in *The Prisoner*, another man who could never be "briefed, debriefed", typecast, numbered or controlled. Steve Ashley sits at the other end, in patched jeans and long hair, while Simon wears a weird boiler suit and braces. Royston Wood also stands, arms crossed, his lined face that of someone from an older generation. Sue is dressed in patchwork, while a denim-jacketed Mattacks looks grim and wears a medallion around his neck. Tyger, lacking flares or patches or long hair, looks as if teleported down from a more stylish era, the 1980s at least. It's interesting in that Steve thought it was actually Royston's band. "I suppose Royston had presented it to me in that way. "I've got this band" and I'm sure that Ashley would question that. I hadn't realised the sensitivity or politics of the band. I just thought that it was a great bunch of guys and it should be fun."

The band had brought along their own suggestions for a group name – among them, Royston Wood's Conspiracy, Sally Racket and Simon Nicol's anagram of Albion, "Obnail". But they chose a name that was already identified with Shirley Collins in the public mind. To be fair, this is hardly *No Roses* Part Two, with Royston playing only a peripheral role on that first album, and Steve and Sue no role at all. The focal point of the new band was to show itself as the visceral combination of Steve and Royston's vocal harmonies, far away from Shirley's soft charms. It is hard to see her, in retrospect, as a third harmony singer: her voice is too individual, and her reputation too high to be restricted to such a role. Even so, one can understand her annoyance at being excluded. Nicol said at the time that "Shirley was never a runner for the band – we just like the name, although there's guaranteed to be confusion". With Shirley having led a band of the same name for live gigs a few months before, this is an understatement. As to *Morris On*, that too is largely unconnected. "That was just a joint project by the musicians involved, and although Tyger and Dave were involved in it, the Albion Country Band is quite independent of that".

This was something new. Steve Ashley finally had the chance to present his songs amongst the live thunder of an electric band. "The idea or ideal perhaps, that we might create some music that was original, that we all contributed to, appealed to me. Obviously I had songs that I wanted to sing, and did some. There were one or two that we did early on – we did '*The Spirit Of Christmas*' for a little while. We had one really nice rehearsal where we did '*The Candlemas Carol*' and Simon did some very nice guitar. But for some reason or other, it didn't materialise. What Ashley I think quite understandably did, was create a gig whereby everybody had a shot – so Royston sang '*Lovely Joan*' and '*Seventeen Come Sunday*' and I would do '*Fire & Wine*' and '*Lord Bateman*', and then Royston and I would do a couple of songs together. '*The Ramblin' Sailor*' was one. Simon sang a couple of Richard's and we played some of Sue's tunes. The others rehearsed '*It Was One Morning In The Spring*' for a long time. Royston sang it beautifully and Sue played the viol. And I thought it sounded great. Because I wasn't playing on that one, I listened to it in the bathroom or in the garden."

Rather than a workman's cottage in Wiltshire, or a rented vicarage, this time the band kept things in the family. Steve remembers that "we went to Simon's house which had a big gatepost at the front with "Fairport" written in creosote on the front. It was in Thrapston, Northamptonshire. A big house – a nice place to rehearse. Ashley had already sorted himself. He knew he wanted to do the Morris stuff. As the thing evolved, he had the idea of bringing on the Chingford Morris Men. Which again was very exciting. Ashley knew I played the penny whistle. I don't think they realised that I also played the mouth-organ, so they were playing a tune, and I joined in on the mouth-organ, just for the craik. The point is, I was a blues harmonica player, I didn't often play a straight harp. But I then started to play straight across it, so I was playing bluesy rhythms and things.

"I remember that Ashley was really amazed and excited by this. I think we all were. It was also a much more sympathetic rhythmic support to Sue's fiddle, much more in tune with her cultural background. A little coincidence, a little moment where "cross-over", a little ahead of its time, where blues mouth-organ played against the fiddle, was an exciting thing. I think that's what probably decided everybody – "It's Steve! He sings, writes songs, plays guitar and he can play the mouth-organ!" It was a better deal…" Four for the price of one. "But it was also necessary for me to play a lot of the morris tunes in a regular way as well as cross harping on the reels. I found it difficult at first. I'm an intuitive kind of player. But people that play tunes, it's a different kind of thing. It requires a precise technique. I did it, but it was a lot of work for me. So I bought a mouth-organ with a button on it, because some of the tunes have got accidentals in them. So I had to do this Larry Adler thing.

"An accidental is a semi-tone really. Most of those country dance tunes tend to be very straightforward, four-squared, but occasionally – what is an example, '*Jockey To the Fair*' was one. So it needed the button." Steve, who didn't read music, learned some tunes from a tape that Ashley had made. He was using his own knowledge of traditional music to write original songs, as at this time were Richard Thompson and Lal Waterson: "I don't think that anybody would have seen it as a movement. It was wonderful for me to be singing and playing to audiences that were Fairport audiences if you like, who were so incredibly passionate and interested. That was great. And I did take to Ashley and felt confident in his organisational skills. I liked him. I felt it was mutual, I think that we liked each other. The others were fun to work with too, so it's a shame that we never made an album. But it's a long time ago and we've all moved on since."

Ashley Hutchings looks back on the first Albion Country Band as being a "fragile" entity. "It wasn't a confident band and maybe that's colouring my perspective when I say that we weren't that good, or we didn't raise much dust. For a start we had two fragile people – Steve Ashley and Sue Draheim, who were kind of like butterflies. They were very easily blown over. And Royston Wood who was used to singing unaccompanied in a trio. His first time with an electric group. So that's 50% of the band who were unsure of themselves. And then you had Simon, Mattacks and me, who should have been very sure of themselves as we'd done it before. But of course, if you think about the roles of the six people, we were the rhythm section and the other three were the leaders if you like. They were the lead instruments or lead singers. So if you were going to carry anyone, it would have been better to carry a rhythm guitarist or a bass player. Not a lead singer or fiddle player. So that's the picture that I've got in my mind. Simon sang a bit, but there's no question that Steve and Royston were the two lead singers, and very fine singers in their own separate ways. What I can remember of that line-up is unsure performances, but when I hear the tapes, like you I think, "Oh that's rather good, or that arrangement's very interesting".

"It's a line-up that seems to be growing in stature as time goes by. It's almost a beginning, it's very fresh. It's a much rougher sound than Steeleye. It's wonderfully English, even though you've got an American fiddle player. It hasn't dated a second. It really is something that is very revolutionary music. It's not rock music. It's not improvised. It's structured. It's not Steeleye. It's a new direction."

Another crucial part of the line up was the Albion Morris. Robin Denselow saw the Albion Country Band's legacy in having achieved "one break-through, and that was to drag that much satirised part of the folk tradition, Morris dancing, into the twentieth century. The Albions' set always included a set of Morris dance tunes, and a team of Morris men would leap on and perform to an electric folk accompaniment". Those watching were "favourably amazed at the sight of grown men performing ritual prancing and banging sticks together. As an exercise in both rock theatrics and popularising a tradition, it was just as important a move as Steeleye's mummers' plays". For Denselow, the pity was that "the Albions could never stay together or produce a record on time. A shame too that Tyger got so involved with it all that he wouldn't let his band play other music".

Once they had made a collective decision to play Morris tunes, within two weeks "Tyger turned up with a tape recorder and a load of these incredible tunes. I don't know where he got them from, well I do know, but I'm not going to tell". Royston was not a great fan of *Liege & Lief* – "you can really kick the guts out of English music if you are not careful". Indeed, "I still take issue with Tyger over this. I don't think all the things on the album treated English music well". It had taken at least a year after hearing the album that the idea came to Royston that "I could be involved in electric folk".

Unlike Steeleye Span, who, with the exception of '*Rave On*' and a couple of other such pastiches, restricted themselves to traditional material only, the Albion Country Band planned also to draw on songs by Steve Ashley, Lal Waterson and Richard Thompson, songs which use traditional material as a jumping off point, just as – say – Led Zeppelin took off from the delta blues. Thirty years on, Thompson explained why he felt English traditional music now seems to be in such a parlous state, despite all their best efforts. Richard puts this down to "the troubled nature of England, a post-colonial malaise." He jokes that '*The New St George*' would now make a good soccer hooligan anthem. "I think the music of England had died away more than in Scotland. It was more precarious. Politically English music has always been very suppressed. As Martin Carthy will tell you. Its popularity is very regional. In Northumbria you have a strong folk scene because people like Alastair Anderson have really worked at it. Lancashire has a strong tradition. In Sussex there's a strong tradition. There's little pockets. Suffolk? Is there anything left out there? It's almost died out. It's very patchy. It was never totally successfully revived. Fairport tried to do that. Steeleye tried to do that. The Albion Country Band tried to do that. It was shakier."

Ashley asks what few others would dare, if Richard had found it difficult to write songs after the trauma of the M1 crash. Richard opens up, like daylight penetrating a locked room. "I think right up to the mid-seventies I found it very hard to be an honest song writer to tell you the truth. To put your heart on your sleeve. To say "I love you" or something. To actually bare your personal life in song I just found very hard, so I would definitely draw veils over songs. To just keep it one step removed from decipherment if you like. I don't want people to know this is really about me. It's in code."

Thompson now thinks that he needed to go through such "abstract ideas" to settle into writing more naturally. "It's much easier to have a concrete idea that you can then put layers on, if you have that desire and skill." Even so, many devotees – including the two authors – actually prefer Thompson's songwriting when it was in code. After all, surely all literature works through veils, or through structures, or through narratives. It was Bob Dylan who most notably brought this kind of writing to popular song. Getting away from simple songs about 'I love you' or moon in June.

Richard counters that "unlike poetry or a novel, popular music is supposed to be done at a certain level. It's supposed to be accessible at a very basic level. So you are held to that as an ideal. The great songs of popular music are very, very simple. Hank Williams songs, Buddy Holly songs are very, very simple songs. If you want a song with some modern morality behind it, or politics behind it, then you really do have to layer it somehow on top of that real simplicity, otherwise it's not popular music. You seem pretentious. You've gone bombastic, and you've done the concept album. Having just done one I know exactly what it feels like!" The answer to this is that there are good concept albums, and bad concept albums, and the work of Rick Wakeman. Just as one could argue that *Hamlet* is a play based around the concept of delay, or Monet's late watercolours deal with the concept of light, so Ashley's finest work – whether *Morris On* or *By Gloucester Docks* or *Street Cries* – is usually based around a concept of his own devising.

Even so, Ashley feels that back in the early seventies "we were trying a bit too hard to be New St Georgian. I'm not putting it all on Richard, but I'm saying that we were very earnestly going down this path. The Albions were as well." Richard feels that "folk-rock" got itself stuck in a rut. "It just became very hackneyed. That's the reason most people got bored with it. I know I got bored with it. It came to a dead end. There wasn't a willingness to explore any further. I think that the later Albion Bands, through going to early music, and going to dance music, broadened the horizon considerably."

Simon Nicol felt much the same. Of his decision to leave Fairport, the band he co-founded, Simon Nicol says "it was becoming an institution, and who wants to live in an institution. The Albion Country Band came together in order to give us something to do in the cold winter evenings". Simon has a cutting wit, edging towards the brutal, but he does sound serious when he says that "I just kept my ear to the ground for people who I liked to form the group". It is more a question of having sympathetic workmates than any huge desire to play in a particular style, or with a pre-set agenda. "I don't know if I ever take it seriously enough: I'll play anything I'm able to play and I'm fully aware of my limitations."

'Electric morris' was just one element in the new band's repertoire, a mix of traditional music, and some contemporary material. Sue Draheim brought some of the fiddle tunes she has acquired on her travels – "I used to play with an old guy I knew in San Francisco and learnt some Irish music as well as the American stuff I was playing". Shades of Steeleye Span. In addition, Royston Wood has been learning concertina with Dave Bland. The band as a whole announced it would draw from "disparate periods of time": this has in many ways been the template for all of Ashley Hutchings' varied projects which he has so determinedly pursued over the three decades since. The Dr Who of folk rock.

"With the Morris Men it's pure Show Biz. When we had The Albion Morris, they came dancing on, a roar would go up from the audience. I can hear it to this day. The band played a set, half an hour or whatever, and then we brought the Morris on, and the place would erupt."

Hutchings' musical journey has often seemed to have parallels with William Morris and the Arts and Crafts Movement, part of a social trend towards equality, which he is updating. Ashley: "I think actually we did think of ourselves as a modern day equivalent of Morris' Movement in the seventies, and for a time, there was I thought, some kind of cohesive movement. Unfortunately nowadays it's fragmented so much that it doesn't exist anymore as a movement, or as a common drive. So I just do what I can to follow my instinct. It's sad in a way. It was lovely to feel a part of a movement and to know that there were souls out there who had the same attitudes. We talk about the family. The family isn't the family anymore.

The Fairport, the Steeleye, the Albion family. It's too fragmented now. We've all got different ideas, we've all gone in different directions. But there was a time in history when we were all pulling together, consciously. And it felt great to be a part of that."

The Albion Country Band's public debut was at Sussex University, close to Ashley's home, on June 9th 1972 and ten days later they were at the BBC recording their first session for John Peel. Four days on, they made their first London appearance at King's Cross Cinema, as part of the 'King Sound' midnight to six a.m. extravaganza. For Ashley and Simon it must have been like Middle Earth revisited. Support acts were Medicine Head and 'Wild' Willy Barrett. 'Sounds' came courtesy of hippie veteran Andy Dunkley and lights – or 'environment' – by Sweet Puff. It was just the kind of slightly cobwebby venue from which ex-mime artist and acousto-hippy David Bowie was emerging at the time in costume and make-up, playing for the kids, and blowing through the tatters of the Woodstock

SUSSEX UNIVERSITY UNION presents on FRI., 16th JUNE, at 8 p.m.
THE FIRST PUBLIC APPEARANCE OF
ALBION COUNTRY BAND
(Ashley Hutchings, Royston Wood, Steve Ashley, Dave Mattacks, Simon Nicol, Sue Draheim)
PLUS — SPIROGYRA
at SUSSEX UNIVERSITY, FALMER HOUSE, FALMER, BRIGHTON.
TICKETS: 50p AT DOOR/40p IN ADVANCE FROM VIRGIN RECORDS, BRIGHTON, OR UNION OFFICE

Sussex University debut gig advert. 16th June 1972

King's Sound – London debut gig advert. 23rd June 1972

dream like a hurricane.

It is of interest that the Albion Country Band were playing a rock venue, rather than a folk club. The previous weekend had seen the jazzy rock of Manfred Mann's Earth Band. The next night saw a barely-known Roxy Music as a support band, the following weekend the Electric Light Orchestra, pop with violins. All for £1 a night. The Albions were part of this eclectic musical menu. Karl Dallas was still awake when the Albions appeared on stage at 2am, and "it was as if the whole assembly had been wafted miles into the Cotswolds". As Royston

Wood led the band into an unaccompanied song about St George, sourced from a mummers play, "it seemed as if Ashley Hutchings' developing infatuation with English traditional music had completely taken over", but the ensemble then launched into a full electric assault on Thompson's '*The New St George*' . The centuries dissolved, and Ashley's modus operandi began to come into focus.

Hutchings summed up the live experience of that original Albion Band: "We were rough and ready, but somehow it doesn't matter, does it? When people make original music for the first time, you don't care that it's rough and ready. This is traditional music taken out of mothballs, with a truly contemporary approach. Because of Sue Draheim's jazzy fiddle playing the feel is more of American country than straight English". Hutchings' new venture is translating its various sources into "the pop idiom". Ashley's alchemy is not quite in place, so that as yet "songs by the various vocalists don't seem to hang together with a coherent style. Once Steve Ashley has learnt properly how to sing with a full band, he will be a 'monster talent'." He leads the ensemble into a "remarkable full-length version of '*Lord Bateman*", one more to add to the list of "electric folk classics". Fortunately, a tape survives, and as we will find with the Albion Country Band, it is only because of fanatics hiding tape recorders under their pullovers that much of the story can be told at all.

Here, the audience sound half comatose, befitting the hour, and Steve Ashley quips "the people who are still asleep would appreciate it if you were all a little quieter". The band certainly sound disjointed at times. Simon Nicol sings '*The New St George*', and the "full orchestra" are present and correct on 'Lord Bateman' – taking their lead from Mattacks' drum kit. They stay silent during Royston's and Steve's duet on '*Babylon*', part of the sacred harp tradition. Tyger jokes that "we have a wet blanket in the group" – Simon Nicol – who doesn't want to come back to play some dance tunes as an encore. Hutchings describes '*Paddy on the Railroad*' as an "Irish American tune", and the audience at last show some signs of life, clapping along. The biggest surprise of this set is the inclusion of '*Cuckoo's Nest*'.

'*St George He Is For England*' is sung 'Eng-er-land, like a bunch of football hooligans. Unaccompanied, except by vocal harmonies, it takes us back to a time

> *"When danger stalked the land*
> *and serpents ploughed the sea*
> *it was the bold and brave St George*
> *the dragon made to flee".*

There are references to Lancelot du Lac, Saint Denis and King Arthur. A heartbeat's pause, then straight into the electric ensemble performing Thompson's '*The New St George*', like a call to arms. Never has its line 'St George's tune is calling you on" sounded so apposite. The slightest of pauses, and we are into '*St Anne's Reel*', a sprightly violin-led instrumental. Mattacks wastes not a drumbeat, and the rest rattle along in support, with percussive harmonica and a simple but perfect bass riff. The whole thing seems to speed up slightly at the end. As to the Morris medley, there is the same bouncy, rhythmic thrust as the *Morris On* album, with plenty of instrumental interplay, but no actual dancers. The Chingford Morris have yet to make their debut.

Now the Albions hit the road with serious intent. In July, *Melody Maker* carried a reader's letter which reckoned that thanks to the original line-up of Fairport imploding, "we now have six electric folk bands and 28 musicians. Keep moving,

Tyger Hutchings and all the rest of you, but leave us something to remember you by each time you settle".

The Albions played London in August, and by now '*St George, He Is For England*' had a new verse: "from countryside we've lately come, St George is our command". It gives the whole thing a more revolutionary feel. Someone complains that "this microphone keeps biting me", and calls for a chair for the lead guitarist, "so he can play his erotophone". Thompson's '*The Poor Ditching Boy*' is sung delicately over an ornate bass riff, with a harmonica lead break.

Steve introduces as "with the human voices only, a folk song collected from a record by Bert Lloyd". He and Royston launch into the unaccompanied '*When A Man's In Love*', with their voices chasing each other like two kittens after the same ball of wool. '*Rolling Through The Rye Grass*' is introduced as an Irish reel, and they claim it as "probably the height of bad taste" for the way it moves into a Las Vegas finale. This is not a band who take themselves too seriously. The music itself can be as serious as your life. They visit the four seasons in a medley which brings together the ominous '*Spirit of Christmas*', an unaccompanied '*Royston's Song*', the stately '*Floral Dance*' and the anthemic '*Fire and Wine*', followed by a long instrumental coda. There is also a snatch of '*We Three Kings*', odd for a gig in the middle of summer. On '*Lovely Joan*', a recorder weaves around Steve's vocal; shades of the debut Fairport album.

Hutchings reckons "We need a touch of Morris", and introduces a medley starting and ending with '*Fieldtown Processional*'. Even more important, he talks about how a few weeks before the Albions had played with the Chingford Morris dancing in front of them, at a festival in Suffolk. "It seems a bit bare after that", and he asks the audience to imagine the dancers. Shortly afterwards, these same dancers were to reform as the 'Albion Morris Men'. Hutchings also delivers a spoken recitation, feyly declaimed in humorous couplets. The band sound full of zest, and much of their material is stitched together into medleys. It is a process which Ashley has always followed, constantly rejigging the running order between gigs, balancing sad with merry, slow with sprightly.

In discussing the public reaction to the band, Hutchings stated: "The public were slightly bemused. They loved in general, the Morris Dancers. But there came a point, where we thought that the Morris Dancers were saving the show. Everyone goes bananas, and we end up getting an encore. That's cheating really. Those performances seem to be valued more than they were at the time." Another thing was the shortness of the actual performances. "They were very short. An hour tops, maybe less. We played some material from *Morris On* in the set list, but it was tunes more than anything."

The Albion Country Band arrived "hot-foot from Holland" to top the bill at the Courtyard Arts Trust Festival. Things open with a violin-led instrumental, like the dawn of a fine summer morning. '*The New St George*' is now a slow march, sung with intent. '*Lovely Joan*' opens with funereal chords, around which concertina and violin wind like serpents, with Steve's deliberately English vocals tender and insistent. On '*Lord Bateman*', *S*teve Ashley sings unaccompanied, then once Bateman is imprisoned, the band crash in – Simon predominant – and the vocals grow harsher, more guttural. Bateman escapes, drums pound, and the ensemble power into a stately instrumental based on Guillaume de Machaut's '*Triple Ballade*' as seven years pass. Steve comes back in, accompanied by solo violin, then the music swells as the gaoler's daughter sets out for England, and justice. The porter's speech is omitted, and Steve sings the final line unaccompanied, with particular emphasis on the last word: "did set him FREE". No lead guitar break. The song has the same driven quality as '*Tam Lin*', and its arrangement here is similarly insistent, like someone being slowly throttled.

'*Babylon*', the American gospel song, looks forward to the day of judgement: "the day long expected … of full release". The demonising of Babylon, modern life, is presumably a sentiment which Bob Marley would have had no difficulty agreeing with. Steve Ashley and Royston Wood's naked voices rise in praise, lifting to a shout: "Babylon is fallen, to rise no more". Hutchings resurrected the song for *The World Turned Upside Down*. "We sang it in that production. It's a rousing clarion call, song from that period of the English Civil War. It's certainly unusual for an electric band. Unique I would say."

A review of the show in *Melody Maker* reckons that this is "a tougher, grittier band than Fairport. They seem to be

Dutch tour poster. 28th July 1972

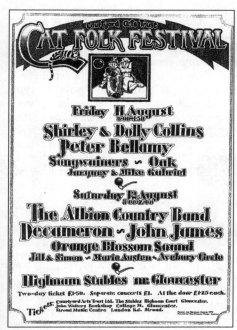

Courtyard Arts Trust Festival gig poster. 12th August 1972

having a good time too". This despite a sudden downpour, with the audience "sitting on their straw bales, waiting for a treat". This is a band that can "morris like hell!", and Hutchings, ever the scholar, takes pains to give precise descriptions of where each tune has come from. Andrew Means singles out Sue Draheim for not only "looking pretty good" – but for the way "her fiddle soars, sings, punches and colours all this music": in a closing '*The New St George*' she hauls the band through chorus after chorus. Behind her, Dave Mattacks drums "as cleanly and thoughtfully as ever".

The 'Albion Morris Men' were part of the entertainment when the band headlined a concert at the Shaw

Theatre in London in mid-September. Neil Philip remembers the Albions as "stupendously good. Sue Draheim was fantastic, almost as fluid a fiddler as Vassar Clements. The band was very strong as an ensemble – it didn't feel like something about to fall apart, though there was a sense of confusion and perhaps even rivalry about who was the lead singer."

For Karl Dallas, "if anyone has been thinking of getting together an English National Folk Ensemble they need look no further. For in the Albion-plus-Chingford combination – "we have already got a group just as theatrically exciting as any Eastern European troupe". This certainly comes as a shock to "anyone used to the more restrained playing and dancing one normally comes across in villages at Whitsun". Hutchings pretended to leave Steeleye to form a "real, dyed in the Cotswold wool traditional English band, whereas what he is running is a good old-fashioned rock-and-roll group". Less positively, Robin Denselow reckons that the Albions seem "to have been assembled by a wayward computer", seemingly without rhyme or reason. The task they face is to sound different from both Fairports ("brash and exciting") and Steeleye ("more delicate, with emphasis on arrangements"). At the Shaw Theatre, they "struck a middle balance. Their playing was low key, smooth, and surprisingly dependent on the lesser known players of the band".

One of these is Steve Ashley and in an interview which *Disc* published at the end of September, he points out, ominously, that the views he is about to express are his own and "not necessarily those of the group". "The Country Band should have their own group album released in the new year. They begin recording next month, and intend to mix (new) with old songs".

One of the ironic things is that Hutchings had two very good, contemporary songwriters in the band. Royston and Steve. Ashley agrees with the criticism that they were underused. "We could have used loads of Steve's songs. They were suitable, English and rooted in the tradition. I was still under the spell of traditional music at that point. Still very much locked into research and coming up with interesting traditional songs and tunes. Had it been a few years later, it would have been a totally different story." Steve Ashley confesses that he too enjoyed playing Morris tunes, "especially with the mouth-organ. Because with Sue and I, it was a nice thing. The fiddle and the mouth-organ were good together. Also, the rhythm section was great, the bass lines were very strong and Dave was really inventive.

Simon's a great guitarist. I think it was a good band. Royston and I got on very well and he was great to sing with. But I felt each one of us had our little party-piece". Meanwhile, he was learning to play electric guitar. Sue was taking on a whole load of new disciplines, all of them challenging for someone trained as a country fiddle player. "Everybody in the band was working hard and we made some great music but unfortunately we didn't get round to working together to

Keele University poster. 13th October 1972

create something new."

In late October, this line-up of the Albion Country Band imploded. Robin Denselow later reckoned that "they sounded like a collection of individuals, not a band." One of their final gigs was at Westgate Hall in September 1972. It doesn't sound like a band falling apart, though at times there is a sense of musicians going through the motions. Acoustic and electric instruments now mesh properly, but they lack some of the rough energy of a few months before.

Freshest of all is the Morris medley, which Hutchings meticulously introduces. He sounds fey and scholarly, wrapped up in the importance of what his band is attempting. There's '*Old Woman Tossed Up In A Blanket*' from Headington – during the spoken passage it is suggested that the old woman is

Medway Folk Music Festival, Rochester Castle poster. 16th October 1972

Steve Ashley! A minute or so of tuning up follows, then the medley, tuneful and somehow timeless, with Royston's concertina and Sue's fiddle taking the musical lead. At times '*Princess Royal*' threatens to mutate into '*Johnny Todd*', the theme to *Z Cars*.

There is an interesting introduction to '*Rambling Sailor*', "a traditional naughty song, about a young man who goes in search of female company". She leaves him "a receipt in the form of an unmentionable condition. Presumably he survives it long enough to tell this story". Next up, Tyger humorously intones

> "*Greensleeves and Pudding Pies*
> *tell me where me mistress lies,*
> *and I'll be with her before she rise*
> *fiddling all together*'.

Cue Sue. Later, Simon attempts a limerick, beginning "There Was A Young Man From Japan", and an even worse one written by WS Gilbert, culminating with a hornet. Nicol also sings '*The New St George*', followed by reels on which Steve's mouth organ chatters and Sue's fiddle floats. The rhythm section chugs along like a steam train, speeding up just towards the end.

The band encore on '*Babylon*'. Royston indicates that all is not well behind the scenes. "I don't really think we deserve that reception tonight. Steve and I are going to go a bit folky for you, and sing some American gospel". It is symbolic that this last number leaves the band out completely.

On one of the very last gigs, at the London School of Economics on 14th

October. Simon warns the rowdy crowd that "I think you might be subjected to a night of what happens when a band is put on at 10.45 and has four hours drinking time". Nicol's breezy introductions are much as they were with Fairport. "Here's an autumn song that we've been playing all summer". All sounds chummy. Steve adds that "for the last three weeks we've been making that introduction – it's been a long autumn. It was going to be called 'fire and retsina', but it didn't scan".

The '*Old Woman Tossed in a Blanket*' verse is read out in an accent straight out of Jethro Larkin in the Archers, to audience delight. Introducing what turns out to be a sombre and extremely emotional rendition of '*Seventeen Come Sunday*', Simon – still recovering – reckons that the day after your birthday is a flat day, with a whole year to look forward to the next one. "This song is courtesy of Harry Cox of Norfuk". Royston adds that he will 'beep' out all the naughty words: "when I was in the Young Tradition you couldn't sing any words like 'bugger'". There is much banter before '*Babylon*'. There is also much audience hilarity as the three try to get it together: genuinely sounding like chums, not musicians two of whom are about to be sacked. One jokes that singing out of tune is "very ethnic, very important for an ethnic group". Simon goes cockney after one false start, then the thing starts in earnest, the extra voice giving extra resonance, prefiguring the 'typhoon of sound' of later. There is a short burst of rock guitar during Steve's introduction to the 17 verse 'Lord Bateman' – "*shut the door!*" This is close to the arrangement which is later to grace *Stroll On*: muscular and unrelenting.

Two live instrumentals survive to grace Hutchings' *The Guv'nor* CD box set. Steve's harmonica is a dead ringer for the theme tune to *The Navy Lark*. The ensemble slow down and speed up in unison, well drilled by their bass supremo. Although no producer is listed, if this is all live – and it's got that looseness – it's certainly straight from the soundboard. *The Guv'nor* also boasts what sounds like a studio take of '*Rambling Sailor*' with Royston Wood and Steve Ashley striking sparks off each other, two men on the razzle. Sue Draheim's fiddle weaves around them like a snake. Thompsonesque, almost. The rhythm section keeps things basic, the power house behind a band whose potential was never to be fulfilled, but burnt brightly.

Robin Denselow had long seen "the writing on the wall". He found it ironic that their only studio recording turned up on "the solo album of someone the band chucked out", Steve Ashley's long-delayed *Stroll On*, released two years later, in 1974. '*Lord Bateman*' is "straight Albion and it's long, but imaginatively treated, with an instrumental section in the middle where the story leaps seven years. Steve sings well, the always self-effacing Simon plays extremely fine guitar, and Sue's fiddle playing is silkily smooth. It shows what the Albions could do". Steve Ashley: "When the band split, I regretted that we had not recorded '*Lord Bateman*' as it had taken so much work and was undoubtedly a highlight of our gigs. It seemed like a nice opportunity for us to get together one more time and do something positive. I was really pleasantly surprised that everybody was up for it."

3:5
TAKING CARE OF BUSINESS

Melody Maker carried a vitriolic interview, in which the usually inscrutable Tyger talked of the frustrations, economic and artistic, of a year trying to get a genuinely English electric folk band off the ground. "For the past year as far as I'm concerned, Albion had been a total waste of time, artistically. The only worthwhile thing that has come out of it has been the incorporation of the Morris men into the performance. I don't think anything we've done songwise has been any great shakes. Albion hasn't developed at all, therein lies the problem."

This is an angry man. "I'm frequently disgusted by the lack of fire in the musicians' bellies, the ones that I play with, and they know that, so I'm not telling them anything new by saying it. If you compare the standards of playing and singing in folk music, principally electric folk music, in this country with other forms of music, in pop music, light music, classical or jazz, then we're nowhere, we're absolutely nowhere. We're all a bunch of amateurs. And until we can put on as good a performance on our level that will match up to the best from any other field, then I won't be happy, personally."

News of the upheaval within the Albion Country Band broke at the end of October. The band were back on the main news pages, because splits are always more newsworthy than formings, and the piece led over a Stackridge panto, Phil Seamen's funeral, and Three Dog Night cancelling a tour. "A major shake-up took place on Saturday night, resulting in vocalists Steve Ashley and Royston Wood leaving the band immediately. Fiddler Sue Draheim is to leave eventually, but will stay until a replacement is found". Hutchings reckons that the band had gradually fallen apart. "It wasn't like BANG! That's the end of that. The group will now reform. It kind of drifted apart and Steve and Royston realised that it wasn't going to work, with our promptings, and backed out.

Steve Sheldon – who now runs the Albion Band's web site – recalls: "I was Social Secretary at Trent Polytechnic and we put the Albion Country Band with Plainsong supporting at a venue in Nottingham. I went backstage after the gig to do my usual socialising and pay the money. In those days I collected autographs. To my surprise, Ashley added "ex-Albion Country Band" to some people's names."

Steve Ashley was severely taken aback. "At the time I remember there was a real excitement about what was going on, particularly from the audience's perspective. And it was continually changing. When the split occurred Sue, Royston and I were absolutely amazed. It was so sudden. But we had a couple of months worth of gigs left and I was perfectly happy to work them out." Hutchings wasn't. "I just went back to London and sat and thought about it. The phone rang and it was Karl Dallas. I didn't want to say anything negative. To me, that was the honourable thing to do. It was our private business – we'd split up for reasons that were obvious to probably everybody. We were pulling in different directions. And I felt – well OK, now we'll go our separate ways and hopefully I'll be able to get my album out and get on with my life." A brief statement from Royston made it clear that departing members had been pushed, rather than chosen to jump. "The three ex-Fairports have decided that they can get on without the rest of us".

Sue Harris also felt that the band weren't pulling together as a musical unit. "There was a little divisiveness going, we three and those three. After all they had a history together long before we three came into the picture so it wasn't surprising. I remember a lot of good laughs and a lot of fun. I've always loved Steve's songs. I wish we could have worked together again. The break up was not fun!"

Ashley had given them the bullet as he had earlier done with Judy Dyble, and was to many times more in the future. Part of the cost of being a driven personality is that others get squashed if they block up the road.

Shirley Collins: "Ashley made a huge mistake with the manager he got. It was Keith Roberts, somebody who'd managed Fairport very early on. And he was a disaster. He was an old friend. I'll tell you what it was about him that I hated – he drove too fast. I sometimes went to rehearsals and gigs and we had a very close call at one point. After the crash, the last thing you want is somebody who drives dangerously. He and his wife were the sort of people who would stop the car and dump the ashtray in the kerb." Steve Ashley: "There wasn't management as such. There was a nice chap called Keith who was somebody's friend, he came in later on but to me he wasn't a real manager." Later, Jo Lustig attempted to sign up the Albion Band to a management deal, but Hutchings walked away from it. "I could see us losing our autonomy". Ever since then of course, he's done it himself.

In the *NME*, an Albion spokesman explained that "the music lacked the quality expected, and the band were being held back by this. But the split was at a musical level only". Both Steve and Royston "are now expected to make solo albums". Steve Ashley set up the short lived New Merlin's Cave a year later in October 1973, a London club which was run partly by performers who were all in some way involved in songwriting which was inspired by traditional music.

Steve: "One nice, positive thing came out of the split – having had a taste of playing in a band, I met Richard Byers and we formed Ragged Robin, which was almost like a rebirth. Again we only lasted a year and I was really broke by then. I had the idea of creating a club in London which in some ways could emulate say "The Singers' Club" or "Les Cousins". A club in London for songwriters to drop in and try out new songs. So I asked Richard Thompson who was then working with Linda and Simon Nicol in Sour Grapes, Robin and Barry Dransfield, and Lea Nicholson if they would like to take part. Heather Wood and Anthea Joseph offered to do the door and organise things and we had a meeting at the venue and we got it together. It was a direct continuation of what the first Albion Country Band could have been.

"Robin and Barry were busy at the time and obviously Sour Grapes could fly off and do a tour at any minute, so it was going to fall to me, Lea and Bunny (Richard Byers) and maybe Robin and Barry alternating as residents. And then each week, we would each have turns in choosing who the guests would be. It was a fantastic little experiment. The first night it was Sandy Denny – and you couldn't get near the club for all the cars and people, it was just amazing. We later had The Young Tradition – they performed as three individuals. My choice was Bert Lloyd and that night was great. Sandy Denny was there. He got up and sang a few songs and absolutely mesmerised everybody. He was so good. He did this version of '*Young Tambling*'. It absolutely terrified the wits out of everyone, the last line: "and stuck in two eyes of wood". Merlins suddenly came to life. It was electrifying. Merlins lasted about six weeks or maybe two months. I know Dick Gaughan and The Etchinghams with Ashley came and did it. Then it just folded up. People were getting more and more gigs, and eventually there was a lack of impetus and it fell away." Where was it? In a pub? "Near King's Cross." It had previously been the venue for Ewan MacColl and Peggy Seeger's "The Singers' Club" back in the '60s.

As to the remaining members of the original Albion Country Band, Royston subsequently joined Swan Arcade and then moved to the States where he died in a tragic road accident in 1990. Dave Mattacks rejoined Fairport "after months of pestering from the Midlands". Sue Draheim: "After Steve and Royston had left, I stayed with the "Caretaker" band for a while. But I can't recall doing more than a few gigs with Richard and Linda." Simon Nicol puts it carefully: in November, she "contracted pneumonia and didn't rejoin us after her convalescence, owing to a premonition of bad vibes". She had sufficiently recovered a month later to form the John Renbourn Group, alongside Jacqui Mc Shee, Tony Roberts and Keshav Sathe.

Tyger's own long and strange journey into the heart of traditional music had many twists and turns yet to go before he was to resurface, musically and artistically refreshed, on the other side. A news story in *Melody Maker* announced that The Fairport axis – Hutchings, Nicol, Mattacks – were to be joined as "a purely temporary measure" by another old colleague, Richard Thompson, along with his partner Linda Peters on vocals. Thompson had already "turned down other invitations to join the band", but he was not about to leave his mates in the lurch.

Reading between the lines, it was obvious that Hutchings already had the template for a future Albion line-up: "eventually it is expected that accordion wizard John Kirkpatrick and his wife Sue will join, possibly with the addition of Martin Carthy". Meanwhile Ashley had to continue gigging, or starve. "When Royston and Steve left we had these gigs and Simon and I couldn't exist, nor could the roadies and the management, without fulfilling the gigs and getting the money. We wouldn't have done it if we hadn't thought we could have a reasonably decent group, so we bolstered ourselves up with Richard and Linda, just to see us through to the end of the year." In a statement to *Sounds*, Keith Roberts reveals that Richard Thompson and Linda Peters have only joined "until the end of the year". It was time enough for some extraordinary gigs.

Sometimes Matthews Southern Comfort drummer Roger Swallow was one of a nucleus of musicians who helped Ashley through the rest of his 1972 gig sheet: Simon Nicol reckoned that "we need a drummer with great verve and enterprise and someone with a wide musical variety and flexibility. Dave Mattacks came from the world of dance band music and there may be others like him". Roger Swallow fitted like a glove, alongside the likes of Richard and Linda, Simon Nicol, Barry Dransfield, John Watcham, and – at the very end – Shirley Collins. This temporary line-up of the Albion Country Band is in some ways the most legendary and fleeting of all: some of us see it as far more of a missing link to an English contemporary folk music than the official line-up that went before. Fans who witnessed this moveable convention remember its few gigs with pride and a sense of excitement which outweighs nostalgia.

Hutchings merely remembers that "we had gigs we had to fulfil. It was as simple as that. Rather like the National Theatre a few years later, bringing in whomever I could find. We had a certain number of gigs that we had to fulfil over a very short period. Maybe nearer eight than ten. It wasn't necessary the same line-up at all those things. I can remember changing the drummer. I can remember one night that we couldn't get a drummer. And Dots Daultrey, who is one of the leading dancers in the Albion Morris, came along, did a couple of dances, and played drums. It was a real kind of busking time. There must have been a certain amount of magic with Simon, Richard and Linda, me, Sue. Barry Dransfield also played on some. You know it was a weird thing. It had to be fluid if suddenly someone couldn't be there. It was an interesting, fascinating footnote. It was Polytechnics and Colleges. The 1973 Albion Country Band was being set up, so we knew that it was a temporary thing. But that didn't stop us from getting some enjoyment out of it."

"Although it was fun, it was also fraught for me when so and so couldn't make a gig, or who was going to play drums tonight. Did he know the repertoire? But apart from that, the first Albion Country Band was not fun. Whatever it was, it was not fun. And Simon I'm sure would agree with me." Simon: "It was a bit chaotic when we were recruited for those Christmas gigs at The Howff. It was obvious that Ashley was beginning to lose his grip in terms of directing it."

The 'Caretaker Band' was the one electric outing for the songs on *Henry The Human Fly*, until the Thompsons played the Festival Hall in 1975. Great as it was to hear the duo playing acoustic sets at folk clubs, it was even more exciting to hear the same songs performed with an electric band. Richard himself is characteristically modest. "I'd no idea. The stuff from that part of my career is a bit sketchy you know. I've got a tape in the post that was very cryptically labelled. It just turned up and I stuck it on a machine and I thought it sounds like Leadbelly 1952 or something from Alan Lomax's folk collection. I couldn't recognise the song, I couldn't recognise the singer. It took me two minutes to realise that it was me singing in a folk club, with the Ex, singing some song that I haven't sung since 1973. One of those like *'Dragging the River'*. I could not recognise it. It was fantastic. It was the weirdest feeling as if it were coming from Mars. Being beamed from another galaxy."

When Neil Philip saw the caretaker band at Reading Town Hall, "they were playing a funny mixture of stuff, Richard was still singing *'Dragging the River'*, Hutchings sang *'Don't Make It 54'*, a weird C&W parody about John Wesley Harding in a fake American accent". *'Nadine'*, revisited. "They were great fun to watch, but not really a group with a sense of direction". For all the fluffs and false starts, this band proved to be – much like early Fairport – a seed bed, various elements of which would flower later, and elsewhere. The most joyous reunion is of Thompson with his old rhythm section: something about Hutchings' bass and Nicol's rhythm brings out the best in his own guitar playing. Simon was to join Richard and Linda as a trio in the following year, while Mattacks' precise drums, when present, also act as a spur. Anyone expecting labyrinthine guitar breaks would have been disappointed, though. This is Ashley's show, and he remains in complete control.

What he *had* achieved by thinking to ask the Thompsons on board for ten weeks was to capture them at the height of their early glory. Here were the startling songs which made up *Henry* and the long delayed *I Wanna See The Bright Lights Tonight*. Even better, these performances contained oddities like *'Dragging the River'*, *'Shady Lies'* (later covered by Iain Matthews) and *'Napoleon's Dream'*. Here too were songs and tunes left over from the set list of the Albion Country Band One, and a few pointers to Hutchings own creative future.

The debut gig by the 'caretaker' band took place at University College, London on 25th October, barely two weeks after the 'official' Albions imploded. Thompson sings lead on a tentative *'Nobody's Wedding'* in his folkiest voice, and the whole band swing into the instrumental passages. Ashley plucks away on bass. He addresses the crowd, sounding laid back, almost contemptuous. "Now we've broken the ice, this is the first song this line-up has ever done. We're doing a lot of Richard's songs". The next one, he suggests, comes courtesy of Merle Haggard. *'Shady Lies'* "puts the 'country' back in 'Albion Country Band'". Then he is offered a five pound note, or has one thrown on the stage. "Oh there's a fiver, I don't have to play, I'll go. It's more than I'm getting paid". Linda takes lead vocal, and the band thump along like the pride of Nashville. There is nice country fiddle from Barry Dransfield.

Ashley introduces *'Poor Ditching Boy'* as sounding like an American song but based on a Shetland tune. It opens almost acoustically, like Boys of the Lough, then in comes bass and drums and Richard's clotted voice, somewhere between a peasant and a lout. The chorus soars, half anthem, half bitter complaint. Richard and Linda duet unaccompanied on their folk club favourite *'Napoleon's Dream'*. The Left Banke's *'He May Call You Up Tonight'* has Ashley on nimble bass and a full electric backing. Lots of drums and power chords from Richard and Simon, even a short lead guitar break. Wonderful, but hardly the English traditional music which Ashley had left first Fairport and then Steeleye to perform.

The tone changes for some "rock n'roll with the Albion Morris" although they are still called the Chingford Morris because their new Albion logos have yet to arrive: an early example of consumer branding! Simon and Ashley carefully clear the space in front of the stage for the dancers to emerge. John Watcham – "the plain clothed Morris man" – joins in with the band on concertina. *'Winster Processional'* begins as more of a plod, with lots of slow handclaps from the audience, for encouragement, not in complaint. The dance set picks up speed and energy. Dransfield is peerless and four of the main participants in *Morris On* can at last put that album's music – and dancing – into a decent live setting. One can hear the band picking up pace, and there is a splendidly ragged male chorus on the "Incapable Morris".

Linda Thompson returns for *'Has He Got A Friend For Me'*, one of Richard's most plangent songs. Her full-on, highly emotional rendition is matched by the band, with lots of melancholy violin and mournful guitar. It is nice for the song's creator to finally join in on *'New St George'* with the Albions, though the lead vocal sounds more like the vocally harder-edged Simon Nicol. Hutchings addresses the audience. "How are we doing? As long as you can tolerate the wrong chords, as you probably realize the official set is now over. This is a jam, we've got about an hour. We'll do a country and western song about John Wesley Hardin. This one I'm afraid I'm going to grunt my own way through. He was reputed to have killed 53 people in a gun fight ... he used to machine gun them". The song lopes, with Ashley talk-singing in a ludicrous John Wayne mumble about a killer who did it "Texas style". The song is full of daft rhymes, and Linda joins in on the chorus, less Peters than Ronstadt. "If there's a gunman's Valhalla/he's right up there with the rest". The band are in on the joke, plodding from chord to chord, with lachrymose fiddle circling above it all like a vulture.

The only possible comparison to this song is Viv Stanshall's *'Bad Blood'*, also set in the baddest of the boondocks, about a gunman who could tell the time by the "gravy ... running down ... his legs". Ashley: "*'Don't Make It 54'* is a very, very obscure song about John Wesley Hardin which I unearthed and sang in a kind of sing-songy way. A real mish mash, but fun. And with the pressure off to a large extent." *'Break My Mind'* closes things, set to a throbbing beat. Linda's voice is at its hardest, and Thompson's guitar interpolations similarly cutting. He plays a short but startling lead break, while Ashley punches away underneath. This is folk music only in the sense that human beings are performing it.

At Brunel University, the band sounds smoother, and muster a cool Nashville swing to '*Shady Lies*', with Ashley's bass predominant, and delicious country guitar fills. Hutchings apologises for the feedback then introduces Simon on electric dulcimer, for '*The Poor Ditching Boy*'. Tuneful, but restrained. '*He May Call You Up Tonight*' could almost be early Fairport, with Ashley playing a counter-melody on bass, and no sharp edges. Next up is the electric Morris. The band retune and Linda comes back for a haunting '*Has He Got A Friend For Me*', using every ounce of her voice's innate sadness. '*New St George*' is like a truck driving down the highway. After cheers of approval, they encore on '*Break My Mind*', "a rock n'roll song" written by John D Loudermilk. The Albion Country Band sound like, of all people, Status Quo as they boogie behind Linda's spirited vocal. Ashley has got his drapes on, metaphorically, and Richard solos as only he can, soaring amidst the high notes.

At the barn-like main refectory of Oxford Polytechnic (as was), Brian found his musical deities of the time looking slightly uncertain, but blazing out in spurts and patches, like a forest fire. The running order has changed quite considerably. Ashley drawls that "last time we played here was at an all day festival around five years ago. Free were the first band on: there were four of them". Richard adds in his cheekiest voice that neither the acoustics nor heating system have improved since. '*Nobody's Wedding*' is stately, carefully enunciated, followed by some equally measured jigs and reels. No false histrionics here.

Thompson's '*Little Beggar Girl*' has just been added to the set, and Hutchings points out that "it's quite a triumph". Thompson undercuts this with his quip "it's about taking money from people under false pretences, rather like this evening". Linda gets fully into the role of a street urchin. Within ten years the song will have begun to come true, with the streets of London littered again with the homeless. The song acts, like so many early Thompson compositions, as a parable, in which all history joins to form a timeless present tense. A couple of the Albion Morris now dance to '*Old Woman Tossed Up In A Blanket*', which as Ashley points out was first collected at Headington, just down the road. The dancer's feet clatter on the wooden stage, like tap dancers. Normal service is resumed with '*Has He Got A Friend For Me*', effortlessly sad, with violin mournful as a Sally Army band. '*New St George*' evokes William Morris, himself deeply connected with Oxford, then dissolves the tension with a waltz. The band encore with a sprightly instrumental. There is no sign of anyone demanding their money back, despite Thompson's gloomy forebodings.

The last gasp of the pick-up Albion Country Band was at three successive nights at the Howff, a club newly opened by Roy Guest, just off Regents Street in London. These ran through from 29th

Howff xmas gigs advert. 29th-31st December 1972

December to New Years' Eve, 8pm to midnight on the first two nights. *Melody Maker* announced that "a compilation of music, long-sword, rapper and Morris dancing, mummers' plays and seasonal tradition". This all sounds like a cross between Royston Wood's idealistic ideas for the Albion circus, and some of Ashley's later Christmas shows. On the first night, the biggest surprise was a rollicking version of Thompson's *'Little Beggar Girl'*, sung with urchin glee by Linda, and with the pick-up Albion band swinging like crazy behind her. An electric dulcimer, presumably struck by Simon (it has his rhythmic insistence) leads into a spirited Richard vocal, and again the band thumps behind like an English version of Neil Young's Crazy Horse. Had Ashley gathered around him the greatest band of his career, one that could have taken English contemporary song onto a new and higher plane, and just not realised it?

Another rare Richard Thompson delight, his wittily cruel *'Dragging The River'*, which another band member jokes has nothing to do with Ralph McTell's *'The Streets of London'*. Richard itemises exactly how he will dispose of his girlfriend, to her face. Linda joins in with the chorus of a song which seems to be about her. There is a strong bass line, or possibly the foot-operated keyboard which Richard used to drag around with him to the clubs. Techno starts here. A lovely, lonely, subtle and resolutely acoustic *'Has He Got A Friend For Me'* follows.

Now it is time for Shirley Collins to take the stage in this musical glamour contest. She opens with an unaccompanied song, in which her mellow Sussex vowels finally drag a chorus out of the audience. For *'Lovely Joan'*, the Albion Country Band plug in again to accompany her, in their usual bouncy fashion. There is a stern and lengthy electric guitar solo, no frills, presumably by Simon.

Next up is the electric Morris show. One can clearly hear the bells on the dancers' legs jingle louder as they approach the stage, like Christmas come early. John

Photo: John Bryan

Second night at the Howff. 30th December 1969

Watcham's concertina leads the musical ensemble. Not a note is wasted, and of course there are no instrumental solos. This is music to a specific purpose, aiding the lords of the dance. Thrilling all the same. The dancers exit, and the greatest surprise is left to the end, a majestic version of '*A Calling On Song*' from the first Steeleye album. Shirley Collins' voice floats over a sonorous backing, then Simon takes over, and finally Linda Peters soars heavenwards. Ashley's bass anchors everything, and one can imagine him smiling.

The advert for the three date Howff residency pleaded politely that "not everyone attends on the final night, as the premises have a relatively small capacity". Neil Philip remembers that on that unforgettable evening "first we had Richard Thompson and Linda Peters on their own, then Shirley Collins, then Barry Dransfield came on and did some songs , and then he joined the original group for the Morris section. After that came a Mumming Play. All this took about three hours, and when it was finished, after two encores, the audience started filing out. We couldn't believe it was finished, and, filling my lungs with one gargantuan gasp, I let out a really long spaced-out scream for "More!" We all stamped our feet, joined gradually by the sorry remainder of the original audience. Our persistence was then rewarded by a one and a half hour set of old rock and roll songs, Everley's stuff, and things, for which none other than Dave Pegg and Dave Mattacks took the stage. Ashley Hutchings pissed off somewhere. All the music that evening was good, and the atmosphere was really great – boozy and relaxed. Simon Nicol even played drums at one point. I got the feeling that Hutchings wasn't all that enthusiastic about all this – as if playing this fun stuff was maybe diluting the music that had gone before, but that may be imagination. He didn't get up to sing '*Nadine*'."

Robin Denselow however recalls a memorable outburst from Ashley, just after midnight: "The place was packed, celebratory drinks were flying to and fro, and an exceedingly good band up on stage was improvising around the statutory '*Auld Lang Syne*'". One of the band now launched into a Chuck Berry riff. Ashley reacted "in a most unexpected way. He ripped out the plugs from the band's equipment, and stormed off with them into the night". The audience had to wait until replacements were found, and then the band – without Hutchings – boogied late into the night.

Ashley: "This has gone into legend now. Really, it was like a party for three nights. The Howff wasn't that big. It held a good few hundred. Well, you know I love rock & roll. Periodically it's raised its head down the years – *The Bunch*, *Twangin' n' Traddin'*, certain items on the *Shuffle Off* album. Rock & roll keeps coming up. But the final night descended, and I use that word advisedly, into a ridiculous jam, past closing time, of Chuck Berry style Rock & Roll. I'd had enough and I didn't want to know anymore. I'd left the stage and let them get on with it. And after a certain amount of this rock & roll I just thought: "Come on, let's call it a day guys". And I pulled the plug, that's true. We all do silly things and on the scale of silly things that's not very important." It seemed pretty symbolic. "You'd better put that in." Did they put the plug back in? "I don't think so. That was it." It was very symbolic.

Richard Thompson remembers it clearly. "He pulled the plug, yes. He was right in a wrong sort of way." Simon Nicol thinks it was the same night when Phillipa Clare "did the balletic version of *A Young Person's Guide To The Orchestra* wearing a lampshade. Phillipa is a mysterious woman whose life "interweaves with Fairport down the years." Richard adds, "with or without any consent."

Shirley Collins memory is more down to earth. "They had opened up to do this New Year's gig, and they hadn't got any food for the audience. For some reason, I'd volunteered to do some cooking. So I spent the early part of the evening, rushing around the shops. So I was cooking and singing and going home with Ashley who was cross. It was a GREAT New Year!!!"

Later a band member explained that "Tyger thought it blasphemous that anyone should use the Albion Country Band and all it stood for to play that stuff". This from a man who still boasts a fine collection of rock'n'roll 45s. Obviously for Ashley, his new band – and his career at this point – was part of a serious and single-minded enterprise to save English music, perhaps even from itself. As Eric Winter wrote about these three legendary nights, "almost everything the band and dancers did has been done (perhaps more prissily) by the EFDSS. But try and get that swingin' audience into the hallowed and clinical portals of Cecil Sharp House". There was some "vigorous morris with the band really hitting the music very hard indeed", while the sword-dancing proceeded at a pace "that seemed (almost literally) cut throat". His review is accompanied by shots of a wild-haired Ashley singing, and Thompson bending stoop-backed over his electric guitar. They are all caught in the spotlight, like wild creatures in the lights of an approaching car. For Andrew Means, it was "the nearest thing to traddie-cabaret yet to emerge from the folk-rock jungle".

In the *Folk Review*, Shirley Hutchings is interviewed back in the English countryside, at Red Rose Cottage in Etchingham. The accompanying photos are a series of idyllic snapshots of life as lived by the intellectual descendants of William Morris. She wears flared trousers and a patterned top, messes around in the garden, sits on a swing, thrashes around with a badminton racket, and stands close to Ashley in his steel glasses and rustic shirt. The most important things are "my love and respect for Ashley, my love for my children and my love for English music. That's what *really* matters to me".

December finally saw the release of *Bright Phoebus*, the album of contemporary songs by Mike and Lal Waterson. A review in *Melody Maker* spoke of how the album's arrangements are "in the imaginative hands of Martin Carthy and Ashley Hutchings": they are "surprisingly, ridiculously broad". People were reassessing the importance of the Watersons to the English folk revival. The same applied to Fairport, whose *History* double album also appeared in time for Christmas. The album came complete with a family tree by Pete Frame, but by the time of printing it was already out of date. The branch representing the Albion Country Band was just about to burst into flower, yet again.

For the third Albion Country Band line-up, Martin Carthy rejoined his old colleague from Steeleye Span. Ashley asks himself why. "Maybe he was missing being up there with the 'big sound', and the comradeship of a band. Because it's very lonely travelling around by yourself doing folk clubs. And he's a non-driver. One of the legendary non-drivers along with John Tams and myself. He was a train frequenter. It's a lonely business and so I can understand why he'd want to be in a band."

Hutchings had asked John and Sue Kirkpatrick a year before, but they had other commitments. "That's exactly right. And so on paper it was a damn good line-up. But interestingly Carthy came into it with his acoustic guitar. He didn't revert to the electric

which he had fallen in love with during Steeleye. And there was a very different sound, a very definite demarcation line. Simon played the electric guitar and Martin played the acoustic guitar. It was again a unique line-up. To have oboe, squeezebox, and guitars – there you go – another different sound." Certainly Sue's playing on '*I Was A Young Man*' gave the band an extraordinary dimension. Roger Swallow had played with Ian Matthews. Carthy remembers that " Hutchings had phoned him up out of the blue. "It was really all of a sudden. We put together a repertoire in one or two weeks. I know we started on the 1st of January." Hungover from the Howff, no doubt.

Martin was looking forward to "getting back into the band scene, especially with Ashley". As he later told the *Terrascope*, "we rehearsed for two weeks and went straight out on the road. For the first month we were turning up at gigs and having to argue our way on stage, saying 'just give us a chance to play and if you like what you hear then pay us'". So what exactly was the problem? "Partly to do with the previous line-up" – Mk 1, not the

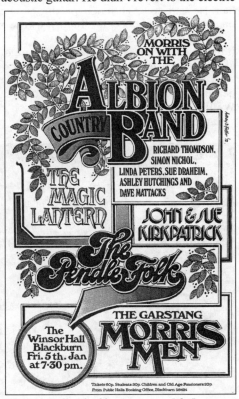

Winsor Hall, Blackburn poster. 5th January 1973

caretaker band – "and partly to do with the fact they'd booked a band with six members and the band turned up with two of the members they'd booked. They didn't give a shit about the pedigree of the new people". Many times, "we'd play and they'd come over and say 'thanks very much, here's your money', that happened a lot".

Shirley: "But, I wanted to be in the band at first. John wanted Sue, his wife, to play and work with him. Her oboe was fabulous, it's stunning. But she can't sing very well. I don't like her singing. So I had to back out and let Sue in. And I resented that at the time. But for the good of the band, you step aside..." Sue Harris would keep her maiden name – and identity – with the band, and "the combination of her woodwind with his reeds will add an interesting dimension". John points out that he plays the "push-pull" Anglo-German concertina and button accordion, "both of which play a different note when you push the bellows in and pull it out". It is jerkier to play than the English concertina but less "sluggish". He also remembers that this line-up "wasn't a very relaxed sort of group", a sentiment shared by Ashley: "No, it wasn't relaxed at all."

Folk Review carried some superb photos by John Bryan of the new band rehearsing at the Quaker House, Stourbridge. The whole band pose amongst the pews – Ashley stage centre, Simon grinning like a naughty schoolboy – and play in a circle. Hutchings has an electric bass strapped to his waist, and also sings into a microphone: he wears white shirt and dark trousers, clean shaven with steel glasses and long curly hair. He stares over at Simon, picking at a Fender. The Kirkpatricks talk to each other on concertina and oboe, lost in their own world.

Tyger – as he is still called – gave a rare interview to *Melody Maker*, warning that if things did not work out this time, he might break up the band completely "and start afresh". "At least members of the new band are all aware of each others' music, but "I'm still not happy that Martin and John and Sue will be working their solo gigs, because superficially there's not that much difference between that and Steeleye. We'll still not be able to rehearse as much as we should". If things do not work out, "I'll make a complete break. Not from the music but from the clique that's become

Albion Country Band 3 at Quaker Meeting House, Stourbridge. 1973. l-r: Ashley, Simon Nicol, Martin Carthy, Roger Swallow, Sue Harris, John Kirkpatrick

associated with it. There's no other kind of music I want to play, but I'll see if I can find some completely unknown musicians with a fresh approach". Etchingham beckons, and indeed the rest of Ashley's future career. But not quite yet.

Karl Dallas reviewed their appearance at the City University, concluding, "Now this is more like it". The vocal harmonies were a little uncertain, and the arrangements sometimes over elaborate, "put together as if the players have more of an eye on Vaughan Williams than either the English or the rock traditions". They had nevertheless established their own "musical vocabulary", right from the start. This was most noticeable on two songs by Richard Thompson: no longer there in person. '*Poor Ditching Boy*' and '*Nobody's Wedding*' which incorporated "a touch of Mendelssohn's '*Wedding March*' and a conga which almost brought the house down". The band's instrumental power was already awesome, though there was little room for improvisation. "Is it rock? Probably not. Is it folk? Well, perhaps. It's a bit classical in its feeling. Is it good music? Certainly".

When they played Harrow Polytechnic, '*Poor Ditching Boy*' is slowed down, sung by Carthy as if in a dream. Next up, some electric Morris, drum-heavy. '*I'll Go And* '*List For A Sailor*' begins as solo Kirkpatrick, then bass enters for emphasis, and finally the whole band thumps in. The sound balance is like lumpy pudding. '*Princess Royal*' sounds even worse, bombastic rather than punchy. The delicacy of the two previous line-ups has blown to the wind. Clogs thunder to '*I'm Forever Blowing Bubbles*'/'*Old Bull and Bush*', and the band grinds on, remorselessly. A gig at the Northern Polytechnic in early April opens with the Morris medley, though again the rhythm section is out of control. The primal drum bashing almost drowns out Carthy on '*Gallant Poacher*'. '*High Barbaree*' has its theme outlined by Sue, like an overture. Suddenly, the Albions are in focus. The song winds down with Sue's slithering coda. Ashley adds occasional bass notes like a coffin descending into the earth.

Later in April, the Albion Country Band returned to a favourite venue, the Shaw Theatre. Many hopeful of getting tickets were turned away, but reviews were mixed. Eric Winter found the gig patchy, "not tight but neither was it uptight. Albion seems to prefer its songs to be raw at the edges, like unfinished seams". This "angularity" undercut Sue's melodious oboe playing". The real triumph was the Albion Morris, with a "bit of good clog" at the end, and a sword dance "at something like one and a half times its normal speed". Their morris set was illuminated by "a hobby horse in

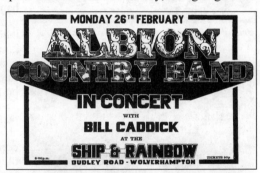

Ship & Rainbow, Wolverhampton poster. 26th February 1973

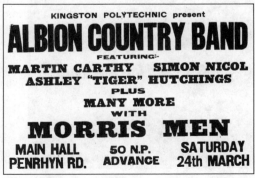

Kingston Polytechnic poster. 24th March 1973

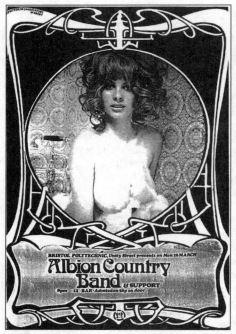

Bristol Polytechnic poster. 26th March 1973

Shaw Theatre gig advert. 15th April 1973

the shape of a lion, with a head as golden and awe-inspiring as the King Tut topknot". This was dancing which showed "tremendous dignity without being stuffy", and the music would be just the same "when it has had another month or so to settle".

Karl Dallas was far less enthusiastic. He believed that Ashley's previous ventures had always come good, "given time". This time though, "I find myself asking if Ashley hasn't got himself off on an entirely wrong tack, so wrong that he ought really to quit and start again in a different direction. The looseness which has always been a pleasantly relaxed aspect of their appearances, has degenerated into positive anarchy". Roger Swallow's drums were sometimes so out of sympathy with Ashley's bass lines "that he might have almost been playing with another band".

Dallas's major criticism, though, is their "constant attempt to turn folksongs into monstrous cinematic epics, complete with overtures (usually on Sue Kirkpatrick's oboe) and music to be played behind the closing titles and cast list". He notices that the audience begin by joining in on the choruses, "but by the end the unnecessarily complicated arrangements had bludgeoned them into silence". However, the band went off "to a rousing reception" and encored with a "tight, funky, simply arranged instrumental that was the most exciting thing of the evening".

Martin Carthy was still talking about this review years later, and believes it can only have hastened the band's demise. "You just get shitty gigs occasionally. And there was this one bloke in particular who was just waiting to shoot us down". If the critics were agreed on one thing, it was their praise for the Albion Morris. Richard Thompson composed 'Albion Sunrise' "specifically to marshall the morris dancing troupes" and Dolly Collins wrote an enthusiastic appraisal of 'Albion's Electric Morris' for *Folk Review*. The dancers are photographed in a church hall, frozen as they leap in the air, proud in their lion insignia, and full of youthful enthusiasm.

The band returned to the BBC on May 9th to record a session for the Bob Harris radio show. A superb '*Hanged I Shall Be*', which really rocks as it builds to its climax, was left unheard. Simon injects some great guitar. Ashley notes that it all sounds "natural and immediate. A bit raw, like the band on-stage". '*I'll Go And List for a Sailor*' has the interesting dynamics one has grown to associate with Hutchings, along with a real village band feel. The same is true of the instrumentals, tight but loose. Carthy's dark voice, Sue's oboe and Kirkpatrick's rich accordion mesh nicely with Ashley's bass. Only the drummer is sometimes heavy handed.

Later in May, the Albions headlined a gig at the Royal Festival Hall in London. A tape of the gig shows a band who have largely resolved the problem of integrating acoustic and electric instruments into a live mix. Swallow belongs to the 'nail-it-to-the-floor' school but is OK as long as the band is thundering along with him. The audience reaction is equally thunderous. Simon Nicol plays the comic front man, so that '*Gallant Poacher*' is "a song from Dorset, a warning to anyone tempted by their next door neighbour". On '*When I Was A Young Man*', the rhythm section is almost Led Zeppelin-like in its intensity. This urgency communicates itself to the rest of the band, who boogie along. '*Hanged I Shall Be*' is a couple out walking and "all of a sudden, he murders her". The audience laugh along, then are chilled by Carthy's rendition, closer to the Velvet Underground than to Pentangle. There is lengthy tuning up as Kirkpatrick points out a problem, his melodeon and concertina are at "totally different pitches". '*Forever Blowing Bubbles*' is now a frothy concoction: Ashley sternly enjoins the audience to stamp along.

For Robert Shelton, "as a sort of electrified, antiquarian, mobile carnival, the Albions deserve to be recognised as one of the

Folk Song '73 gig advert, Royal Festival Hall. 14th May 1973

Carnegie Theatre, Workington poster. 11th June 1973

best eighteenth century bands to be heard in the twentieth. "They are quite marvellous in their invention, their use of the oboe against the concertina, and the very crisp electric outbreaks they used to change mood and tempo. The electric dulcimer in *'When I Was A Young Man'* was so imaginative as to unnerve many a rock band". By comparison, Richard Thompson & Linda Peters were "morose", and Shirley Collins "not in voice".

Eric Winter also refutes Karl Dallas's earlier assessment of the Albions now: "they seem to have got it together in a highly professional way". There were no gaps between songs, and they left Winter "entranced by their weaving patterns of music and song". Dallas returns to the fray in a his review of the Norwich Folk Festival. The Albions "did such a rotten afternoon set that they asked for a chance to redeem themselves in the evening concert, and did so, more than adequately".

Martin Carthy: "It was a great band, I look back with enormous pleasure, and a lot of fury, because we were quite misunderstood. And not helped by certain people who were in a position of influence" – a reference to Karl Dallas of whom he says, "He made life very difficult. He wrote a review that finished us off basically. He reviewed us at Norwich Festival. We did one gig that was awful, and we asked to do another set. And we did a blistering second set but he wasn't there. And I was blazing. This review came out and said we were basically shite. I never forgave him for that. I'm rather good at bearing grudges, I do admit. It was so unfair. And from that moment on, we were a good band. It was a case of breaking the ice. It was like with Steeleye – give a month or two months and then we break the ice, we break through and you're playing what we want to play. The sound is right."

The band gigged in Holland at the end of June. The Albions were booked for the 9th Cambridge Folk Festival in late July, along with Steve Ashley's Ragged Robin. Ironically, the band headlining were Steeleye Span, just back from a successful tour of the USA. They encored in authentic 50s gear, with Maddy Prior in a "bouffant wig and waspie waist". As *NME* put it, Steeleye post-Hutchings "take traditional folk music and blast it into the 1970s . The trouble is that such music *still* sounds as if in a time warp, whereas Ashley's best music still sounds timeless." Time, though, was about to be called on his latest band. *Sounds* mentions in passing "Ragged Robin and the Albion Country Band, both of whom are breaking up".

Ashley: "Something did seem to go wrong. Maybe it was that particular